Law, Memory, Violence

The demand for recognition, responsibility, and reparations is regularly invoked in the wake of colonialism, genocide, and mass violence: there can be no victims without recognition, no perpetrators without responsibility, and no justice without reparations. Or, so it seems from law's limited repertoire for assembling the archive after 'the disaster'. Archival and memorial practices are central to contexts where transitional justice, addressing historical wrongs, or reparations are at stake. The archive serves as a repository or 'storehouse' of what needs to be gathered and recognised so that it can be left behind in order to inaugurate the future. The archive manifests law's authority and its troubled conscience. It is an indispensable part of the liberal legal response to biopolitical violence.

This collection challenges established approaches to transitional justice by opening up new dialogues about the problem of assembling law's archive. The volume presents research drawn from multiple jurisdictions that address the following questions. What resists being archived? What spaces and practices of memory – conscious and unconscious – undo legal and sovereign alibis and confessions? And what narrative forms expose the limits of responsibility, recognition, and reparations? By treating the law as an 'archive', this book traces the failure of universalised categories such as 'perpetrator', 'victim', 'responsibility', and 'innocence', posited by the liberal legal state. It thereby uncovers law's counter-archive as a challenge to established forms of representing and responding to violence.

Stewart Motha, School of Law, Birkbeck, University of London, UK.

Honni van Rijswijk, School of Law, University of Technology Sydney, Australia.

Law, Memory, Violence

Uncovering the Counter-Archive

Edited by
Stewart Motha and
Honni van Rijswijk

LONDON AND NEW YORK

First published 2016 by Routledge

2 Park Square, Milton Park, Abingdon, Oxfordshire OX14 4RN
711 Third Avenue, New York, NY 10017

a GlassHouse book

Routledge is an imprint of the Taylor & Francis Group, an informa business

First issued in paperback 2017

Copyright © 2016 selection and editorial matter, Stewart Motha and Honni van Rijswijk; individual chapters, the contributors

The right of Stewart Motha and Honni van Rijswijk to be identified as the authors of the editorial material, and of the authors for their individual chapters, has been asserted in accordance with sections 77 and 78 of the Copyright, Designs and Patents Act 1988.

All rights reserved. No part of this book may be reprinted or reproduced or utilised in any form or by any electronic, mechanical, or other means, now known or hereafter invented, including photocopying and recording, or in any information storage or retrieval system, without permission in writing from the publishers.

Notice:
Product or corporate names may be trademarks or registered trademarks, and are used only for identification and explanation without intent to infringe.

British Library Cataloguing in Publication Data
A catalogue record for this book is available from the British Library

Library of Congress Cataloging-in-Publication Data
Law, memory, violence : uncovering the counter-archive / edited by Stewart Motha, Honni van Rijswijk.
pages cm
Includes bibliographical references and index.
ISBN 978-1-138-83063-9 (hardback) — ISBN 978-1-315-73715-7 (ebk)
1. Archives—Law and legislation. 2. Public records—Law and legislation. 3. Restorative justice. 4. Transitional justice. 5. Victims of crimes—Legal status, laws, etc. I. Motha, Stewart J. (Stewart John), 1970- editor. II. Rijswijk, Honni van
K3560.L39 2015
344'.092—dc23
2015034089

ISBN: 978-1-138-83063-9 (hbk)
ISBN: 978-1-138-57043-6 (pbk)

Typeset in Baskerville by
by FiSH Books Ltd, Enfield

Contents

Notes on contributors   *vii*
Acknowledgements   *ix*

Introduction: A counter-archival sense   1
STEWART MOTHA AND HONNI VAN RIJSWIJK

1   **A counter-archival sensibility: Picking up Hannah Arendt's 'Reflections on Little Rock'**   16
JENNIFER L. CULBERT

2   **Listening to the archive: Failing to hear**   34
JILL STAUFFER

3   **(Un)remembering: Countering law's archive – improvisation as social practice**   50
SARA RAMSHAW AND PAUL STAPLETON

4   **Animating the archive: Artefacts of law**   70
TRISH LUKER

5   **The file as hypertext: Documents, files and the many worlds of the paper state**   97
MAYUR SURESH

6   **Counter-archive as staging dissensus**   116
KARIN VAN MARLE

7   **Constitutions are not enough: Museums as law's counter-archive**   140
STACY DOUGLAS

vi Contents

8 Archiving victimhood: Practices of inscription in international
criminal law   156
SARA KENDALL

9 The conspiracy archive: Turkey's 'deep state' on trial   177
BAŞAK ERTÜR

10 Making a treaty archive: Indigenous rights on the Canadian
development frontier   195
MIRANDA JOHNSON

11 Schmitt's *Weisheit der Zelle*: Rethinking the concept of
the political   215
JACQUES DE VILLE

Index   232

Notes on contributors

Jennifer L. Culbert is an Associate Professor in the Political Science department at Johns Hopkins University, US, where she teaches courses in political theory and jurisprudence. She is the author of *Dead Certainty: The Death Penalty and the Problem of Judgment* (Stanford University Press, 2008).

Jacques de Ville is Professor in the Department of Public Law and Jurisprudence at the University of the Western Cape, South Africa. He is the author of *Jacques Derrida: Law as Absolute Hospitality* (Routledge, 2011).

Stacy Douglas is Assistant Professor of Law and Legal Studies at Carleton University in Ottawa, Canada, where she teaches legal and political theory, and constitutional law. She has published academic and political commentary in *Law and Critique*, *Law, Culture and the Humanities*, *Radical Philosophy*, as well as the *Australian Feminist Law Journal*.

Başak Ertür is a Lecturer at the School of Law at Birkbeck, University of London, England. Her current research focuses on trials, performativity, political violence and memory. She is the editor of *Manual for Conspiracy* (Sharjah Art Foundation, 2011), and the co-editor of *Waiting for the Barbarians: A Tribute to Edward Said* (Verso, 2008).

Miranda Johnson is a Lecturer in the Department of History at the University of Sydney, Australia. Her book, *The Land is Our History: Indigenous Claims and the Transformation of the Settler State*, is forthcoming with Oxford University Press.

Sara Kendall is a Lecturer at the University of Kent, England, where she co-directs the Centre for Critical International Law. Her research seeks to bring approaches from critical theory and the interpretive social sciences to bear upon the field of international law.

Trish Luker is a Chancellor's Postdoctoral Research Fellow at the Faculty of Law, University of Technology, Sydney, Australia. She works in the areas of socio-legal research and critical legal theory, maintaining a research focus on interdisciplinary approaches to law and the humanities.

viii   Notes on contributors

Sara Ramshaw is a Senior Lecturer at the University of Exeter, School of Law, England. She is the author of *Justice as Improvisation: The Law of the Extempore* (Routledge, 2013) and Principal Investigator on an AHRC-funded project on musical improvisation and child protection law in Northern Ireland.

Paul Stapleton is an improviser and sound artist. He is also a Senior Lecturer at the Sonic Arts Research Centre, Queen's University Belfast, Northern Ireland, where he co-directs the Translating Improvisation research group with Sara Ramshaw and the QUBe music collective with Steve Davis. www.paulstapleton.net

Jill Stauffer is Associate Professor and Director of the concentration in Peace, Justice and Human Rights at Haverford College, Pennsylvania, US. She is author of *Ethical Loneliness: The Injustice of Not Being Heard* (Columbia UP 2015) and is on the Board of Directors of the oral history book series Voice of Witness.

Mayur Suresh is a Lecturer at the School of Oriental and African Studies, University of London, England, and has previously practised law in India. He is currently completing his doctoral thesis at the School of Law, Birkbeck, England. His research emerges out of an ethnography of terrorism trials in Delhi's courts.

Karin van Marle is a Professor in the Department of Jurisprudence, University of Pretoria, South Africa. She is also a fellow at the Stias Institute for Advanced Study, Stellenbosch. Her research focus over the past two decades has been to reflect on and investigate the multiple narratives, theoretical directions and paths of and for a jurisprudence post 1994, in the aftermath of apartheid, and she has published widely on these topics.

Acknowledgements

This collection grew out of a conference stream presented at the Critical Legal Conference 'Reconciliation and Reconstruction' at Queen's University Belfast in September 2013. We would like to thank the conference organisers, Sara Ramshaw, Yvette Russell, Bal Sokhi-Bulley and Catherine Turner for providing such a rich and productive space, and those who attended the panels and so helped develop the conversation of the counter-archive.

Thank you to Colin Perrin and to Laura Muir, for their assistance in developing this collection.

We are very grateful to Yvette Wajon for her editorial work on this volume.

Our thanks also to the artist Judy Watson for permission to use the image on the cover, and in Chapter 4.

Introduction

A counter-archival sense

Stewart Motha and Honni van Rijswijk

The demand for recognition, responsibility, and reparations is regularly invoked in the wake of colonialism, genocide, and mass violence. There can be no recognition without victims, no responsibility without perpetrators, and no justice without reparations – or so it seems from law's limited repertoire for assembling the archive after the 'disaster'. Law's memorial function harbours the problem of legal systems founded on violence. Law as archive serves to delimit a violent past, and seeks to inaugurate the future. In modernity, there are social and political expectations that acts of violence will be adjudicated by law: that 'evil' acts will be declared unlawful, that responsible perpetrators will be punished and injured victims will be compensated. Transitional justice processes have sought new forms of addressing 'extraordinary' acts of violence,[1] increasing law's jurisdictions. Law's role here is necessarily bound up with state power and state violence.[2] These processes are central to the constitution of law's archive of harms.

The archive has been theorised by writers from Walter Benjamin to Jacques Derrida, and has recently been subject to a resurgence of interest in law and humanities scholarship as a way to approach law's failures in judging and responding to historical and contemporary violence. The essays gathered here build on critical legal scholarship in the area of transitional justice, as well as conversations regarding the role of representation, affect, memorial practices, and imagination in the ongoing relationship of law and sovereign violence.[3]

The archive traditionally delineates the site from which the law is drawn, and manifests the space of law's authority. From its root in *arkheion*, the residence of the *archons* or superior magistrates, the archive is also where official documents were deposited. As Derrida reminds us, the *archons* had the power to make, represent, and interpret the law (Derrida 1995: 2). In

---

1   On the roles of legal and literary modernism in responding to the harms of modernity, see Manderson (2012); Reichmann (2009); Felman (2002); and Van Rijswijk (2012).
2   For readings of law's relation to violence, see Sarat (2001); and Kahn (2008).
3   See Slaughter (2007); Meister (2012); and Van Marle and Motha (2013).

contexts of transitional justice, law serves as a repository or 'storehouse' of what needs to be gathered and recognised. Legal decisions performatively produce the archive of sovereign violence when they distinguish a legal order from an unjust past, and reorient the law in the wake of histories of violent sovereign impositions. Law's command and commencement is intimately associated with sovereign appropriations of space. Archival and memorial practices are thus central to contexts where transitional justice, the redress of historical wrongs, or reparations are at stake.

The essence of this collection is to refuse to take law's archive for granted, and to thereby interrogate the teleological narratives of progress that law constitutes after violent events. The book moves beyond a thematic exploration of the archive to question its constitution, boundaries and materiality. This is achieved by considering the logics and practices of representation through which the archive is established. The task of this book is, then, to locate the multiple forms, genres, sites and practices that manifest law's *counter-archive*. We examine law's implicit assertions of authority in staking out domains of adjudication through the constitution of archives of violence. What unfolds is a 'sensibility', as Jennifer Culbert so aptly puts it, which uncovers the richness of events or 'happenings' that can remain 'strange' while 'interrupting or even challenging prevailing wisdom' (see Chapter 1, pp. 16–23).

The essays gathered here are drawn from multiple jurisdictions and address the following questions: which forms of violence and suffering resist being archived, and what is their political significance? What spaces and practices of memory – conscious and unconscious – undo legal and sovereign alibis and confessions? And what narrative forms expose the limits of responsibility, recognition, and reparations? The counter-archival strategies deployed here show the failure of universalised categories, such as 'perpetrator', 'victim', 'responsibility', and 'innocence' posited by the liberal legal state, to fully adjudicate violence and suffering.

Counter-archival practices disrupt the linear unfolding of time, and the delimitation of space (as jurisdiction or community) that law inscribes when it deals with historical crimes or mass violence. Counter-archives function as critical intervention within and beside legal processes. They challenge established forms of representing and responding to violence.

Archival forms

The form of the archive has been discussed in a number of disciplines. The anthropologist Ann Laura Stoler (2009) promoted a move beyond the conventional view of the archive as a collection of documents no longer in use. In attending to what is 'not written', Stoler is not seeking a hidden message, but instead distinguishing between 'what was "unwritten" because it could go without saying and "everyone knew it", what was unwritten because it could not yet be articulated, and what was unwritten because it could not be said' (Stoler 2009: 3). The unwritten 'looms largest', however, in 'making colonial ontologies themselves' (ibid.). Drawing on Ian Hacking's *Historical Ontologies*, Stoler refers to 'ontology' as the:

> *ascribed* being or essence of things, the categories of things that are thought to exist or can exist in any particular domain, and the specific attributes assigned to them. Ontologies... refer to 'what comes into existence with the historical dynamic of naming.'
> (Stoler 2009: 4, citing Hacking 2002: 26)

Pursuing such historical ontologies involves the 'identification of *mutating* assignments of essence and its predicates in specific time and space' (Stoler 2009: 3). And, colonial ontologies of racial difference, for instance, show that 'essences' are 'protean, not fixed, subject to reformulation again and again' (ibid.).

Stoler suggests that we attend not only to colonialism's archival content, but to the principles and practices of governance lodged in particular 'archival forms' (Stoler 2009: 20). By 'archival forms', she means: 'prose style, repetitive refrain, the arts of persuasion, affective strains that shape "rational" response, categories of confidentiality and classification, and not least, genres of documentation' (ibid.). She focuses on 'archives-as-process' rather than 'archives-as-things' (ibid.). Archives are regarded as 'condensed sites of epistemological and political anxiety rather than as skewed and biased sources'; with colonial archives serving 'transparencies on which power relations were inscribed and intricate technologies of the rule in themselves' (ibid.). Taking these provocations seriously, we have sought to multiply the sites of the archive with particular attention to opening up what is regarded as archival *material*. What emerges is not only a sense that the archive is a technology of rule, but that the problem of archiving violence is closely tied to the deeper root of technology as *techné*. The counter-archival move is then informed by a sensibility of the archive as art, fiction, and fabrication.

For Verne Harris, the work of record-keeping is 'justice and resistance to injustice' (2007: 256). Drawing on Derrida, justice, like democracy, is open and always to come. The work of justice cannot be enclosed. Harris draws an analogy between this notion of justice and the archive: '[t]he call of justice resists the totalization of every such enclosure. It resists, if you like, what is traditionally regarded as the fundamental archival impulse – contextualization. It is open to the future and to every "other"' (Harris 2007: 257). Harris argues that:

> justice requires us to re-imagine archival contextualization. Conventionally understood, contextualization has to do with the

disclosing of all relevant contextual layers. That is to pin down meaning and significance. But [...] context is infinite, ever-changing, and permeable to 'text', so that contextualization can only ever be about a preliminary and highly selective intervention, in which pinning down is not a possibility.

(Harris 2007: 257)

The accessibility of the context of a past event is a major frontier of dispute about what it means to do justice to the past. Many historians argue that all that can be done in relation to the past is not 'justice', but a gradual revealing of the 'context' in which particular social, economic, and political struggles took place.[4] There is then no 'justice' to be done in relation to the past – only partial truths to be revealed now. We resist this historicist impulse of the contextualist approach.

As part of Derrida's investigations into the nature of the archive, he considers certain figures of responsibility that create and protect the archive, and considers, too, the ways in which the archive mediates responsibility of these guardians towards others. This question of the relation between authority and archive was raised by Derrida in his essay, 'Scribble (writing power)' (1979), which describes the archival violence of the hoarding actions by archival priests. The priests concealed the codes they curated from view, and in their concealment, in their guarding, the priests not only preserved knowledge, but also derived power:

... for custody of meaning, the repository of learning and the laying out of the archive – encrypts itself becoming secret and reserved, diverted from common usage, esoteric. Naturally destined to serve the communication of laws and the order of the city transparently, a writing becomes the instrument of abusive power, of a caste of 'intellectuals' that is thus ensuring hegemony, whether its own or that of special interests: the violence of a secretariat, a discriminating reserve, an effect of scribble and script.

(Derrida 1979: 124)

Law can be found '*there* where men and gods *command, there* where authority, social order are exercised, *in this place* from which order is given' (Derrida 1995: 9). It is the *archons* ('men and gods') who have the power to interpret the archive (ibid.). The *archons* are those who 'possess the right to make or to represent the law' (ibid.: 10). Law's archive determines the possibilities and limitations of 'legitimate' legal violence; it determines forms of legal and social relation.

---

4   For a critique of such historicism in legal and political thought, see Motha (2015).

However, the key to understanding the relation of archive to law and to legal relation, is to acknowledge that the archive is not somewhere over 'there' but rather 'here', now. State law is an implicated archive, and we are 'implicated subjects' in relation to it. Michael Rothberg's (2014) term 'implicated subject' is an attempt to think through a subject position, politics and ethics beyond the binary figures of perpetrator and victim in the imaginary of responsibility for violence (Rothberg 2014; see also Sanders 2002). The term 'implication' marks the ways in which we belong to legal contexts of injustice – not as criminally responsible perpetrators, but not as innocent bystanders, either. Rather, we are the inheritors and beneficiaries of legal, economic and social systems. This means thinking beyond the archive as object or even site, to include our relation to it and our role in its constitution and powers. This collection is concerned with the archives of legal violence proximate to such implication. It examines the ethics of encounters or spacings between subjects and violence.

On the counter-archive

Derrida's *Archive Fever: A Freudian Impression* (1995) ranges from the origins of psychoanalysis to the implications of new technologies such as the internet and email for archiving. Derrida identifies a malady, a fever, which is associated with a destructive drive – the death drive. The desire to go back, to repeat, is a compulsion towards death (Steedman 2001: 6). The desire for origins, for going back, and repetition are all aspects of a psychoanalytic process that seeks the pre-linguistic and pre-representational. As Derrida puts it, we have no 'concept' of the archive (Derrida 1995: 9); in the archive we confront an *aporia*, the impossibility of saying in advance what is the archive, what is archiving, and what is archivable. The archive relates to the future – it is an address to the future. In this dialectic of remembering and forgetting, how are we to conceive of the archive, and indeed the counter-archive? Let us begin by recalling Derrida's influential response to this question.

Derrida is concerned with the entropic and doomed search for origins. Archive fever is 'a compulsive, repetitive, and nostalgic desire for the archive, an irrepressible desire to return to the origin, a homesickness, a nostalgia for the return to the most archaic place of absolute commencement' (ibid.: 91). Archive fever also signifies the relation of the archive to '*le mal radical*' (ibid.: 13), with evil itself. These two arguments are intertwined. Derrida's essay investigates *mal* as the doomed 'fever' of archival origins, and also the *mal* that refers to the archiving and adjudication of violence. This second meaning tracks the significance of the archive's imbrications with law's heightened interest in adjudicating violence.

Assertions of exclusivity are key to law's assertion of authority. State law speaks with one voice and one authority, guarding its singularity. Derrida explains the protection of this singularity within the archive through the metaphor of the exterior and interior, and by the ways in which the boundary between them is guarded from intrusion: there is 'no archive without outside' (1995: 11), and the archive is a 'place of election where law and singularity intersect in *privilege*' (ibid.: 10). Law's insistence on its singularity, and its singular authority, are at the core of its archival violence: the 'power' of 'consignation' lies in the act of '*gathering together signs*,' in the coordination of 'a single corpus,' refusing heterogeneity (ibid.). The singularity of this technique is crucial to ways in which the legal archive is vested with authority and uniqueness, law refusing to engage with other authorities (Aboriginal, 'international', 'refugee').

Carolyn Steedman opens a different register in relation to *Mal d'archive*. She suggests that 'fever' has a 'faintly comic' connotation in English, whereas the French 'mal' (with the aid of an insert in the French edition of *Mal d'archive*) evokes 'trouble, misfortune, pain, hurt, sickness, wrong, sin, badness, malice, and evil' (Steedman 2001: 9). The insert to the French edition pointed to:

> The disasters which mark the end of the millennium, are also *archives of evil*: hidden or destroyed, forbidden, misappropriated, 'repressed'. Their usage is at once clumsy and refined, during civil or international wars, during private or secret intrigues.
>
> (Steedman 2001: 15)

More than feverish attention to origins, Steedman emphasises 'real' maladies – anthrax and other diseases conveyed by 'dust' in the archive. She finds a different sickness, and also a different magistrate. This magistrate is none other than History – the history of the 'resurrectionist historian' who exhumes the dead (Steedman 2001: 38). The Magistrate effects the resurrection through the work of history – here citing Jules Michelet (1982: 268):

> Yes, everyone who dies leaves behind a little something, his memory, and demands that we care for it. For those who have no friends, the magistrate must provide that care. For the law, or justice, is more certain than all our tender forgetfulness, our tears so swiftly dried. This magistracy, is History. And the dead are, to use the language of Roman law, those *miserabiles personae* with whom the magistrate must preoccupy himself. Never in my career, have I lost sight of that duty of the historian.
>
> (Steedman 2001: 39)

Rather than Derrida's Greek *archon*, Steedman suggests that Michelet's 1872–74 image of 'History, (or the Historian or both)' are charged with

A counter-archival sense 7

care of the forgotten and the dead. Derrida's Magistrate, for Steedman, is the wrong one (Steedman 2001: 40).

French inquisitorial judges of the late eighteenth and nineteenth centuries, and English judges in their petty sessions charged with administering Poor Laws, assembled the 'real archive' – not the archive of *Archive Fever*, which is reduced to a repository of documents (Steedman 2001: 45). These were 'enforced autobiographies', and Steedman associates them with the emergence of the notion of literary character. The counter-archive is then produced by the French and English magistrate of the eighteenth and nineteenth centuries through the stories gathered as inquisitor, mediator, and amanuensis of the poor. This archive is never just the repository of official documents. And importantly, 'nothing starts in the Archive, nothing, ever at all, though things certainly end up there. You find nothing in the Archive but stories caught half way through: the middle of things; discontinuities' (ibid.). The emphasis on 'stories' gathered 'half way through' is important, but surely it is precisely the 'auto' (of autobiography) that is lacking if the magistrate becomes the amanuensis of everyday life? The essays in this volume focus on stories gathered from a variety of fragments, state practices, and affective responses to violence. These are only sometimes found in courts and other sources of state records. Our interest is less the source and rather the sensibilities though which they become cognisable, audible, and visible.

The interrupted stories caught 'half way through' that Steedman alluded to are not without benefit to historians. Foucault observed that 'discontinuity' has changed in status and become one of the fundamental elements of historical analysis (1998: 299–300). It used to be that when events were recognised as scattered and discontinuous, the task of the historian was to repress this. Historians now practice the 'systematic introduction of discontinuity' (ibid.: 300). The identification of 'rupture' becomes a practice of the historian. For Foucault, our concern should be 'how is it that this statement appeared rather than some other one in its place' (ibid.: 307). Such statements are events and they have a singular specificity. What are the conditions under which those statements appear in a given society at a given time? How do statements appear, circulate, get repressed, forgotten, destroyed and reactivated? (Foucault 1998: 309). An *archive* is:

> ... not the totality of texts that have been preserved by a civilization or the set of traces that could be salvaged from its downfall, but the series of rules which determine in a culture the appearance and disappearance of statements, their relation and their destruction, their paradoxical existence as *events* and *things*. To analyze the facts of discourse in the general element of the archive is to consider them, not at all as documents (of a concealed significance or a rule of construc-

tion), but as *monuments*, it is – leaving aside every geological metaphor, without assigning any origin, without the least gesture toward the beginnings of an *arch* – to do what the rules of the etymological game allow us to call something like an *archaeology*.

(Foucault 1998: 309)

Foucault's *Madness and Civilization* (1961), *The Birth of the Clinic* (1963) and *The Order of Things* (1966) all embody this problematic. They ask what the relation is among and between statements. What are counter-archival statements, and where are they encountered? The essays in this volume approach this question by developing a counter-archival sense.

A counter-archival sense

What encounters or events engender a counter-archival sense? In Chapter 1, Jennifer Culbert provides an account of Hannah Arendt's counter-archival sensibility. Arendt's 'Reflections on Little Rock' (1959) was inspired by what caught her eye in a photograph of a black girl in a bus on her way home from a school integrated in the wake of *Brown v Board of Education of Topeka*, 347 U.S. 438 (1954). It is not facts and context that inform Arendt's analysis, but the 'ambiguous character of the phenomenon' that prompts her to write. Culbert points to the features of Arendt's phenomenological approach – a concern not for ascertainable facts, material, or the 'real thing' – but rather the *sense* to grasp 'flickering events' or 'happenings' (p. 18). A counter-archival approach seeks to cultivate this sensibility. Arendt was not trying to establish the 'truth' of what happened in that bus in Little Rock, but to draw on the fragment or shard of history that is the photograph to fashion a story. Arendt's narrative dismayed the emerging 'good sense'. Drawing on Walter Benjamin, Culbert emphasises that the power of the photograph was not what it disclosed, but the very power of its *citation*. Torn from its context, the photograph enabled Arendt to disrupt the self-satisfaction of the present. This counter-archival sensibility harbours the possibility of natality – 'a spontaneous inaugurating act, an uncaused commencing, an initiating deed that starts something' (p. 27). Although the archive has been identified as the site of command and commencement, what the essays in this collection seek are instances of this 'uncaused commencing'.

Narratives of violence are thus revealed to be a problem of time, audience, and ways of seeing, hearing, and listening. Jill Stauffer argues that 'some injustices are made of a failure of hearing', and that these failures occur in the very 'institutions *designed* for hearing' (p. 35). Stauffer draws on examples of the reception of testimonials by survivors of the Holocaust, from Truth and Reconciliation Commission proceedings and of inmates subjected to solitary confinement in the United States. While

A counter-archival sense 9

acknowledging that 'those who are put in the place of the hearer of testimony may have reasons for not hearing well' – they may be constrained to adhere to facts, laws and procedures that silence some stories; 'may have a political interest in a restorative discourse' (p. 37); 'may be overwhelmed by how far the demand for help exceeds their capacity to offer assistance' (p. 37); or they may be protecting themselves from 'the trauma of hearing' (p. 37) – Stauffer calls for an ethics and politics of reparative responsibility in acts of listening. If we think of listening as a site of responsibility, Stauffer argues, 'as the duty to respond or to be responsive', then other possibilities, beyond existing forms of law, may present themselves (p. 35). These new forms require us 'to learn how to hear better what is being said' and so transform law's archives (p. 35).

This volume demonstrates the vitality of archival genres of law, literature, music, ethnography, and political theory drawn from multiple geographical sites. Spatialising time through multiple aesthetic genres is a key contribution the book makes to interdisciplinary studies on law, violence and memory. While transitional justice archives link wrongs and failures with reconciliation and apology, Sara Ramshaw and Paul Stapleton turn to improvised musical practice as counter-archival practice. Musical improvisation provides an allegory and counter-point to modes of transitional justice. In improvised musical space, they argue, mistake in improvisation 'does not necessitate apology' but rather points to future accountability, and to words rather than deeds – 'un-remembering rather than re-inscribing' (p. 50). This flexibility is offered as a radical alternative to the tired, existing forms of transitional justice. Abolishing the need for apology, an archive of a different kind might be created. What is at stake in this exploration of law *as* improvisation is the refusal to depict legal decision-making 'as uncreative and static, as a kind of necessary deadness or dead archive' (p. 63). Ramshaw and Stapleton offer a depiction of the creative life of law as a 'dynamic social phenomenon', enacted in non-linear time – law informed by the aesthetics of 'surprise' (p. 52).

Legal time is usually found in a variety of official papers and files. Several essays in the collection seek to reorient the nature of the file. These essays build on the groundbreaking work of Cornelia Vismann (2008). The artistic work of Judy Watson, who uses documents from the archive of colonial assimilation as the basis of a material critique, and who has provided the cover image to this collection, instantiates this practice. Taking a materialist approach to law's archive, Trish Luker, inspired by the artwork of Judy Watson, presents us with a counter-archive of artefacts previously undetected in their performance as 'objective' sources of evidence in legal proceedings, and encourages us to read in ways that attend to 'the possibility of documents as having performative capacity in the production of knowledge practices' (p. 94). Rather than considering archival sources as documentary text or representation, Luker argues, they are better understood from an ethnographic perspective – as 'imprints or inscriptions of the human on the page' (p. 93). Reading one of the key exhibits in the Stolen Generations case of *Cubillo v Commonwealth* (2000) 174 ALR 97, alongside Watson's artwork, Luker offers a counter-archive of legal evidence, relocating it instead as 'evidence of the symbolic and material force of colonial rule and the assertion of sovereignty' over Indigenous peoples.

Mayur Suresh provides an ethnography of the life-cycle of legal files amassed in Delhi courts in the trial of Mohammed Hanif[5] and 21 other co-accused, charged with setting off explosive devices. Suresh follows the ways in which these files are constantly copied, transcribed, translated and reorganised. Through his reading, the files are revealed to have a disturbing agency, as well as a dense materiality:

> Reams of paper of different colours and thickness, printers, paper punchers, empty files, balls of string to bind files, pens of various colours and pencils all point to the crucial position that paper occupies. It is as if the very structure and layout of the court is premised around paper and the production and maintenance of files. In most courts throughout India, the digital world stops at the courtroom doors. Paper jealously guards its primary position in the judicial process – it alone can record what happens inside a courtroom.
>
> (Suresh, this volume: 97)

The file has a material presence that is 'world absorbing and world creating'. Suresh questions the 'movement between the file and the world', and the file's power over the world (p. 100). Suresh describes the way in which the defence strategy in the trial 'involves bringing in more and more of the world into the file' (p. 100). The file is thus not only an archive *of* the world, it also produces unforeseen counter-archives *to* the world, and to legal practices.

A variety of memorial processes re-inscribe and re-claim the meanings attached to familiar violent events, and less well-known incidents. The 'countering' response to these sensibilities can be surprising: interruptions, discontinuities and ruptures of national narratives. Karin van Marle, in her interpretation of the metaphors of post-apartheid memory in South Africa, draws on the work of Svetlana Boym and offers 'reflective nostalgia' and 'memorial remembering' as resistant counter-archival practices and politics: 'nostalgia and remembrance that do not celebrate what they long for and remember, but are embodied and embedded in disappointment' (p. 116). Since 1994, many metaphors have come to play a role in post-apartheid

---

5   The names of places and persons have been changed by the author to maintain confidentiality.

discourses on memory, such as memory as a process of drawing and redrawing, memory as the interplay between narration and authorship, and memory as the movement between memorial and monument. A critical approach to memory, through nostalgia and remembering, Van Marle suggests, may serve to surpass the limits of the invention of the legal archive, which presents a master narrative derived from a selective past. These processes provide the possibility of a counter-archive, made from 'the same narratives, memories and symbols' (p. 122), but which tell different stories through critical readings and reflections. Van Marle ends with a case, 'a jurisprudential archive of sorts' (p. 117), the case of *Baphiring Community v Tshwaranani Projects* (2014 1 SA 330), considering what kinds of nostalgia and remembrance might be at play, and what can be made of the community's refusal to accept compensation in exchange for their land. The issue of land reform is considered within the broader discourse on the shifts and changes required for political, social and legal transformation in South Africa. In these contexts, reflective nostalgia can be seen as a politics of resistance by going against the grain; it neither opposes change nor avoids responsibility. And, 'in contrast to restorative nostalgia it does not seek for a homecoming, but remembers the past with irony and in a way that does not stand in the way of transformation' (p. 116).

Stacy Douglas takes up the constitution, which is so often reified as a foundational document of nation states, and also as a common site of critique by legal scholars concerned with community in post-conflict societies. Douglas argues that what is missed in privileging the constitution in critical analyses is the role of other sites, such as museums: 'museums, when paired with constitutional reform, can act as law's counter-archive, helping to create imaginations of political community that resist simple narratives of "community" amidst contested histories' (p. 140). While the cultural site of museums can also be colonial and imperialist, their forms and structures offer a 'reflexivity' of the communities they represent; these possibilities are inherently more constrained through constitutional forms, whose 'task is to delimit community' (p. 146). Thus the museum can serve as law's counter-archive, doing the 'interruptive work of community' that is not available through the constitutional form. Douglas examines the District Six Museum in Cape Town, South Africa, as one such example, which attempts to re-imagine the country as anti-apartheid and anti-capitalist, by re-considering the very categories of politics, language and meaning through which South Africans have been taught to think.

This collection reveals how state violence arises through adjudications in ways that are not available through law's own accounts. As Sara Kendall describes it in the context of her study of the inscription of victimhood within the International Criminal Court, legal *techné* transforms the lived experience of suffering into something stripped of its texture and rich meanings, as 'data to be contained and managed in relation to juridical time' (p. 157). Kendall argues that international criminal law's restorative turn is limited at those sites in which law introduces the figure of 'the victim' within a fundamentally punitive field:

> '... the abstract victim is invoked to shore up the authority of international criminal law, while the [victim's] corporeal body is subjected to a calculus that will include or exclude based upon categories that appear arbitrary from outside the legal frame'.
>
> (Kendall, this volume: 157–8)

Kendall considers how this inscription of victimhood arises through the genre of the application form, which is then filed and adjudicated, and which either bestows the category of 'victim' upon the applicant, or denies them of that status. Kendall then turns to the 'emblematic wound', an outgrowth of juridical logics, as a way 'to unsettle this archive through revealing its biopolitical implications' (p. 158). She also considers a letter of withdrawal from a large group of court-recognised victims, which, she argues, contests the form of justice carried out in their name.

Başak Ertür examines the 'conspiratorial imagination' of the 'deep state' in trials concerning the assassination of Armenian-Turkish journalist Hrant Dink in 2007 and the Ergenekon trial of 2008–2013 (p. 178). The 'deep state' refers to:

> ... a state within the state, a network of illegitimate alliances crisscrossing the military, the police force, the bureaucracy, the political establishment, the intelligence agency, mafia organisations and beyond; lurking menacingly behind the innumerable assassinations, disappearances, provocations, death threats, disinformation campaigns, psychological operations, and dirty deals of the past several decades.
>
> (Ertür, this volume: 177)

The Dink and the Ergenekon trials, both concerning the extra-legal activities of the state and its crimes, each implicate the 'deep state' in entirely different ways. But the cases reveal the problem of producing knowledge about the deep state, as well as the performative production of the state through these trials. The legal archive hides the truth of the state's violence:

> Beyond all the noise and commotion, the accusations and counter-accusations of conspiracy, this consensus produces the 'deep' state as something of a fetish in the scene of the trial. The state is co-produced and reproduced through the case file that functions as a conspiracy archive.
>
> (Ertür, this volume: 190)

Ertür argues that a counter-conspiratorial practice is required to overcome this conspiratorial imagination:

> The counter-conspiracy works with and against law: rather than staking claims on the legal spectacle and therefore allowing it to fulfil or frustrate (and thus orchestrate and co-opt) the desire for truth and justice, it mobilises law's archive against itself. The aim is not only to seek the truth of past violence but also to discern the traces of the forces, patterns, imaginaries and affective investments that facilitate the perpetuation of particular forms of violence.
>
> (Ertür, this volume: 192)

The manufactured sense of transparency in the trial hides more than it reveals.

Miranda Johnson re-examines and reinterprets the role and significance of testimony provided by Canadian Dene leaders in the early 1970s concerning land treaties made in the early twentieth century. In 1973 Dene leaders in the Northwest Territories brought their first-ever legal case claiming treaty and aboriginal title rights. The case drew on and enlarged what Johnson terms a 'treaty archive' that was being created by a Dene organisation in the context of land rights, economic development, and political activism in Canada. The archive had two major purposes: to counter assumptions of the Canadian government that Dene people had no customary rights, and to enhance Dene self-determination and peoplehood. The treaty archive is both a historical artifact and, Johnson contends, a repository from which new historical narratives can be made. The treaty archive offers a number of narrative possibilities – inaugurating a new present while preserving some aspect of the past. Further, the treaty archive transformed law's archive by countering the official story of treaty-making told by the Canadian state about treaties with indigenous peoples, augmenting an Indian perspective of the treaties, gathering documents scattered across the country, and expanding on oral histories of Dene leaders.

Jacques de Ville provides a reinterpretation of the counter-archival sense within the context of constitutional theory. De Ville reads the work of Carl Schmitt and Jacques Derrida to investigate the self-destructive force of a counter-archive, calling for 'a certain "radicalisation" of the notion of counter-archive' (p. 216). Schmitt contends in *Constitutional Theory* (1928) that the political component should guide the understanding of the constitution. Schmitt suggests the self, and by implication the concept of the political, is haunted by a force of self-destruction. For de Ville, at stake in the counter-archive is not 'something against, counter to, or opposed to the archive, which perhaps still remains too complicit in archive production, but perhaps rather some "thing" archive destroying' (p. 216). He suggests that 'Constitutional theory, through its inevitable engagement with law and with the political, has no option but to navigate between the force fields of the preservation and the destruction of the archive' (p. 229). On this account 'Man' is malignant, the archive is but a reflection of this malignancy, and presents a double-bind of seeking archival authorisation and being free of it.

The essays gathered here find no freedom or justice in the archive. Partly interrupted and recovered stories create the possibility of commencing again, but always in the grip of traces of the past. A counter-archival sense fosters new proximities to violence and its aftermath – attentive to the space of being in memory and proximity to violence. There is a need to cultivate a jurisprudence of sense not simply as instrumental modes of perception, but as the art of valuing. In this task, and in the archive, we are only ever halfway through.

References

Arendt, H. 2003, 'Reflections on Little Rock', in J. Kohn (ed.), *Responsibility and Judgment*, Schocken, New York, pp. 193–213.

Derrida, J. 1979, 'Scribble (writing power)', *Yale French Studies*, no. 58, pp. 117–147.

Derrida, J. 1995, *Archive Fever: A Freudian Impression*, University of Chicago Press, Chicago.

Felman, S. 2002, *The Juridical Unconscious: Trials and Traumas in the Twentieth Century*, Harvard University Press, Cambridge.

Foucault, M. 1961, *Madness and Civilization*, Union générale d'éditions, Paris.

Foucault, M. 1963, *The Birth of the Clinic*, Presses Universitaires de France, Paris.

Foucault, M. 1966, *The Order of Things*, Editions Gallimard, Paris.

Foucault, M. 1998, 'On the Archaeology of the Sciences: Response to the Epistemology Circle,' in J. Faubion (ed.), *Michel Foucault, Aesthetics, Method, and Epistemology: Essential Works of Foucault 1954–1984*, vol. 2, Penguin Books, London.

Harris, V. 2007, *Archives of Justice: A South African Perspective*, Society of American Archivists.

Kahn, P.W. 2008, *Sacred Violence: Torture, Terror, and Sovereignty*, University of Michigan Press, Ann Arbor.

Manderson, D. 2012, *Kangaroo Courts and the Rule of Law: The Legacy of Modernism* Routledge, London.

Meister, R. 2012, *After Evil: A Politics of Human Rights*, Columbia University Press, New York.

Motha, S, 2015, 'As If – Law, History, Ontology', *UC Irvine Law Review*, vol. 5, pp. 327–348.

Reichmann, R. 2009, *The Affective Life of Law: Legal Modernism and the Literary Imagination*, Stanford University Press, Stanford.

Rothberg, M. 2014, 'Trauma Theory, Implicated Subjects, and the Question of Israel/Palestine', *Profession*, viewed 20 July 2015, <https://profession. commons.mla.org/2014/05/02/trauma-theory-implicated-subjects-and-the-question-of-israelpalestine/>.

Sanders, M. 2002, *Complicities: The Intellectual and Apartheid*, Duke University Press, Durham.

Sarat, A. (ed.) 2001, *Law, Violence and the Possibility of Justice*, Princeton University Press, Princeton.

Scott, D. 2014, *Omens of Adversity: Tragedy, Time, Memory, Justice*, Duke University Press, Durham.

Slaughter, J.R. 2007, *Human Rights, Inc.: The World Novel, Narrative Form, and International Law*, Fordham University Press, New York.

Steedman, C. 2001, *Dust: The Archive and Cultural History*, Rutgers University Press, New Brunswick.

Stoler, A. L. 2009, *Along the Archival Grain: Epistemic Anxieties and Colonial Common Sense*, Princeton University Press, New Jersey.

Van Marle, K. and Motha, S. (eds) 2013, *Genres of Critique: Law, Aesthetics and Liminality*, SUN Press and STIAS, Stellenbosch.

Van Rijswijk, H. 2012, 'Neighbourly Injuries: Proximity in Tort Law and Virginia Woolf's Theory of Suffering', *Feminist Legal Studies*, vol. 20, pp. 39–60.

Vismann, C. 2008, *Files: Law and Media Technology*, trans G. Winthrop-Young, Stanford University Press, Stanford.

Cases

Baphiring Community v Tshwaranani Projects (2014 1 SA 330).
Brown v. Board of Education of Topeka 347 U.S. 438 (1954).
Cubillo v Commonwealth (2000) 174 ALR 97.

Chapter 1

A counter-archival sensibility
Picking up Hannah Arendt's 'Reflections on Little Rock'

Jennifer L. Culbert

As I define it, a 'counter-archival sensibility' is a sensibility informed by the belief that we live in 'broken time' (Herzog 2000: 4), a time when the role once played by tradition has been, in the wake of catastrophe, assumed by archives. Archives assure us of continuity between past and future, preserving the past and legitimating the authorities of the present. How archives keep present what has passed away and, in so doing, underwrite (national or state) power is the topic of subtle and heated discussion (Freshwater 2003; Robertson 2004). Counter-archivists do not participate in this discussion. They do not participate because they reject the positivism that underlies the turn to archives as a solution to the crisis of modernity.[1] Instead of turning to artefacts and history to render final otherwise contestable claims, counter-archivists tell stories that realise the significance of random facts and chance events. When these stories resonate with those who hear them, they are able to achieve a common sense or fellow feeling that both sustains and is sustained by a world (Arendt 1968b: 21).[2]

[1] 'Modernity' refers to both a historical period and a cultural phenomenon. It is identified with political concepts that entail a 'universal and secular vision of the human,' concepts like 'citizenship, the state, civil society, public sphere, human rights, equality before the law, the individual, distinctions between public and private, the idea of the subject, democracy, popular sovereignty, social justice, scientific rationality, and so on' (Chakrabarty 2008: 4). Modernity is also associated with a 'great rupture' or break from tradition (Schinkel 2015: 37). Along these lines, modernity is understood as a period of perpetual crisis, an eternal return of the new in the now. However, when I refer to the 'crisis of modernity' I mean to refer to a particular break in this cycle. In the aftermath of this break, we seek solace in a philosophy that rejects metaphysics and insist that knowledge be grounded always and only in what we can observe, measure, and directly manipulate (Arendt 1998).

[2] In *Hannah Arendt and the Redemptive Power of Narrative*, Seyla Benhabib (1990) uses language with religious connotations to describe the power of storytelling. In so doing, she underscores her interpretation of Arendt's political theory as one based on universal (or universalisable) grounds. By contrast, I suggest the power of storytelling becomes evident when systems of belief in a deity or deities and practices of devotion no longer bind human beings to a shared origin, revealing no absolute undergirds the world, and challenging people to take the initiative to find or make meaning with others without reference to a common authority.

In brief, as I conceive of them, counter-archivists refuse the role that the archive has come to play as the site and source of the revelation of (and sometimes as yet unacknowledged) truth in the modern world. Thus, counter-archivists do not strive to include or uncover more in the archive in the manner of modern archivists who attend to the ghosts that haunt the archive, seeking to acknowledge those who were previously ignored or denied recognition so they may become a part of ('our') history. Instead, they dive into the past to bring up things that have become rich and strange with the passage of time, like a grain of sand that has become a pearl in the gut of an oyster. By bringing up such things, counter-archivists simultaneously recover a lost or forgotten fact – a grain of sand – and occasion the emergence of something new – a precious stone or gem – a beautiful, implausible, provocative thing that contributes nothing valuable to the coffers of information, but stimulates further reflection on the world in which it appears.

In this essay, I suggest that Arendt exemplifies a 'counter-archival sensibility' in the way her work displays the past. To illustrate this sensibility, I turn to Arendt's controversial work on the U.S. Supreme Court's decision in *Brown v. Board of Education of Topeka*, 347 U.S. 438 (1954) (Arendt 2003). This work is often condemned for being based on a lack of understanding of some of the basic facts of American history and the consequences of that history for the present lives of African-Americans. Rather than try to justify Arendt's 'Reflections on Little Rock', I focus on how her essay is inspired by something that catches her eye – a photograph. Such a thing immediately raises the question of 'facticity' or the truth of the events represented in an image captured on film. Unlike others who discuss photographs of the civil rights movement, Arendt does not try to verify what she sees and so validate her claims about what she observes (Berger 2010). Instead, she reflects on what she experiences in her encounter with a picture in the newspapers. Her experience inspires and informs her argument, grounding it in a particular event, and so preserving that event, but also foregrounding the specific point of view from which that event is narrated – occasioning something unforeseen and strange, and interrupting or even challenging prevailing wisdom.

To the extent that foregrounding the point of view from which an event is narrated renders a story suspect as a pernicious, 'interested,' or merely subjective account of history, Arendt's essay may fail to resonate with readers. But to the extent that her reflections are encountered as an attempt to make an event meaningful in the context of a world we maintain only by our wonder about the things that happen and sharing what we experience with one another, 'Reflections on Little Rock' may remind readers to tend more rigorously to the condition of the possibility of common sense or fellow feeling in 'dark times' (Constable 2014).

The power of citation

A counter-archival sensibility appears in Arendt's work when one observes how her reflections are prompted by events whose meaning cannot be settled by determining their veracity. It isn't that Arendt does not recognise facts; she does. According to Arendt, facts are 'brutally elementary data' (2006c: 234) that are 'beyond agreement and consent' (ibid.: 236). Indeed, she insists, 'Even if we admit that every generation has the right to write its own history, we admit no more than that it has the right to rearrange the facts in accordance with its own perspective; we don't admit the right to touch the factual matter itself' (ibid.: 234). Nevertheless, despite their 'domineering' character, Arendt observes that facts 'have no conclusive reason whatever for being what they are; they could always have been otherwise, and this annoying contingency is literally unlimited' (ibid.: 238). Consequently, she concludes that the 'intractable, unreasonable stubbornness of sheer factuality' never decides the meaning of events (ibid.). Only in stories, and in particular histories, do random occurrences become meaningful. In a process 'akin to the poet's transfiguration of moods or movements of the heart', the storyteller transforms 'the given raw material of sheer happenings' (ibid.: 257).

Arendt is moved to take up the 'raw material of sheer happenings' identified with the civil rights movement by a photograph. 'Reflections on Little Rock' begins:

> The point of departure of my reflections was a picture in the newspapers showing a Negro girl on her way home from a newly integrated school: she was persecuted by a mob of white children, protected by a white friend of her father, and her face bore eloquent witness to the obvious fact that she was not precisely happy.
>
> (Arendt 2003: 193)

Arendt's point of departure for her discussion of the integration of public schools is a picture that catches her eye in the newspapers. Arendt describes the image that prompts her to embark on her reflections but, significantly, the image is taken out of context – we do not know what papers she was looking at or the date(s) of publication. Even the description of the picture itself raises unanswered questions: Who is the girl in the picture? Where is her school? What is the mob of children doing exactly? Who is the white friend? How does Arendt know this person is a friend of the girl's father?

These questions seem to call for traditional archival work. We might start with a study of the newspapers of the day or the papers Arendt was known to read to find an image that fits the description. We might then examine the accompanying caption and story to see what light, if any, is shed on the identity of the girl, the location of her school, and the name of the photographer who took her picture. We might even try to arrange a visit to the archives where we can look through Arendt's personal papers in hopes of finding a clipping from the newspaper accompanied by notes in Arendt's own hand about the picture.

Before undertaking such work, however, we might pause to consider the task we aim to perform and what prompts us to do it. In this instance, a pause would reward us with the observation that the questions that set us on a path to the archive reflect not so much our uncertainty about a fact or set of facts – uncertainty that might be relieved by handwritten notes on a piece of yellowing newsprint – as the ambiguous character of the phenomenon that prompts Arendt to write.

A photograph seems to capture a moment in time and thereby provide direct access to what 'really happened' at that moment, representing the facts of a situation that otherwise may have escaped our attention in the heat of events or that have become contentious as they fade from memory. In other words, a photograph seems to promise definitive answers to our questions. In so doing, a picture in the newspapers can (and often does in readers of 'Reflections on Little Rock') infect us with what Jacques Derrida calls 'archive fever' (1995), an intense desire to get to the bottom of things, to settle things once and for all with the authority bestowed by (proximity to) the authentic, the original, the true. At the same time, however, that which we seek eludes us as we pursue it to an origin. Photography famously unsettles any confidence we have in the success of such pursuits. The medium makes us acutely aware that any representation of reality is a manufactured re-presentation, subject as much to chance (in the form of mechanical failure, for example) as to manipulation (see Berger 2011).

All of this is to say the photograph that prompts Arendt's 'Reflections on Little Rock' is not as transparent as it might first appear. The picture in the newspapers may tempt us to believe it contains the information we need in order to know the truth of what happened that day in that place, if only to be able to show how Arendt's prejudices, personal experiences, and academic assumptions distort her view of the particular scene, and by extension, the civil rights movement (Gines 2014). However, the photograph in Arendt's essay both invites the viewer to take the facts of the picture to refer to realities in the world, and *at the same time*, denies the viewer the satisfaction of being able to accept that invitation.

As I have already suggested, Arendt's primary concern in her work is not with confirming or settling the matter of what Roland Barthes calls 'the *necessarily* real thing' (1981: 76). Instead, her concern is with making sense of phenomena that catch her eye, flickering events, persons or objects that animate and inspire her to think and fashion, rather than find, meaning. A list of these phenomena would include Sputnik (Arendt 1998), as well as the constitution of the United States (Arendt 1990), and the trial of Adolf Eichmann (Arendt 1994). In all of these instances, Arendt transforms 'the given raw material of sheer happening' into something else – something provocative in an unanticipated way.

In 'Reflections on Little Rock', Arendt transforms what she sees into a story about a black school girl's 'not precisely happy' face (2003: 193). As Arendt tells the tale, the United States Supreme Court makes a poor decision: it chooses to mitigate or compensate for the effects of 'the original crime in this country's history' – the crime of slavery – by integrating public schools (ibid.: 197). First, this decision violates the inalienable right of parents to raise their children in 'idiosyncratic exclusiveness' (ibid.: 211). Second, it puts the burden of working out a problem that adults for generations have confessed themselves unable to solve on the shoulders of both black and white children (Arendt 2003: 203; Allen 2004: 197). The girl's indefinite expression in the photograph testifies to the significance of this burden. Finally, and only to add insult to injury, the Court chooses to ignore legislation that continues to make criminals of people who do nothing wrong except flout social convention by marrying others who are identified as being of a different race. By leaving these laws unchallenged the Court stands by while racial legislation perpetuates a wrong.

According to Arendt's story, the Court may not be able to correct such a wrong but it can avoid continuing it. To be able to do that, however, the Court must observe the distinctions that characterise different spheres of life and respect the exclusivity of the principles that rule these different spheres. That is to say, the Court must discriminate *properly* – it must engage in *critique* (Koselleck 2006: 358–359). As Arendt would have it, in the political sphere the government can – indeed *must* – act always and only in the name of equality. In the social sphere, however, the government cannot force people on one another. The government is constrained, Arendt claims, because in this sphere, the right to free association, and therefore to discrimination, is more important than any other principle, including the principle of equality. Unfortunately, the Court does not observe these distinctions and so does not decide *Brown v. Board* (1954) well.

As Jill Locke has observed, Arendt's argument in 'Reflections on Little Rock' (Locke 2013: 536) sounds a lot like the argument made by the Supreme Court in *Plessy v. Ferguson*, 163 U.S. 537 (1896). In that case, the Court acknowledged that the object of the Fourteenth Amendment to the U.S. Constitution was 'undoubtedly to enforce the absolute equality of the two races before the law' but defended segregation nevertheless on the grounds that 'in the nature of things [the Fourteenth Amendment] could not have been intended to abolish distinctions based upon color, or to enforce social, as distinguished from political equality' (*Plessy v. Ferguson*

(1896) p. 544).[3] Observations of the similarity between Arendt's language and the Supreme Court's language in 1896 reinforce the position of critics like Robert Bernasconi (1996) who, in his reading of Arendt's 'Reflections on Little Rock', suggests that she embraces a surprising number of clichés in her discussion of *Brown v. Board* (1954) and the civil rights movement. Among these clichés are what Bernasconi calls 'the Disneyland version of events' of the American Revolution (Bernasconi 1996: 4), the ancient Greek distinction between the social and the political (ibid.: 5), and the assumption that ethnic homogeneity is necessary for the establishment of a common world (ibid.: 17). According to Bernasconi, Arendt's embrace of these platitudes prevents her from comprehending and adequately addressing what he refers to as the 'racial issue' in the United States (ibid.: 4). In brief, because Arendt does not reach beyond these clichés she fails to acknowledge and imagine the experience of African Americans in the world she shares with them in the United States.

Bernasconi does not say so exactly, but Arendt's failure to reach beyond such clichés is particularly damning in light of her comments about 'empty talk' – an inability to speak that Arendt connects with an inability to think from the standpoint of somebody else (Arendt 1994: 49). In her report on the trial of Adolf Eichmann, Arendt attributes such talk to Eichmann, claiming that his repetition of slogans and stock phrases served as 'the most reliable [safeguard] against the words and the presence of others, and hence against reality as such' (ibid.).

In these instances and many others like them, criticism of Arendt's argument focuses on her failures of knowledge, and traces these failures to various sources in her life, including her European (elitist, racist, and/or German) background and her childhood experiences as a Jew in Germany (Ellison 1964; Bernasconi 1996; Weissberg 2012; Morey 2014). These are certainly valid criticisms in their own terms. However, what they overlook is that Arendt may not be trying to establish the *truth* of what happened in Little Rock. This view of 'Reflections on Little Rock' is supported by the observation that the phenomenon that draws her attention is not a record of the past but a shard of history. With this fragment, Arendt fashions a narrative that upsets expectations and dismays 'good' sense.

That the point of departure for her reflections is not a transparent presentation of historical events is made obvious in recent discussions of the

---

3 The first section of the Fourteenth Amendment reads: 'All persons born or naturalized in the United States, and subject to the jurisdiction thereof, are citizens of the United States and of the State wherein they reside. No State shall make or enforce any law which shall abridge the privileges or immunities of citizens of the United States; nor shall any State deprive any person of life, liberty, or property, without due process of law; nor deny to any person within its jurisdiction the equal protection of the laws.'

photograph that prompts her to write.[4] According to Arendt's story, the girl in the picture has been abandoned by her family and the National Association for the Advancement of Colored People (NAACP) to face a hostile crowd on her own. In *Hannah Arendt and the Negro Question*, Kathryn Gines claims that while the girl's father is not in the frame of the photograph, he is not far away (2014: 17). Such details may not be immediately apparent – Gines admits that some of them are made clear only in the captions and stories accompanying the pictures on the front page of the *New York Times* (ibid.: 18) – but some of them seem to require no more research than a second glance at the photograph. For instance, Gines claims, the man who accompanies the girl in the picture is not white, as Arendt states, but black. Curiously, it is with reference to 'the white friend' in the picture that Danielle Allen in *Talking to Strangers* (2004) also takes issue with 'Reflections on Little Rock'. However, Allen has a different objection to Arendt's discussion of the image. While the title of Arendt's essay refers to a particular city, according to Allen the picture published in the *New York Times* that best fits the description of the photograph Arendt provides is actually taken in Charlotte (Allen 2004: 197). Arendt's description of the friend as white, together with Gines's claim to knowledge that the friend is black, and Allen's eloquent silence about the issue – she visibly cites (with quotation marks) Arendt's description of the friend but makes no comment – raises the vexed question of racial identity and attribution. How do we know the person in the photograph is black or white?[5]

In brief, in Arendt's essay, as well as in criticism of it, a photograph does not represent the African-American struggle for civil rights but repeats it with a difference. The power of the photograph, then, is not the power of disclosure but of *citation*. Arendt claims her friend Walter Benjamin discovered the power of citation when he realised that 'the break in tradition and the loss of authority which occurred in his lifetime were irreparable, and he ... had to discover new ways of dealing with the past' (Arendt 1968c: 38). According to Arendt, when Benjamin realised the present no longer gave any weight to the past, he despaired. Specifically, he despaired of 'the mindless peace of complacency' of a period of time that understood itself to be *sui generis*, unique and of its own kind, so that no other period of time could or should have anything to teach it (ibid.). How then to relate to the

---

4   Indeed, it would appear there is no photograph but instead 'a distilled image drawn from the series of photographs taken by Will Counts' (Hinze 2009: 46n34).

5   Recent revelations about Rachel Dolezal and the controversy that continues about her self-identification as black indicate the contentiousness of this question. Its unique power to generate controversy is suggested by the response to revelations of other cases of 'ethnic fraud'. Discussing the case of Andrea Smith who claimed affiliation with the Cherokee, Joanne Barker (2015) suggests, 'it seems the entire nation demands accountability of someone pretending to be Black ... but doesn't seem to give one iota of concern about those who pretend to be Indian.'

past? According to Arendt, Benjamin discovered a strange, destructive power in the ability to tear things out of context. By tearing things out of context, the self-satisfaction of the present is disrupted. But the power of citation is not only damaging, it is also optimistic. For the power of citation, Arendt observes, also 'contains the hope that something from this period will survive – for no other reason than that it was torn out of it' (1968c: 39). In other words, by ripping things from familiar settings and citing them in alien locations, Benjamin worked to subvert expectations, disrupt 'business as usual', challenge common sense and destroy 'peace of mind'. At the same time, and with the same gesture, he saved that which he so violently removed and re-situated from passing away unnoticed in a perpetual present of moments presumed to be always already understood in accordance with conventional wisdom.

Reciting the archive

The tradition Benjamin saw broken in his lifetime was instituted in Europe in the mid-nineteenth century when the archive was established as 'a symbol of truth, plausibility, and authenticity' (Freshwater 2003: 730). Of course, archives have existed since at least the Greeks; 'archive' comes from the Greek *arkheion*, 'initially a house, a domicile, an address, the residence of the superior magistrates, the *archons*, those who commanded' (Derrida 1995: 2). Until the French Revolution, documents were preserved in a variety of administrative agencies, as well as, later, institutions of the church (Posner 1940: 5). Only during the first years of the French Revolution was the possibility of an actual centralisation of all records in the one national archive considered. Then, with the rise of the modern state, the archive and its administration came to play an important role in the formation and legitimation of the nation itself (Featherstone 2006: 592). Indeed, the archive came to be seen as 'the repository of the national history and the national memory' (ibid.; Brown and Davis-Brown 1998: 20).

It was the development of the discipline of history that fostered the sense that it was possible to '"tell history as it was" through careful scrutiny of the treasure-house of material from the past, accumulated in the archive' (Featherstone 2006: 592). This discipline was professionalised in the 1830s with the work of the French sociologist August Compte, who prescribed a positivist methodology for the collection, examination, and interrogation of documentary evidence modelled on the rigorous observation of phenomena in the natural sciences. Most famously, the German historian Leopold von Ranke proposed three principles of historical investigation – the objectivity of the historian, the close analysis of archival material, and the importance of history documenting the past '*Wie es eigentlich gewesen*' ('as it really was') – that guided historical research in the social sciences until the 1950s (Freshwater 2003: 730).

During the second half of twentieth century, empiricist approaches to history such as those prescribed by Compte and Rank were seriously challenged, however. The processes of creation, rationalisation, and administration of archives – processes that enabled history to be described as 'an enterprise devoted to classifying, fixing, stabilizing, and authorizing memories' distinguished from other forms of memory by 'the production of truthful evidence and facts' (Robertson 2004: 460) – were closely examined and critically dismantled. In *The Archaeology of Knowledge* (1972), Michel Foucault famously redefines the archive as 'first the law of what can be said, the system that governs the appearance of statements as unique events,' and second, as 'that which determines that all these things said ... are grouped together in distinct figures, composed together in accordance with multiple relations, maintained or blurred in accordance with specific regularities' (p. 129). Other scholars reconceive of archives in terms of a more simplistic and straightforward 'realist' sense of power. Joan Schwartz and Terry Cook, for instance, comment that 'Archives have always been about power, whether it is the power of the state, the church, the corporation, the family, the public, or the individual. Archives have the power to privilege, and marginalize. They can be a tool of hegemony; they can be a tool of resistance' (2002: 13; cited in Trundel and Kaplonski 2011: 408–409; see also Brown and Davis-Brown 1998: 21–22).

The power exercised in the construction and manipulation of the archive is made more complicated by the observation that the choice to find something worth archiving (or not) need not be a conscious one (Hardiman 2009: 31. Eric Ketelaar 1999: 57 calls the conscious or unconscious choice to consider something worth archiving 'archivalisering'). Drawing on psychoanalytic theories elaborated by Gaston Bachelard and D.W. Winnicott, Carolyn Steedman describes the archive as 'a place that is to do with longing and appropriation' (1998: 76). In the mid-twentieth century, she claims, 'the past is searched for something (someone, some group, some series of events) that confirms the searcher in his or her sense of self, confirms that searcher as he or she wants to be, and feels in some measure that he or she already is' (ibid.: 73). Indeed, with the title of an article about the responsibility of professional archivists to appraise their collections, the archivist scholar Terry Cook observes to his colleagues, 'We are what we keep; we keep what we are' (2011). Noting that this 'we' is more often than not 'a white, middle-class, well-educated, and not very diverse group' (ibid.: 175), Cook proposes that instead of aspiring to a 'value free', 'hands off' approach, archivists should acknowledge how archiving is subjective and culturally bound so they might 'disarm' themselves of exclusive power and, for the benefit of society, learn to share this power collaboratively (ibid.: 185).

Returning to Foucault's account of the archive as 'discursive practices, systems that establish statements as events (with their own conditions and domain of appearance) and things (with their own possibility and field of use)' (1972: 128), critical scholars of the archive remark how the archivist is reliant on other schemes perhaps related to but also other than identity, as well. For instance, when Featherstone comments that 'a discriminating gaze' isolates an event out of a mass of detail and accords that event significance, he calls attention to how such a gaze depends on an aesthetics of perception (2006: 594). To the extent that human beings make sense of the world based on the 'coordination of patterns' – patterns that are present in material 'environments' as well as in 'interior spaces of affective thinking' (Valsiner 2008: 67) – aesthetic sensibilities may influence the decision about what to collect, but also what to store, what to throw away, and what to catalogue (see Pickett 2009 on aesthetic education in response to the Little Rock crisis).

At the end of the twentieth century, these and other critical observations about the archive contributed to a 'subtle shift in the archival mind-set' (Cook 2011: 179). According to Cook, 'The focus of archivists shifted from being centered around archives as 'truth', evidence, authority, defending the integrity of the record, to archives as story, as narrative, as part of a societal and governance process of remembering and forgetting' (ibid.). With this shift the role of the archivist changes from 'being the curator of what was left over' to 'co-creating the archive' (ibid.). There are historians who explicitly challenge this idea, particularly when the shift in roles is understood to contribute in some way to a politically progressive or inclusive project. Ann Burton, for example, asks, 'If the archive...is not only partial but also complicit in the subordination of various group, how can the kind of inclusionary or exemplary stories that liberal social Historians seek be produced?' (cited in Robertson 2004: 462). In effect, Burton points out how the focus on narrative, no matter how well intentioned, may lead archivists to forget or disregard the limits and the unreliability of the archive.

In brief, the history of the archive is a history of loss. For some, this signals the end of History. For others, like Burton, it does not because 'loss itself is nothing more or less than the subject of history, in whatever form it takes' (cited in Robertson 2004: 462). And, of course, without the threat of loss, death, and destruction, as Jacques Derrida argues (1995), there would be no archives, for without that threat there would be no reason to collect and preserve what remains of the past with an eye to maintain and protect it for the future. But even when the traditional legitimacy of these collections has been challenged, and the 'sanctum' (Brown and Davis-Brown 1998: 21) has become a site of 'conflicted signification', we still have to return to the past (Freshwater 2003: 751). Indeed, according to Freshwater, 'the contemporary awareness of historical indeterminacy is at the heart of our desire to return to the archive as a source of knowledge' (ibid.). That is to say, the more critical we are of our grasp of the past and

26 Jennifer L. Culbert

the legitimacy of the stories we (are able to) tell about it, the more powerful our need to return to our sources. Despite all the criticisms, then, we
keep going back to the archives 'in search of some partial and provisional
truths' (ibid.: 740) in order to attempt a cautious, conditional reconstruction of the past (ibid.: 751).

A counter-archival sensibility

The counter-archivist resists the urge to go back. In part, as I have already
suggested, the counter-archivist rejects the positivism on which the epistemological power of the archive rests. With a shift in focus from 'recorded
products' to 'record-creating processes' Cook acknowledges that 'core
theoretical formulations about archives will change', but what he means by
that is 'the core intellectual work of archival science should focus more on
illuminating the functional and structural contexts of records, and their
evolution over time, and on building knowledge systems capable of capturing, retrieving, displaying, and sharing this conceptual-provenance
information as the basis of all archival decision-making' (2001: 24). The
styles of reasoning that are authorised by, and in turn support the status of
the archive as a process focused (rather than product-focused) legitimating
authority, do not suit the counter-archivist who tells stories. The narratives
endorsed by modern archivists continue to rely on what Projit Mukharji
calls 'information' (2010: 90). Information is about 'things and events
defined solely by their *plausibility*' (ibid.: 90–91). Plausibility is a conventional or popular standard of veracity, derived as it is from Latin, and
meaning deserving applause or approval. The humility of the modern
archivist thus more or less obscures her reliance on commonly approved
practices. By contrast, at least according to Mukharji, stories told by the
counter-archivist are indebted to 'the communication of personal experience of events' (ibid.: 90). In other words, what the counter-archivist
recounts in her stories are incidents that occurred to her and that she lived
through herself.

For Mukharji, such incidents may occur to the counter-archivist
'through living chains of communications' (ibid.: 90). These lines of trans-
mission are made possible, he claims, by grace of a deity who is 'available
to the world of immediate experience of contemporary devotees and visitors' (ibid.). In other words, the counter-archivist benefits from the
presence of a spirit that connects her to the past. This force allows her to
have personal experience of an event that the modern archivist would
understand to have taken place long ago, or to have a personal encounter
with a person the modern archivist would know died long before the
counter-archivist was even born.

Curiously, the deity of whom Mukharji speaks bears an uncanny resemblance to the principle that Arendt identifies with 'what saves the act of

A counter-archival sensibility 27

beginning from its own arbitrariness' (Arendt 1965: 212). According to Arendt, the 'act of beginning' is a spontaneous inaugurating act, an uncaused commencing, initiating deed that starts something. Whatever is begun with this deed endures by grace of a principle that is born into the world with it. This principle is the 'way the beginner starts,' the *ethos* of the act, as it were. This principle 'lays down the law of action' for those who take up what the beginner has started 'to partake in the enterprise and to bring about its accomplishment' (ibid.: 212–213). The principle inspires the deeds that are to follow, Arendt claims, and remains apparent as long as the action lasts (ibid.: 213). Paraphrasing Plato, Arendt calls the beginning that carries this principle within itself 'a god' (ibid.). Nevertheless, the counter-archival sensibility I attribute to Arendt is not accurately described in Mukharji's terms.

Like Mukharji, Arendt is interested in telling stories about personal experience (Vazquez 2006: 51). Arendt engages the world phenomenologically, not empirically (Parekh 2008: 6); she describes how things appear to her or are given in experience rather than how they are in themselves. Also like Mukharji, Arendt is critical of the methodology of social science and rejects it (Grunenberg 2007: 1021). As Peter Baehr shows, Arendt identifies social science with the rise of the social and structural theories of causality that deny the possibility of human freedom (2010: 4). But unlike Mukharji, Arendt understands the 'living chains of communication' that link the beginning with the present and the future to be broken. There was a time when this was not the case. According to Arendt, in ancient Rome, the Roman senate did not simply represent the men who founded the city but reincarnated them, keeping the founders of the city present, 'and with them the spirit of foundation was present, the beginning, the *principium* and principle, of those *res gestae* which from then on formed the history of the people of Rome' (1965: 201). However, since the Romans, what we call 'tradition' – that which bridges the gap between past and future – has become weaker and weaker, and in the modern age it finally broke (Arendt 2006a: 13). Fina Birulés explains that Arendt understood that 'throughout modernity' the thread of tradition was frayed to the point of breaking, but that it was only after the emergence of totalitarian regimes that Arendt knew the rupture to be irrevocable (2009). According to Arendt, the cleft sprang 'from a chaos of mass-perplexities on the political scene and of mass-opinions in the spiritual sphere which the totalitarian movements, through terror and ideology, crystallized into a new form of government and domination' (2006b: 26). In *The Origins of Totalitarianism* (1973), Arendt identifies what Antonia Grunenberg describes as 'the collapse, or better the self-destruction of the tradition of modernity' (2007: 1004) with the emergence of totalitarianism. Max Horkheimer and Theodor Adorno describe this phenomenon as 'the self-destruction of the Enlightenment' (1972: xiii).

The rupture was irrevocable then because 'From this moment on, the loss of tradition could not be viewed as something only belonging to the speculative field of ideas – as the philosophers who proclaimed the death of metaphysics throughout the twentieth century seemed to think – but, rather, to political history' (Birulés 2009). Thus, when tradition finally broke, the gap between past and future 'became a tangible reality and perplexity for all; that is, it became a fact of political relevance' (Arendt 2006a: 13). Now, according to Arendt, 'each new generation, indeed every new human being as he inserts himself between an infinite past and an infinite future, must discover and ploddingly pave it anew' (ibid.).

Such a task is not easy. Citing Tocqueville, Arendt claims, 'as the past has ceased to throw its light upon the future, the mind of man wanders in obscurity' (2006a: 6). In the preface to *Between Past and Future*, Arendt observes that tradition 'selects and names' and 'hands down and preserves' (ibid.: 5). Without tradition, that is to say, 'outside a pre-established framework of reference' remembrance is helpless, for there seems to be 'only sempiternal change of the world and the biological cycle of living creatures in it' (Arendt 2006a: 5). In these circumstances, it is tempting to try to return to tradition.

In 'dark times,' we give in to this temptation. In the 1968 preface to *Men in Dark Times*, Arendt describes 'dark times' as times distinguished by the absence of light (1968a: viii). The light that is missing is that which is thrown by the public realm on human affairs. According to Arendt, this light is disappeared 'by speech that … under the pretext of upholding old truths, degrade[s] all truth to meaningless triviality' (ibid.). Such 'efficient talk and double talk' fails to illuminate because instead of acknowledging truth – which Arendt defines as evidence of the mind (reason) and senses (facts) (1978: 59) – it clings to 'tradition', the 'guiding thread through the past and the chain to which each new generation knowingly or unknowingly was bound in its understanding of the world and its own existence' (Arendt 2006b: 25). Holding tight to a pale reflection, a shade of the beginning, talk obscures the emergence of new phenomena and the recognition of unprecedented action, stifling the generation of original meanings.

Arendt does not imagine herself as being able to connect directly to the past. Nor does she think of herself as constrained by a principle, let alone the shadow of one. Any principle that emerged with the appearance of something new in the past has been smashed, and to resurrect it out of despair of having no guiding standard or authority would be to risk thoughtlessness. Instead, as Birulés suggests, Arendt 'looks for a thought that, fed in the present, works with fragments taken from the past that, torn from their original context, may have the strength of new thoughts' (Birulés 2009). In other words, what inspires Arendt are bits and pieces rendered odd by the passage of time. Turning these 'left overs' in her mind, she observes how they affect the unfolding of an idea. In this process, Arendt's concerns are less about communicating with the past than about what Michael Shanks calls 'an archaeological poetics' – 'Invention; non-identity and the necessity of going beyond what I have found; being drawn into metaphor and allegory' (1992: 180).

Appreciating Arendt's reflections

One need only recall Eric Hobsbawm's critique of *On Revolution* to appreciate how this kind of approach to the past directly challenges established conventions of remembering, representing, and responding to events (1973: 205). In that critique, Hobsbawm observes: 'The historian or sociologist, for instance, will be irritated, as the author plainly is not, by a certain lack of interest in mere fact. This cannot be described as inaccuracy or ignorance, for Miss Arendt is learned and scholarly enough to be aware of such inadequacies if she chooses, but rather as a preference for metaphysical construct or poetic feeling over reality' (cited in Vazquez 2006: 45). To this day, Arendt's 1963 report on the trial of Adolf Eichmann in Jerusalem provokes readers who accuse her not only of being a poor historian but also, in the words of one of her first and most damning critics, Gersholm Scholem, of coming 'between us and the events' (1964: 51). Scholem condemns Arendt in particular for drawing attention to herself and away from matters of great importance with the tone she uses to discuss them. He confronts her directly with his disapprobation:

> Why, then, should your book leave one with so strong a sensation of bitterness and shame – not for the compilation, but for the compiler? How is it that your version of the events so often seems to come between us and the events – events which you rightly urge upon our attention? In so far as I have an answer, it is one which, precisely out of my deep respect for you, I dare not suppress; and it is an answer that goes to the root of our disagreement. It is that heartless, frequently almost sneering and malicious tone with which these matters, touching the very quick of our life, are treated in your book to which I take exception.
>
> (Scholem 1964: 51)

Thus, both of these critics of Arendt's work emphasise the incongruity of Arendt's tone or attitude as expressed in her writing and the matters about which she writes.

What they highlight but do not observe is how this tone makes manifest the gap between Arendt and the topic she is discussing. Arendt does not approach the subjects on which she reflects with the assumption or expectation of familiarity or proximity in time or space. She speaks of personal experience but that is to say, she speaks of her own experience of what presents itself to her to see, or what she takes to appear. She does not suppose that what appears to her is something she apprehends completely and knows intimately. What appears to her is never something total but only always something partial. It is remnant or a scrap, a part of something else, and a part that she seizes upon for no apparent reason except, perhaps, because it is strange. What is strange is that which is from elsewhere, foreign and unfamiliar. But what can show itself to be strange need not necessarily be alien. Scholem is confused and hurt by Arendt's 'heartless' tone when she talks about Eichmann's trial in Jerusalem – his impulse is to remind her of *Ahabath Israel* or 'Love of the Jewish people ...' (1964: 51) – because he expects her to identify with what she sees. But, as her tone manifests, Arendt does not identify with that about which she thinks when she cites and resituates it.

When we appreciate how Arendt picks up or cites the photograph that serves as the point of departure for her 'Reflections on Little Rock', we may acknowledge how she lifts the picture out of context and reflects on it from a certain distance. But we may also recognise how in so doing she saves the image that inspires her narration of events in the late 1950s from our indifference or lack of curiosity. Content with our understanding of the past – even if challenged by current events to reconsider how much has really changed for African-Americans in the United States with the civil rights movement and how to go forward – we are moved by Arendt's essay to return to a photograph where we are struck again by the singularity of the girl, her courage, and the intensity of the forces made manifest in her interaction with the crowd – forces of hatred, fear, racism, pride, community organisation, state power, and the press. In turn, we tell stories about the photograph, often to take issue with Arendt's own, continuing the narration.

Of course, this narration does not take the form of a chain novel. Unlike the judge in Ronald Dworkin's narrative of judgment, the counter-archivist does not attempt to pull a common thread out of the stories that precede her own or impose a single purpose over the material being interpreted (1986: 228). Dworkin's judge is creative and curious about what he finds before him to decide, however, as an author and a critic, Dworkin's judge sees himself as contributing to a larger enterprise, taking the responsibilities of continuity seriously (ibid.: 229). Indeed, he interprets and adds to a 'tradition' which he expects other judges to confront (ibid.). By contrast, Arendt's storyteller transforms 'the given raw material of sheer happenings' in a process 'akin to the poet's transfiguration of moods or movements of the heart' so that otherwise random facts and chance events become significant (2006c: 257). Arendt understands facts and events to be the outcome of people living and acting together. Because this is so, facts and events have no conclusive reason for being what they are. Occurring in the flux of human affairs, they are under-determined and contingent; they could always have been otherwise (ibid.: 238). Consequently, they are as actual and impermanent as all human affairs.

The counter-archivist does not attempt to determine the truth of the image so as to resolve its provocations by tracing them back to matters of fact – representations and memories of which are authorised by the historical method. Rather than shut down these provocations, the counter-archivist takes them up to see what is to be made of what has shown itself to her. And with her testimony, the counter-archivist may also hope that what she makes of that provocative shard may persist long enough to contribute to the resilience of a common world so that we may, despite dark times, have a place to say something meaningful.

References

Allen, D. 2004, *Talking to Strangers: Anxieties of Citizenship since* Brown v. Board of Education, University of Chicago Press, Chicago.

Arendt, H. 1965, *On Revolution*, Penguin, New York.

Arendt, H. 1968a, 'Preface', in *Men in Dark Times*, Harcourt Brace & Company, San Diego, CA, pp. vii–x.

Arendt, H. 1968b, 'On Humanity in Dark Times: Thoughts about Lessing', in *Men in Dark Times*, Harcourt Brace & Company, San Diego, CA, pp. 3–31.

Arendt, H. 1968c, 'Introduction', trans. H. Zohn, in W. Benjamin (1968), H. Arendt (ed.) *Illuminations*, Schocken, New York, pp. 1–55.

Arendt, H. 1973, *The Origins of Totalitarianism*, Harcourt Brace Jovanovich, San Diego.

Arendt, H. 1978, *The Life of the Mind: Thinking*, Harcourt Brace Jovanovich, San Diego.

Arendt, H. 1990, *On Revolution*. London: Penguin.

Arendt, H. 1994, *Eichmann in Jerusalem: A Report on the Banality of Evil*, Penguin, New York.

Arendt, H. 1998, *The Human Condition*, University of Chicago Press, Chicago.

Arendt, H. 2003, 'Reflections on Little Rock', in J. Kohn (ed.), *Responsibility and Judgment*, Schocken, New York, pp. 193–213.

Arendt, H. 2006a, 'Preface: The Gap Between Past and Future', in *Between Past and Future: Eight Exercises in Political Thought*, Penguin, New York, pp. 3–15.

Arendt, H. 2006b, 'Tradition and the Modern Age', in *Between Past and Future: Eight Exercises in Political Thought*, Penguin, New York, pp. 17–40.

Arendt, H. 2006c, 'Truth and Politics', in *Between Past and Future: Eight Exercises in Political Thought*, Penguin, New York, pp. 223–259.

Baehr, P. 2010, *Hannah Arendt, Totalitarianism, and the Social Sciences*, Stanford University Press, Stanford.

Barthes, R. 1981, *Camera Lucida: Reflections on Photography*, trans. R. Howard, Farrar, Straus, and Giroux, New York.

Barker, J. 2015, 'Rachel Dolezal and Andrea Smith: Integrity, Ethics, Accountability, Identity', *Tequilasovereign*, viewed 7 February 2015, <https://tequilasovereign.wordpress.com/2015/06/30/rachel-dolezal-and-andrea-smith/>.

Benhabib, S. 1990, 'Hannah Arendt and the Redemptive Power of Narrative', *Social Research*, vol. 57, no. 1, pp. 167–196.

32 Jennifer L. Culbert

Berger, M. 2010, *For All the World to See: Visual Culture and the Struggle for Civil Rights*, Yale University Press, New Haven, CT.

Berger, M. 2011, *Seeing through Race: A Reinterpretation of Civil Rights Photography*, University of California Press, Berkeley.

Bernasconi, R. 1996, 'The Double Face of the Political and the Social: Hannah Arendt and America's Racial Divisions', *Research in Phenomenology*, vol. 26, pp. 3–24.

Birulés, F. 2009, 'Contingency, History and Narration in Hannah Arendt', trans. A. Lomas, *HannahArendt.net*, viewed 21 August 2014, <www.hannaharendt.net/index.php/han/article/view/149/264>.

Brown v. Board of Education of Topeka, 347 U.S. 483 (1954).

Brown, R. and Davis-Brown, B. 1998, 'The Making of Memory: The Politics of Archives, Libraries, and Museums in the Construction of National Consciousness', *History of the Human Sciences*, vol. 11, no. 4, pp. 17–32.

Chakrabarty, D. 2008, *Provincializing Europe: Postcolonial Thought and Historical Difference*, Princeton University Press, Princeton.

Constable, M. 2014, *Our Word is Our Bond: How Legal Speech Acts*, Stanford University Press, Stanford.

Cook, T. 2001, 'Archival Science and Postmodernism: New Formulations for Old Concepts', *Archival Science*, vol. 1, pp. 3–24.

Cook, T. 2011, '"We Are What We Keep; We Keep What We Are": Archival Appraisal Past, Present and Future', *Journal of the Society of Archivists*, vol. 32, no. 2, pp. 173–189.

Derrida, J. 1995, *Archive Fever: A Freudian Impression*, trans. E. Prenowitz, University of Chicago Press, Chicago.

Dworkin, R. 1986, *Law's Empire*, Harvard University Press, Cambridge, MA.

Ellison, R. 1964, 'The World and the Jug', in *Shadow and Act*, Random House, New York, pp. 107–143.

Featherstone, M. 2006, 'Archive', *Theory, Culture and Society*, vol. 23, no. 2–3, pp. 591–596.

Foucault, M. 1972, *The Archeology of Knowledge*, trans. A.M. Sheridan Smith, Vintage Books, New York.

Freshwater, H. 2003, 'The Allure of the Archive', *Poetics Today*, vol. 24, no. 4, pp. 729–758.

Gines, K. 2014, *Hannah Arendt and the Negro Question*, Indiana University Press, Bloomington, IN.

Grunenberg, A. 2007, 'Arendt, Heidegger, Jaspers: Thinking Through the Breach in Tradition', *Social Research*, vol. 74, no. 4, pp. 1003–1028.

Hardiman, R. 2009, 'En Mal D'Archive: Postmodernist Theory and Recordkeeping', *Journal of the Society of Archivists*, vol. 30, no. 1, pp. 27–44.

Herzog, A. 2000, 'Illuminating Inheritance: Benjamin's Influence on Arendt's Political Storytelling', *Philosophy and Social Criticism*, vol. 26, no. 5, pp. 1–27.

Hinze, C.F. 2009, 'Reconsidering Little Rock: Hannah Arendt, Martin Luther King Jr., and Catholic Social Thought on Children and Families in the Struggle for Justice', *Journal of the Society of Christian Ethics*, vol. 29, no. 1, pp. 25–50.

Hobsbawm, E.J. 1973, 'Hannah Arendt on Revolution', in *Revolutionaries, Contemporary Essays*, Weidenfeld and Nicolson, London, pp. 201–208.

Horkheimer M. and Adorno, T. 1972, *Dialectic of Enlightenment*, trans. J. Cumming, Continuum, New York.

Ketelaar, E. 1999, 'Archivalization and Archiving', *Archives and Manuscripts*, vol. 27, pp. 54–61.

Koselleck, R. 2006, 'Crisis', trans. M. Richter, *Journal of the History of Ideas*, vol. 67, no. 2, pp. 357–400.

Locke, J. 2013, 'Little Rock's Social Question: Reading Arendt on School Desegregation and Social Climbing', *Political Theory*, vol. 41, no. 4, pp. 533–561.

Morey, M. 2014, 'Reassessing Hannah Arendt's "Reflections on Little Rock" (1959)', *Law, Culture, and the Humanities*, vol. 10, no. 1, pp. 88–110.

Mukharji, P. 2010, 'Babon Gaji's Many Pasts: The Adventures of a Historian in a Counter-Archive', *Contemporary South Asia*, vol. 18, no. 1, pp. 89–104.

Parekh, S. 2008, *Hannah Arendt and the Challenge of Modernity: A Phenomenology of Human Rights*, Routledge, New York.

Pickett, A. 2009, 'Images, Dialogue, and Aesthetic Education: Arendt's Response to the Little Rock Crisis', *Philosophical Studies in Education*, vol. 40, pp. 188–199.

Plessy v. Ferguson, 163 U.S. 537 (1896).

Posner, E. 1940, 'Some Aspects of Archival Development since the French Revolution', in M. Daniels and T. Walch (eds), *A Modern Archives Reader: Basic Readings on Archival Theory and Practice* (1984), National Archives Trust Fund Board, Washington, pp. 3–14.

Robertson, C. 2004, 'The Archive, Disciplinarity, and Governing: Cultural Studies and the Writing of History', *Cultural Studies-Critical Methodologies*, vol. 4, no. 4, pp. 450–471.

Schinkel, W. 2015, 'The Image of Crisis: Walter Benjamin and the Interpretation of "Crisis" in Modernity', *Thesis Eleven*, vol. 127, no. 1, pp. 36–51.

Scholem, G. 1964, 'Eichmann in Jerusalem', *Encounter*, pp. 51–52.

Schwartz, J. and Cook, T. 2002, 'Archives, Records, and Power: The Making of Modern Memory', *Archival Science* vol. 2, pp. 1–19.

Shanks, M. 1992, *Experiencing the Past: On the Character of Archaeology*, Routledge, London.

Steedman, C. 1998, 'The Space of Memory: In an Archive', *History of the Human Sciences*, vol. 11, no. 4, pp. 65–83.

Trundel, C. and Kaplonski, C. 2011, 'Tracing the Political Lives of Archival Documents', *History and Anthropology*, vol. 22, no. 4, pp. 407–414.

Valsiner, J. 2008, 'Ornamented Worlds and Textures of Feeling: The Power of Abundance', *Outlines: Critical Practice Studies*, vol. 10, no. 1, pp. 67–78.

Vazquez, R. 2006, 'Thinking the Event with Hannah Arendt', *European Journal of Social Theory*, vol. 9, no. 1, pp. 43–57.

Weissberg, L. 2012, 'From Konigsberg to Little Rock: Hannah Arendt and the Concept of Childhood', in E. Goeble and S. Weigel (eds), *'Escape to Life': German Intellectuals in New York: A Compendium on Exile after 1933*, Walter D. Gruyter, Berlin, pp. 80–99.

Chapter 2

Listening to the archive
Failing to hear[1]

Jill Stauffer

> To read from a reparative position is to surrender the knowing, anxious paranoid determination that no horror, however apparently unthinkable, shall ever come to the reader *as new*.
>
> (Eve Sedgwick 2009: 146)

Another, less eloquent way of stating what Sedgwick says is: if you read reparatively you open yourself to surprise, to the sometimes unwelcome sense that you do not already have at hand the tools you need for hearing and responding. Such an experience can be unsettling – and so we may understand why what Sedgwick calls 'paranoid reading' so often predominates in critical scholarship. Paranoid reading is a kind of insurance policy against the disappointment that comes with wanting the world to be one way and finding that it is not that way. If, when you analyse the world, its people and events, you arrive at the analysis always already knowing that what you'll find is oppression, violence and abuse of power needing to be debunked, you won't be disappointed when that's what you find. One of Sedgwick's points is that if that's your technique, you may, in your search for the theory-structure that explains the objects of your focus, miss ambiguities haunting the world of those objects. In doing that you may also inadvertently have subscribed to a theory of communication as transparency, where what gets said means only what is said and the truth sets things aright. And if that is your belief you may, as Sedgwick also notes, fail to appreciate that uncovering abuse does not accomplish repair on its own. Sometimes it doesn't even help.

Reparative reading opens the reader to surprise, to finding a world in a state she did not expect, for better and for worse. Persons open to being unsettled may, at certain times and in certain places, be most able to

---

1 This essay is excerpted from a chapter called 'Hearing' in *Ethical Loneliness: The Injustice of Not Being Heard*, by Jill Stauffer. Copyright © 2015 Columbia University Press. Reprinted with permission of the publisher. Parts of the section on Hanna F. also appeared in Stauffer's 'A Hearing: Forgiveness, Resentment and Recovery in Law', 2012.

improvise new responses to harms that no pre-existing remedy fully comprehends. The self with a will to repair needs to be open to being interrupted, to hearing something other than what she expected. And that matters because some injustices are made of a failure of hearing. Such failures may happen even in institutions *designed* for hearing: courts, archives of testimony, truth commissions. When a speaker speaks in an institution designed for hearing, and an audience empowered to listen hears something other than what she says, it can be difficult to determine who is responsible for failed communication, especially if we get stuck thinking that responsibility equates with culpability. If we think instead of responsibility as the duty to respond or to be responsive, other possibilities may present themselves. These possibilities will require of us that we learn how to hear better what is being said in the testimonies that we collect and store away in law's archives.

Hanna F. – Resilience is not the only survival tactic

Toward the end of a 90-minute interview done for the Fortunoff Video Archive for Holocaust Testimonies at Yale, an interviewer asks concentration camp survivor Hanna F. what she felt when liberation finally came. Her immediate response is: 'That I am alone in the whole world' (Feiler 1980). She had nowhere to go, no loved ones left living to reunite with, she could not return to her home in Poland, and so she was 'simply lost without words'. One of the interviewers then asks her how she feels about being Jewish now, given that she spent all of the war either pretending she was half-Jewish or not Jewish at all. She says: 'It took me a while 'til I met my husband after the war that I still had my assumed name. And afterward I went back to my old name, my own identity. To my own Jewishness. And I am Jewish all right'. Then a second interviewer adds, 'And very plucky. You were able to survive because you were so plucky, when you stepped back out …'. The interviewer is referring to how Hanna got out of Auschwitz a second time. Because she had papers that proved she was Aryan, she had been selected to be sent to Germany to work. But once she was in line to board a bus, a soldier told her to get out of the line because her head was shaved – apparently camp officials didn't want hairless women returning to Germany, making the camps look bad. When that soldier looked away she got back in line. He saw her and ordered her out again. Then he left and she got back in line a third time, and made it onto the bus. That makes her 'plucky' in the eyes of one interviewer. But to the suggestion that she is plucky, Hanna responds with a string of 'no's: 'No, dear, no dear, no … no, I had, no …'. She continues: 'How should I explain to you? I know that I have to survive. Even running away, even being with people constantly, especially the second part, the second time being back in Auschwitz. That time I had determined already to survive and you know what? It wasn't luck, it was

36 Jill Stauffer

stupidity'. The interviewer adds, 'And a lot of guts'. Hanna F. corrects her, saying, 'No, no, no. No, but there were no guts, there were just sheer stupidity'. The interviewer counters: 'Well, but you stepped back in line'. Hanna F. responds, 'I just, you know ...', and then one of the interviewers stands up, blocking the camera, and says, 'I am going to take your microphone', ending the interview. It is a curious exchange, one in which failure to hear abounds. An interviewer tells Hanna F. that she was plucky; she hears 'lucky' and responds to clarify that luck had nothing to do with it. The interviewer doesn't catch the miscommunication and so states in other words what amounts to the same thing, 'you had a lot of guts'. Meanwhile Hanna is trying to correct the misperception – to describe what really allowed her to survive – but that is what we do not get a chance to hear from her. Interviewers set up a scene for hearing, and then fail to listen.

Lawrence Langer uses this scene to draw our attention to moments when interviewers encourage certain kinds of testimony and discourage others. In his rendering of the conversation, when Hanna says she survived through stupidity, 'the two interviewers laugh deprecatingly, overriding her voice with their own "explanation", as one calls out, "You had a lot of guts!"' (Langer 1991: 64). Having also watched the tape, I am not certain that that is what happened. It is possible that one of the interviewers is being deprecating, but more likely that she really wants to support Hanna's strength in pushing her way through situations that many did not survive. After all, it is no small thing to get out of Auschwitz, alive, twice. However, either way, the outcome is that Hanna doesn't get heard at precisely the moment when she seems to be opening up the most. It is a scene of failed hearing.

Much of Hanna's testimony is resistant or difficult. She says multiple times, when asked to describe her experiences, things like, 'No, it is very hard to describe it', 'It is very hard to go into every detail', 'I cannot go into the details that you want to. Some of them are so gruesome. I really cannot go back so far. It hurts', or 'Must I go back to those things? I would rather not' (Feiler 1980). She often starts to tell a painful story, then pauses for a long while, then changes the topic, resorting back to a more controlled narrative. That may be because 'lots of survivors compartmentalize the issues and retrieve the memories in disjointed fashion to protect themselves from being overwhelmed by the whole memory,' as psychologist Mary Fabri observes (cited in O'Connell 2005 p. 333). Or she may have other reasons for not answering the questions put to her. In the video it seems clear that she tells the story she wants to tell rather than the one she is being asked for. In her telling, the story is not about being 'plucky'. Hanna's interviewers seem to want redemptive stories about the resilience of the human spirit and the drive to live against all odds. Because that is what they want, that is also what they hear.

Langer points out that, while there may be redemptive stories to tell, many times, survivors of grave abuse do not marvel at the strength of the

Listening to the archive   37

human spirit, especially not their own. Instead they 'mourn its fragility when the isolated self has no support from the surrounding milieu to validate it' (Langer 1991: 202). In other words, if we listened well to what testimonies such as Hanna's try to convey, it might interrupt our preconceptions about what testimony after violence should accomplish. We might also find ourselves face to face with our own responsibility as listeners who have the power to hear or to fail to hear.

Why we may fail to hear

Of course, those who are put in the place of the hearer of testimony may have reasons for not hearing well. They may be constrained to adhere to the facts of the case or the established laws and procedures. They may have a political interest in a restorative discourse. They may be overwhelmed by how far the demand for help exceeds their capacity to offer assistance. Or they may be protecting themselves from the trauma of hearing. After all, stenographers, interpreters and journalists working on South Africa's Truth and Reconciliation Commission (TRC) developed symptoms of post-traumatic stress disorder from listening.[2] One need not even hear the stories in person in order to undergo effects of trauma. Priscilla Hayner reports that 'a number of commissions have found that the staff who are most disturbed by the harrowing tales of torture and abuse are not those taking statements directly from victims, but are instead data entry staff charged with coding and entering the information into the database' (Hayner 2001: 151). It might be someone's job to spend long days entering data in codes for abuses such as: forcible abduction, amputation, beating of head against wall, pulling out of teeth, removal of fingernails, being buried alive, being burned with chemicals, head submerged in water, being forced to watch the torture of others, genital mutilation, gang rape, burning of body parts, disembowelment, and so on. Exposure, even in the abstraction of codes, to the breadth, depth and volume of the terrible things human beings have done to other human beings may take its toll.

Dori Laub (1992: 72) lists six ways in which those who listen to traumatic testimony try to insulate themselves from hearing what it says:

(1) mental paralysis, brought on by a fear of merging with the atrocities;
(2) outrage and anger, unwittingly directed at the victim;

---

2   Antjie Krog, who reported on the TRC, recounts that already in the second week of hearings she felt herself losing language, and thought of resigning her post. The next morning a counsellor addressed the journalists, to warn them that they might experience the same symptoms as victims, finding themselves feeling powerless, without help and without words. Krog writes, 'I am shocked to be a textbook case within a mere ten days' (Krog 2007: 51).

38 Jill Stauffer

(3) withdrawal and numbness;
(4) a flood of awe and fear – the impulse to endow the survivor with sanctity and thereby keep her at a distance, to avoid the intimacy involved in knowing;
(5) foreclosure through facts, circumventing human experience through an obsession with details, or by only hearing what you already know; and, finally,
(6) hyperemotionality, where the testifier is drowned in the listener's defensive affectivity.

So, listeners have a responsibility to hear well. But they may have conscious or unconscious resistances to hearing well. The problem is likely even more complicated than that, however. Why do so many of us want to hear the narrative of resilience rather than the story of destruction? Psychologist Ronnie Janoff-Bulman (1992) has argued, using studies and her own clinical work as evidence, that human beings have a need to assume that the world is benevolent and that responsible actions can lead to good outcomes. That is another way of saying that human beings want to be able to take existence for granted, and so they work very hard – sometimes to the point of denial of reality – to make of the world a place where they might do that. Even though it seems to inhabit the opposite end of a spectrum, the will to believe in the world's benevolence is related to what Sedgwick calls 'paranoid reading', in that it, wilfully or not, structures experience of the world for predictability. Dan Bar-On has shown in his studies of the descendants of Holocaust perpetrators and survivors a will to distance the self from a difficult truth (cited in Herman 2009). In one case a man who had finally asked his father about his job as a train conductor in Germany during WWII learned, after his father's initial denial, that his father had watched a large group of prisoners shot to death on a train platform. A year later when Bar-On re-interviewed the man, he 'did not remember his father's disclosure, or that he had in turn repeated the story to Bar-On' (cited in Herman 2009: 129). Judith Herman, in commenting on this case, describes Bar-On's metaphor of a 'double wall erected to prevent acknowledgement of the memory of crime. The fathers did not want to tell; the children did not want to know' (Herman 2009: 129). That is part of how we shield ourselves from painful knowledge. It is also how we perpetuate the pain of those who lack the capacity to erect such mental shelter. James Baldwin puts it well with regard to racial prejudice in the United States in *The Fire Next Time*: 'This is the crime of which I accuse my country and my countrymen, and for which I nor time nor history will ever forgive them, that they have destroyed and are destroying hundreds of thousands of lives and do not know and do not want to know it' (Baldwin 1990: 5). Baldwin recognises that conditions for apology or reconciliation are not met, and beyond that, that few even recognise their absence.

Herman observes that the human tendency to want a benevolent world can distort the perceptions of bystanders – people who live in a violent or unjust world (this world) but whose daily lives still allow them to think otherwise. She writes that, like the son of the war-time train operator, 'we have been reluctant to know about the crimes we live with every day. We have sought information only when prodded to do so, and once we have acquired the information we have been eager to forget it again as soon as possible' (Herman 2009: 135). We may fail to hear because we are indifferent to what has happened, because cultural difference makes a story difficult to understand, or because it is painful to absorb the truth of violent events. We may also fail to hear because we don't want to be confronted with something we didn't foresee, or because there is no common frame for the experience being described. But Hanna F. wanted to tell a story made up of equal parts resilience and destruction. We need to hear both parts. The paranoid reading approach is certain that the world will only offer up horrors. Wanting to hear only stories of resilience shares with paranoid reading a determination not to be taken unaware by any revelation: nothing will surprise either approach.

Fragility's complication

Janoff-Bulman observes that when a human being undergoes a trauma inflicted by another human being, 'the world is suddenly a malevolent one, not simply because something bad has happened to the victim but because the world of people is seriously tainted. Trust in others is seriously disturbed' (1992: 78). Such violation damages a person's sense of her own self's boundaries and may destroy her trust in the world. Ruth Kluger adds: 'What matters is not just what we endure, but also what kind of misery it is, where it comes from. The worst is the kind that is imposed by others with malicious intent. That's the kind from which no one recovers' (2003: 17). Recovery from such harm can be difficult at least in part because the shattering of the initial view of the world as kind and caring cannot be undone. Those who work to recover from human-caused trauma often face a difficult choice between letting go of old assumptions about how the world works – in particular that it is benevolent and that selves are sovereign – and living with the frightening prospect of building a new world in which one must give up the old security and admit one's vulnerability to harm (Janoff-Bulman 1992: 89–94). Howard Zehr, a founder of the restorative justice movement, argues that victimisation violates 'our vision of ourselves as autonomous individuals in a meaningful world' (cited in Walker 2006: 92). Susan Brison, a survivor of rape and attempted murder, writes that trauma 'not only shatters one's fundamental assumptions about the world and one's safety in it, but it also severs the sustaining connection between the self and the rest of humanity' (2002: 40).

40   Jill Stauffer

If any of us are lucky enough to have remained intact and unviolated, we don't want to hear that no matter what we do we might end up destroyed, that the fabric holding together the world that we experience as relatively safe is very fragile. We don't want to know that, and so we may find it difficult to hear a story where that is the message. That is one complication in how we hear.

There is a further, related complication. A great many of us probably inherit our sense of our own responsibilities from ideas about the autonomous self who is responsible only for actions freely undertaken – in other words, the idea that we bear responsibility only for things we've done and intended. Surely there are sites of human judgment where that is precisely how we should think about culpability. Sometimes individually responsible persons, freely acting and fully intending to cause harm, do bad things to other persons. And we find them blameworthy for that, and that's fine.

But does *that* story about responsibility correspond in any way to the harm undergone by Hanna F.? Even if we could find the person responsible for the years of abuse and dehumanisation she endured – if, say, we could put Hitler or a camp official on trial – would finding him guilty do justice to the way a whole world of meaning had to be orchestrated around hatred and indifference in order to allow what befell Hanna to happen? Not just Hitler, not just Nazis, not just everyday Germans, but the whole world, standing by, saying nothing, doing nothing, many of them hating some people for what rather than who they are, and allowing the ghettoisation, deportation and finally extermination of the people they had abandoned. Recovery from that kind of harm doesn't come from a finding of individual criminal responsibility – which is not to say that such a finding of guilt wouldn't be just or welcome or contribute to a larger program of recovery.

Hearing, time and autonomy

Seven years after her initial testimony, Hanna F. returned to the Fortunoff archive, and was interviewed by Dana Kline and Lawrence Langer (Feiler 1987). In that second interview we learn a bit about what it might mean to her to survive through stupidity. She reveals that throughout the war she kept wanting to believe that someone she loved would survive, and she calls that stupidity. When Langer asks her directly what she meant by 'surviving through stupidity', she explains that she had no fear. She would just do what she had to do. So stupidity seems to mean, for her, a kind of unreflective resistance to what was impossible about the situation in Auschwitz. My sense that this is the case gets partial confirmation from her statement late in the second interview that, 'you see, there was no brains. I had no fear. ... Stupidity. I just made up my mind I have to go by and that's all.'

The interviewers ask her: 'Do you think if you had been smart you would have been afraid?' She responds: 'Scared. I was not scared at all for anything over anybody. Once I put my right foot forward I was determined. I was pushing. I was going'. Interviewers follow up with: 'What do you think made you able to do that? Most people would have been scared.' Her answer: 'Determination'. They follow with: 'What gave you that determination? Something you did for yourself, your upbringing?' And then she reiterates her hope that someone else from her family would survive while also enacting her main strategy of starting to say something difficult, pausing, and turning instead to something manageable: 'I suppose the upbringing helped too. I was hoping that somebody will survive. That ... [pause, and huge sigh] I never went home from work without a few potatoes. It wasn't stealing it was organising'. She tells a story about how, during the war, the verb 'to organise' always pointed to theft.

This second tape, rather than ending abruptly in confusion, ends with Langer thanking Hanna for her story, and Hanna responding, 'you're welcome. Maybe I'll feel a bit better too. I unloaded a bit'. That ending might leave a viewer feeling good, as if something cathartic had just occurred, and maybe the speaker had derived some benefit from speaking and being heard. That may even be what happened. It starts to undo how terrible it feels to watch the first interview's ending. But one can't listen to two interviews held seven years apart, during which a survivor of grave harm narrates exactly the same stories, in very similar ways, and not be moved by what it would mean to have *those* be the stories that underlie the self's sense of its own history. If testimony works, it is not because someone gets to tell a story once, exorcise it, and then move on from past harm.

Nothing will fully repair such loss, but some approaches will do better than others at helping to rebuild worlds. The person whose world and self have been destroyed will need to rebuild a sense of self, of her own sovereignty in the world. That is where theories of the value of personal sovereignty, liberty and autonomy come in handy. But the how and the why of that need for autonomy and what it takes to rebuild a self can't be fully explicated if we begin by assuming that any person's sovereignty is insulated from the surrounding world. No one is sovereign from the ground up. Selves can be destroyed because selves are also built, and built cooperatively, by human relationships of various kinds – rational, affective, intentional, unwitting, chosen and unchosen. Even if selves were more self-sufficient than this intersubjective definition would have us believe, it would still be the case that, before a self could rebuild her own sovereignty, she would need to feel safe. That, in turn, requires a surrounding world where safety is possible, though that is also what is destroyed by violence. A world, a cooperatively authored thing, can't be rebuilt by a person acting alone, especially not one with a destroyed self. It is the job of the wider world to help with the rebuilding. So a person whose world and self have

42 Jill Stauffer

been destroyed may need to rebuild a sense of her own sovereignty, but responsibility for offering conditions, where that is possible, ought to fall very widely. That is so, not only because only very wide disregard allows worlds to be destroyed, but because thinking of responsibility in terms of individual culpability may mend discrete harms but will never fix a broken world.

That is why, at the same time that a person whose world has been destroyed may need rebuilt sovereignty, the person whose world was left intact may need a bit of destruction of her own personal sovereignty. This claim can't be universalised in any simple way because we all carry with us varying amounts of damage and different levels of belief in our own autonomy. But I don't think it's too dangerous to say that a huge number of people could do with some destruction of their idea of the self's autonomy. Just a bit more awareness that the self's sovereignty is a fiction or a partial truth, and that the fiction can be as useful as it can be harmful.

Yvonne Khutwane: An archive does not rebuild a world

Fiona Ross describes the case of Yvonne Khutwane, who in July 1996,

> testified about a variety of forms of violation. In the print media, her testimony was condensed to her experiences of sexual violation. Reported as a 'story' of rape, that framing was taken on and repeated in the Commission's 1998 report, and in a [conference] talk ... by Commissioner Wendy Orr.
>
> (Ross 2003b: 335)

Ross shows how material from Wendy Orr's talk was then reproduced in a scholarly book by Martha Minow (the widely read *Between Vengeance and Forgiveness*, 1998) and then also became part of the basis on which the effects on women of proceedings like the Commission were analysed (for instance, in Priscilla Hayner's well-known book on truth commissions, *Unspeakable Truths*). Ross's telling of Khutwane's story does a good job showing just how far out of the control of the speaker a TRC testimony can spiral. Many people reading this chapter will have read Minow's and Hayner's books, and perhaps a few will have read the transcript of Khutwane's testimony. It doesn't render anyone blameworthy for having encountered Minow or Hayner first. But it does show who has more power over Khutwane's story. Upon reading a transcript of what Yvonne Khutwane said, one is reminded of how much patience and respect the TRC Commissioners showed to so many who testified. Khutwane wanted to tell a story of her humiliation, and she did so on her own terms, which were sometimes meandering or difficult to follow. Her story was difficult to follow (if it was) in part because Khutwane did not wish to tell the story that the Commission most wanted to hear. One can read her testimony as an assertion of agency, a form of resistance to the expected narrative form, and an attempt to reclaim her self by means of her own story. Commissioner Gobodo-Madikizela helped her along and asked some questions designed to bring what harmed her to the fore, and in doing so consistently steered her back to the story of rape rather than to the wider array of harms Khutwane was attempting to narrate. Upon reading the transcript one might surmise that Gobodo-Madikizela had her reasons for doing this – rape was a common reality for women caught up in the struggles around and against apartheid, but gathering data on that abuse was difficult because of cultural taboos around speaking about sexual violence. In addition, the main objective of a TRC hearing on Human Rights Violations was to gather information on such abuses, so Commissioners would, while allowing victims to tell their own stories, consistently work to make sure that those who testified revealed the abuses that would help build the larger truth about South Africa's history and also potentially qualify victims for reparations.

Gobodo-Madikizela did succeed in getting out of Khutwane a story about rape. But the 'guiding' of her testimony at times seemed to make Khutwane impatient. She would remind the Commissioner that she was still telling *her* story. Since Khutwane did not mention rape in her initial written statement, and Gobodo-Madikizela gained this testimony only through persistent (but gentle) questioning, it seems likely that Khutwane had not intended to tell the story of sexual violence in as much detail as she ended up doing.[3] Ross observes, in regard to the rape charges, that Khutwane 'sometimes evaded the questions posed, or answered them briefly. ... She was not reticent in describing the other violations she had experienced. She told of being threatened, hit, beaten with the butt of a gun, strangled, suffocated and squashed (Ross 2003a: 89). She also spoke about being victimised by arson and her child's death, and described feeling alienated from her political community.

Some of the humiliation Khutwane described did include sexual violation, but the point that she comes back to repeatedly in her testimony is that she was dehumanised by young people, the age of her children. They slapped her and touched her inappropriately and generally disrespected her. Since she comes from a culture that respects its elders, the violation of that respect,

---

3   Indeed, Gobodo-Madikizela had not even seen the rape story coming, and once Khutwane described what had happened her, was drawn in to her own memories of having narrowly escaped sexual violence when she was younger. Gobodo-Madikizela writes, of listening to Khutwane's testimony: 'I pictured her in the back of the army truck, her body being violated by a white soldier in camouflage uniform, and I feel every detail of her trauma as if it is something that has happened to me: the intrusive hand of the young soldier, the shame of helplessness, and the humiliation all seem like a painful stab deep inside' (2003: 91).

when added to the other losses and abuses she describes, gives us a fuller sense of what destroyed her world. In her words: 'It was so painful because I couldn't stand it, because these kids were young and they were still at a very age they had all the powers to respect and honor me. They were just the same age as my children and what were they doing to me' (Khutwane 1996). Of course she was harmed by being sexually violated. But the story she wished to tell framed what happened in terms of a broader destruction of world. The TRC let her do that for the most part. The larger world of news media and academic writing then effectively reduced how Khutwane's testimony would be heard outside of the TRC to a narrative of sexual violence. An institution designed for hearing may use procedures that silence some stories, and even when a resistant story gets told and, miraculously, heard, the larger world may not be willing to hear it for what it is.

Colin de Souza: There are different narratives of suffering

It is not only the format of the TRC or the tendency of Commissioners to encourage forgiveness and gloss over resentment that silences resistant testimony. Jan Blommaert, Mary Bock and Kay McCormick, using sociolinguistic discourse analysis to find suffering where it is masked by forms of speech, spend a fair amount of time on the testimony of Colin de Souza before the Human Rights Violations committee of the TRC (Blommaert *et al.* 2007). They worry that his testimony fails to produce an understandable 'narrative of suffering': 'There are few, if any, explicit expressions of emotion; de Souza doesn't cry, but tells his story in a composed, rather flat and factual way, emphasizing more the adventurous side of his experience than the devastating effects it has had on his life' (ibid.: 45). So they set out to interpret the story in such a way that his testimony really does show how someone's life could be destroyed by the struggle against apartheid. But there is something not quite right here. Let's consider some pieces of de Souza's testimony where he describes being imprisoned, chained, and beaten. He reveals how, after his imprisoners throw some teargas canisters into the cell, 'I was still clever of knowing the tricks and the tactics you know of laying down on the ground and that, the tear gas won't get me, so when they came in, they saw that I was still conscious, they were expecting somebody after a half an hour to be unconscious' (de Souza 1996). He takes prides in being able to resist at least some of their abuse. He then continues: 'they undress me and they chained me up... my hands to my feet and they... put me up against this metal gate... then start beating me with the batons over my head, Van Brakel would pull my hair and you know and they was beating me till I was out' (de Souza 1996). There is plenty of that: detailed descriptions of the torture to which he was subjected. A key point for de Souza (on my reading of his testimony) is that his training prepared him for this – he knows how to react to tear gas, etc. On more than one occasion when a Commissioner asks him a question designed to get him to talk about his suffering, he answers factually and then returns to a story of outwitting police or participating actively in the struggle against apartheid. For these and other reasons, Blommaert *et al.* call his testimony 'a story of suffering, disguised as an event narrative (2007: 40).

A question worth asking is: what do we learn from discourse analysis here? Blommaert *et al.* tell us that we learn that 'affect markers are not a stable and closed category, but that any feature of talk can potentially serve an affect-marking function when it is stylistically contrastive with other features' (ibid.: 54). Fair enough. The authors take the time to listen carefully to transcripts of de Souza's testimony so they can appropriately label his speech according to pitch, stress, intonation, pause, and other indicators, and thus we may learn something about how de Souza handles his own suffering in speech form. Anyone who has both witnessed a hearing and read its transcripts knows the very important difference between the two. But what do we fail to hear when we do not take de Souza at his word that part of what sustained him is that he was well-trained, that he was – in his word – clever enough to know how to react to tear gas canisters and being chased and detained and tortured? Blommaert *et al.* worry that 'it is precisely the existence of a public transcript that makes hidden transcripts invisible, obliterates resistance and shapes an image of ideological incorporation' (ibid.: 55). Let me be sure to say that I think it is important that those who read, hear and write about testimony keep these possibilities in mind – to look and listen for them. As Blommaert *et al.* state, 'upon closer inspection, we can see very different versions, rooted in very different traditions of talking and thinking about topics, and very often leading us into a more "subcultural" view of particular representations of reality' (ibid.: 54). Institutions structured to take testimony in certain forms, settings and languages will always make speech easier for some than others, and so those who listen may need to learn how to attend to more than a bare transcript of what is said. The tools of sociolinguistics are surely one of the indispensable tools of this endeavour. But in this case, in finding de Souza's pain in the 'hidden transcript' of how he speaks, Blommaert *et al.* unwittingly obliterate his resistance to making the story only about his suffering. Ross calls this: 'excavating and revealing pain in accounts that expressly set out to disguise it or to shatter normative models' (Ross 2003b: 334). The authors worry that de Souza's testimony says about him that 'he was not one who suffered, but one who struggled' (Blommaert *et al.* 2007: 55). Though I doubt anyone who heard or read his testimony would miss his suffering – from torture and ostracisation, to his continuing mental and physical health problems, and the diverse effects of this on everyone in his life – surely it matters that he chose to tell a story of struggle rather than one only of suffering.

46 Jill Stauffer

Imposed isolation

In the early 1980s in the United States, psychiatrist Stuart Grassian was ordered by a Massachusetts court to evaluate 15 inmates at a Correctional Institution to determine whether their claim that solitary confinement is cruel and unusual punishment, and thus unconstitutional, could be substantiated. While being interviewed by Grassian, one prisoner observed:

> I went to a standstill psychologically once – lapse of memory. I didn't talk for 15 days. I couldn't hear clearly. You can't see – you're blind – block everything out – disoriented, awareness is very bad. Did someone say he's coming out of it? I think what I'm saying is true – not sure.
>
> (cited in Grassian 1983: 1453)

Grassian reported that seven of the prisoners suffered perceptual distortions or hallucinations. Another prisoner reported: 'I hear sounds – guards saying, "They're going to cut [it] off." I'm not sure. Did they say it or is it my imagination?' (Grassian 1983: 1452). The prisoner lacks certainty about what he has heard, but not because he wasn't listening closely enough. As Grassian observes, 'If [the guards] did say [what the prisoner thought he heard], the prisoner is suffering from derealization; if they said something else, or something not directed at him, he is suffering a (paranoid) perceptual distortion; if they said nothing, he is having a hallucination' (ibid.: 1452). But solitary confinement is structured such that no one – not even those to whom it happened – can know what happened. Lisa Guenther points out, 'we don't expect that our most fundamental sense of identity could come unraveled in the prolonged absence of others – but this is because we rely on the support of others at such a basic level that we can take them for granted' (Guenther, cited in Stauffer 2013: 67).

In her remark, Guenther is talking about solitary confinement, but I think her observation has a wider meaning. Identity comes unravelled in the prolonged absence of others – and that isolation does not have to be solitary confinement. What happens when a survivor tries to narrate a destruction of self and world, but what gets heard by those who listen is a redemptive story about resilience or forgiveness? What happens when a woman testifies about a complex experience of humiliation and disrespect and it is reduced to a story of rape, or when a survivor wants to tell a story about his strength, and it is converted into a story about his pain? These are forms of imposed isolation that may happen even in a crowd of people, even in a crowd of supportive people. Many of those supportive people may have failed to hear well because they are stuck in the other part of Guenther's remark: they have relied on the support of others to such an extent that they have taken it for granted. They don't even see that they need it or that it can be destroyed. That is one barrier to hearing well the testimony of those who have lost that connecting thread. Those who listen may not see that when they fail to hear, they also fail to contribute to rebuilding a world, precisely because they have failed to recognise a self who is struggling to be heard on her or his own terms.

Responsibility as response

Human resilience makes a more satisfying story than does a permanently damaged self. Gross human rights abuses are easier to punish than are the diffuse practices of disrespect that also dismantle a person's sense of safety in the world. It is usually easier to support a narrative that rewards the set expectations about how stories and evidence work than it is to find oneself made uncertain by unfamiliar ways of thinking. And tales of suffering may compel sympathy or create nation-building narratives more successfully than do stories about continuing anger or pride in one's violent resistance. Add to that differing cultures, languages, levels of education and familiarity with testimonial forms, and we simply cannot avoid the fact that some stories will always be easier to hear than others. How might those of us who care to listen to what law collects in its archives learn to hear better?

One could hear my earlier assertion, that some of us could use a bit of destruction of our sense of the self's own sovereignty, as provocative. But it doesn't have to be. Anyone hoping to understand what justice or recovery is in the wake of world-destroying violence will also have to get a sense of what it means that worlds and selves can be destroyed. She will have to listen, to be responsive. She'll have to *experience herself as responsive* rather than – or in addition to – autonomously self-sufficient. In listening, she should be ready to hear things that don't accord with her expectations, things she doesn't want to hear, even things that threaten to destroy her idea of how the world works. She will have to be disarmed.

Of course, one could take a very practical stance and say that one simply can't listen to everyone, and that missing a resistant narrative here or there isn't going to stop a nation from transitioning to democracy or keep communities from learning to live alongside one another. That's not entirely untrue. But approaching testimony with a preconceived idea of what it should accomplish might make the breadth or depth of resistance to that settled idea of what should be achieved illegible. When you encourage forgiveness and gloss over resentment, when you only want the facts of the case, when you want to hear only about gross human rights violations, when you think that healing comes from emphasising resilience rather than destruction, or that only propositional claims backed by reasons can testify to what builds or breaks worlds, you will have determined in advance that certain stories may not be heard. And then, even if you listen, you will not have a sense of a whole universe of harms that will be there whether or not they are heard, forming a backdrop to all efforts to move forward. This

48 Jill Stauffer

doesn't only matter for those who don't get heard – especially if the survival of any democratic institutions being built really does rely on the people who will accept or reject those institutions. And it gives us a sense of just how broadly responsibility for recovery, transition and reconciliation must fall. In order for any large and complex recovery to succeed, a wide array of persons must contribute actively to building a world where it is actually reasonable for a survivor to trust that, though she was once abandoned by humanity, it will not happen again. That will involve building institutions, yes, but more is needed. A wide array of persons will have to learn to tell themselves different stories about who they are and how they come to owe things to others. Brison writes that forming new narratives can aid in this 'by opening up possibilities for the future through retelling stories of the past. It does this not by re-establishing the illusions of coherence of the past, control over the present, and predictability of the future, but by making it possible to carry on without these illusions' (Brison 2002: 104). Survivors of grave harm or longstanding oppression often know why such revisions are needed. Those who have been more lucky should learn to listen better to what they say.

References

Baldwin, J. 1990, *The Fire Next Time*, Vintage International, New York.
Blommaert, J., Bock, M. and McCormick, K. 2007, 'Narrative Inequality in the TRC Hearings: On the Hearability of Hidden Transcripts', in D. Anthionissen and J. Blommaert (eds), *Discourse and Human Rights Violations*, John Benjamins Publishing, Amsterdam, pp. 33–63.
Brison, S. 2002, *Aftermath: Violence and the Remaking of a Self*, Princeton University Press, Princeton.
de Souza, C. 1996, *Testimony of Colin de Souza*, Nature of Violence: Detention and Assault by Police, South African Truth and Reconciliation Commission, Case CT/00519. August 5, <www.justice.gov.za/trc/hrvtrans/helder/ct00519.htm>.
Feiler, H. 1980, *Video testimony of Hanna Feiler*, Fortunoff Video Archive for Holocaust Testimonies, Yale, HVT 0018, Interviewed by Laurel Vlock and Miriam Posner, February 11.
Feiler, H. 1987, *Video testimony of Hanna Feiler*, Fortunoff Video Archive for Holocaust Testimonies, Yale, HVT 971, Interviewed by Dana Kline and Lawrence Langer, October 16.
Gobodo-Madikizela, P. 2003, *A Human Being Died That Night: A South African Woman Confronts the Legacy of Apartheid*, Houghton Mifflin, New York.
Grassian, S. 1983, 'Psychopathological Effects of Solitary Confinement', *American Journal of Psychiatry*, vol. 140, no. 11, pp. 1450–1454.
Hayner, P.B. 2001, *Unspeakable Truths: Confronting State Terror and Atrocity*, Routledge, New York.
Herman, J. 2009, 'Crime and Memory', in K. Brown Golden and B. Bergo (eds), *The Trauma Controversy: Philosophical and Interdisciplinary Dialogues*, State University of New York Press, Albany, pp. 127–141.

Janoff-Bulman, R. 1992, *Shattered Assumptions: Towards a New Psychology of Trauma*, Free Press, New York.

Khutwane, Y. 1996, *Testimony of Yvonne Khutwane*, Violation: Torture/Detention, South African Truth and Reconciliation Commission, Case CT00530, June 24, <www.justice.gov.za/trc/hrvtrans/worcest/ct00530.htm>.

Kluger, R. 2003, *Still Alive: A Holocaust Girlhood Remembered*, Feminist Press at the City University of New York, New York.

Krog, A. 2007, *Country of My Skull: Guilt, Sorrow, and the Limits of Forgiveness in the New South Africa*, Random House, New York.

Langer, L. 1991, *Holocaust Testimonies: The Ruins of Memory*, Yale University Press, New Haven.

Laub, D. 1992, 'Bearing Witness or the Vicissitudes of Listening', in S. Felman and D. Laub (eds), *Testimony: Crises of Witnessing in Film and Literature*, Routledge, New York, pp. 57–75.

Minow, M. 1998, *Between Vengeance and Forgiveness: Facing History After Genocide and Mass Violence*, Beacon Press, Boston.

O'Connell, J. 2005, 'Gambling with the Psyche: Does Prosecuting Human Rights Violators Console Their Victims?', *Harvard International Law Journal*, vol. 46, no. 2, pp. 295–346.

Ross, F. 2003a, *Bearing Witness: Women and the Truth and Reconciliation Commission in South Africa*, Pluto Press, London.

Ross, F. 2003b, 'On Having Voice and Being Heard: Some After-Effects of Testifying Before the South African Truth and Reconciliation Commission', *Anthropological Theory*, vol. 3, no. 3, pp. 325–341.

Stauffer, J. 2012, 'A Hearing: Forgiveness, Resentment and Recovery in Law', *Law Review of the Quinnipiac University School of Law*, vol. 30, no. 3, pp. 517–526.

Stauffer, J. 2013 '"What is the Experience of Isolation?" An Interview with Lisa Guenther', *The Believer*, vol. 11, no. 5, pp. 67–70.

Stauffer, J. 2015, *Ethical Loneliness: The Injustice of Not Being Heard*, Columbia University Press, New York.

Sedgwick, E. 2009, 'Paranoid Reading and Reparative Reading, or, You're so Paranoid, You Probably Think This Essay is About You', *Touching Feeling: Affect, Pedagogy, Performativity*, Duke University Press, Durham, pp. 123–152.

Walker, M.U. 2006, *Moral Repair: Reconstructing Moral Relations after Wrongdoing*, Cambridge University Press, Cambridge.

Chapter 3

(Un)remembering

Countering law's archive – improvisation as social practice

Sara Ramshaw and Paul Stapleton

> Nothing is a mistake. There's no win and no fail, there's only make.
> John Cage (sic)[1] (Kent 2008: 176)

> [T]he act of improvising also tells us something about ourselves and the world we share. It transforms contingency into necessity, while simultaneously reminding us of the necessity of contingency.
> (David Borgo 2014: 48)

A mistake made during an improvised musical performance may be aesthetically unpleasant, but is rarely lethal or dangerous. Members of the listening audience (and perhaps even the other musicians on stage) may not even notice the gaffe. A mistake in law, by contrast, can have dire consequences. Wrongly convicted persons can be imprisoned, sometimes for life. Those mistakenly freed are at liberty to commit further crimes, including violent ones. That said, lawyers and legal academics have much to learn from musicians regarding their approach to mistake in ephemeral performance. Transitional justice studies[2] often link failures and wrongs with apology and reconciliation (Barkan and Karn 2006; Teitel 2006). Yet, when viewed through the practice and techniques of improvisation, failure does not necessitate apology. In improvisation, it is more about recognising failures and being accountable through future actions, rather than archiving the mistake(s) and apologising for such. Doing rather than saying. Un-remembering rather than re-inscribing. Responding to the new situation with knowledge and confidence, without the weight of guilt.

This chapter takes its inspiration and substance from ephemeral performances, or 'improvised doings' as Landgraf calls them (2011: 21), which resist the compulsion towards the archiving of mistakes for which

---

1 This quote is often attributed to John Cage. However, after extensive investigation, it appears that it actually originated from educator and artist Sister Corita Kent, as part of a class she taught in 1967–68.
2 For a critical summary of transitional justice studies, see Turner (2013).

apology is subsequently demanded. Improvisation is theorised here as a *social practice* (Fischlin and Heble 2004: 11), one that can be applied to the discipline or field of law (Ramshaw 2013a). Improvisation as social practice envisions 'possibilities excluded from conventional systems of thought' (Fischlin and Heble 2004: 11) and thus is an 'important locus of resistance to orthodoxies of the imagination (knowing), of relations with others (community), and of relations to the materials of the world around us (instruments)' (ibid.). Law, as Ramshaw elsewhere notes, is fundamentally improvisational, requiring a constant negotiation between the freedom of the judge to take account of the otherness or singularity of the case *and* the existing laws or rules that both allow for and constrain that freedom (2013a: 3). What this chapter explores is how to reconcile this conception of law as improvisation with its archival elements and what thinking about law through musical improvisation adds to the discussion of law's counter-archive.[3]

First, it is important to clarify that musical improvisation is not completely unarchivable. The improvised act is never one of pure immediacy. Instead, it retrospectively develops and builds on its own history (Landgraf 2011: 17). To improvise well requires great skill, discipline and technical knowledge, as well as an attention to 'background, history, and culture' (Lewis 2004: 153). Thus, rather than eschewing all formality and structure, the improvised act can only be understood in relation to the pre-existent (and the archive), be it the original melody, theme or musical tradition. In the words of Charles Mingus, '[y]ou gotta improvise on *somethin'* (cited in Kernfeld 1995: 117, emphasis added). To do otherwise would make its recognition *as* improvisation impossible (Ramshaw 2013a: 43). Moreover, an essential aspect of musical improvisation is that it 'archives historical practices and speaks to a community about its past and present' (Fischlin and Heble 2004: 7): 'Improvisation as remembrance', Fischlin and Heble write (2004: 11).

That said, improvisation is simultaneously *counter*-archival in nature. As the 'sound of surprise' (Fischlin *et al.* 2013: 203), it is oriented towards the 'unknown' (Corbett 1995: 225). Improvisation involves practices that cannot, by their very nature, be 'readily scripted, predicted, or compelled into orthodoxy' (Caines and Heble 2015: 2; see also Fischlin *et al.* 2013: 203; Fischlin and Heble 2004: 22). And this can result in the unsettling of 'comfortable preconceptions' and cast doubt on 'fixed and stable ways of seeing, and hearing, the world' (Fischlin *et al.* 2013: 203). What follows takes as its starting point Fischlin, Heble and Lipsitz's question about what is at stake in improvised musical performances and to whom (Fischlin *et al.*

---

3   As musicians are best placed to provide in-depth knowledge of the practices of improvisation, and one of the authors is himself a sound artist and musical improviser, this chapter focuses extensively on musical improvisation.

2013: 203), interrogating the significance of risk and mistake in 'improvised doings'. Abolishing the need for apology, an archive of a different kind is created and the question then turns to what is at stake for law and justice when theorised through the 'ethics and aesthetics of surprise' (ibid.: 204).

Mistake

'Erring is essential to human endeavour' (Peters 2012: 6). It is the constant 'trying something out', which, as Gary Peters notes, 'becomes less and less hit and miss ... and becomes instead a task that gains in consistency and intensity. This process transforms, over time, if not the nature then certainly the feeling of certitude necessary for an improvisation to take place' (ibid.: 6). Mistake invites certitude, which enables improvisation.

The notion that improvisation is in any way related to or dependent on certainty and predictability appears to go 'against the grain of most writing on improvisation, which very much places the emphasis on the unfixing of fixed structures' (Peters 2012: 6). As mentioned above, performances based on an ethics and aesthetics of surprise resist memory, disengaging with the 'politics of memorialisation' (McNamee 2009: 50), and the archival process more generally. As David Borgo writes, it is the exploration of *uncertainty* that is the *raison d'être* of improvising musicians: 'Improvisers not only welcome but they worship the sound of surprise. They revere the uncertainties of new techniques, new conceptions, and new performance occasions, groupings, and venues' (2005: 14). And, as Borgo articulates elsewhere, improvisers often seek out contingency: 'Creative use of the accidental or the unexpected – as comments from countless improvisers will attest – helps to keep the music fresh' (2014: 38).[4]

Yet, as also stated in the introduction, one of most common myths or misconceptions surrounding improvisation is that it is structure-less (Alterhaug 2004: 103) and devoid of 'law', adhering to 'neither convention nor protocol', tolerating 'no system of constraint' and requiring 'no prior thought' (Fischlin and Heble 2004: 23). In actual fact, improvisation is only made possible through a thorough knowledge of the tradition in which it is taking place and much practice or dedication to learning the skills of the art of improvisation (Demsey 2000: 789; Bailey 1992: xii). Why else do many improvisers – John Coltrane being a telling example (Fischlin *et al.* 2013: 95) – spend so much time rehearsing for an improvised performance, or preparing to be spontaneous? This work or discipline is 'necessary

---

4   Improvisation, in accordance with this view, is conceived as 'the creation and development of new, unexpected, and productive cocreative relations among people. It cultivates the capacity to discern elements of possibility, potential, hope, and promise where none are readily apparent' (Fischlin *et al.* 2013).

to the extent that it allows the improviser, at the decisive moment, to begin and sustain a work with a degree of certitude that belies the uncertainty of its origin and gestation' (Peters 2012: 6).

Peters perhaps goes farther than others to label most improvisation as *predictable.* In his article, 'Certainty, Contingency, and Improvisation', he explains that the 'pleasure' associated with improvisation actually stems from a 'shared certainty' as between the audience and the improviser(s) regarding the fact that 'quite strictly prescribed things are likely to happen', as opposed to the 'much-heralded *uncertainty* that so effectively fuels the risk-taking agenda and the edgy virtuosity that accompanies it' (2012: 6, emphasis added). He continues by saying that 'it is precisely the improviser's desire for certainty that does indeed protect formal structures from any serious disruption or deconstruction—that's the point... *[I]f you want uncertainty then stay away from improvisation'* (ibid.: 6, emphasis added).

Assertions of predictability or inevitability in improvisation are extremely controversial (Borgo 2014: 38). Improvisers, on the whole, are reluctant to acknowledge or speak about inevitabilities in improvised performance (ibid.: 39). As Borgo shrewdly articulates: 'Few would subscribe to the pejorative notion that *anything goes* in improvisation, but many hold dear to the notion that *anything can happen*' (ibid.: 39, emphasis in original). That said, Borgo acknowledges that, 'as an improvisation progresses, artists and audiences alike are in a state of continually wanting to know what will happen next. Improvisations create a movement whose direction we want to see continued' (ibid.: 45). The sense of inevitability thus comes from the '*narrowing* of possible choices' (ibid.: 45, borrowing from Landgraf 2009), enabling us 'to predict, to forecast, so that we can be prepared for what comes next' (Borgo 2014: 45). Borgo reconciles the paradoxical conceptions of improvisation as both contingent and predictable by describing 'successful' group improvisation as having the feeling of '*improbable inevitability*': 'The various contingencies and adaptations that emerge through the process of improvising become "inevitable" only when the music successfully integrates them into itself' (ibid.: 45).

The 'improbable inevitability' of 'successful' improvisations, can, as Fischlin, Heble and Lipsitz point out, 'encourage people to take new risks in their relationships and collaborations with others, to work across various divides, traditions, styles, and sites, and to hear (and see) the world anew' (Fischlin *et al.* 2013: 204). But not every improvisation is successful. What is at stake, then, when improvisation fails, and to whom? And even when improvised encounters fail, can they 'actually provide listeners with an important model for rethinking how and why they need to find productive ways to address encounters with difference'? (ibid.).

What does it mean to fail as improvisers? Fischlin *et al.* (2013: 205) list some instances in which a musical improvisation may not be seen (or heard) to succeed:

(1) The music fails to surprise us; it simply resorts to clichés, or relies on 'habitualized gestures'
(2) The musicians are unwilling or unable to listen to one another
(3) Authoritarian musical gestures are deployed, or
(4) The musicians are more focused on the development of their own virtuoso techniques than with the collective endeavour.[5]

We would also add that improvisation might fail when the audience does not have a context or experience to properly engage with the performance. Improvised music, especially that of the more experimental variety, can be challenging to listen to (Glouberman and Sorbara 2004). Thus, audiences also need to practice and hone their skills of listening. However, as Fischlin, Heble and Lipsitz note, 'even in so-called failed improvisations there always remains the spark of what might have been: the fact that chances were taken (or not) and that the performative agency enacted, however successfully, can still teach the listener something valuable' (2013: 205).

Why, then, might the failures of musical improvisation be of interest to critical legal theorists? When musical improvisation does not work, the result is often thought of in terms of a musical or aesthetic failure (Fischlin *et al.* 2013: 205). But if we consider the complex ways in which improvised musical practices 'inhabit the *social* landscape', and how problem-solving in improvised music corresponds with that in other areas of human experience, then the implications of improvisational failure in music may be far more wide-reaching and profound than first imagined (ibid., emphasis added).

Christopher Small, in his book *Musicking*, writes that '[w]hen we perform, we bring into existence, for the duration of the performance, a set of relationships, between the sounds and between the participants, that model ideal relationships as we imagine them to be and allow us to learn about them by experiencing them' (Small 1998: 218). Thus, acts of 'musicking', in determining their success or failure, should be judged on their 'success in articulating (affirming, exploring, celebrating) the concepts of relationships of those who are taking part' (ibid.: 213). 'We may not like those relationships', as Small points out, 'but we should understand that our opinions are as much *social* as they are purely aesthetic. ... That is to say, we are passing an opinion not merely on a musical style but on a whole set of ideal relationships that are being articulated by the musical performance' (ibid.: 213, emphasis added). Thus, when an improvisation fails, the participants (musicians and audience members alike) gain an understanding of how relationships in general can fail. But

---

5   According to John Stevens, 'The thing that matters most in group music is the relationship between those taking part ... Good and Bad become simply a question of how much the musicians are giving, that is the music's form' (cited in Scott 2014: 95).

(Un)remembering   55

as critical improvisation scholars suggest, if we listen closely we can find meaning in what might have been, glimpsed in momentary instances where connections take place or are even simply imagined (Fischlin *et al.* 2013: 204). These failures can aid in the realisation of ideal possible futures, a process of both learning from and un-remembering the past and present. It is in this manner that improvisers become experts at forgetting mistakes, as they are only stepping stones to more certain (or confident) successes.

As such, often the 'unforeseen antagonisms' that emerge from an 'act of improvisation gone wrong' generate 'their own surprising turn of events, out of which new forms of alliance, new and unforeseen kinds of community-building ... take place' (Fischlin *et al.* 2013: 218). As critical improvisational theorists remind us, 'even in failed instances of improvisation, the social significance of the failures becomes the locus for new dialogue, however tense, that is productive of new forms of engagement, new ways of understanding agency and social practices that test the limits of the listener's ability to interpellate dissidence and difference' (ibid.: 219). This is because it 'teaches the listener that in the surprise of the unexpected lies the potential for new understanding, for necessary, though not always easy, self-examination, and for renewed and unrelenting efforts to attempt to negotiate difference' (ibid.).

Unremembering the archive: The trauma of memory

The archive is commonly characterised as an unfaithful representation of the ephemeral art experience, with documentation often conceived negatively in relation to the knowledges embodied in live events. This formulation was questioned by the 'Dialogic Evidence: Documentation of Ephemeral Events' project,[6] which aimed to reconcile the archive with ephemeral performance by exploring the possibility (and the limits) of a productive co-existence between sonic art, performance art and documentation practices (Stapleton 2008). The project championed the (often undervalued) provisional nature of the knowledge embodied in performance, and developed archival strategies which made explicit the unstable nature of documentation. This section further interrogates the concepts of 'liveness' and 'rememberings'[7] in relation to the (counter) archive in both

---

6   Paul Stapleton was the Principal Investigator of this 10-month long research project, active from mid-September 2006 to mid-July 2007, which was supported by the Arts and Humanities Research Council's Small Grants in the Creative and Performing Arts Scheme and the University of Central Lancashire. For more information, see http://gtr.rcuk.ac.uk/project/54C60FBB-7382-432D-A1AF-B526CFE15C40.

7   'Rememberings' was suggested by Simon Ellis, a participant in the Dialogic Evidence project, as an alternative to the term 'documentation' or 'archive'.

music and law. Here, we argue that the acceptance of archival doubt, as a suspension of disbelief, is a necessity in the aporia of the performative moment where the past fails to fully account for the present, and the present fails to accurately represent the past. Yet an ephemeral performance does not exist without the past, and the past is only understood through the living present.

In *Archive Fever*, Jacques Derrida troubles the distinction between the 'psychic archive' and 'spontaneous memory' (Derrida 1995: 19). Derrida claims: 'There would indeed be no archival desire without the radical finitude, without the possibility of a forgetfulness which does not limit itself to repression' (ibid.). Derrida goes on to say that such archive fever 'verges on radical evil' (ibid.: 20). However, it is not only in death (of oneself or the archive) that ~~forgiveness~~ forgetfulness is possible. For improvisation, unremembering (of self, memory, history and social conventions) is an impossible and necessary evil.

Two distinct, yet interconnected, examples, document this. In the first instance, celebrated jazz saxophonist, Ornette Coleman, attempts to escape the trauma of memory and 'short-circuit the habitual aspects of his saxophone playing' by taking up the violin and the trumpet (Frisk 2014: 157). Habit, as 'embodied memory', can both 'allow for freedom and limit the space for it' (ibid.: 157, 153). Coleman thus sought to shake off habit, the goal being to 'create as spontaneously as possible – "without memory," as he has often been quoted as saying' (ibid.: 157, citing Litzweller 1992: 117). With no formal instruction on how to play the violin or trumpet, he was free to 'play and improvise in a manner that his memory made it difficult for him to do on the saxophone' (Frisk 2014: 157).[8] Frisk explains: 'Freedom from memory and freedom from influence from extra-musical parameters – these "unknown" instruments gave Coleman a sense of *internal* freedom, liberated from the physical memory associated with his saxophone playing' (ibid.).

A second, somewhat related, example has Derrida being invited by Coleman to perform a 'solo' on stage with him and pianist Joachim Kühn at the Jazz a la Villette festival in Paris in 1997. Timothy Murphy describes this event: 'On the appointed evening, Derrida took the stage with Coleman and Kühn and began to perform his composition, but press reports indicate that the audience jeered him so loudly that his words could

---

8   It might be of interest to readers that trumpeter Miles Davis was extremely angry about Coleman's attempt to play the trumpet. In his autobiography, he writes: 'I don't know what's wrong with him. For him – a sax player – to pick up a trumpet and violin like that and just think he can play them with no kind of training is disrespectful toward all those people who play them well' (Davis and Troupe 1989: 250). Thanks to Maurice Macartney for alerting us to Davis's comment.

(Un)remembering 57

hardly be heard' (Derrida 2004: 331). The archived memory of this event is quite traumatic for Derrida, as he details at a Q and A session with the audience at the premier of the film DERRIDA at Film Forum in New York City in October 2002: 'And once onstage, I started reciting this special text that I'd written for this occasion as he accompanied me, improvising. But his fans were so unhappy with this strange man coming onstage with a written text that they started, uh, whistling? [Booing?] ... So it was a *very painful experience*' (Dick and Ziering Kofman 2005: 115, emphasis added).

Despite the painful nature of this 'failed' performance, Derrida went on to publish his pre-composed text in full (Derrida 2004). It is in this document that Derrida's understanding of the tense relationship between preparation, as that which is necessarily archival in nature, and improvisation, as that which counters the archive, is revealed: 'As all of you see, I have here a sort of written score, you think I am not improvising, well, you are wrong. I am pretending not to improvise, I just pretend, I play at reading, but by improvising' (ibid.: 332). Just as an actor knows her lines and yet must still deliver them *as if*[9] for the first time, Derrida's performance here is both rehearsed and new in the performative moment.[10]

Reflecting on this event in *Counterpath* (with Catherine Malabou), Derrida seems to suggest, however, that there is something about improvised *music* that offers a counterpath in relation to the archive: 'Music always travels "further closer" than words. The brief "rehearsal" that preceded the improvisation, Coleman's or my own, in no way resembled what took place before the audience ... [T]he event comes, as always, after the event' (Malabou and Derrida 2004: 97). And, in the 'improvised' text he (attempted to) read on stage: 'it's that music, that which happens where it wasn't expected, well, it must create, well, it must create, it must create, it must be created where it is expected without expecting' (Derrida 2004: 334). On the other hand, Coleman's seeming hostility towards memory is not complete when it comes to improvised music: '... in jazz', he explains, 'you can take a very old piece and do another version of it. *What's exciting is the memory that you can bring to the present*' (Coleman and Derrida 2004: 322, emphasis added). As these examples reveal, there is a move towards reconciliation without apology as between liveness and rememberings, performance practices and archival documentation (Stapleton 2008: 2). What this means in relation to the time of the apology in law and improvisation will be explored in the following section.

---

9 For more on the fictive nature of the 'as if', see Motha (2013).

10 For more on this event in relation to the aporia of performative immediacy, see Ramshaw (2013b).

Rememberings (into) the present

Erlend Dehlin, focusing on organisational improvisation,[11] conceptualises improvisation as 'an inextricable feature of human practice', a 'fundamental, everyday phenomenon' (Dehlin 2008: x). For Dehlin, every act of decision or sensemaking becomes 'more or less improvised'[12] and thus it is only in terms of 'purity' that improvisation in music and law would diverge. Dehlin (2008: xi) posits that the 'purity' of improvisation varies in two regards:

(1) The degree of spontaneity, and
(2) The genuineness of creativity.

In relation to the former, spontaneity is measured in accordance with the 'perceived distance between thought and action. The shorter the delay, the more spontaneous the appearance of the action' (Dehlin 2008: xi). The genuineness of creativity is a qualitative measure in which sensemaking goes beyond 'technical problem-solving and routine' (ibid.).

Assertions of 'purity' or 'genuineness' in improvisation can be extremely dangerous.[13] And, following Morrow, as well as Fischlin and Heble, we are reluctant to offer any 'authentic' conception of improvisation, which would then limit the *potential* such a concept invites (Fischlin and Heble 2004: 31). That said, it is almost impossible to think about improvisation in law and music without framing it in terms of temporality or degrees of spontaneity. According to Borgo, '[t]he act of improvising produces a temporal and sensual immediacy, it allows complexity to emerge from a simple and contingent beginning'[14] (Borgo 2014: 46). However, the 'action of response' in improvisation 'happens quicker than consciousness can grasp, and the formation of expectations often occurs on non-conscious levels' (ibid.). As such, 'any interpretation of the music, whether by performers or

---

11 For more on this, see the special issue of *Organization Science* on 'Jazz Improvising and Organizing' (1998), which explored the adaptive capabilities of organisations. It emerged from a symposium in Vancouver, Canada on 'Jazz as a Metaphor for Organizing in the 21st Century'.

12 For more on this conceptualisation as it applies to improvisation in architecture, see the video footage of Timothy Waddell and Ruth Morrow's (2014) talk entitled 'Translations: Improvisation / Architecture' which took place as part of the Translating Improvisation Research Group (TIRG) 2014–15 Seminar Series at Queen's University Belfast on Friday 7 November 2013. See www.translatingimprovisation.com.

13 This comment emerged from a personal communication with Professor Ruth Morrow, School of Planning, Architecture and Civil Engineering (SPACE) at Queen's University Belfast on 13 November 2014.

14 As Derrida reminds us, *arkh*, from which the archive comes, means both a *commencement* and a *commandment* (Derrida 1995: 1).

listeners, can only come *a posteriori*, and is therefore subject to the same misinterpretations as all human memories and utterances' (ibid.).[15]

This characterisation of improvisation, as quicker than consciousness or un-conscious, can be quite problematic. That improvising musicians 'dig into their unconscious minds and bypass more conventional modes of intellection' (Gabbard 2004: 300) has very 'racist' (Derrida 2004: 332) origins: 'Various versions of this myth have circulated since the beginning of jazz history when the predominantly African-American musicians were considered too primitive to be playing a music mediated by intellect' (Gabbard 2004: 300). Moreover, according to Gabbard, '[t]he trope of the improvising jazz artist as the unthinking explorer of the unconscious is still very much with us' (ibid.: 301).

While not wishing to return to racist conceptualisations of the unconscious improviser, there does seem to be more of an acknowledgement or exploration in contemporary writings on improvisation of the varying degrees of spontaneity, which, in Dehlin's words, influences the 'purity' and 'flow' of the improvisation, and which, following Csikszentmihalyi (1990), can lead to 'radical transformation happen[ing] in real time' (Dehlin 2008: xi). For example, Franziska Schroeder blogs that, after much thinking about and observing herself in the process of 'free' improvisation, '[o]ne thing has become clear': 'I seem to take two quite different approaches when aiming to play "free"' (Schroeder 2014). She terms these two different ways of playing and engaging with one's instrument as: 'found improvisation' and 'determined or predetermined improvisation' (ibid.). In relation to the former, Schroeder desires her 'body to "find" the music inherent in the instrument and in [her]self (it does work and does happen – even if it sounds a little clichéd!)' (ibid.). She writes: 'I aim to improvise spontaneously, where I ask my body and instrument to produce the outcome, rather than me deciding what music will be; it is a bodily attitude where I try to be very much in the moment and fluid, where I can be relaxed and fully present; something that I guess is more *unconscious*' (ibid., emphasis added). As with Dehlin, Schroeder, following Csikszentmihalyi, likens this to a 'state of "flow"', that is, 'a deep focus on the activity of music playing to an extent that we are no longer concerned with the physical

---

15 A version of this chapter was presented on the afternoon of Friday 6 September 2013 as part of the Law's Counter Archive parallel session at the annual Critical Legal Conference, which took place at Queen's University Belfast. The pre-scripted text was performed by Sara Ramshaw and was intertwined with live music improvisations by Paul Stapleton (Bonsai Sound Sculpture) and Michael Speers (percussion), in an attempt to create a dance between constative and performative *sayings* and *doings*. Our rememberings of this event are gathered together in the Appendix to this chapter. They are preferably to be read aloud, thus inviting you (the reader) to inhabit our first-person perspectives.

instrument itself, the environment, or individual aspects of playing', 'a state where thoughts and any concerns disappear', 'an optimal balance between skills and challenge in the activity of musical performance' (ibid.).

Schroeder distinguishes 'found' improvisation from more conscious or 'determined' improvisation: 'My body and instrument relation change immensely when I put myself into this state where I want to know everything what [sic] is going to happen, where I aim to anticipate every musical step and idea (is this possible, you will probably ask?)' (2014). The 'self-reflexive awareness required of performance' (Soules 2004: 280), or 'performative-consciousness' (Soules 2004: 281, citing Schechner 1988), evident in Schroeder's 'found' improvisation evidences the possibility of 'accomplished' improvisers learning (and practising) 'codes that connote freshness, looseness, and a feeling of spontaneity' (Gabbard 2004: 315). Such learned procedures 'create a pattern so complex that we get an illusion of randomness' (Nachmanovitch 1990: 27).

The illusion of spontaneity in musical improvisation plays with time and temporality, just as the illusion of temporal constraint in Western systems of law and justice produces a vision of legal decision-making as extremely measured and linear in nature. The ideal of the rule of law in Western democratic society tells the story of predictability, equality and certainty, both in process and judgment. The common law, for instance, relies on the device of legal precedent in order to ensure that like cases are treated alike and similarly situated individuals share the same legal outcome. Judges are not supposed to make pronouncements based on their own personal inclinations or whims. What is lost, though, in this focus on certainty and predictability is the fact that judgment, if truly just or justified, must necessarily be somewhat uncertain and unpredictable. Put more simply, if the outcome of the judging was known in advance, there would be no need for judgment or decision. The Western common law tradition is based on the notion that everyone deserves his or her day in court. But there would be no point having one's case adjudicated or heard unless there was the possibility, however slight, that the judge may find in one's favour. Legal judgment then, by its very nature, demands a degree of improvisation and unpredictability. Justice cannot be known or determined in advance and any such knowledge of or influence on a particular outcome would certainly be construed as unjust, corrupt and unfair (Ramshaw 2006; 2013a).

To be truly just, or justified, each judgment would have to break with the past – as well as any future that is based on the past – and offer an absolutely unique interpretation that no existing decision could or ought to guarantee absolutely (Derrida 2002: 251). This, of course, is impossible, especially in the *time* available for judicial decision-making. Judgment thus entails both a (singular) act and a (general) process: the uniqueness of each problem can only be addressed or understood through pre-existing structures of language/thought/problem-solving abilities or techniques/etc., and the

(Un)remembering 61

temporality of judgment rests on the paradoxical relation between the singular and the general. Judgment as paradox means that no legal decision can ever be completely just or justifiable: we can never have all the information or knowledge necessary to make a judgment that is fully faithful to the singularity of a particular situation; we can never have thought through an issue from every single angle, perspective or viewpoint (Derrida 2002: 255). There is always an element of justification that is beyond comprehension and knowledge. This deficiency, though, is not necessarily a bad thing. The unknown outside that is always inside the time of judgment is actually what enables law and society to adapt or change. In other words, if everything was always fully explainable or completely justified, there would be no call for change in society, no call for judgment. Eventually legal judgment would find itself redundant (Fitzpatrick 2005: 9). The continued legitimacy of law thereby rests not on its having all the answers, but on its uncertainty and incompletion.

In his essay, 'Melody and Law's Mindfulness of Time', Gerald Postema plays with the temporality of law by offering *melody* as a 'metaphor and model' in which to 'understand the role of time in law's characteristic normativity' (2004: 205). To the existing dominant models of law's normativity in jurisprudence, namely those of *nomos* (reasons) and *thesmos* (commands), Postema adds melody or *melos* (ibid.: 207). This third model is of particular value to lawyers and legal academics for it 'highlights the temporal dimensions of law's normativity that the other models leave in the shadows' (ibid.). Melody, argues Postema, orders time through the constituent elements of '*attention, memory, and anticipation*': 'Deciding cases governed by precedent is like grasping a melody as it is being played. ... It involves *attention* to present circumstances, *memory* of past decisions, and *anticipation* of the direction in which the rule or *ratio* is moving. The past is essential to precedent-sensitive reasoning, but it is not simply backward-looking' (ibid.: 208, 214, emphasis added). According to Postema, '[l]aw's memory is always bent to the present in anticipation of the future. Equally, its focus on the future is from the threshold of past and present. At any point in the arc traced by the *ratio* decision-makers interact with decision-makers going before them and coming after them' (ibid.: 214).

Postema's conceptualisation of the melodious time of law, while intriguing, is somewhat limited for our purposes for it remains tied to *linearity*, even if the past, present and future interact in a complex fashion (2004: 214). In contrast to the linear sensemaking typically employed in law, Dehlin advocates '*improspective*' decision-making, that is sensemaking that looks *into* the present – '*in* the present, *on* the present' (Dehlin 2008: 59) – rather than *backwards* at the past (Dehlin 2008: x). Improvisation, following Weick (1979, 1995 and 2001) and Schön (1991), becomes a *process* of 'evolving, ongoing action involving varying degrees of creativity and spontaneity' (Postema 2004: 15).

As with law and legal judgment, time plays a key role in improvisation. In Ellen Waterman's 'Some Strategies for Improvisation in Collaborative Writing', she lists some of the skills or techniques necessary for 'good' improvisation, all of which involve a temporal blurring of past, present and future in order to create a paradoxical meeting place in which the most 'just' music occurs (2009).

'Good' improvisation, says Waterman, involves, for example, 'deep listening' (2009: 2). Deep listening is a philosophy and practice developed by 'improvising composer' Pauline Oliveros and entails the ability to both send and receive ideas and be self-reflexive and sympathetic in one's response (2005: xix). This requires not only knowledge of what has gone on before in the past and attentiveness to the present moment, but also sympathy for the future or for the unknown (Fischlin and Heble 2004: 11). Another key element is 'a sophisticated knowledge of form and structure' which enables a call and response structure and allows for the emergence of variation and counterpoint or contrary ideas (Waterman 2009: 2). Again, the present collides with the past of tradition in order to respond in a manner that is forward-looking. The *ability to* 'code switch' is also extremely important, meaning having more than one way of proceeding at one's disposal and being flexible and responsive to the tones, languages and approaches of others (ibid.). Once more, knowledge of tradition is crucial, along with an ear to future proceedings in the present moment. 'Good' improvisers are 'committed to a non-hierarchical process', one that demands sustained focus, respect and attention to the process itself and a shared responsibility for the outcome (ibid.). Time in this process or the process of time melds together past, present and future in order to create a more just and loving relationship to the other. Finally, Waterman mentions the need for 'trust in others (and the process)', which involves learning strategies to build trust within and among communities and various stakeholders and the unlearning of lifelong habits (ibid.). The past thus becomes a tool in the present for future change. Together these elements, when applied to law, envision a process that looks beyond a strict application of a dead document, dead in the sense that, regardless of scope, it cannot respond fully to the singular life of each individual situation, to a more dialogic and responsive decision-making, one that, like improvisation, involves risk-taking and collaboration in an attempt to achieve justice or make for a more just result.

~~Apology~~ (or, sorry, no time to apologise)

Apology is an inefficient use of time in musical improvisation. It slows things down, sidetracks and disrupts movement forward. Viewing law as fundamentally improvisational in nature allows for a certain level of abstraction in which the present bows down before another place in time, where, at least potentially, there is another time in place. This re-framing of the question of judgment and justice in terms of temporality is a familiar Derridean idea, the notion that judgment is often out of time, that the times are out of joint. The idea can be conveyed more simply, and more musically, by noting that, whatever the substantive merits or otherwise of the multiple co-factors that go into judgment, sometimes it is obvious that the timing is all wrong. To rework this idea back from the mundane to the abstract, the issue might be phrased as a question: how could the timing ever be right when the past and the future by their nature are never accessible in the present?

Musical improvisation, which can be taken as a continuing and profound examination of the issue of timing, occurs, *plays* even, in the paradoxical space where the present so resonates with the past and the future that this might be considered a 'meeting'. This is obviously impossible, and yet equally obviously constitutes exactly the nature of this art form. The premise of this section is that thinking through the relationship between improvisation and time is useful to those interested in critical legal theory and law for it enables a view of the temporality of judgment or justification as far less static and linear. Musical time in improvisation is somehow a gift outside of worldly time, outside of the economy of exchange and restitution. The timeline given by the jazz rhythm section to the improvising soloist may change in character in response to changes in the character of the improvising solo (Monson 1996: 82–83). Time responds to change and in so doing changes time. By giving time to justice in this manner, a more nuanced conception of judgment and justification may be possible.

Critical Studies in Improvisation (CSI) theorises improvisation as a complex and dynamic social phenomenon, one that interrupts traditional orthodoxies of judgment and takes on a shared responsibility for participation in the community, all the while accepting the challenges of risk and contingency. To say then that law as archive improvises or that it ought or needs to improvise should not be regarded negatively. What is needed in contemporary critical legal theory is a conceptualisation of law *as* improvisation, as a creative social phenomenon that is similarly complex and dynamic and, when truly just or justified, aims at all the things Waterman says above of 'good' improvisation. Although it is beyond the scope of this chapter, more critical work is needed on what it actually means to improvise in relation to the archive that is law. To do this, unpredictability must be viewed not as random unpredictability but as improvisation critically conceived or what we like to call 'just unpredictability'. What is at stake in this exploration is the continued depiction of legal decision-making as uncreative and static, as a kind of necessary deadness or dead archive; as opposed to a depiction of the creative life of law as a dynamic social phenomenon, one that pertains to the life-affirming vibrancy of the musical extempore in which the past, present and future dance together in a never-ending paradox of living and learning, justice and social change.

Appendix: Remembrances of the event

Paul Stapleton: I'm worried that Michael is not here yet. I've set up and sound checked, but Michael has yet to arrive and the session is about to begin. I know he has just flown back from NYC and that he thought he was arriving into Dublin yesterday morning, and not today. He got the time change backwards. I also know he would be driving on little sleep, having to pick up his drum kit somewhere in Portadown before heading here, room 6B on the third floor of the Peter Froggatt Centre at Queen's University Belfast. I really don't like performing as a soloist, so I hope he makes it here in time. More importantly, I hope he is ok. During sound check I noticed that my turntable attachment stopped working due to a loose wire. The rest of my custom-made instrument, the Bonsai Sound Sculpture (or BoSS) seems to be working ok. This will be the second time Michael and I have played together as a duo, and the first time we have played together in front of an audience. And this is not your usual improv gig audience. And this is not a typical performance space. Actually, I'm thinking of this more as a trio. Sara will be reading our co-authored text (also our first publicly presented collaboration) and we will be intervening with music. We won't be performing over Sara's speech, but we still will be in a three-way dialogue. No idea how this will turn out. We have never done this before. But I am excited by this risky situation. Will a critical legal audience respond well to our musickings? I don't think I even know what a critical legal audience is. The unusual nature of the space we are performing in, where I am standing now, does not bother me. I don't believe in neutral performance spaces. The space is another partner in the improvisational dialogue, offering both physical (acoustic) affordances and social expectations. I am set up at the back of a medium-sized classroom. Standard room layout with PowerPoint projection facility and chairs facing forward. Windows on the left and door on the opposite corner from where I am standing. We are warned that we can't be too loud as a parallel session will be happening in an adjacent room. This will be an interesting constraint for Michael and I. The only other time we have played together was in a recording session at the Sonic Arts Research Centre last month that we plan to release as an album (www.paulstapleton.net/portfolio/michaelspeers). In this previous recording session we were trying to make Merzbow sound like Kenny Rodgers (i.e. we made music at a volume and intensity level that literally shook the building). It will be interesting to see how we respond to this volume constraint today. I'm all for reduced playing, but Michael and I have never done this together. Michael arrives! He is now setting up a minimal kit. The session starts in a few minutes. He looks tired. I tell him about the volume constraint and the structure of: Musical Introduction (5 minutes); Reading of written text Part 1 – Mistake (6 minutes); Musical Intervention (5 minutes); Reading of written text Part 2 – Apology (3 minutes); Musical conclusion (1 minute). He nods his head.

We haven't rehearsed this and we are not watching clocks, so the timings will be approximate. We set no other explicit constraints on the content of our playing. But we both know we are not going to decide what we play out of nowhere. I've known Michael for three years and we both have seen each other improvise many times before. We know how to listen to each other, how to allow for space, how to blend together, how to clash, how to make the other change direction. How to expect the unexpected, how to anticipate surprise, and how to cope with being challenged by the unknown. We are on last, so we will first have to sit through two other talks before we perform. Michael and I sit towards the back of the classroom. This must be strange for Michael. He doesn't even really know Sara or anything about this conference. I have at least looked at the program, and Sara and I are well aware of the points of connection in our research and have started collaborating over the past year. Michael was in New York less than a day ago, he rushed to get here, and now he has to sit for 45 minutes listening to people talk about subject areas for which he has little context. Yet, he has read our paper and I'm fairly sure he gets what we are going for. Before the talks begin I text him the following message: 'My turntable stopped working. Loose wire. Can be fixed, but not today. 2 papers before our performance. We are on at 2.40pm to 3pm, followed by questions for 30min. This must be the most surreal start to a gig [...]'. I'm surprised by how engaging the talks are, and time is passing quicker than I thought it would. I wonder how the ideas of the speakers before us will effect our playing, how their language might be used as source material. Will we respond to their words? It is now time for our performance. Michael and I stand up and move to our instruments at the back of the room. Sara is at the front of the room. The audience of about 25 people is looking back and forth, between Sara at the front and us at the back. Michael and I make eye contact briefly, take a breath, and then start simultaneously to make sound … That feels like about 5 minutes. We stop playing together at the same time. And now Sara begins speaking. Mistake. I know that quote is commonly attributed to John Cage, but I forget when and where he said or wrote it. Dialogic Evidence. The Archive. The live archive. How do we apologise for mistakes in our performance? How are mistakes even possible in improvisation? Did we make any mistakes just then? Who decides? Who cares? Does our performance really require that kind of judgment? Is not asking forgiveness a precondition of improvisation? Who am I in this act? Who have I become? Who will I become? How do I un-remember who I am? 'It is in this manner that improvisers become experts at forgetting mistakes, as they are only stepping stones to more certain (or confident) successes.' Sara stops talking and we start playing again … My preconscious flow is broken for a moment when I wish my turntable was working. I pause briefly then reach for a bow just as Michael does the same … I remember something about '**inscribing** the lived experience of **suffering** into legally recognizable categories' ... 'what forms of **silence** or **deafness** re-victimize survivors or **undermine** reconciliative efforts, and what forms of **hearing** truly do **justice**?' ... 5 minutes, thereabouts. We find an ending and Sara starts again. Apology. '[...] 'unforeseen antagonisms [...] In improvisation, it is more about recognizing failures and being accountable through future actions, rather than apologizing. Doing rather than saying. Un-remembering rather than re-inscribing.' Inevitability. 'Without guilt.' Sara stops. We play for approximately one minute. One last quiet moment. And end.

Sara Ramshaw: Our 'paper' followed the launch of my newly published book, *Justice as Improvisation: The Law of the Extempore*, which was introduced by my former PhD supervisor, Professor Peter Fitzpatrick. His generous and kind words, and the pressure of having to say something about my research to a crowd that included some of the most important and revered critical legal scholars in the world, left me feeling very self-conscious and exposed. I had not thought much about Michael's lateness as I had confidence in Paul's solo improvisational abilities. Only later did I find out that Paul does not enjoy performing as a soloist. I trusted him and his skills completely, though, and thus put zero thought into the logistics of their set-up or performance. I was more worried about how their music would be received by the audience of critical legal scholars. I was still a fairly inexperienced and naïve listener of experimental improvised music and did not fully understand many of the decisions or sounds made by Paul on his BoSS myself. And yet I was/we were, in a sense, *forcing* such music on an audience of, what I could only assume, were even less experienced listeners. Starting to feel *very* nervous. I remember that the table at the front of the room could not fit all the speakers behind it. As I was the final speaker, I situated myself to the left of the table for the other talks and remained there for our presentation. After two amazing papers by Jill Stauffer ['Reconciliation as Repair (in a world where some things remain broken)'] and Sara Kendall ['An Uneasy Ethics of Redemption: Oppenheimer's *The Act of Killing* as Transitology'], it was our turn. We had prepared the written text in advance and the approximate temporal length of the improvisations – I am continually amazed at musicians' acute awareness of and accuracy in relation to time – but I had no idea what they were planning to play, although I had heard Paul on his BoSS before. I remember that I was wearing long clunky Fleuvog boots and a knee-length skirt. With no table dividing me from the audience, the feelings of exposure and self-consciousness returned, even stronger than at the book launch. Luckily, I had the set text to guide me. During the improvised musical sections of the 'paper', most of the audience remained facing the front of the room, even though Paul and Michael were playing behind them. I saw some struggling with the sounds, not knowing where to look or what to do; others had their eyes closed, focusing intently on the sounds coming from the back of the room. I kept wondering whether we had made a huge mistake. I was scared to end for fear of the lacklustre response we may get. But, at the same time, wanting Paul and Michael to finish faster so that the uncomfortableness caused by the unfamiliar sounds would cease. I ended: 'what if one could repeat a mistake enough times such that it sounded inevitable. Is this a hiding of a mistake, an admission of mistake, a means of reconciling a mistake with what should have been, or is it simply not a mistake at all? And what role do you, as audience members listening to the repeated mistake, play in making conscious, in archiving, the mistake for which we – without guilt – will not apologise?' Paul and Michael played for one final minute. The response from the audience and the Q & A discussion that followed was unbelievable, far exceeding our most optimistic expectations.

References

Alterhaug, B. 2004, 'Improvisation on a Triple Theme: Creativity, Jazz Improvisation and Communication', *Studia Musicologica Norvegica*, vol. 30, pp. 97–118.

Bailey, D. 1992, *Improvisation: Its Nature and Practice in Music*, 2nd edn, Da Capo Press, New York.

Barkan, E. and Karn, A. 2006, *Taking Wrongs Seriously: Apology and Reconciliation*, Stanford University Press, Stanford.

Borgo, D. 2005, *Sync or Swarm: Improvising Music in a Complex Age*, Continuum, New York and London.

Borgo, D. 2014, 'What the Music Wants', in F. Schroeder and M. Ó hAodha (eds), *Soundweaving: Writings on Improvisation*, Cambridge Scholars Publishing, Newcastle upon Tyne, pp. 33–51.

Caines, R. and Heble, A. 2015, 'Prologue: Spontaneous Acts', in R. Caines and A. Heble (eds), *The Improvisation Studies Reader: Spontaneous Acts*, Routledge, New York, pp. 1–5.

Coleman, O. and Derrida, J. 2004, 'The Other's Language: Jacques Derrida Interviews Ornette Coleman, 23 June 1997', *Genre*, Summer 2004, pp. 319–28.

Corbett, J. 1995, 'Ephemera Underscored: Writing Around Free Improvisation', in K. Gabbard (ed.), *Jazz Among the Discourses*, Duke University Press, Durham, pp. 217–40.

Csikszentmihalyi, M. 1990, *Flow: The Psychology of Optimal Experience*, Harper and Row, New York.

Davis, M. and Troupe, Q. 1989, *Miles: The Autobiography*, Simon & Schuster Paperbacks, New York.

Dehlin, E. 2008, *The Flesh and Blood of Improvisation: A Study of Everyday Organizing*. Doctoral Thesis, Norwegian University of Science and Technology, viewed 16 November 2014, <www.diva-portal.org/smash/get/diva2:174512/FULLTEXT 01.pdf>.

Demsey, D. 2000, 'Jazz Improvisation and Concepts of Virtuosity', in B. Kirchner (ed.), *The Oxford Companion to Jazz*, Oxford University Press, Oxford and New York, pp. 788–798.

Derrida, J. 1995, *Archive Fever: A Freudian Impression*, trans. E. Prenowitz, University of Chicago Press, Chicago.

Derrida, J. 2002, 'Force of Law: The "Mystical Foundation of Authority"', trans. M. Quaintance, in G. Anidjar (ed.), *Acts of Religion*, Routledge, New York and London, pp. 230–298.

Derrida, J. 2004, 'Play – The First Name', trans. T.S. Murphy, *Genre: Forms of Discourse and Culture*, vol. 37, no. 2, pp. 331–40.

Dick, K. and Ziering Kofman, A. 2005, *Screenplay and Essays on the Film Derrida*, Manchester University Press, Manchester.

Fischlin, D. and Heble, A. 2004, 'The Other Side of Nowhere: Jazz, Improvisation, and Communities in Dialogue', in D. Fischlin and A. Heble (eds), *The Other Side of Nowhere: Jazz, Improvisation, and Communities in Dialogue*, Wesleyan University Press, Connecticut, pp. 1–42.

Fischlin, D., Heble, A., and Lipsitz, G. 2013, *The Fierce Urgency of Now: Improvisation, Rights, and the Ethics of Cocreation*, Duke University Press, Durham and London.

Fitzpatrick, P. 2005, 'Access as Justice', *Windsor Yearbook of Access to Justice*, vol. 23, no. 1, pp. 3–16.

Frisk, H. 2014, 'Improvisation and the Self: To Listen to the Other', in F. Schroeder and M. Ó hAodha (eds), *Soundweaving: Writings on Improvisation*, Cambridge Scholars Publishing, Newcastle upon Tyne, pp. 153–169.

Gabbard, K. 2004, 'Improvisation and Imitation: Marlon Brando as Jazz Actor', in D. Fischlin and A. Heble (eds), *The Other Side of Nowhere: Jazz, Improvisation, and Communities in Dialogue*, Wesleyan University Press, Connecticut, pp. 298–318.

Glouberman, M. and Sorbara J. 2004, 'The Return of Open Cobra', viewed 16 November 2014, <www.room101games.com/cobra/details.html>.

Kent, C. 2008, *Learning by Heart: Teachings to Free the Creative Spirit*, Allworth Press, New York.

Kernfeld, B. 1995, *What to Listen for in Jazz*, Yale University Press, New Haven and London.

Landgraf, E. 2009, 'Improvisation: Form and Event – A Spencer-Brownian Calculation', in B. Clarke and M. Hansen (eds), *Emergence and Embodiment: New Essays on Second-Order Systems Theory*, Duke University Press, Durham, pp. 179–204.

Landgraf, E. 2011, *Improvisation as Art: Conceptual Challenges, Historical Perspectives*, Continuum, New York and London.

Lewis, G. 2004, 'Improvised Music after 1950: Afrological and Eurological Perspectives', in D. Fischlin and A. Heble (eds), *The Other Side of Nowhere: Jazz, Improvisation, and Communities in Dialogue*, Wesleyan University Press, Connecticut, pp. 131–162.

Litzweiler, J. 1992, *Ornette Coleman: A Harmonic Life*, Morrow, Inc., New York.

Malabou, C. and Derrida, J. 2004, *Counterpath: Traveling with Jacques Derrida*, trans. D. Wills, Stanford University Press, Stanford.

Mc Namee, E. 2009, 'Eye-Witness: Memorializing Humanity in Steve McQueen's Hunger', *International Journal of Law in Context*, vol. 5, pp. 281–294.

Monson, I. 1996, *Saying Something: Jazz Improvisation and Interaction*, University of Chicago Press, Chicago and London.

Motha, S. 2013, 'AS IF: Constitutional narratives and "forms of life"', in K. Van Marle and S. Motha (eds), *Genres of Critique: Law, Aesthetics and Liminality*, Sun Press, Stellenbosch.

Nachmanovitch, S. 1990, *Free Play: Improvisation in Life and Art*, Jeremy P. Tarcher/Putnam, New York.

Oliveros, P. 2005, *Deep Listening: A Composer's Sound Practice*, iUniverse, Lincoln.

Peters, G. 2012, 'Certainty, Contingency, and Improvisation', *Critical Studies in Improvisation*, vol. 8, no. 2, p. 8.

Postema, G. 2004, 'Melody and Law's Mindfulness of Time', *Ratio Juris*, vol. 17, no. 2, pp. 203–226.

Ramshaw, S. 2006, 'Deconstructin(g) Jazz Improvisation: Derrida and the Law of the Singular Event', *Critical Studies in Improvisation* vol. 2, no. 1, p. 19.

Ramshaw, S. 2013a, *Justice as Improvisation: The Law of the Extempore*, Routledge, London.

Ramshaw, S. 2013b, 'The Paradox of Performative Immediacy: Law, Music, Improvisation', *Law, Culture and the Humanities*. Advance online publication, August 16, 2013, doi: 10.1177/174387211349804.

Schechner, R. 1988, *Performance Theory*, Routledge, New York.

Schön, D.A. 1991, *The Reflective Practitioner: How Professionals Think in Action*, Prentice Hall, Englewood Cliffs.

Schroeder, F. 2014, 'Found and Determined Improvisation', in F. Schroeder, *Improvisation in Brazil 2014* (weblog), viewed 16 November 2014, <www.improvisationinbrazil.wordpress.com/2014/05/01/found-and-determined-improvisation/>.

Scott, R. 2014, 'The Molecular Imagination: John Stevens, The Spontaneous Music Ensemble and Free Group Improvisation', in F. Schroeder and M. Ó hAodha (eds), *Soundweaving: Writings on Improvisation*, Cambridge Scholars Publishing, Newcastle upon Tyne, pp. 95–109.

Small, C. 1998, *Musicking: The Meanings of Performing and Listening*, Wesleyan University Press, Connecticut.

Soules, M. 2004, 'Improvising Character: Jazz, the Actor, and Protocols of Improvisation', in D. Fischlin and A. Heble (eds), *The Other Side of Nowhere: Jazz, Improvisation, and Communities in Dialogue*, Wesleyan University Press, Connecticut, pp. 268–297.

Stapleton, P. 2008, 'Dialogic Evidence: Documentation of Ephemeral Events' *Body, Space and Technology Journal*, vol. 7, no. 2, viewed 16 November 2014, <people.brunel.ac.uk/bst/vol0702/paulstapleton/>.

Teitel, R. 2006, 'The Transitional Apology', in E. Barkan and A. Karn (eds), *Taking Wrongs Seriously: Apology and Reconciliation*, Stanford University Press, Stanford, pp. 101–114.

Turner, C. 2013, 'Deconstructing Transitional Justice', *Law and Critique*, vol. 24, no. 2, pp. 193–209.

Waddell, T. and Morrow, R. 2014, 'Translations: Improvisation / Architecture', Translating Improvisation Research Group (TIRG) 2014–15 Seminar Series, Queen's University, Belfast, 7 November.

Waterman, E. 2009, 'Some Strategies for Improvisation in Collaborative Writing', Prepared for the Improvisation, Community and Social Practice (ICASP) Improvisation and Social Policy Workshop, McGill Law School, 17–18 June.

Weick, K.E. 1979, *The Social Psychology of Organizing*, 2nd edn, McGraw-Hill, New York.

Weick, K.E. 1995, *Sensemaking in Organizations*, Sage, Thousand Oaks.

Weick, K.E. 2001, *Making Sense of the Organization*, Blackwell Publishers, Oxford.

Chapter 4

Animating the archive
Artefacts of law

*Trish Luker**

Introduction

This chapter investigates law's counter-archive through a reflection on the materiality of archival sources and the significance of objective status when such sources are presented as evidence in legal proceedings. It suggests that rather than regarding archival sources simply as documents, they might better be understood as *artefacts* – 'the imprint or inscription of the human on the object, the page or the body' (Ezell and O'Brien O'Keeffe 1994: 3). Understanding documents as artefacts requires a materialist approach that takes heed of their existence as specific forms of written and printed inscription, the characteristics of which facilitates their privileged status and contributes to their agentic power (Latour 1986). This chapter investigates these issues with reference to documentary evidence tendered in a legal claim for compensation taken by members of the Stolen Generations in Australia in the case of *Cubillo v Commonwealth* ('*Cubillo*').[1] Thinking of archival sources not as legal documents, but as artefacts with specific agentic powers, draws attention to the material conditions of their creation and demonstrates the way they are productive of colonial relations. In particular, this chapter will consider the status of administrative *forms*, the proforma documents that remain as traces of the embodied encounters between state officials and the subjects/objects of governance.

The investigation of the legal historical archive is supplemented by reflections on counter-archival artistic practice that redeploys archival documents in contemporary creative work, to produce historical documents in the present. As the work of a number of contemporary Australian

---

* I am grateful to the referees and Georgine Clarsen for useful comments on an earlier draft and to Judy Watson for kind permission to reproduce her work.
1 (2000) 174 ALR 97 ('*Cubillo*').

Animating the archive 71

Indigenous artists demonstrates,[2] taking an anti-colonising stance in relation to material from colonial archives can animate the past, and in this way contribute to historical understanding. By moving between material artefacts from the historical archive and the redeployment of archives in creative practice, this chapter raises questions of the materiality of law. In this way, it engages with the notion of the counter-archive not only as a metaphor for practices that destabilise law's claims to authority, but also as objects which themselves have performative and productive capacity.

In Australia, there is inconsistency in judicial decisions about the evidentiary value of sources of historical knowledge and insufficient judicial understanding of approaches to interpretation of archival documents.[3] These decisions have led to contentious debates about the inadequacy of colonial archives and their predisposition to reproduce colonial relations, particularly as sources of evidence for claims made by Indigenous people. They exemplify the extent to which law's engagement with archival sources gives rise to legal reasoning and jurisprudential outcomes which often pay too much attention to content, but which fail to appreciate the significance of material qualities – characteristics such as the genre and format of a document, whether it is handwritten or typed, its legibility, whether it is complete or incomplete, as well as its possible life trajectory or "career". Documents are not simply representational, and the significance of their materiality changes over time – a document created initially as a medium of communication inevitably becomes an historical artefact once it is collected and preserved in an archive or a museum.

Is it the ontological character of archival sources, the fact that they have existed in other times and places, and their proximity to past events that facilitates the authority accorded to them as a foundation for the resuscitation of historical events and subjects? In the area of colonial history, studies of material culture have helped challenge the textual dominance in historiography, offering new ways of thinking about the past. Penelope Edmonds points to the productive tension that may emerge when historians of colonialism read objects as *texts*, exploring their contradictions and ambiguities in relation to other archival material as evidence of the inherent uncertainty and instability of the colonial space. She argues that it is in the juncture

---

2 In this chapter, I will examine the work of Judy Watson. Other Australian artists engaged in work which uses archival material or ethnographic modes of viewing the Indigenous subject include Brook Andrew, Richard Bell, Gordon Bennett, Fiona Foley, Danie Mellor and r e a. See Jane Lydon (2014) for an investigation of the appropriative use of historical photographs to tell Aboriginal stories.

3 Such as the first case heard under native title legislation, *Members of the Yorta Yorta Aboriginal Community v Victoria and Ors* [1998] FCA 1606 (18 December 1998), the landmark action in relation to claims by members of the Stolen Generations in *Cubillo*, and the key case in relation to Indigenous cultural heritage *Kartinyeri v The Commonwealth of Australia* [1998] HCA 22.

72 Trish Luker

between written archival sources and the life of material objects that the tensions and discontinuities of empire are revealed (Edmonds 2006: 84). In addition to reading objects as texts, it is also possible to read texts as objects, as more akin to artefacts. Such an approach is productive not only because it reveals asymmetry and contradiction, but also because it undermines the self-evident authority attributed to text, nowhere more apparent than when colonial archival sources are tendered as evidence in legal proceedings.

Thinking of evidentiary sources as artefacts requires us to see them less as records of information and more as cultural objects. It resists the epistemology of evidence law by which information contained in documents may acquire the status of fact. An ethnographic approach to archival documents attends to material characteristics such as structure, form and aesthetics. It engages in analysis of the careers or political genealogies of documents to demonstrate how they function as agents in the production of knowledge, with political, legal and social consequences (Trundle and Kaplonski 2011).

When archival sources appear as evidence in legal proceedings, such as in claims concerning historical injustices, they are commonly accorded authority based on their content, on the character of documents as storehouses of information, with scant attention to their material existence and form. Such an approach facilitates law's objectifying stance. However, a far more nuanced approach is called for when dealing with archival sources, one which takes account of the production of the archive as well as its materiality, and which recognises the contribution that can be made by other interpretative frames, such as those of artistic practice, as informing our understanding of the past in the present: a process which might be characterised as counter-archival. In this way, 'contemporary art also contributes productively to the revision of history that has been standardised by the political interests of the past' (von Zinnenburg Carroll 2014: 4).

Recovering archives

In a work entitled 'under the act' (2007), Australian artist Judy Watson uses archival sources such as letters, photographs, reports and other official documents that she found in the Queensland State Archives in government files concerning her great-grandmother and grandmother, whose lives were controlled under the *Aboriginal Protection and Restriction of the Sale of Opium Act of 1897* (Qld).[4] Included in this work is her great-grandmother's

---

4   Judy Watson (Waanyi), whose matrilineal family is from country in north-west Queensland, is one of Australia's leading contemporary artists. The work 'under the act' was exhibited in *Culture Warriors*, the National Indigenous Art Triennial 2007 at the National Gallery of Australia and in *Taboo* at the Museum of Contemporary Art in Sydney, curated by Brook Andrew. It is available as numero uno publications in an edition of 20 plus 5 artists' proofs from Grahame Galleries, Brisbane.

'exemption card', referred to by Aboriginal people as 'dog tags', which permitted them to work outside missions and reserves, and which they were required under the legislation, to carry at all times. There is correspondence between her grandmother, Grace Isaacson, and the Director of Native Affairs concerning her application for exemption from the Act and a report on her eligibility (see Figure 4.1); letters of objection from various people to the authorities when Watson's grandmother was seeking permission to marry a white man; and the subsequent report by the regional Protector of Aboriginals on her character, level of education, living conditions and with whom she associated; as well as Grace's application to have access to her bank balance, held by the government 'in trust'. The documents include the use of the blood-based racial categorisations ('full blood', 'half-caste', 'quadroon', 'octroon') used to describe Aboriginal people at the time. Watson said that she thought she was the first person from her immediate family to have accessed her grandmother's personal welfare file in the State Archives and that she was shocked by the derogatory language used to describe Aboriginal people (Watson and Martin-Chew 2009: 76). 'under the act' follows an earlier work titled 'a preponderance of aboriginal blood', which also uses documents from the Queensland State Archives as the basis of the work, including letters and official correspondence concerning the electoral franchise, which denied the vote to Aboriginal people deemed to have 'a preponderance of Aboriginal blood'. Watson had been commissioned by the State Library of Queensland to produce work to celebrate the Queensland Centenary of Women's Suffrage and Forty Years of Aboriginal Suffrage.[5]

Watson's powerful and personal work demonstrates a counter-archival artistic practice that redeploys archival sources. Each of the archival documents has been photocopied onto thin paper, and using *chine-collé*, are overlaid with etched images of blood made out of pigment, drawing attention not only to the terminology of racial categorisation, but also references the warfare, violence and death that frequently occurred on the frontier in Australia. The use of the form of an artist's book enhances the familiar intimacy of the archival records and points to the significance of the relationship between the artist and the material, as if they might perhaps have been family heirlooms discovered in an attic. The reproduction of the archival material in their original size and format also accentuates the material and visual character of the historical sources. When I saw the work exhibited, it appeared in glass display boxes, thereby referencing the archival collection from which the documentary material

---

5   Judy Watson (2005) 'a preponderance of aboriginal blood', published by the artist and available as numero uno publications in an edition of 5 plus a special edition commissioned by the State Library of Queensland.

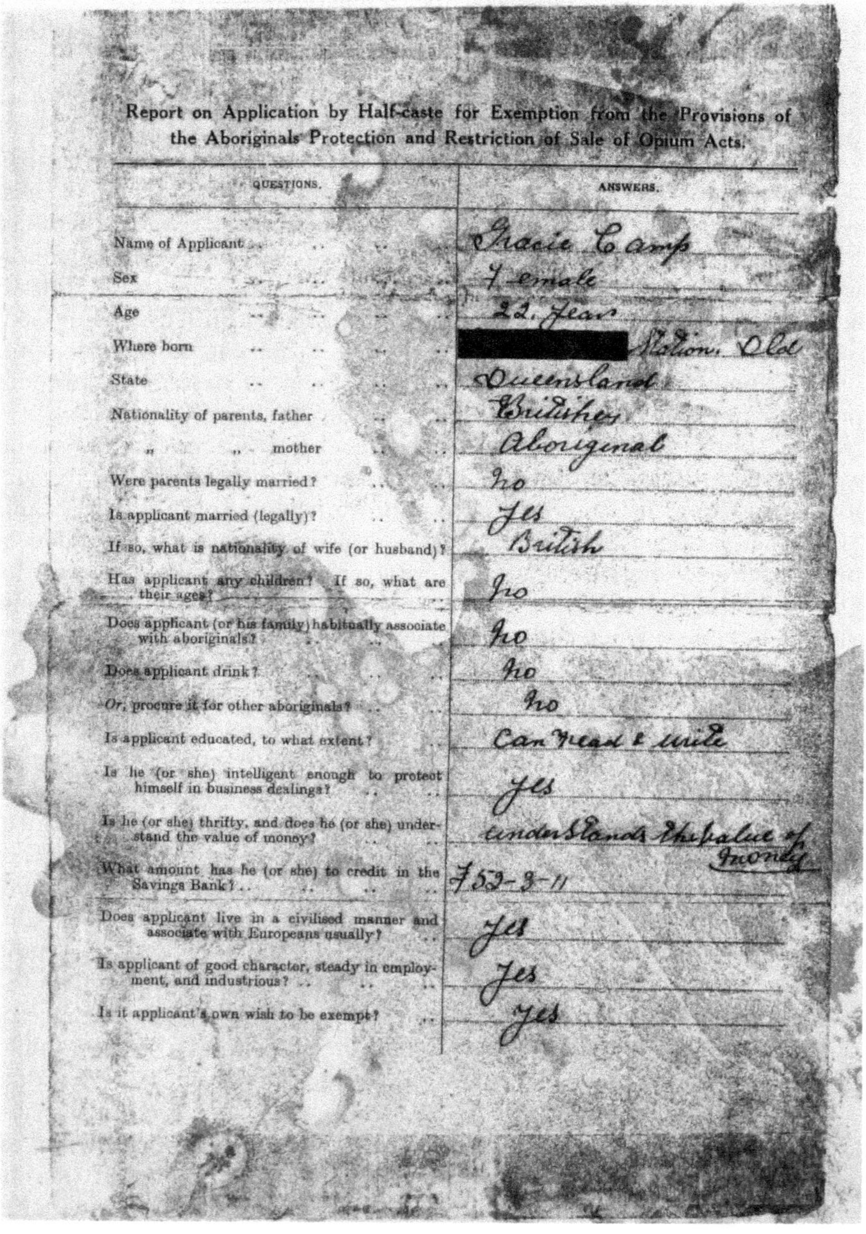

Figure 4.1 Judy Watson, page 12, *under the act* (2007), etching with chine collé, 30.5 × 42.0 cm. Courtesy of the artist and grahame galleries + editions

is originally drawn. Such a curatorial approach suggests a museological aesthetic, and in this way offers a direct critique of ethnographic modes through which Aboriginality is constituted and objectified in the discourses represented by the documents.

Watson has described the material from the archives as already having 'latent power', saying that as a result of this, she didn't want to change very much and that the leakage onto the page was enough (Watson 2005). The suggestion that the archival documents have latent power brings to mind the type of agentic capacity described by Jane Bennett as the 'curious ability of inanimate things to animate, to act, to produce effects dramatic and subtle' (2010: 6). As with Watson's work, it is often the materiality of archival sources that draws our attention – visual traces of the past found in documents, letters, notebooks or maps, where we might encounter torn fragments, stains or imprints, suggesting the possibility of a close relationship to subjects of history.

It is not surprising that Watson was able to locate so many personal records relating to her family in the Queensland Archives. Bureaucratic record-keeping is a well-established technology of control and the colonial venture in Australia amassed an enormous archive of documentation relating to the regulation of Aboriginal people. Written documents – including reports, correspondence, photographs, maps, certificates, applications, declarations, surveys, calculations, inventories, registrations and other administrative records, in addition to legislation, regulations and legal judgments – are intrinsic to the armoury of colonialism. Colonial nations produce administrative records for national purposes in the affirmation of sovereignty. Indeed, it is these bureaucratic and legal records through which much of the force of colonial power and authority is wielded. As Achille Mbembe reminds us, there is no state without archives (2002: 19). In this way, archives are understood as institutions that exert power over all aspects of society, including the administrative, legal and financial accountability of government, corporations and individuals (Schwartz and Cook 2002).

Despite the fact that the colonial archive is largely constituted by legal and governmental records, there has been far less attention to archival theory within legal scholarship. Where scholarly interest in the relationship between law and history is emerging, it is generally associated with postcolonial perspectives, examining the role of law in imperialism and in the construction of the colonial subject (Darian-Smith and Fitzpatrick 1999; Kirkby and Coleborne 2001; Stoler 2009; Ford 2010). Postcolonial approaches to historical scholarship have contributed to the understanding that archives cannot be considered simply as repositories of information, but as historical agents themselves, 'less as stories for a colonial history than as active, generative substances with histories, as documents with itineraries of their own' (Stoler 2009: 1). Following

Foucault's methodological approach to reading the archive, and his genealogy of historiography, the archive is now understood as 'first the law of what can be said, the system that governs the appearance of statements as unique events' (1972: 129). The notion of the archive as a site of epistemological struggle is taken up in work that explores the encounter with the archive itself, its promises of verification, revelation or intimacy, played out as romantic tussles between researcher and the materiality of history (Steedman 2001; Farge 2013). In these 'archive stories', historians and other researchers narrate physical encounters with collections, institutions and historical figures in their search for historical knowledge (Burton 2005). These are fruitful approaches to reconsidering the archive as they contribute to deconstructing its monolithic status as arbiter of historical truth.

The production of administrative documents requires buildings to house the records, bureaucrats to administer the imperatives demanded therein to classify, locate and relocate, as well as inspectors and officers to regulate and police legislative proscriptions. As Ann Laura Stoler puts it: 'accumulations of paper and edifices of stone were both monuments to the asserted know-how of rule, artefacts of bureaucratic labor duly performed, artifices of a colonial state declared to be in efficient operation' (Stoler 2009: 2). Tony Ballantyne argues that the entire system of modern empire building was 'underpinned by the shuffling and shuttling of paper' (2014: 20). Accentuating the importance of the mobility of paper to the creation of empire, he suggests that rather than thinking about texts as 'words' or 'ideas', they might be understood as material forms manifest as paper and writing designed to be mobile, 'to be shared, to be sent, to be stored and retrieved', which by their nature lent themselves to colonial governance, including law (Ballantyne 2014: 21).

Genealogical approaches to historiography are productive because they attend to the operation and circulation of power/knowledge through discursive constructions. They also may lead to consideration of materiality and form in the constitution of historical knowledge and interest in thinking about archival documents as artefacts of knowledge production (Riles 2006). This attention to documentary practices assists in revealing the 'agentive quality of documents' (Trundle and Kaplonski 2011), recognising the way they participate and operate in webs of material and discursive relations. To engage in an ethnographic approach to the colonial state archive contributes to understanding the way the state actually 'produces, adjudicates, organizes, and maintains the discourse that become available as the primary texts of history' (Dirks 2002: 58–59).

Postcolonial scholarship has contributed to critical engagement with the reception of history's archive as a source of evidence about what went on in the past and how to value different forms of historical knowledge, examining the role of law in imperialism and in the construction of the colonial subject (Kirkby and Coleborne 2001; Stoler 2009). However, when archival evidence is presented in legal claims in courts, law has remained largely impervious to these critical approaches, maintaining a positivist attitude to interpretation of historical sources, which privileges impartiality, neutrality and objectivity. Questions about the nature, extent and accuracy of the colonial state archive has come into sharp relief in 'postcolonising'[6] settler states particularly as a result of Indigenous legal claims in relation to historical injustices. However, as Adele Perry points out, 'the archive is at best an unreliable ally in postcolonial struggles' (2005: 327). On the one hand, the extent of the colonial archive is evidence of the hyper-surveillance of Indigenous people in colonial and neo-colonial times; on the other, it is an entirely inadequate source, largely written from the perspective of the colonial state, where Indigenous voices and perspectives are absent or retrospectively inserted through critical artistic practice, such as in Watson's work.

Colonial archives produce and reproduce hierarchical categories of evidence. While oral history has become increasingly acceptable to historians over recent decades, law remains attached to the claims of originality and objectivity associated with the materiality of the documentary form, endowing it with stability and legitimacy and granting it status as an arbiter of truth. The materiality of the archive, by which I mean both what is and is not to be found there, is in this way determinative of the legal outcomes of those who most seek to draw on its sources for remediation of historical wrongs. In some contexts, the notion of an oral archive has emerged as a result of legal claims, such as in the Truth and Reconciliation Commission in South Africa (Harris 2002). However, in other contexts, including Australia, oral evidence has been valued only to the extent that it can verify the written record.[7]

Miranda Johnson points out that the juxtaposition of oral and written history in the way that occurs in law serves to understate the varieties of historical resources and interpretative possibilities of re-reading and re-contextualising colonial archives (2008). For example, the performance in court by witnesses and the subsequent transcription of Indigenous elders'

6   I am using this term to describe the condition of ongoing colonial relations, but when the legitimacy of the settler colonial state has been challenged. See Aileen Moreton-Robinson (2003).
7   In significant Australian legal decisions, archival records have played a central role as evidence. For example, in claims for native title, historical evidence is used to address the requirement that title-holders prove an ongoing traditional connection to the land in question. However, in the first judicial decision in relation to a claim for native title, *Members of the Yorta Yorta Community v State of Victoria* (1998), Justice Olney drew on the diary entries of a pastoral squatter as evidence, finding that the claimants had lost their traditional connection to country. In doing so, he effectively reversed the legal principle attributing authority to the oral form of evidence, determining that archival texts would serve as the basis for interpretation of testimonial evidence.

78 Trish Luker

testimony and their cross-examination produces a documentary record that transgresses these forms. She suggests a practice of 'listening to documents', or interpreting the 'written-oral, *as oral*', serves to overcome some of the assumptions embedded in the dichotomy written/oral (ibid.: 116). Such a practice 'transforms local pasts into public histories by producing a text and a set of textual practices out of such past so that they can circulate beyond the bounds of a particular community' (ibid.: 110).

Law's documentary practices

Clearly, written records are central to the operation of law. After all, documents, and the paper that constitutes them, are fundamental mediums of law and function as a source of legal authority. Common law archives itself ceaselessly. Indeed, it exists in order to create an archive, which assists in determining its future direction. However, it is not only finalised court decisions that constitute the legal archive, but also the products of parliamentary processes, police and prison records, bureaucratic records, evidentiary and litigation materials as well as court administrative material.

In an account of the history of the emergence of written records in England, Michael Clanchy points to the political function of writing and reading in his contention that lay literacy developed out of bureaucratic and legal requirements, rather than any particular demand for knowledge (1993). Clanchy identified legal procedures, such as oral summons and pleadings, as exemplary of the continuing privileging of the spoken word, despite the increasing proliferation of documents. He points to the historic function of the *narrator* or *conteur*, the precursor to barristers, who 'spoke on the litigant's behalf in his presence' as 'an extension of the litigant's faculty of speech' (Clanchy 1993: 274). According to Clanchy, '[w]riting shifted the emphasis in testing truth from speech to documents', but the privileging of oral testimony over documents 'shows how cautiously – and perhaps reluctantly – written evidence was accepted' (ibid.: 275, 263).

However, Cornelia Vismann suggests that in theorisations about the origins of law, undue attention has been paid to the orality/literacy binary (2008). She argues that it is the functional logic of administrative processes represented in the documentary forms of law that 'contribute to the formation of the three major entities on which the law is based: truth, state, and subject' (ibid.: xii). In particular, Vismann elaborates on the importance of the media technology of files, and their precursor, lists, as basic functional, process-generating administrative procedure, conforming 'neither to orality nor to literacy', in the production of legal systems (ibid.: 5). She suggests that files, by virtue of their capacity to be updated, appearing 'live, ever-changing, acting and inexhaustible', take on ontological qualities along the lines of speech (ibid.: 10).

Vismann argues that files are the foundation of legal activity, but that they 'remain below the perception threshold of the law' and have received scant attention from legal theorists (2008: 11). It is only when they are removed from their administrative context, such as when they appear as evidence in court, that they become objects of scrutiny, because it is here that a determination is made as to whether they fulfil the requirements of evidence and attention is directed to their probative force. It is at this point in the trajectory of files, Vismann argues, that truth claims emerge. Once files move from the status of personal notebooks to become documents kept in public places, ultimately entering the courtroom, they acquire a different speech act status, moving from an imperative, prescriptive form to an evidentiary descriptive one. She says:

> Here the regime of literalness arises with the question of truth: is what was written down an accurate recording of what was said? Does what is stored correspond to what took place? Is it complete? It becomes necessary to establish criteria for the reliability of written records and to furnish means to authenticate them.
>
> (Vismann 2008: 52)

In this way, Vismann argues that files are performative and fact-producing. Law generates its own reality through the production of files: indeed, she suggests that for law, what is not on file is not in the world. Law believes only in its own literality; it is impossible to prove the non-existence of something (ibid.: 57).

This is a radical genealogical approach to the history of law, tracing the evolution and role of one of its primary products, files. It is an overtly materialist approach to legal history that suggests the need for close attention to documentary genre in analyses of organisational paradigms and documentary forms as artefacts of modern knowledge practices. In the context of the development of the modernist 'automation of order' during the late nineteenth century, with the emergence of mechanisation in reproducible communication, such as the invention of the typewriter, we might ask, following Vismann, what significance should be attributed to administrative *forms*, that is, pro forma documents, as media central to the bureaucratisation of governmental processes, or governmentality? Forms, by which I mean documents based on or replicating a formula, and the demands they place on subjects to complete them, epitomise the media of late modern legal agency and proliferated in colonial contexts.

Archival forms as evidence

Thousands of archival documents were tendered as evidence in the trial of *Cubillo*, a landmark legal action taken by Lorna Cubillo and Peter Gunner against the Australian Government. Cubillo and Gunner had been removed as children from their families and communities in the Northern Territory of Australia during the 1940s and 1950s under policies of assimilation implemented with respect to Aboriginal people and resulting in what is known as the Stolen Generations. The evidence presented included federal government correspondence, letters and memoranda between officers and the Director of Native Affairs, patrol officers' diaries and reports, records and correspondence of the institutions where the claimants resided, welfare and medical files, education and employment records of the claimants, government reports, conference proceedings, newspaper articles and parliamentary statements, and maps and photos. The documents spanned a period of over 50 years.

The applicants argued that the Commonwealth was vicariously liable for their removals from their families and communities as children and subsequent detentions. There were four causes of action: wrongful imprisonment and deprivation of liberty, breach of statutory duty, breach of duty of care and breach of fiduciary duty. They argued that under the legislative regime in force at the time, the Commonwealth (via the Director of Native Affairs and his officers) was vicariously liable for the acts of its employees and that there had been a general policy of removal of 'part-Aboriginal' children from their families and communities, without regard to their individual circumstances. Justice O'Loughlin found that the Commonwealth was not vicariously liable because the relevant legislation in force at the time, the *Aboriginals Ordinance 1918* (NT), gave the Director of Native Affairs the power to undertake the care, custody and control of a 'part-Aboriginal' child if, in the Director's opinion, it was necessary or desirable, in the interests of the child. Under section 17 of the *Welfare Ordinance 1953* (NT), the Director of Welfare had the power to take a 'ward' into custody and to order that he or she be removed to and kept within a reserve or institution.

Justice O'Loughlin found that there was neither enough evidence to support a finding of a general policy of removal of 'part-Aboriginal' children, and that, even if there had been, the evidence presented in the proceedings did not justify the conclusion that it was implemented in respect to the applicants. He found that there was a prima facie case of wrongful imprisonment of Lorna Cubillo, but that the Commonwealth was not liable because the burden of proof had not been satisfied, highlighting the incompleteness of the history and the lack of documentary evidence. In the case of Peter Gunner, however, Justice O'Loughlin found that there were several pieces of documentary evidence that 'pointed strongly to the Director, through his officers, having given close consideration to the welfare of the young Peter'.[8] In particular, Justice O'Loughlin identified a

---

8   *Cubillo*, Summary of Reasons for Judgment, [11].

Animating the archive 81

form of consent with the purported thumbprint of his mother, Topsy Kundrilba, which he interpreted as a request that Peter be removed to St Mary's Hostel. The form of consent was crucial to Justice O'Loughlin's decision in relation to Peter Gunner. While the judge determined that it was not possible to make findings of fact about the circumstances of Gunner's removal from his family, he nevertheless found the form of consent a sufficiently persuasive exhibit that it formed the basis for the court's rejection of the claim. Justice O'Loughlin determined that it functioned as documentary evidence that Topsy Kundrilba had given her informed consent to the removal of her son.[9]

The archival documents tendered as evidence in the *Cubillo* case exemplifies what Renisa Mawani describes as the 'double logic' of law's archive (2012). Arguing that law's archive operates through both symbolic and material force, as well as document and documentation, Mawani suggests that '[l]aw's archive is a site from which law derives its meanings, authority, and legitimacy, a proliferation of documents that obscures its originary violence and its ongoing force, and a trace that holds the potential to reveal its foundations as (il)legitimate' (ibid.: 337). The existence and volume of the archival records pertaining to the claimants in *Cubillo* is certainly evidence of the symbolic and material force of colonial rule and the assertion of sovereignty. As artefacts of colonial knowledge production, it also demonstrates the function of documents and documentation as instruments of legal and governmental practices. However, there are also ways in which these documents can be read as evidence of uncertainty and doubt, marking 'anxieties about subject-formation, about the psychic space of empire, about what went without saying' (Stoler 2009: 25).

Exhibit A21: Form of Consent

Exhibit A21 was identified in the proceedings as a 'Form of Consent by a Parent'. The exhibit is a simple, typed pro forma document of apparent legal character, akin to a statutory declaration, where names are inserted into a narrative statement that is phrased in the form of a request (see Figure 4.2). The declarant, Topsy Kundrilba, is defined pursuant to the *Aboriginals Ordinance 1918–1953* (NT), and she requests the Director of Native Affairs to declare her 7-year-old son, Peter Gunner, to be an Aboriginal under the same Ordinance. Four grounds are listed: that he is of Part-European blood, his father being a European; that she desires that he be educated and trained in accordance with accepted European standards, to which he is entitled by reason of his caste; that she is unable to

9   I have discussed this exhibit using a different analytic framework in a previously published article: Luker (2009).

FORM OF CONSENT BY A PARENT

I, TOPSY KUNDRILBA being a full-blood Aboriginal (female) within the meaning of the Aboriginals Ordinance 1918–1953 of the Northern Territory, and residing at UTOPIA STATION do hereby request the DIRECTOR OF NATIVE AFFAIRS to declare my son PETER GUNNER aged seven (7) years, to be an Aboriginal within the meaning and for the purposes of the said Aboriginals Ordinance. MY reasons for requesting this action by the Director of Native Affairs are:-

1. My son is of Part-European blood, his father being a European.

2. I desire my son to be educated and trained in accordance with accepted European standards, to which he is entitled by reason of his caste.

3. I am unable myself to provide the means by which my son may derive the benefits of a standard European education.

4. By placing my son in the care, custody and control of the Director of Native Affairs the facilities of a standard education will be made available to him by admission to St. Mary's Church of England Hostel at Alice Springs.

SIGNED of my own free will
this
day of 1956
in the presence of

TOPSY

her mark

KUNDRILBA

Figure 4.2 National Archives of Australia: Welfare Branch; F1, Correspondence files, annual single number series, 1956–57, 1956/2077, "Welfare Branch Declaration to be a Ward Peter Gunner". Tendered as evidence by the respondent in relation to Peter Gunner in *Cubillo v Commonwealth* (2000) 174 ALR 97 as "Form of Consent by a Parent". Reproduced with the permission of the Federal Court of Australia.

Animating the archive   83

provide the means by which her son may derive the benefits of a standard European education; and that by placing her son in the care, custody and control of the Director of Native Affairs, the facilities of a standard education will be made available to him by admission to St Mary's Church of England Hostel at Alice Springs. The document holds the purported thumbprint of Gunner's mother and includes the statement 'signed of my own free will this ___ day of 1956 in the presence of ___ ', but the gaps have not been filled in. The typed words 'her' and 'mark' appear on either side of the print, and 'TOPSY' and 'KUNDRILBA' above and below. The document is undated, unwitnessed and bears no official letterhead, seal or insignia. It had been sourced in the National Archives of Australia. As such, it was regarded as a public document, making further evidence as to its authenticity unnecessary.

The document was apparently produced under the policy of assimilation to classify Peter Gunner as an Aboriginal and declare him a ward of the state subject to legislation under which he was removed from his family and placed in St Mary's Hostel in Alice Springs. However, under the *Aboriginals Ordinance 1918*, the Director of Native Affairs had power over all Aboriginal people, including the discretionary power to remove children. Under section 7(1), all Aboriginal children were deemed to be subject to the legal guardianship of the Chief Protector of Aboriginals, notwithstanding that they had a parent or other relative living. Section 6(1) gave the Chief Protector discretion to undertake the care and control of any Aboriginal person or 'half-caste', including an adult, if it was considered necessary or desirable in the interests of the person. Under the subsequent *Welfare Ordinance 1953–1957* (NT), any Aboriginal person in the Northern Territory of Australia could be declared a ward of the state. The Welfare Ordinance introduced the legal framework for the policy of assimilation. It facilitated the removal of children from their families based on their purported need of care, rather than race.

Heather Douglas and John Chesterman point out that prior to the introduction of the 1953 legislation, a census was conducted of all Aboriginal people and that this was a critical tool in the implementation of the assimilation policy (2008). Inclusion in the census led to Aboriginal people being created as legal subjects, as wards of the state, and subsequently as subjects of legal regulation under the assimilation policy (ibid.: 376). Clearly, defining the legal status of Indigenous subjects has political and symbolic significance for colonial and neo-colonial rule. I have argued elsewhere that the form of consent functioned to interpellate both Kundrilba and Gunner as subjects of colonial regulation and demonstrates the colonial production of legible subjects and of patronymic legal identity (Luker 2009). Here, I am less interested in the semiotic and more with the material and archival nature of exhibits. As Annalise Riles explains, approaching documents as ethnographic objects or artefacts engages with

84 Trish Luker

questions of temporality, form and genre, authorship and agency (2006: 18–22). In particular, I am interested in the function of documentation and archivisation as a process of fact production and as an aid in the rationalisation of decision-making as technologies of colonial rule.

Gunner was removed from his mother in 1956, the year after the *Welfare Ordinance 1953* came into effect.[10] Under the new legislation, the definition of 'Aboriginals' was revised to exclude 'half-castes'. However, a new subsection was introduced that empowered the Director of Native Affairs to declare a person, if one of their ancestors came within the statutory definition of 'Aboriginal', to be deemed an Aboriginal if the Director considered it to be in their best interests, and the person requested it. Despite the power available under the legislation at the time Gunner was removed, Justice O'Loughlin concluded that as Gunner was himself only a child at the time, the authorities had perceived the need for his mother to request the declaration.[11]

Justice O'Loughlin's conclusion is possibly a response to the document's unofficial and rudimentary appearance. While it seems to be a 'pro forma', it is the fact that the typewriter font used for both generic and inserted text is the same which gives it the appearance of uniformity and coherence. This is not a document that has been officially designed and printed by a government department. It is more likely that the document was originally produced and subsequently completed on the same typewriter, in the same office by the same person, perhaps the patrol officer responsible for the community residing at Utopia Station. It appears that the authority responsible, most likely the local patrol officer, believed that some form of documentation was called for to facilitate the removal of Gunner and his admission at St Mary's Hostel, although we do not know who this was, because the form has not been witnessed. While the names, residence, relationship and gender of Peter Gunner and his mother, Topsy Kundrilba, apparently have been inserted into a template, it may just as readily have appeared as a piece of correspondence unique to these individuals.[12]

---

10 The *Welfare Ordinance 1953* (NT) commenced in May 1957, repealing the *Aboriginals Ordinance 1918*.

11 *Cubillo* [139].

12 In the trial, Harry Kitching, patrol officer in the area covering Utopia Station at the time and considered by Justice O'Loughlin probably to be responsible for Gunner's removal, said he recognised the form, but could not recall anything about Peter Gunner's situation at Utopia, nor the reasons for his recommendation that he be admitted to St Mary's. In his affidavit, he said 'I had no recollection of being present when Topsy marked the form. I note that it was not signed or dated': Kitching's affidavit, [82]–[84], cited in transcript, 7 August 1998, p 95. Yet documentary evidence that referred to Gunner, recorded by Kitching, was presented in the trial: Exhibit A15, Memo from Evans to Acting Director, dated 4 November 1954, includes copies of an inspection report of Utopia conducted by Kitching in June 1954; Exhibit HSK4 contains extracts from Kitching's diary reports of visits to Utopia between January–June 1955, in which he notes that when he arrived at

Justice O'Loughlin acknowledged that many questions remained unanswered as to how or whether the contents of the document were explained to Kundrilba, or whether they were explained at all; in which case, he asserted, that the document would probably be a nullity.[13] On the balance of probabilities however, the judge found that the 'line of documents' favoured a positive conclusion that Kundrilba gave her informed consent to her son going to St Mary's. It is this apparently individualised treatment that facilitated the conclusion that Justice O'Loughlin reached, that he could not find evidence of a general policy of removal of Aboriginal people in the documentary sources.

Notwithstanding a lack of clear provenance, the document was stored, together with many other records, in a departmental welfare file created for Peter Gunner. It survived for over 50 years before being tendered as evidence in the case. At the time of the legal proceedings, it was preserved in the National Archives of Australia. Within archival theory, the principle of provenance, or *respect de fonds*, means that records are preserved to reflect the arrangement employed by the organisation, administration or individual responsible for their creation. This is said to enhance the authenticity and integrity of the records, and ensures that they maintain a close relationship to the administration that produced them. According to John Ridener, one of the distinctive characteristics of modern archival theory is that it endorses a key public role for archives as participants in the creation of government efficiency and accountability (2008: 81). While nineteenth century archives were collections of records for use by historians and other scholars, arranged chronologically without regard to the source, during the early twentieth century, government records became more important as national governments consolidated their rule through the spread of colonial enterprises over the world. This reflected an enhanced value being placed on documentary records as forms of evidence, as a paper trail providing verification and details of government action and activity. In this way, archival practices of collection, storage and management of material records respond to and reflect geopolitical movements. This rationale is particularly evident in the role of archives in the propagation of imperial rule.

The development of modern archival theory coincided with the period during which standardisation of forms was introduced in an attempt to ensure efficiency in administrative and classification functions and to impose order on record keeping (Ridener 2008: 93). The advent of

---

the camp on 4 April 1955, the 'children fled into scrub'; Exhibit A17, Undated Memorandum from Mr McCoy to the Director of Welfare (September 1955), written by Kitching, included the suggestion that he had met with Kundrilba and Gunner and that Gunner was willing to attend St Mary's.

13   *Cubillo* [788].

86 Trish Luker

mechanical reproduction had a profound effect on archival theory and practice. As Ridener explains, the ability to create multiple copies of documents quickly, 'the technological innovations wrought through the typewriter multiplied issues of duplication and authenticity' (ibid.: 12). Unlike handwritten documents such as letters, authorial provenance is far more difficult to establish with typewritten documents. Furthermore, mechanical reproduction resulted in a dramatic increase in the production of administrative records, resulting in changes in the meaning of the archive and approaches to archival practice.

As Latour has demonstrated, the materiality and movement of documents is central to law (2010). In his ethnography of the French Conseil D'État, he describes in detail the generation, compilation and circulation of legal files resulting in their ultimate 'ripening' into useful pieces of evidence in a case (ibid.: 75–76). In this way, law is a process of movement – 'weaving', 'shaping' and 'formatting' – of material objects, including files, texts, litigants and decision-makers. Indeed, Latour claims that it is the fabrication and circulation of files that facilitates the movement of the people engaged in legal processes which actually produces 'legal effects' (ibid.: 80). This dynamic of 'transition, movement or metamorphosis' (ibid.: 129) of files and textuality is also channelled in the interactions of legal decision makers. In this way, law 'is largely a *documentary network* through which the social is arranged and assembled' (Levi and Valverde 2008: 818, original emphasis).

Files were central to colonial administration in Australia, particularly in the documentary practices employed for the regulation of Indigenous people. The early twentieth century was characterised by a burgeoning colonial administration, producing an enormous archive of bureaucratic records, documenting information about identity (births, deaths, marriages, racial classifications); health, welfare and medical records; residential location, movement and removal; educational achievements; employment; police and prison records. In *Cubillo*, the evidentiary status of the form of consent was enhanced by virtue of it being one in a line of documents that had been compiled in the Native Affairs Branch and preserved in Gunner's welfare file, including diaries prepared by patrol officer Harry Kitching and correspondence between the offices in Alice

---

14 The exhibits included Exhibit HSK9: Letter from Mr McLeod, station owner Utopia, to Mr Evans, Acting District Superintendent (14 November 1953); Exhibit HSK2.1: Census (1954); Exhibit HSK3 and HSK4: Diary extracts of Mr Kitching (January–June 1955); Exhibit A13: Mr Richards Memorandum (25 February 1955); Exhibit A14: Letter from FJS Wise; Exhibit A15: Memo from Evans to Acting Director (4 November 1954); Exhibit A16: Letter dated 21 February 1955; Exhibit A17: Undated Memorandum from Mr McCoy to the Director of Welfare; Exhibit HSK13: Correspondence from Mr Giese to Acting Director, Alice Springs (1 April 1955); Exhibit R6: Report of AE Richards (12 April 1955); and Exhibit R9: Document dated September 1955.

Springs and Darwin of the Director of Native Affairs, the Director of Welfare and the District Superintendent.[14]

As the claimants acknowledged, under the legislation in force at the time, the Director of Native Affairs had the power to remove Gunner from his mother, if he deemed it to be in the child's best interests. However, it is apparent that the local patrol officer responsible for his removal believed that a documentary record including evidence of the purported consent of Kundrilba was necessary to authorise the removal. In this way, not only was the form of consent a material agent in the subjection of Gunner to the legislative framework in force at the time, it was also a folio in a file containing other documents that together functioned to record and rationalise the actions of the colonial authorities in controlling many aspects of Gunner's life. As Hannah Robert points out, it removed the requirement to invoke the statutory provisions of the Aboriginals Ordinance in force at the time, and therefore transferred the responsibility of removal and subsequent detention from the state to the mother (2002: 6).

Perceived materially, as an administrative file containing an accumulation of bureaucratic knowledge, it is possible to ascertain a level of anxiety on the part of the authorities about the implementation of colonial rule in the volume of correspondence recorded and preserved. In this way, the generation of documentary records was part of a process of fact-production designed to rationalise the practice of removing children. For example, patrol officer Harry Kitching thought it necessary to record that, when he visited on 4 April 1955: 'The majority of children on Utopia all disappear as quickly as possible' when he approached, noting that he made 'no attempt to chase them but have tried to build the confidence of the remainder in native affairs officers being [sic] in mind the coming census and the need for an accurate count'.[15] At a later date, a further note records that on 14 September 1955 when he returned to compile the census: 'Two children, Florie Ware, and Peter, were seen with their parents, and it now appears that they will both be willing to attend school and to go to St Mary's Hostel in the coming year'[16] and that he had promised that the children would be able to come home at Christmas.[17] In between these two occasions, correspondence between Kitching's superior, Mr Richards, and the Director of Welfare which supported 'Kitching's judgment as to the inadvisability of chasing the half-caste children', resulted in a response from Mr Giese, the Acting District Welfare Officer, which stated that: 'Every endeavour should however be made to gain the confidence of these half-caste children, as I feel that this branch is responsible for their future. I would

15 Transcript, cross examination of Kitching, 6 August 1998, referring to exhibit of letter dated 6 April 1955.
16 Exhibit HSK15, Transcript, cross examination of Kitching, 6 August 1998, p. 78.
17 Exhibit HSK15, Transcript, cross examination of Kitching, 7 August 1998, p. 103.

88 Trish Luker

like to be advised of the progress made by Patrol Officer Kitching in this matter'.[18]

Ultimately, it was this 'line of documents' which, compiled together as a welfare file, produced a narrative, which Justice O'Loughlin found sufficiently convincing that consideration had been given to Gunner's well-being. As Latour points out, documentary evidence always carries the mark of other institutions, which are already capable of producing law, for when a decision is made, 'it has only pronounced itself on a file which is composed of documents that have already been profiled so as to be ... "judgment-compatible"' (2010: 75). As he reminds us, any document may be mobilised as a piece of evidence, and it is because it is mobilised in a legal claim that it takes on a legal form. He points out, however, that this only occurs retroactively: 'Still, if they have been able to slip into the file so easily it is because they had been preformed and pre-folded to respond to this type of contestation' (ibid.: 77).

The form of consent is part of the colonial administration's bureaucratic paper trail, produced to counter political concerns about the removal of Aboriginal children. Such concerns were by then increasingly being expressed to the federal government by citizens and humanitarian organisations. As an expert witness, and the only historian ultimately called to provide evidence in the case, Professor Ann McGrath, stated that her research of the period 1946–62 revealed 'disquiet, sometimes deep concern', evident within the Australian community, including amongst white women, Aboriginal protection groups, unionists and other groups including the YWCA, and a wide array of individual people.[19] She said she had also found evidence of 'government people who were deeply concerned about the policy ... of child removal' and that she was 'surprised, in looking at all these primary sources, by the amount of activism in the community ... to get the Government to change the legislation because 'they felt that something cruel and inhuman was happening to Aboriginal mothers and their children'.[20] McGrath concluded that she did not find 'overwhelming evidence saying that that policy – that that actual way of implementing assimilation by a removal of children from their mothers was endorsed by the wider community to any significant degree'.[21]

Exhibit R93: Form of Information of Birth

Peter Gunner's welfare file, produced as the Applicant's exhibit A45, released by the Territory Health Services for the purposes of the litigation,

---

18 Exhibit HSK14, Transcript, cross examination of Kitching, 6 August 1998, p. 77.
19 Transcript, cross-examination of Dr McGrath, 24 September 1999, p. 3353.
20 Ibid.
21 Ibid.

contains many further documents, including forms, records, notes and correspondence pertaining to Gunner's health, scholastic progress, movement and employment. Another exhibit tendered as evidence in the proceedings was a *Form of Information of Birth*, also displaying the purported thumbprint of Kundrilba (see Figure 4.3). This is a more formal document than the form of consent, produced pursuant to the *Registration of Births, Deaths and Marriages Ordinance 1941* (NT) and states that it is to be furnished to the District Registrar within twenty-one days of the date of birth, failing which, it required a solemn declaration of the facts to be made before a Magistrate. However, with this form, there is a striking anomaly in the dates: the date of birth is recorded as 19 September 1948, but the form is dated and signed as 17 May 1956. The file includes correspondence from the Acting District Welfare Officer, Mr McCoy, to the Director of Native Affairs discussing the 'forms of information of births of Aboriginal children Kathleen and Jeffrey and Peter Gunner'; a request to the Administrator for approval of the registration of the births; a letter from McCoy to the Director concerning admission of Gunner to St Mary's Hostel; a letter from Harry Giese to the Administrator requesting that Gunner be declared an Aboriginal in accordance with the provisions of the Ordinance; and a letter, dated 24 May 1956, from Mr McCoy to the Director with details of Gunner's proposed admission to St Mary's.[22]

This correspondence suggests that the creation of the record of Gunner's birth, making him subject to legal regulation, was necessary to facilitate his institutionalisation at St Mary's Hostel. The particulars of the birth certificate, its retrospective creation and existence in the file together with the correspondence, further demonstrate the way the process of documentation not only facilitated state regulation of Aboriginal people, but was also regarded as a necessary adjunct to the actions being taken. Richard Harper argues that for institutions 'documents provide resources whereby objectivity can be achieved. This objectivity provides the materials which organizational actors can use to "see", "recognise" and "constitute" the rational basis for choosing one course of action over another' (1998: 33). In this way, the creation of multiple records all held on an official file – birth certificate, letters, request, approval, admission – contributes to rationalise and legitimise a process that was otherwise contrary to legislative requirement. As a documentary practice, it also provided an explanatory rationale acceptable to Justice O'Loughlin when it was presented as legal evidence.

---

22 Transcript, opening address by the respondent, 3 March 1999, pp. 416–20.

THE NORTHERN TERRITORY OF AUSTRALIA
Registration of Births, Deaths and Marriages Ordinance 1941

Form of Information of Birth
(To be furnished to the District Registrar)

District _____ Alice Springs

Name of Place where born _____ Utopia Station

CHILD (If twins, state which is elder born.)

* Date of Birth _____ Tuesday 19ᵗʰ September 1948

Christian Name ( ) _____ Peter, Gunner _____ Sex _____ Male

Christian Name ( ) _____

Surname _____

Occupation _____ Unknown European

Age ( ) _____

Where born ( ) _____

When Married { (To Mother of Child her as mentioned) the _____ day of _____ 19

Where Married { ( ) _____

FATHER OF CHILD

Previous Issue of present marriage only. Give full Christian name and age of each child living, in order of birth.

Names	Ages	Names	Ages	Names	Ages

Deceased: No. of Males _____ ; No. of Females _____

MOTHER OF CHILD † If married more than once write each married surname in order.

Christian Name ( ) _____ Topsy

Maiden Surname† _____ Kundrilba

Age ( ) _____ 27

Where born ( ) _____ Utopia

Usual Residence _____ Utopia

Name of Doctor _____

Names of Nurse and other person present at Birth _____ Native Midwife

and Addresses _____ Utopia

I CERTIFY that the above Statement of Particulars is correct, for the purposes of being inserted in the Register of Births—

Signature of Parent _____ Topsy Thumb Right Thumb Print Kundrilba

Father or Mother ( ) _____ Mother

Present Residence _____ Utopia Station

* Date _____ 17ᵗʰ May _____ 1956

Witness to the Signature of Informant _____ H. J. Kitching

Protector

To the District Registrar

at _____

* NOTE—If twenty-one days have elapsed from the date of birth, the law requires a solemn declaration of the facts to be made before a Magistrate by one of the parents, or by some person present at the birth, prior to registration; for this purpose separate forms are provided, on application to the Principal Registrar. Stillbirths are to be registered as a birth and as a death.
Informant should see that he receives a receipt for this Form of Information, on a printed form, signed by the Registrar.
Any person wilfully giving false information is liable to a penalty of Ten Pounds.

Figure 4.3 "Form of Information of Birth", tendered as evidence by the respondent in relation to Peter Gunner in *Cubillo v Commonwealth* (2000) 174 ALR 97. Reproduced with the permission of the Federal Court of Australia.

Creative anachronism

Archival practices that preserve documents in original and rationally ordered form are not the only way to reconstitute sources of historical knowledge as evidence of the past. As the work of Judy Watson and other artists demonstrates, there is increasing interest in use of archival materials as the basis of creative works that productively engage with documentary and archival practices to critique epistemological premises underlying the production of modern knowledge. When artists appropriate archival sources in creative work, they are able to create material objects that accentuate details we may not otherwise observe, instil resonance between subjects, places and institutions, reframe established ways of understanding our own relationship to the past, and thereby rewrite history from the present. As Khadija von Zinnenburg Carroll suggests, contemporary artists working with and appropriating from the colonial archive engage in a productive form of anachronism which facilitates the possibility of a conversation across time and the opportunity 'literally to see the past in the present' (2014: 14).

The creative use of archival documents by Watson demonstrates this productive form of anachronistic dialogue. Notwithstanding their now faded and fissured formality, the aesthetic quality of bureaucratic Times Roman typeface and black ink on the archival documents functions to interpellate Kundrilba and Gunner within historically specific colonial relations of power.[23] In contrast, the blood-coloured pigment employed by Watson in her contemporary creative work obscures the details of the archival documents, and in this way engages in a counter-archival practice to undermine their apparent historical authority.

Contemporary Indigenous art that draws on archival material often uses images to overtly critique the foundational disciplines of anthropology and ethnography and their objectifying stance, challenging the epistemological foundations of Western knowledge practices. Ethnographic images have particular valency because of the significance attributed to the power of representation and photography to accurately portray and 'capture' its subjects. However, these contemporary artists are able to refigure subjects, animating their existence and in this way contribute to new and critical approaches to historiography. The use of archival sources in contemporary artistic work demonstrates the mobile character of documents, the way they travel though space and time, shuffled through bureaucratic and archival processes, now to be found in newly animated form on display in art galleries across the world.

---

23 I have discussed this in more detail elsewhere, arguing that the exhibit functions as a somatechnic site: see Luker (2009).

92 Trish Luker

In Watson's artistic work 'under the act', two of the archival documents have been superimposed with photographs of members of the artist's family (see Figure 4.4). Peering out from the formality of the official letters, and washed over with blood-coloured pigment, are the strikingly animated faces of women and children, Watson's great-grandmother Mabel Daly, her mother's cousin Mavis Pledger and her grandmother, Gracie Isaacson, then a baby. The correspondence over which these faces appear is from the Director of Native Affairs to the Protector at Mt Isa, Queensland. It is in response to Gracie's request that the money she had earned and which was held by the department be made available to her. The labour of Indigenous people has been exploited in Australia since the early years of colonisation and has been largely subject to legally sanctioned government control under Protection Acts.[24] Such practices have come to be known as 'stolen wages'. Under the *Queensland Aboriginals Protection and Restriction of the Sale of Opium Act 1897* (Qld), governments exercised extraordinary levels of control over all aspects of the lives of Aboriginal people, including employment. Government appointed protectors, usually police officers, had the power to make decisions as to whether Aboriginal people were permitted to be employed and negotiate agreements with employers, including wages. As an artistic work, it is not possible clearly to read the text of the letters because they have been washed over in the blood-coloured ink and superimposed with the images of people whose lives were regulated by the documentary regime represented. The treatment of the archival sources by Watson functions as a form of palimpsest where the official documents are scraped away and used again to bring new truth to the surface. It constitutes a counter-archival practice that animates the document with the subjectivities of the colonised, its materiality returning what remains unspoken in their deployment as an artefact of legality.

Conclusion

Colonial archives are a rich source of historical material and are often drawn upon as evidence in legal claims in relation to historical injustices. In considering archival sources as evidence of events that have occurred in the past, attention should be given not only to their informational content, but also to their materiality, including the rationale for the creation of the

---

24 Practices include indentured labour, non-payment and underpayment of wages, underaward payments, withholding and mismanagement of wages, savings and pensions alleged to have been placed in trust accounts, and compulsory redirection of welfare payments and other entitlements. For a discussion of avenues pursued for compensation for stolen wages, see Thornton and Luker (2009).

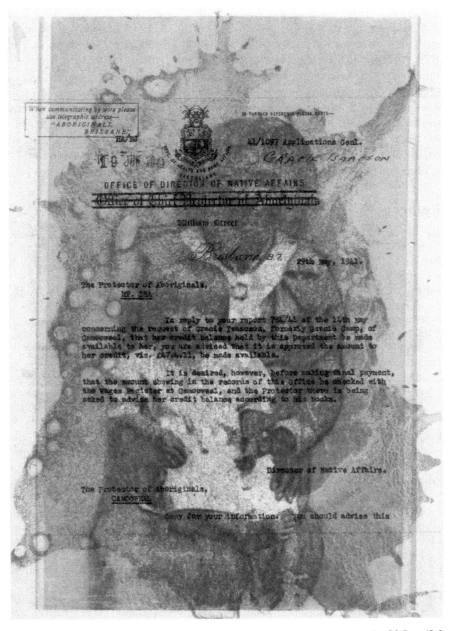

Figure 4.4 Judy Watson, page 2, *under the act* (2007), etching with chine collé, 30.5 × 42.0 cm. Courtesy of the artist and grahame galleries + editions

document, principles of provenance, the process of archivisation and ultimate storage on files in proximity to other records, as well as features such as genre and format, when assessing the evidentiary significance. Rather than considering archival sources as documentary text or representation, they are better understood from an ethnographic perspective, as artefacts, or imprints or inscriptions of the human on the page, and in this way, attend to the possibility of documents as having performative capacity in the production of knowledge practices. As Watson's artistic work demonstrates, a counter-archival engagement with archival sources can lead to seeing them as having 'latent power', which may lead productively to new understandings of the past.

References

Ballantyne, T. 2014, 'Mobility, Empire, Colonisation', *History Australia*, vol. 11, no. 2, pp. 7–37.

Bennett, J. 2010, *Vibrant Matter: A Political Ecology of Things*, Duke University Press, Durham and London.

Burton, A. 2005, 'Introduction: Archive Fever, Archive Stories' in A. Burton (ed.), *Archive Stories: Facts, Fictions, and the Writing of History*, Duke University Press, Durham and London.

Clanchy, M. 1993, *From Memory to Written Record: England 1066–1307*, 2nd edn, Blackwell, Oxford.

Darian-Smith, E. and Fitzpatrick, P. 1999, *Laws of the Postcolonial*, University of Michigan Press, Ann Arbor.

Dirks, N.B. 2002, 'Annals of the Archive' in B. Axel and D. Keith (eds), *From the Margins: Historical Anthropology and Its Futures*, Duke University Press, Durham and London.

Douglas, H. and Chesterman, J. 2008, 'Creating a Legal Identity: Aboriginal People and the Assimilation Census', *Journal of Australian Studies*, vol. 32, no. 3, pp. 375–391.

Edmonds, P. 2006, 'Imperial Objects, Truth and Fictions: Reading 19th Century Australian Colonial Objects as Historical Sources' in P. Edmonds and S. Furphy (eds), *Colonial Histories: New and Alternative Approaches*, RMIT Publishing, Melbourne.

Ezelle, M. and O'Brien O'Keeffe, K. 1994, *Cultural Artifacts and the Production of Meaning: The Page, the Image, and the Body*, University of Michigan Press, Ann Arbor.

Farge, A. 2013, *The Allure of the Archives*, trans. T. Scott-Railton, Yale University Press, New Haven, CT.

Ford, L. 2010, *Settler Sovereignty: Jurisdiction and Indigenous People in America and Australia, 1788–1836*, Harvard University Press, Cambridge.

Foucault, M. 1972, *The Archaeology of Knowledge and The Discourse on Language*, trans. A.M. Sheridan Smith, Pantheon Books, New York.

Harper, R. 1998, *Inside the IMF: An Ethnography of Documents, Technology, and Organizational Action*, Academic Press, Elsevier.

Harris, V. 2002, 'The Archival Sliver: A Perspective on the Construction of Social Memory in Archives and the Transition from Apartheid to Democracy' in C.

Hamilton, V. Harris, J. Taylor, M. Pickover, G. Reid and S. Razia (eds), *Refiguring the Archive*, Kluwer, Dordrecht.

Johnson, M. 2008, 'Making History Public: Indigenous Claims to Settler States', *Public Culture*, vol. 20, no. 1, 97–117.

Kirkby, D. and Coleborne, C. (eds) 2001, *Law, History, Colonialism: The Reach of Empire*, Manchester University Press, Manchester.

Latour, B. 1986, 'Visualisation and Cognition: Drawing Things Together', in H. Kucklick (ed.), *Knowledge and Society: Studies in the Sociology of Culture Past and Present*, vol. 6, Jai Press, Greenwich.

Latour, B. 2010, *The Making of Law: An Ethnography of the Conseil d'Etat*, trans. M. Brilman and A. Pottage, Polity Press, Cambridge.

Levi, R. and Valverde, M. 2008, 'Studying Law by Association: Bruno Latour goes to the Conseil d'Etat, *Law and Social Inquiry*, vol. 33, no. 3, pp. 805–825.

Luker, T. 2009, 'Reading the Evidentiary Void: The Body at the Scene of Writing', *Griffith Law Review*, vol. 18, no. 2, pp. 298–312.

Lydon, J. 2014, *Calling the Shots: Aboriginal Photographies*, Aboriginal Studies Press, Canberra.

Mawani, R. 2012, 'Law's Archive', *Annual Review of Law and Social Science*, vol. 8, pp. 337–365.

Mbembe, A. 2002, 'The Power of the Archive and its Limits', in C. Hamilton, V. Harris, J. Taylor, M. Pickover, G. Reid and S. Razia (eds), *Refiguring the Archive*, Kluwer, Dordrecht.

Moreton-Robinson, A. 2003, 'I Still Call Australia Home: Indigenous Belonging and Place in a White Postcolonizing Society' in S. Ahmed, C. Castañeda, A-M. Fortier and M. Sheller (eds), *Uprootings/Regroundings: Questions of Home and Migration*, Berg, Oxford pp. 23–40.

Perry, A. 2005, 'The Colonial Archive on Trial: Possession, Dispossession, and History in Delgamuukw v. British Colombia' in A. Burton (ed.), *Archive Stories: Facts, Fictions, and the Writing of History*, Duke University Press, Durham and London.

Ridener, J. 2008, *From Polders to Postmodernism: A Concise History of Archival Theory*, Lutwin Books, Minnesota.

Riles, A. 2006, *Documents: Artifacts of Modern Knowledge*, University of Michigan Press, Ann Arbor.

Robert, H. 2002, '"Unwanted Advances": Applying Critiques of Consent in Rape to *Cubillo v Commonwealth*', *Australian Feminist Law Journal*, vol. 16, no. 1, pp. 1–23.

Schwartz, J.M. and Cook, T. 2002, 'Archives, Records, and Power: The Making of Modern Memory', *Archival Science*, vol. 2, pp 1–19.

Steedman, C. 2001, *Dust: The Archive and Cultural History*, Rutgers University Press, New Brunswick.

Stoler, A.L. 2009, *Along the Archival Grain: Epistemic Anxieties and Colonial Common Sense*, Princeton University Press, Princeton and Oxford.

Thornton, M. and Luker, T. 2009, 'The Wages of Sin: Compensation for Indigenous Workers', *The University of New South Wales Law Journal*, vol. 32, no. 3, pp. 647–673.

Trundle, C. and Kaplonski, C. 2011, 'Tracing the Political Lives of Archival Documents', *History and Anthropology*, vol. 22, no. 4, pp. 407–11.

Vismann, C. 2008, *Files: Law and Media Technology*, Stanford University Press, Stanford.

96   Trish Luker

von Zinnenburg Carroll, K. 2014, *Art in the Time of Colony*, Ashgate, Surrey.

Watson, J. 2005, 'a preponderance of aboriginal blood', *Grahame Galleries*, viewed 24 June 2015, <www.grahamegalleries.com.au/index.php/judy-watson-a-preponderance>.

Watson, J. 2007, 'under the act', *Grahame Galleries*, viewed 24 June 2015, <www.grahamegalleries.com.au/index.php/judy-watson-under-the-act>.

Watson, J. and Martin-Chew, L. 2009, *Judy Watson: Blood Language*, The Miegunyah Press, Melbourne.

Cases

Cubillo v The Commonwealth of Australia (2000) 174 ALR 97

Kartinyeri v The Commonwealth of Australia [1998] HCA 22

Members of the Yorta Yorta Aboriginal Community v Victoria and Ors [1998] FCA 1606 (18 December 1998)

Legislation

Aboriginals Ordinance 1918 (NT)

Aboriginal Protection and Restriction of the Sale of Opium Act of 1897 (Qld)

Queensland Aboriginals Protection and Restriction of the Sale of Opium Act 1897 (Qld)

Registration of Births, Deaths and Marriages Ordinance 1941 (NT)

Welfare Ordinance 1953 (NT)

Chapter 5

The file as hypertext
Documents, files and the many worlds of the paper state

Mayur Suresh[*]

Introduction: The gravitational pull of paper

Paper is everywhere in courtrooms. Files upon files sit on clerks' desks. Massive filing cabinets occupy much of the floor space in courts. Reams of paper of different colours and thickness, printers, paper punchers, empty files, balls of string to bind files, pens of various colours and pencils all point to the crucial position that paper occupies. It is as if the very structure and layout of the court is premised around paper and the production and maintenance of files. In most courts throughout India, the digital world stops at the courtroom doors. Paper jealously guards its primary position in the judicial process – it alone can record what happens inside a courtroom.

Allow me to highlight the gravitational power that paper has in the courtroom through an ethnographic vignette from the trial of Mohammed Hanif[1] and his co-accused. I followed Hanif's case for about 14 months as a part of the fieldwork for my doctoral thesis. Hanif and 21 others are accused of setting off explosive devices in Delhi and another western Indian city, Surat. They are being held at the jail in Surat and are 'present' for their trial at Delhi via a video-conferencing facility.

The anti-terror police in Delhi, called the 'Special Cell', claimed that Hanif had gone to a southern city, Manipal, where he met a handler who provided him with the explosives. The police claim that in order to contact this handler, they used a public telephone that was operated by a witness, Anthony. During the course of the investigation, after the police had arrested him, the Special Cell say they took Mohammed Hanif to Manipal where he pointed out the public telephone from where he telephoned his handler. The police then prepared a 'Pointing Out Memo' stating that Hanif had pointed out the public phone. This memo was signed by the

---

[*] I would like to thank Stewart Motha, Honni van Rijswijk, Piyel Haldar, Laura Lammasniemi and the anonymous reviewers for their comments on earlier drafts of the paper. I would also like to thank Yvette Wajon for her very helpful editorial assistance.

[1] The names of places and persons have been changed to maintain confidentiality.

police officers present that had witnessed Hanif's pointing out of the telephone booth. The Special Cell say they then asked Anthony, the witness, whether he recognised Hanif, who then stated that he recognised Hanif as having made a telephone call from his phone booth. The police then prepared an 'Identification Memo' in which they stated that Anthony had identified Hanif. This too was signed by the police officers present that had witnessed Anthony identifying Hanif.

Four years later Anthony was summoned to the court to identify the person who made the call from his telephone booth. When Anthony appeared before the Delhi trial court it was clear that he did not understand or speak Hindi or Urdu, the languages spoken in Delhi's trial courts. The examination began in a mixture of English and Hindi, which Anthony struggled to understand and to speak, but somehow managed.

In the crowded courtroom, he was 'helped' through his deposition by an officer from the Special Cell who stood extremely close behind Anthony and it was evident to the defence counsel that the officer was whispering the answers to Anthony. Some of the defence counsel kept telling the officer to stand away from Anthony. He stepped away only to move back in several moments later.

Soon the moment came for him to identify the persons who came to his telephone booth and each of the accused appeared on the screen, one after the other. When one particular person came on screen, a police officer closest to Anthony, gently kicked the back of Anthony's leg. Anthony let out a muffled, yet startled cry, and began nodding vigorously. The defence counsel, noticing the kick, began to shout that the police officer was prompting the witness and asked that the judge record that the witness was being prompted. The judge ignored these objections by saying that he did not see anything and merely recorded:

> At this stage, Ld. Addl. PP[2] has asked the witness to point out from the screen of the video conferencing as to who out of the six persons visible on the screen was accompanying the police on the aforesaid date, in the year 2008. Thereupon the witness has correctly identified Mohd. Hanif, accused present at No. 4 from the left as visible on the screen of the video conferencing. (Objected to by learned defence counsel on the mode of identification).[3]

The Public Prosecutor then dictated (to the stenographer) the rest of Anthony's deposition. Here Anthony states that the police prepared an

---

2   Learned Additional Public Prosecutor.
3   The witness statements and other documents of this case are on file with the author. The case number and other document numbers have been withheld to maintain confidentiality.

Identification Memo, which states that he previously identified the accused person during the investigation. Anthony is now authenticating that Identification Memo:

> On <date>, police prepared memo when I identified the identity of Mohd. Hanif as the person who had come to my PCO on <date> and made phone call. I identified my signatures on the memo prepared in this regard. Same appear at Point C. The memo is **ExPW 78/F**.

Next came the turn of the defence counsel to cross-examine Anthony. The defence counsel questioned the witness about his ability to read and write English (the language in which the Identification Memo was written in) and his ability to accurately remember the events on the day he identified Mohammed Hanif during the investigation. Anthony, who by this time was sweating nervously, kept looking down at his palms, and it became evident that he had something written on his hands. The defence lawyer suddenly reached over and took hold of Anthony's hand and held it up for all to see, shouting that his answers had not been from memory but from the information written down on his hand. One of the defence lawyers started shouting that he should be immediately taken to the photocopy machine so that his hand could be photocopied and the photocopy of his palm be placed on the court file. Another defence lawyer, intending to intimidate the witness, and making reference to the rule that requires parties to tender only original documents, said 'No photocopy, we need the original. Just cut off his hand and put it on the file'.[4]

The judge tried to calm things down, but kept saying that he could not see anything written down on Anthony's palm. The lawyer who was still holding the witness' hand dragged the witness towards the judge's platform. The prosecutor shouted at the defence lawyers, telling them not to manhandle his witnesses. The witness was taken behind the judge's desk, his sweaty palms held upwards, for the judge to see. The judge merely said, 'I can't read anything written here'.[5] The defence lawyers argued that Anthony had the answers written on his hand and demanded that the judge document in that day's proceeding record that the witness was not deposing from memory, but was referring to information written on his palm. Perhaps because the writing had been sweated away, or because the judge did not want his court file to be marked by such farcical events, the judge merely replied that whatever was written on his palm was not legible and hence he could not record that the witness was reading off answers written on his palm.

4 As recorded in my field notes.
5 As recorded in my field notes.

From this dark comic scene, observe how the proceedings revolve around the file. While it initially occupies a background role, the file slowly emerges as the focal point of the proceedings. The file is the only record of what transpired in court on that date. For something to have happened (the witness having information written down on his palm, for example), it must have been recorded on paper. Observe how the defence lawyers try to get the judge to place that day's events on record. Since the judge refused to provide a record the events in his courtroom, those events – officially – never happened. Even if they were recorded, to have any juridical value, it must be recorded in the file in the proper way ('No photocopy, we need the original [hand]'). The court file itself refers to other documents prepared in advance of the file actually coming into court, including the Identification Memo and the Pointing Out Memo). Even as the world is utilised to contest the contents of the file (the questioning of the witness's memory of events) it is tentatively translated into paper, put through the rigour of form, and that paper itself, in turn, exerts a certain power. It is almost as if the paper and the file exert a gravitational pull over everything and everyone else present in the courtroom.

There is a complicated relationship between the file and the world. What is the nature of this relationship? How do we describe its power over the world? In the first part of this essay I consider some academic modes of accounting for this relationship. In these accounts, the logic of the file is intimately attached to the rise of bureaucratic state, and hence closely tied up with modes or production of juridical truth, discourses of state accountability, and the rule of law. Despite this, the institution of a rule based on paper is rendered unstable as paper could be copied, forged, lost and recontextualised. I argue that these renderings have not paid enough attention to how the world is translated into the file, and in turn, how the file produces the world.

In the sections that follow, I attempt to provide an account of this movement between the file and the world – as world absorbing and world creating. I follow one piece of evidence – a branch of a tree – from Hanif's case and provide an account of how the file is made and, in particular, how Latour's idea of the circulating reference (1999) can help us understand how the world enters the file. Thereafter, I look at how the defence strategy – to create reasonable doubt – involves bringing in more and more of the world into the file. I argue that this strategy of bringing in plausible scenarios into the file, to undermine the prosecution's narrative, not only signals the way in which the world circulates and enters the file, but also allows us to think of the file as speaking against itself. The file emerges as a sort of heterotopic space, which is intimately connected to the world, but in which the world is represented and contested at the same time (Foucault 1986: 24).

In the last and concluding section I look at the implications of under-

The file as hyptertext 101

standing the file as not only a textual space but as a hypertextual one. The word *hyper*-text implies that something outside or beyond the text is, nevertheless, connected to the text. I offer the term as a way of thinking both about the world that is beyond the file, being brought into the file, and also the world that is produced as a result of the file.

What is the relationship between the file and the world?

Historians of the Indian colonial state have argued that the production of documents and files, containing the various modes of official writing such as records and reports, were central to imparting a civilised form of government. Government by paper established the colonial state's claim to accountability, and hence were an essential feature of the rule of law (Mill 1990, cited in Moir 1993). Further, files for the colonial state were imagined 'photographs – of the ruled for the rulers' (Smith 1985: 154). In this view, the file contained true and accurate representations of society, and that governmental power was derived from an 'accurate knowledge and efficient use of these facts' (ibid.). The production of files entailed the production of knowledge of the people and places allowing the colonial state – in Calcutta or London – to ostensibly know and participate in the rule of distant territories and people.

Crucially, a file is that which determines and is determined by the form of law (Vismann 2008; Raman 2012; Ogborn 2007). The form of law determines the semiotic value of the files and at the same time, the files become the locus through which discourses on the production of juridical truth about the world, accountability and the rule of law, pass through. Others have argued that files are emblems of state power. Whether one looks at the semiotic ideologies of paper (Hull 2012; Vismann 2008), or conceives of the state – reminiscent of Franz Kafka's *In the Penal Colony* (1919/2006) – as a performative writing machine (Gupta 2012), the file symbolises sovereign power. Thus in these various scholarly renderings, files, government reports and other official documents are simultaneously signs of state power, essential to the rule of law, which serve to provide an accurate account of the world in documentary form through their ability to authenticate and produce juridical truth, and more fundamentally, determine the form that the law will take.

Nevertheless, what concerns the producers of state documents and the scholars who study them is their fragility. Whether conceived as determinative of the form of law, as establishing measures of accountability, or as a mode of production of juridical truth, once a state institutes forms of governance through technologies of writing, it simultaneously institutes the possibility of forgery, imitation and the mimetic performances of its power (Das 2004: 227). The state runs the risk that its written utterances may be grafted on to other chains of signification (ibid.: 244) or be recontextualised (Hull 2012: 24). Whether it was with the colonial state's anxiety over the 'duplicity of paper', engendered by a 'crisis of attestation' (Raman 2012: 137) or the 'theft or mislaying' (Hull 2012: 23) of files in contemporary Pakistan, or the 'unpredictability' of government paper in revolutionary France (B. Kafka 2012: 9), rhetoric of the stability of a rule based on paper has constantly betrayed its material instability.

The power of the file

Despite this fragility of the file, or perhaps because of it,[6] the file exerts a power over those who encounter it. What sort of power does the file have and what sort of power does the file enable? One of the phrases that came up several times in the course of my fieldwork was the term '*kagazi case*' or 'the paper case'. It was often uttered both as a form of surprise (that the only evidence that the police could bring was all written down in a file) and as a term of derision (that the 'evidence' in the file was as flimsy as the paper it was printed on). Echoing what Emma Tarlo calls 'paper truths' (2003: 9), the ambivalent term conveys the impression that the case can be easily shredded – just like paper – but as it is written, it has the capacity to become 'true'. Statements from accused persons – like 'I have the paper to prove it', 'What proof? All there was, was paper!' – indicate the range of powers that paper exercises. These statements indicate that file has a power beyond its content – that there is something else about the files, that accounts for their power.

Ben Kafka has criticised some academic treatment of files as merely looking *through* paperwork – at their content – but failed to pause to look *at* files (B. Kafka 2009: 341). He points to the 'psychic life of paper work' and argues that files are indicative of the ways in which we are attached to the sovereign power (B. Kafka 2012: 15). Kafka explores files – their unpredictability, their slippery nature – as a way of understanding the psychic investments that are made in the state, and the slips of the file (so to speak) as ways of accessing the unconscious attachments to nation and state building (B. Kafka 2012: 16). Files themselves exercise no power of their own, but represent what the state means to various actors. Kafka offhandedly dismisses Bruno Latour's argument on the agency exercised by the file by stating:

> ... no matter how much I learned about the [file's] materiality, I was never going to come around to the argument that things have agency

---

6   Using ethnographic insights into post-Sikh-riot Delhi, Das argues that the fact that state documents can be copied, forged, and transplanted into different contexts is not a sign of the vulnerability of state power, but rather how state power circulates in communities (2004).

The file as hyptertext 103

like people do ... Rather ... I am committed to the idea that people are ruled by unconscious processes which is simply not true of even the most 'agentic' of things.

(B. Kafka 2012: 14)

Latour's argument is that the case file draws a constellation of other actors, institutions and the documents they produce and puts them into a format legible – both literarily and discursively – to the court (2010). Latour does not argue that the file has agentic or purposive capacity like that of a human. Instead he argues that the file draws together documents from different sources, which may have otherwise not come to be arranged together, and the people who encounter the file constantly act and react in relation to the file, and in this sense the file seems to act (Latour 2010: 77). Elsewhere, Latour argues that 'if action is limited a priori to what "intentional" "meaningful" humans do' then nothing apart from humans could be said to act (2005: 45). He therefore describes an actor as 'anything that does modify a state of affairs by making a difference' (Latour 2005: 71).

Elaborating on Latour's argument, Matthew Hull, writing about bureaucratic practices in contemporary Pakistan, argues that 'documents engage (or do not engage) with people places and things to make other bureaucratic objects' (Hull 2012: 5). Further, in accounting for the power of documents, he argues that 'graphic artefacts' of the bureaucracy are simultaneously constituted and constitutive of broader associations of people, places and other things (Hull 2012: 18). He argues that the circulation of documents creates associations of people regardless of organisational structures and formal bureaucratic practices, and by drawing other materials and things into the realm of state power. This account of the file goes some way in accounting for the power of the file. However, the power of the file lies not simply in its hubristic ability to provide an accurate picture of the world, or in the fact that it organises things around itself, but also in its ability to create multiple worlds.

In his short story *Tlön, Uqbar, Orbis Tertius*, Jorge Luis Borges chances upon the *First Encyclopaedia of Tlön Vol. XI*. This encyclopaedia provides an account of the philosophy, language and history of a hitherto undiscovered world. Borges is now holding a 'vast and methodical fragment of an unknown plant's entire history. ... And all of it articulated, coherent, with no visible doctrinal intent or tone of parody' (Borges 1964: 23). Years later, Borges discovers that the encyclopaedia was an elaborate hoax, produced by generations of scholars acting in secret. The encyclopaedia was patronised by an ascetic millionaire who left them his mountains of wealth on one condition: 'The work will make no pact with the impostor Jesus Christ' (ibid.: 31). The millionaire 'did not believe in God, but he wanted to demonstrate to this non-existent God that mortal man was capable of conceiving a world' (ibid.: 31). Soon objects from this fantastic world intrude into the real world: a metallic case engraved with the alphabets of Tlön; a cone the size of a die but of intolerable weight, images of divinity in certain regions of Tlön. Soon Tlön begins to disintegrate this world. Schools begin teaching the language of Tlön, with English, French and Spanish disappearing from the globe. The encyclopaedia not only describes Tlön, but also begins to literally *produce* Tlön in our world.

The power of the file lies precisely in this power to produce one world to replace another. One of the common refrains I heard during my field-work was 'The police made me sign blank sheets of paper', indicating that the police themselves wrote the confession on these signed blank pages. The fear here is not merely that the police have produced a false confession, but that the 'confession' might become 'true'. The file therefore not only attempts to mirror the world, but actively produces it. In this sense, the file occupies what Foucault would call a heterotopic space (1986). In the world produced by the file, 'real sites...are simultaneously represented, contested and inverted' (Foucault 1986: 24). Like the mirror, the file is absolutely connected with all that it organises around itself, but at the same time is 'absolutely unreal' since the world that it produces is located nowhere (ibid.). Similarly, while the file is intimately attached to the world that surrounds it, it not only provides a picture of the world, but at the very same time contests, and upends the world by producing another.

In the next sections I will attempt to show how the file not only pulls the world into it, but in doing so, produces not just one, but multiple heterotopic worlds.

The making of the file

The paper lives of a case in Delhi are governed by a several Rules, Laws, Codes and Manuals: Punjab Police Rules, still in force today, promulgated under the Indian Police Act of 1861, the Delhi High Court Rules, 1967, the Code of Criminal Procedure, 1973 and the Indian Evidence Act, 1872. These various laws prescribe the paperwork that the police and the courts must undertake in their daily lives, including the form to be filled out when conducting an arrest, the maintenance of records of First Information Reports, Daily Diaries which record the movements of a police officer in that station, how witness testimony is to be recorded, and how court records are to be maintained. The idea behind these documentary rules is that police actions ought to be accountable to the judiciary and that the judicial record of the lower courts ought to be legible to higher courts.

Each file maps the progress of a case. Let's take the example of Hanif's case and his alleged conspirators. The bomb blast first takes documentary form in the guise of an entry in the Daily Diary of the Police Station in Gole Market. As the name suggests, this diary records certain events that happen in the jurisdiction of that police station, including the commission of

The file as hyptertext   105

serious offences. The DD (as the 'Daily Diary' is known in police parlance) is recorded on carbon paper (so that there are duplicates of every entry) and are recorded by the designated Station House Officer. According to this DD entry No. 15/A dated 14.10.2008:

> At about 7:17 in the evening ... Lt Constable Geeta <badge no.> gave information that a strong explosion had taken place in the M.C.D. Market, Gole Market.

The DD records that the copy of the entry was then being sent with Constable Suraj Chand to Sub Inspector Mahinder, who was posted at a police booth near a temple close to the spot where the blasts were reported.

The next document that records the occurrence of the bomb blast is another document called a Rukka,[7] which was prepared by Sub Inspector Mahinder, and is sent to the police station, which in turn results in the registration of the First Information Report (FIR). A copy of the FIR is then sent back to Sub Inspector Mahipal and all subsequent paperwork that results from the investigation must bear the FIR's number: 176/2008. In this FIR No. 176/2008 PS Gole Market, the Sub Inspector Mahinder is figured as the complainant and he details what happens after he received the copy of the DD entry from Constable Suraj Chand. He says when he reached the spot he found a number of people 'in injured condition', who were shifted to hospitals with help from the public. Soon police vans, ambulances and fire brigade vehicles arrived on the scene. Sub Inspector Mahinder also said he saw one auto-rickshaw with license plate number ending 1438 that was in a badly damaged condition with a part of it hanging from a nearby pipal tree. He says he saw a damaged fuel cylinder from this auto-rickshaw. He further says that he saw several other damaged vehicles and lists their license plate numbers. There were spots of blood on the ground around the blast site, and nearby shops and their goods were badly damaged. The FIR then records that investigation should proceed for offences under sections of the Indian Penal Code, 1860 (attempt to murder, causing hurt, waging war against the State), the Explosive Substances Act, 1908 (causing an explosion, likely to endanger life, attempt to cause an explosion, possession of explosives) and the Unlawful Activities

---

7   A Rukka is a report written by the police officer at the site of the incident to the local police station detailing the incident and requesting any further action. A carbon copy of the Rukka is prepared and the original Rukka is sent to the local police station with a police officer. At the police station, the duty officer on reading the Rukka, registers a First Information Report in the FIR Register. The Duty Officer then makes an endorsement on the Rukka stating what action has been taken.

Prevention Act, 1967 (membership of an unlawful association, punishment for unlawful activities).

At this stage, there is a split in the paper avatars of the bomb blast between the court file and the police file. When the police register an FIR, they send it to a magistrate to be authenticated. A copy of the complaint is kept on the Magistrate's files and the authenticated original is sent back for investigation (to ensure that the police make no additions later on to the FIR). The court file now only consists of a few pages of the FIR. If the police make an arrest, the court file reflects this in the form of an Arrest Memo and Applications for Remand made by the police. This file will also contain the order by the Magistrate, allowing or refusing remand. Over the course of the following weeks, the police may make applications asking the court for permission to take voice, handwriting, and body tissue samples or ask for further time to interrogate the accused. These applications are made in writing and kept on the court file. If the accused has a lawyer, often the court will ask the defence for their replies to these applications, which will be placed on this file, as will the Magistrate's final decision on them. The court file, slowly, yet surely, expands in girth.

In parallel, the police maintain a case diary, which must be periodically presented to the Magistrate for the latter to monitor the investigation. They also compile their own records documenting the progress of their investigation. We have already encountered two of these documents: the Pointing Out Memo and the Identification Memo. Let's meet a third: the 'Seizure Memo.'

Returning to the scene of the bomb blast near Gole Market, let's follow one particular part of the scene – the pipal tree. The police claim that by this time, the area had been cordoned off to 'preserve' the scene. The investigation has now been handed over to a senior officer, Inspector Akash Thakur. Recall that Sub-Inspector Mahinder had seen an auto-rickshaw that was badly damaged and parts of it had been thrown into a nearby pipal tree. The parts of the auto-rickshaw, the branch in which parts of it are lodged, what appear to be pieces of shrapnel, ball bearings, blood samples, pieces of burnt cloth are all seized by the police. The various things that are seized are rendered into documentary form by a Seizure Memo, which describes the article seized, and is signed by the police officer seizing it and by one police witness.

Let's look at the Seizure Memo of the tree branch (see Figure 5.1). At the head of the memo is the FIR number to indicate in which case this seizure is being made. The Memo is titled '*Fard Magboojgi* (seizure memo) Big Wooden Piece of Pipal Tree'.

The memo is then signed by the officer making the seizure, Sub Inspector Rakesh Kumar Singh and is witnessed by his superior officer Inspector Akash Thakur. Similar Seizure Memos are prepared for the damaged TSR (official parlance for an auto-rickshaw), the blood samples,

The file as hyptertext 107

Case FIR No 176/08 dt. 14/10/2008 u/s 307, 323,121 IPC, 3,4,5 Explosive Substances Act 1908 & 10, 12, 13, Unlawful Activities (Prevention) Act, 1967, PS Gole Market New Delhi

Seizure Memo Big Wooden Piece of Pipal Tree

Below mentioned witness states that just after the bomb blast occurred on of <name of road> in between shops no. 33 and 34, near the MCD market, Gole Market, New Delhi, Expert teams immediately came to the scene. After they had taken samples and performed certain tests, it was noticed that there was a pipal tree standing where the blast had taken place. A side portion of the TSR with registration no. ending 1438 was lodged on a branch of that tree. A portion of the branch of 1.5 feet length and 16 inch diameter was taken. In order for the piece of the branch to be tested for IED traces, it was put into a polly bag. The polly bag was placed in a pulanda and sealed with the seal AT and the details of FIR No.___ was written on it and the article was seized vide this memo and the article was sent to MHC(M).
What is stated above is true.

Witness
-signed-   -signed
SI Rakesh Kumar Singh   Akash Thakur
PS. Gole Market   Sub Inspector Investigation
New Delhi   PS Gole Market
                                                   New Delhi
                                                   14/10/2008

Figure 5.1 Seizure Memo of a tree branch of a pipal tree, Gole Market New Delhi

ball bearings, shrapnel and other things seized from the scene of the blast. Each item is packaged most often in a cloth bag called a *pulanda*, and then sealed with wax and stamped with the seal that bears the initials of the investigating officer, in this instance A.T.

Every step, every movement that the seized articles subsequently take are rendered into paper. After their seizure, the branch and other articles are deposited in an evidence storeroom, called the *malkhana* or the MHC(M), which again registers the details of the articles deposited. When the materials are taken to the Central Forensic Science Laboratory for analysis, here again there is a register describing what has been transferred. At serial number 14 of this list is the piece of the tree:

> One transparent Poly pouch containing one wooden piece having one metal piece sealed with the seal of A.T. and marked as L.

After a certain period of time the police will file the final report, more commonly known as the chargesheet, before the Magistrate's court. Now the parts of the police's file will merge with the court's file. This chargesheet contains the brief facts of the prosecution's case, the offences with which they want to charge the accused, the list of all witnesses, their testimony as told to the police, and all documentary evidence relied upon by the police, including memos that document the seizure of certain evidence, the results of a search by the police, the interrogation of witnesses, along with many other papers that document the activities of the police. At this stage, the court file dramatically expands in girth and weight, with the chargesheet often running into volumes of hundreds of pages each.

After the proceedings before the Magistrate have concluded,[8] the trial commences before a Sessions Court, or in Hanif's case, before the Additional Sessions Judge, Mr Navin Kumar. During the course of the trial, the prosecution must present all physical evidence seized during the course of the trial. The police must prove first, that the material was collected and seized in the manner they said it was, second, that the police in no way tampered with the evidence, and third, that the subsequent forensic analysis of the evidence was competent and accurate. But the court cannot rely on these documents in reaching a judgment, and can only rely on things said in court that have been duly recorded by it in evidence. As a result, the police's file must be translated by the court into its own file.

In order to prove that the branch, the blown up auto-rickshaw (and other things) were seized by the police in the manner that they said it was seized, Sub Inspector Rakesh Kumar Singh is summoned to court to depose[9] to this effect. He is witness number 143. He first states the time and

8   After the police file the chargesheet (under Section 173 of the Code of Criminal Procedure, 1973) in the Magistrate's court, the Magistrate must go through the chargesheet to ascertain that a clear case is made out against the accused and if there is such a case, the Magistrate is said to take cognisance of the case (under section 190 of the Code of Criminal Procedure, 1973). After the Magistrate takes cognisance of the case, the process of scrutiny of documents begins. During this process, each of the accused persons is given a copy of the chargesheet and all supporting documents, and under Section 207 of the Code of Criminal Procedure, the Magistrate must ensure that all the documents filed by the police are handed over to the accused and that these copies are legible. In the case of terror offences (which are triable by a superior court, the Court of Sessions) after all copies have been supplied to the accused, the Magistrate is said to commit the case to the Court of Sessions for trial.

9   What happens in an examination-in-chief and a cross examination is this: the lawyer (the prosecutor in the case of a prosecution witness or the defence lawyer in the case of a defence witness) or judge first asks a question to the witness, the witness replies. The concerned lawyers and/or the judge will then dictate to the stenographer the answer of the witness. A similar process happens during the cross examination of the witness. The witness examination-in-chief and his cross examination are not (usually) recorded in a question an answer format but in the form of a narrative, despite the fact Section 276 of the Code of Criminal Procedure states:

The file as hyptertext 109

manner in which he reached the blast site and what he saw (the area cordoned off, bomb disposal squad and special security guards present). His deposition then says the following:

> At the spot, we also noticed many vehicles including cars, motorcycles, rickshaw lying damaged. We could see blood stains scattered at places. We also noticed a TSR (official parlance for an auto-rickshaw), in severely damaged condition lying under a pipal tree on the side of <...> road leading to <....> road. A portion of the TSR was seen hanging from the said tree. On seeing the TSR, one could say that the bomb had been planted in the said TSR. We could easily see signs of splinters on the cylinder of the TSR. The TSR was having registration no. ending 1438.

The police witness then describes seizing our piece of wood from the spot:

> From the spot, we also collected one piece of wood with an iron piece embedded in it. Also from the spot, we picked up two plastic pieces. These were turned into separate parcels and sealed with the seal bearing impression of A.T. i.e. of Inspector Akash Thakur. These were then seized vide memo **ExPW143/F**.

So here we see first the that facts – the fact that he noticed a part of the rickshaw on the branch, the fact that he seized the branch, the fact that he prepared a memo documenting that he seized the branch – are inserted into the court's record. But this is not enough, as at this point all the Sub Inspector has managed to tentatively establish is that he has prepared the Seizure Memos. The material that he says he seized must be presented in court, as the court must be shown the material to prove their existence. The fact that they physically exist must, in turn, be recorded in the court file. Hence at a later point in the deposition (after he has tendered all the seizure memos in evidence) the Sub Inspector states that he can identify the material that he has seized. At this point, the representative from the

---

276. Record in trial before Court of Session

(1) In all trials before a Court of Session, the evidence of each witness shall, as his examination proceeds, be taken down in writing either by the presiding Judge himself or by his dictation in open Court or, under his direction and superintendence, by an officer of the Court appointed by him in this behalf.

(2) Such evidence shall ordinarily be taken down in the form of question and answer; but the presiding Judge may, in his discretion, take down or cause to be taken down, the whole or any part of such evidence in the form of a narrative.

(3) The evidence so taken down shall be signed by the presiding Judge and shall form part of the record.

police evidence depository, (in unofficial court parlance known as the *malkhana* and officially known as the MHC(M)) presents the various articles associated with this case number. The court record then reads:

> At this stage, representative of the MHC(M) from PS Gole Market has produced in court one parcel bearing particulars of the case FIR No. 176/08 and bearing seals of FSL CBI. It is opened and one piece of wood is taken out of it and shown to the witness. Who states that this piece of wood is of the pipal tree as a part of the TSR registration no. ending 1438 was found lying embedded in it and this part had to be cut off from the said tree. This piece of wood is **Ex143/4**.

Here we see how the piece of wood has travelled from being part of a tree, to being first rendered into documentary form by the Seizure Memo, to being sent to the *malkhana* where it is again registered, to being sent to the Forensic Science Laboratory, where again it leaves a documentary trace, to its actual physical presence in court, to once again being transformed into a document by this last excerpt.

Latour gives us the concept of a 'circulating reference' by which he describes how scientific practices 'pack the world into words' (1999: 24). Latour considers the 'old settlement' on the relation between language and the world – where the chasm between the two domains was only connected through a 'risky correspondence' (ibid.). Instead, Latour, by giving us the idea of the circulating reference, suggests that there was never a gap in the first place, but the constant, chain-like, translation of the material world into language, where material objects are turned into objects of study. Similarly, the piece of wood simultaneously exists of itself, but nevertheless is transformed through these documentary forms – from the branch of the tree to evidence of a bomb blast. The piece of wood has several documentary iterations and in turn each one of these documentary iterations leaves a trace on the court record.

The file contests itself

In her book on files, Cornelia Vismann argues that files did not merely record what was in the world, but gained the power to determine what the world is (2008). She argues that the Latin maxim – *quod non est in actis, non est in mundo* ('what is not in the file is not in the world') that comes up in literary and judicial texts referring to the written foundation for Roman court proceedings – summarises the performative operation of the law in constructing reality. According to this idea, reality is what is found in file, and if the file and the world do not coincide, it is up to the world to prove that something not on file indeed exists. Files in this picture are not merely recording devices, but 'protocols of reality that consume everything outside the law' (ibid.: 56). Since the law only believes what itself has written down, 'the world, does not have a dissenting voice; it has to bow to file performances' (ibid.: 56). I like Vismann's idea of a world-consuming file – to an extent. I hope to show in this section that while the court file does determine reality, the world is drawn to the file and enters the file in unpredictable ways. The file is not only what determines the world, but the world enters the file, as if to cause the file to undermine the world that it itself has created.

Let us return to the courtroom where the Sub Inspector is now to be cross-examined by a defence lawyer. The defence lawyer's strategy is two pronged. First, since it would be pointless to contest that a bomb blast had in fact taken place, it is aimed at contesting the claim that the items were seized in the manner stated by the police officer. Take for example:

> It is correct that the area where the occurrence took place is a public case (sic) where there are many shops. It is correct that I did not join anyone from the public during the investigation conducted by me at the spot.

Here the defence is asking if there were any non-police witnesses who could independently verify that the search and seizure actually did take place. The underlying logic behind this line of questioning is this: If there were independent public witnesses who were around the blast site, why were they not made to officially witness the seizure? The answer must be: because the seizure was not conducted in the manner stated by the police.

The defence then tries to suggest that the memos could not have been written, and the parcels could not have been prepared, because the police officer did not have any of the requisite materials with him:

> At the time I left the police station for the spot, I was empty handed. The material used in preparing parcels at the spot was requisition by me through my staff (sic). But I do not know as to from where my staff had arranged the same.

This point is made more directly later on when the transcript states: 'It is wrong to suggest that the entire writing work was done at the police station and not at the spot'.

The second aim of the defence is to suggest that the police manufactured the memos and conducted a partial seizure only to implicate her client. Take for example, the following excerpt:

> In addition to the above referred TSR, one or two other vehicles had suffered severe damage while other vehicles were partially damaged. I did not taken (sic) any steps as to who were the owners of these other

vehicles which suffered damages. I also did not collect any certificates of registrations of other vehicles which suffered damage.

By suggesting that the police did not seize the other vehicles severely damaged in the blast, the defence is trying to create doubt as to which vehicle contained the explosive. The defence further is attempting to suggest that the police came up with the 'explosives in the auto-rickshaw' theory as a preconceived plan to implicate the accused. Pushing this argument further, the defence then questions the police officer's expertise or ability to state that the explosion had taken place in the auto-rickshaw:

> I am a graduate in Economics. However, during in service training, I have learnt to assess explosives. It is wrong to suggest that I have no such expertise even in service training. It is wrong to suggest that I had no expertise to say that "on seeing the TSR, one could say that bomb had been planted in the said TSR." It is wrong to suggest that no part of the said TSR was found embedded in the tree as stated by me in chief examination. It is wrong to suggest that evidence was introduced falsely to show that bomb had been planted in the said TSR with a view to falsely implicated the accused persons.

Defence lawyers will often speak of their strategy more generally as creating or teasing out 'contradictions' in the prosecution witness's testimony, which consists of not only contradicting and contesting the prosecution's version of events as seen above, but as if almost to make the prosecution's narrative to speak against itself. As Tarlo suggests, this ability to create contradictions within the file, to make it undermine itself is allowed only because the regime of paper truths:

> ... highlight the ever present gap between what is implicitly known and what is officially recorded, a gap open to both negotiation and exploitation as people's experiences ... make clear.
>
> (Tarlo 2003: 9)

In the case of the cross examination, as we can see above, the defence lawyer repeatedly inserts things that could have plausibly happened in the world – the lack of public witnesses, the other damaged cars, the lack of knowledge of explosives – in order to bring the police officer's testimony into question. But in order to do so, she has to bring it on record. This alternative, plausible, world is inserted into the court file in order to create reasonable doubt into what was recorded by the file just some moments before. In this way, the court's record, and the world it creates, is made to speak against itself.

Conclusion: The hypertextual file

Look at the facsimile of a page from the court's transcript of SI Rakesh Kumar Singh's testimony (Figure 5.2).

The parts of the page that are in bold text refer to other physical items, like pieces of the rickshaw or to other documents such as the seizure memo prepared by the police. One way of thinking of this page is to look at the court file as exerting a gravitational force that draws disparate things into it. But as we saw earlier, the world is drawn into the file, and appears to enter the file, and the bold text marks the points at which the world has entered the court's file. The bold text refers to something that is outside this page. If you are reading this on a computer you might be tempted to hover your cursor over the bold portion to see where or to what they link to. What we could have here is not merely text, but hypertext, with each bold phrase linking the page you are reading to something outside of it. Each one of these phrases not only represents where the world has entered the court file, but also is a new fulcrum around which the case can be read. The multiplication of these bold phrases, these hyperlinks, means not only that the world has entered the file in different ways, but also that the world the file is creating may not be singular. Instead, in making the file speak against itself, the defence strategy – to create reasonable doubt – is to make the worlds that the file creates speak against each other.

9

the same parcel

At this stage, representative of the MHC(M) from PS Gole Market has produced in Court one parcel bearing particulars of the case FIR No. 176/08 and bearing seals of FSL CBI. It is opened and from it one transparent jar marked 19 is taken out from it. The transparent jar contains a metallic piece but the witness submits that this metallic piece does not pertain to the investigation carried out by him. According, the same has been put back in the same parcel.

During investigation at the aforesaid spot on 15/10/2008, I also picked up one iron piece i.e. Bottom portion of the above referred to TSR which is **ExPW143/20**, one metallic piece of the said TSR which is **ExPW143/21**, a metallic [*sic*] of the said TSR bearing owner's name which is **ExPW143/22**, from the front portion of the TSR having its registration number which is **ExPW143/23**, CNG cylinder having striking marks made by pellets which is **ExPW143/24**, three tyres of TSR which are **ExPW143/25 to 27**. Steering portion having mudguard which is **ExPW143/28** and 15-16 metallic pieces which are collectively **ExPW143/29** were seized by me vide memo **ExPW 143/G**. All these items were found scattered in the area.

Figure 5.2 Facsimile of a page from the court's transcript of SI Rakesh Kumar Singh's testimony

In his fictional short story *The Garden of Forking Paths* Borges (1941/1998) describes the mysterious legacy of Ts'ui Pen, an illustrious ancestor of the protagonist of this story, Yu Tsun. Ts'ui Pen had retired as the governor of a province to do two things: to write a vast and complicated novel and to construct an equally vast and intricate maze, one in which 'all men would lose their way'. When Ts'ui Pen died, there was no labyrinth and the drafts of the novel were 'contradictory jumble of irresolute drafts' (ibid.: 82). A scholar of Ts'ui Pen's legacy, Stephen Albert unravels this mystery when he reads Ts'ui Pen's will, where it says 'I leave to the various futures (not to all) my garden of forking paths' ((ibid.: 82). And this, for Albert was the key to understanding Ts'ui Pen's legacy. Albert says:

> In all fictional works, each time a man is confronted with several alternatives, he chooses one and eliminates the others; in the fiction of Ts'ui Pen, he chooses – simultaneously – all of them. He creates, in this way, diverse futures, diverse times, which themselves also proliferate and fork. ... In the work of Ts'ui Pen, all possible outcomes occur; each one is the point of departure for other forkings. Sometimes, the paths of this labyrinth converge: for example, you arrive at this house, but in one of the possible pasts you are my enemy, in another, my friend.
>
> (Borges 1941/1998: 83)

The concept that Borges described here – in several layers of the story, but most directly in the combination book and maze – is that a novel can be read in multiple ways, a 'hypertext novel' as argued by media theorist Nick Montfort (2003). Borges, according to Montfort was describing a theory of the universe based upon the structure of such a novel, a universe in which everything that is possible does indeed occur in some branch of reality.

Similarly, can we conceive of the court file as a hypertextual space? In the limited universes created by the file, does everything that is possible occur in particular readings of the file? We have seen how the world is drawn to the file and enters it, causing the file to speak against itself. In the file several worlds are created: one world may counter another, a second world may contest reality. Each time the world enter the files, the file itself creates another world. Each point at which the world enters the file is itself a point of departure for other forkings, a new fulcrum around which the file may be read. The file is not only an archive of the world, but produces several counter-archives. Files yield worlds that could not be foreseen, their meaning in a flux, like Borges' novel, producing several worlds, all at the same time.

References

Borges, J.L. 1941/1998, 'The Garden of Forking Paths', *Collected Fictions*, trans. A. Hurley, Penguin Books, London.

Borges, J.L. 1964, 'Tlön, Uqbar, Orbis Tertius' in D. Yates and J.E. Irby (eds), *Labyrinths: Selected Stories and Other Writings*, New Directions Publishing Corporation, New York.

Das, V. 2004, 'The Signature of the State: The Paradox of Illegibility' in V. Das and D. Poole (eds), *Anthropology at the Margins of the State*, School of American Research Press, Santa Fe.

Foucault, M. 1986, 'Of Other Spaces', *Diacritics*, vol. 16, no. 1, pp. 22–27.

Gupta, A. 2012, *Red Tape: Bureaucracy, Structural Violence and Poverty in India*, Duke University Press, Durham.

Hull, M. 2012, *Government of Paper: The Materiality of Bureaucracy in Urban Pakistan*, University of California Press, Berkeley.

Kafka, B. 2009, 'Paperwork: The State of the Discipline', *Book History*, vol. 12, pp. 340–353.

Kafka, B. 2012, *The Demon of Writing: Powers and Failures of Paperwork*, Zone Books, New York.

Kafka, F. 1919/2006, 'In the Penal Colony' in *The Metamorphosis and Other Stories*, trans. W. Muir and E. Muir, Schoken Books Inc, New York.

Latour, B. 1999, 'Circulating Reference: Sampling the Soil in the Amazon Forest', *Pandora's Hope: Essays on the Reality of Science Studies*, Harvard University Press, Cambridge, pp. 24–79.

Latour, B. 2005, *Reassembling the Social: An Introduction to Actor-Network Theory*, Oxford University Press, Oxford.

Latour, B. 2010, *The Making of Law: An Ethnography of the Conseil d'Etat*, trans. M. Brulman and A. Pottage, Policy Press, Cambridge.

Moir, M. 1993, '*Kaghazi Raj*: Notes on the Documentary Basis of Company Rule 1773–1858', *Indo-British Review: A Journal of History*, vol. 21, no. 2, pp. 185–193.

Montfort, N. 2003, 'Introduction: The Garden of Forking Paths' in N.F. Wardrip and N. Montfort (eds), *The New Media Reader*, MIT Press, Cambridge.

Ogborn, M. 2007, *Indian Ink: Script and Print in the Making of the English East India Company*, University of Chicago Press, Chicago.

Raman, B. 2012, *Document Raj: Writing and Scribes in Early Colonial South India*, University of Chicago Press, Chicago.

Smith, R.S. 1985, 'Rule-by-Records and Rule-by-Reports: Complementary Aspects of the British Imperial Rule of Law', *Contributions to Indian Sociology*, vol. 19. no. 1, pp. 153–176.

Tarlo, E. 2003, *Unsettling Memories: Narratives of India's Emergency*, Permanent Black, New Delhi.

Vismann, C. 2008, *Files: Law and Media Technology*, trans G. Winthrop-Young, Stanford University Press, Stanford.

Chapter 6

Counter-archive as staging dissensus

Karin van Marle

Introduction

The aim of this chapter is to draw tentative lines, or maybe to weave fragile threads, between nostalgia and the possibility of dissensus, in order to contemplate the (im)possibilities of a counter-archive, of countering the archive or even an archival countering. In the same vein as the understanding of nostalgia expanded on below, the argument is intended to seduce, rather than to convince.

I want to consider a notion of nostalgia that, following Simon Critchley, identifies 'disappointment' and not 'wonder' as starting point (Critchley 2004: 2, Antaki 2012: 1). Staying with the idea of a counter-archive, I toil with the task of how to tie or think together nostalgia, specifically 'reflective nostalgia' (as nostalgia of disappointment) and a politics of resistance (Boym 2001). Could 'reflective nostalgia' be seen as a staging of dissensus, as 'putting two worlds in one and the same world'? (Rancière 2004 p. 306). The countering at play is more of an opening up than a clear or clean counter. The argument accordingly unfolds messily, and is not as systematic and synthesised as some readers might prefer.

How could reflective nostalgia be seen as a politics of resistance, or phrased differently in which way could dissensus be staged by reflective nostalgia? I tentatively argue that reflective nostalgia can be seen as politics of resistance in two senses. First because it goes against the grain, against the critiques that regard nostalgia as such as conservative, opposing change and absconding responsibility. And second, in contrast to restorative nostalgia it does not seek for a homecoming, but remembers the past with irony and in a way that does not stand in the way of transformation.

I start with a reflection on nostalgia – in particular the work by Svetlana Boym, paradoxically titled *The Future of Nostalgia* (2001) – after which South African writing on nostalgia, memory and archive is drawn in. I consider various notions of nostalgia and different ways in which to remember, and ask if a politics of resistance could be evoked by reflective nostalgia and memorial remembering, nostalgia and remembrance that do not celebrate what they long for and remember, but are embodied and embedded in disappointment.

Jacques Rancière and his view on the possibility of staging dissensus come next and are considered briefly. Could reflective nostalgia be seen as creating opportunity and possibility for countering, for resisting, for bringing dissensus to forced consensus?

I end with a case, a jurisprudential archive of sorts, the case of *Baphiring Community v Tshwaranani Projects* (2014 1 SA 330) and ask what kinds of nostalgia and remembrance might be at play, and what we can make of the community's refusal to accept compensation in exchange for their land. Peter Goodrich, in response to Stanley Fish's description of judgment as an activity based on forgetting in order to preserve law's autonomy, has argued that the very act of forgetting opens simultaneously a return of memory, of recollection that 'allows for a history of resistance to the fiction of the autonomy of law' (1995: 137). The complexities and ambiguity, the equivocation of memory, the archive and nostalgia are manifested in this case. Lastly and maybe belatedly I refer to the notions of spatiality and spatial justice. I do not delve deeply into them, but invoke them merely as traces to be considered in thinking about nostalgia and dissensus.

A nostalgia of disappointment

In this section I draw on Boym's work on nostalgia before I turn to some South African writing on memory and nostalgia. I am particularly interested in Boym's distinction between restorative and reflective nostalgia.

I want to relate the distinction that she draws to a distinction between two ways of remembering that was applied to not only the South African process of and experience of dealing with the past, but also to a reading and understanding of the South African Constitution. Even though a thorough discussion of the theme falls beyond the specific scope of this chapter, a brief exposition of the discussion on monumental and memorial constitutionalism is needed for my aim to think about this distinction through the one drawn by Boym on nostalgia. South African philosopher Johan Snyman, drawing on examples from post-war Germany, made a distinction between two ways of remembering, one monumental the other memorial (1998: 312). The former celebrates victory in grand fashion; the latter memorialises the losses and victims of war and struggle. Lourens du Plessis, following Snyman, related this distinction to the South African constitution and argued that both monumental and memorial are present in it (2000: 385). Both the 1993 (interim) and 1996 (current) constitutions,[1] for

---

1   South Africa's 1994, or interim, Constitution (formally the Constitution of the Republic of South Africa, Act 200 of 1994) was adopted by the apartheid parliament in 1993, to serve as the legal basis for the transition from apartheid and the drafting of a 'final', post-apartheid constitution. This 'final' constitution (the Constitution of the Republic of South Africa, 1996) was adopted in 1996 and is the current constitution of the country.

example, illustrate that the South African constitutional endeavour is 'hardly modest', claiming among other things the achievement of a 'peaceful transition' and a 'non-racial democracy' (Du Plessis 2000: 385). Du Plessis describes also the entrenchment of the values of dignity, equality and freedom as 'monumental flair' (ibid.). He cites a number of cases in which the Constitutional Court responded to the monumental beckoning of the constitutional text. However, Du Plessis also highlights the constitution as restraint, as memorial (Du Plessis 2008: 193). With reference to the notion of subsidiarity, he argues for an understanding of the constitution that does not put itself – and with it, the Constitutional Court – up as the first call in all cases, but rather allows legislation and lower courts and bodies to tackle issues (ibid.: 194). The memorial constitution is aware of its own limits and of the fact that it can play only a part in the process of transformation.

What is valuable in Du Plessis' analysis is that he shows how both monumental and memorial moments are present, and that we are left with an unresolvable tension or paradox. The constitution's entrenchment of memory, what Karl Klare refers to as its 'historical selfconsciouness', opens up the possibility for a monumental and memorial way of engagement (1998). This distinction served as a framework for a number of other writings to explore the (im)possibilities of constitutional transformation in South Africa after 1994. In my own thinking, the constitution as memorial or memorial reflections on constitutionalism held some possibilities for a critical engagement with what was perceived as a 'common' or 'shared' embrace of the constitutional project and human rights in South Africa. More and more voices questioning the adoption of the constitution and the notion of constitutional transformation are raised. My own position is to consider these voices as well as the firm defenders of the constitution through Boym's work on nostalgia. Of course engagements with the constitution are multiple, and I do not want to attempt to divide them into two neat groups of those defending and those opposing the constitutional project. I am interested to reflect on the play of nostalgia, memory and the past that underlies these positions.

Boym describes nostalgia as utopian, although not directed to the future or the past but rather 'sideways' (2001: xiv). The nostalgic for her is someone who 'feels stifled within the confines of time and space' (ibid.). Nostalgia has been criticised from various angles. Boym refers to Michael Kammen, for whom 'nostalgia is essentially history without guilt' that comes down to 'an abdication of personal responsibility, a guilt-free homecoming, an ethical and aesthetic failure' (ibid.). For Boym, nostalgia, although a longing for a place is also a longing for a different time, is 'a rebellion against the modern idea of time, the time of history and progress' (ibid.: xv). She identifies an interesting paradox inherent to nostalgia: It could bring forth a certain empathy toward others, but should not be used as an attempt to restore a kind of belonging or rediscovery of identity. '*Algia* – longing – is what we share, yet *nostos* – the return home – is what divides us' (ibid.: xv–xvi). The danger inherent in nostalgia is that the ideal to restore an original home could limit and subdue critical thinking and engagement. She warns against confusing the actual home with the imaginary one, yet underscores the loss of home and longing for a different time as central to the modern condition (ibid.: xvi). For my purposes of thinking about nostalgia in the vein of a counter-archive, and for creating a space and time for dissensus, it is important to note that nostalgia is not only about the past but influences the future and that it has a public nature. In this vein Boym distinguishes nostalgia from melancholia, the former being concerned with both individual and collective memory, the latter confined to individual consciousness.

Boym identifies a tradition of critical reflection that she calls 'off-modern', that stands sceptical towards the modern celebration of everything that is new as well as the supporters of traditions (2001: xvi). She explains that in the 'off-modern tradition, reflection and longing, estrangement and affect go together' (ibid.: xvii). Her understanding of nostalgia is underpinned by the impossibility of homecoming. It is also significant to note the interdisciplinarity of the study of nostalgia, encompassing for example psychology, sociology, literary studies, philosophy and computer science. Nostalgia is also fundamentally insatiable, ambivalent and fragmented. Boym refers to the need for a 'dual archeology of memory and of place, and a dual history of illusions and actual practices' (ibid.: xviii). As alluded to above, her distinction between restorative nostalgia and reflective nostalgia is of value for my argument. Boym explains the distinction with reference to the roots of the word – restorative nostalgia highlights the *nostos* and searches for a lost home, reflective nostalgia highlights the *algia*, the longing (ibid.). Restorative nostalgia is involved in making truth claims and in restoring tradition and is associated with national and religious revivals globally (ibid.). Reflective nostalgia accepts the ambivalences of longing and belonging and is interested in thinking about multiple homes and time zones (ibid.). Boym reflects on the time involved in studying nostalgia itself, saying that it slows us down (ibid.: xix).

I have called for slowness previously and appreciate and value the weaving together of the notion of slow time, 'time-out-of-time', with nostalgia as a possible refusal of the traditional archive, and opening of a space and time for dissensus (Van Marle 2003: 239). My tentative exploration involved a comparison with law's time and other concepts of time. I was interested in two responses to law's time. First, a disruption of a chronological and linear conception of time that could disclose multiple truths and fluidity of meanings, and second, a slower time, slowness, where difference and particularity could be explored that is often missed in the way law speeds past in its embrace of generalisation and universalisation (ibid.). Drawing

120 Karin van Marle

on Milan Kundera's novel *Slowness* (1996), I argued for a support of an embodied and embedded recollection impossible in the flight of speed (Van Marle 2003: 241).

In my own following of Du Plessis' work on the constitution as monument and memorial, and in support of the latter, I related the memorial constitution to slowness. The memorial constitution takes time to acknowledge its own limits and the impossibility to recognise difference fully. The memorial constitution could enhance what lies at the heart of the call for slowness namely reflection, thought. In this sense a call for slowness accepts Hannah Arendt's insight that thoughtlessness could give rise to evil, albeit banal (Arendt 1963). However, slowness for me is not only linked to a memorial understanding of the Constitution, there is more to it. The attention inherent to slowness also relates to a politics of refusal.

A politics of refusal simply refers to a way in which we can say no to any expectation of a practice or response that will continue merely what has come before, in other words a blind following of business as usual. I have used Adriana Cavarero's rewriting of *Penelope* (1995) as an example of such a politics of refusal. Penelope, by weaving by day and unweaving by night, refused the order that was forced upon her by patriarchal society. South African author Njabulo Ndebele in a novel titled *The cry of Winnie Mandela* (2003) tells the story of four women who, like Winnie Mandela, waited on their husbands to return. Underlying their coming together to share stories of waiting is a refusal, and a politics of refusal, of saying no to what is expected. 'No. Resist. Stay away from the trap of obligation. Turn obligation into serene detachment. Become a woman with her thoughts. A woman who observes' (Ndebele 2003: 80). At the same time this refusal could open up possibilities of other ways of being. 'A woman of detachment who observes and holds on to her options, which suddenly rush at her like a tidal wave. Savour the passion of enormous possibility. ... Hold on to your options and the freedom to choose between them' (ibid.: 82; Van Marle 2008, 2009). I read Boym's articulation of reflective nostalgia as resistance, as a way of countering the traditional archive and, as I explore below, a staging of dissensus. I propose that it could be understood also as a way to open a politics of resistance, thereby opening a range of possibilities.

Boym's observation on mapping as a specific modern obsession is important for a reflection on archive/counter-archive. For the early modern state it was important to demarcate spaces and territory to assert various forms of power – tax collection, recruitment of soldiers, expansion of territory through colonialism. The modern world aimed to universalise by bringing a 'diversity of maps' to a 'shared world' (Boym 2001: 11). At a time of globalisation the longing for the local came to the fore, flowing from new understandings of space and time. The project of re-mapping, of challenging the Westphalian world view, is part and parcel of countering traditional histories and the traditional archive. Nostalgia, as already noted, is not only drawn to the past but also works sideways. It converses not in the language of philosophy or science but rather in poems and in fragments. '[I]t remains unsystematic and unsynthesizable; it seduces rather than convinces' (ibid.: 13). Boym describes how in the mid-nineteenth century nostalgia was institutionalised by the construction of museums and memorials. 'The past was no longer unknown or unknowable. The past became heritage' (ibid.: 15). Of interest are the different responses to restoration. On the one hand, defenders of total reconstruction who wanted complete reconstruction, attempting to remake the past, and on the other hand, those who loved 'unintended memorialism' who 'allowed one to experience historicity affectively, as an atmosphere, a space for reflection on the passage of time' (ibid.: 15). Boym notes a paradox of institutionalised nostalgia. If the loss or the longing for a different time is very strong, it is often met with overcompensation and idealisation (ibid.: 17).

In a chapter on 'The angel of history: Nostalgia and modernity', Boym calls the modern opposition between tradition and revolution 'treacherous' (2001: 19). Going back to the roots of the words she notes that tradition means both 'delivery – handing down or passing on a doctrine – and surrender or betrayal. Traduttore, traditore, translator, traitor' (ibid.: 19). Revolution also has a dual meaning: 'cyclical repetition and the radical break' (ibid.: 19). She concludes: 'Hence tradition and revolution incorporate each other and rely on their opposition' (ibid.: 19). Thinking about tradition and revolution in this way could have interesting implications for the notion of a counter-archive and the various understandings of memory, but also the memories themselves. It links with the notion of nostalgia as unsystematic and fragmented. The metaphor of the palimpsest so often invoked in the context of memory also resembles this kind of layering and intertwinement between not only past, present and future, but between tradition, revolution, homelessness and home. The critical tradition of off-modern also connects with this troubling of the distinction between tradition and revolution. Different from both anti-modern and anti-postmodern, off-modern seeks to revisit the unfinished critical project of modernity. It holds an alternative vision of time and temporality by viewing it 'not as a teleology of progress or transcendence but as a superimposition and coexistence of heterogenous times' (ibid.: 30).

Before I turn to some South African texts on nostalgia and memory, let us take another brief look at the distinction between restorative and reflective nostalgia and the kind of ethics invoked by the latter. As Boym explains, these two nostalgias should not be seen as absolutes, but as tendencies, ways in which we give shape and meaning to longing (2001: 41). I alluded above to restorative nostalgics who understand their own project as one of seeking truth, supporting nationalist revivals all over the world, engaging in modern myth-making and sometimes constructing conspiracy theories. These nostalgics want to see total reconstructions of monuments and differ from reflective nostalgics who dwell on ruins and dream about other places and times (ibid.: 41). Relying on Eric Hobsbawn's distinction between 'age-old customs' and 'invented traditions', Boym distinguishes between 'habits of the past' and 'habits of the restoration of the past' (ibid.: 42). What these distinctions highlight is that customs followed by 'traditional' communities were not inherently or necessarily conservative, and that invented customs are. Invented customs rely on the loss of a sense of community and cohesion and offer a comfort and solace to feelings of longing. Two interesting paradoxes emerge. First, the faster and stronger the urge for modernisation, the more conservative and static the invented traditions; and second, the stronger the claim of continuity and authenticity the more selective is the past that is presented (ibid.: 42). Where restoration is done with the aim to re-establish, to return to some notion of origin, reflective nostalgia accepts flexibility, the impossibility of recovery and human finitude (ibid.: 49). Absolute truth is not sought, history and the passage of time is meditated on. Restorative and reflective nostalgia could focus on the same narratives, memories and symbols, but the stories they tell differ (ibid.: 49). Reflective nostalgia defers an ultimate homecoming, values 'shattered fragments of memory' and is ironic and humorous (ibid.: 49). From the vantage of reflective nostalgia the past, or memory of the past, opens a multitude if potentialities, 'nonteleological possibilities of historic development' (ibid.: 50).

According to Boym, reflective nostalgia holds a certain ethics – it is this ethics that for me is crucial in linkages between nostalgia, memory, the archive and the constitution. The ethics reflected here opens the space for a politics that could resist and counter the pervasive orders of the day, be they late advanced capitalism, neo-colonial constitutionalism or other hegemonies.

> [T]he ethical dimension of reflective longing consists in resistance to paranoic [*sic*] projections characteristic of nationalist nostalgia, in which the other is conceived either as a conspiring enemy or as another nationalist. The ethics of reflective longing recognizes the cultural memory of another person as well as his or her human singularity and vulnerability.
>
> (Boym 2001: 337)

Boym invokes Emmanuel Levinas and his notion of 'anarchic responsibility' – 'responsibility for the other individual in the present moment and "justified" by no prior commitment' (2001: 338). She mentions Vladimir Nabokov's distinction between 'sensitivity' and 'sentimentality' (ibid.: 339). Sensitivity, according to this distinction, means to be attentive and curious, tactful and tolerant but, unlike sentimentality, it does not amount to a moralism or fixed set of rules (ibid.: 338). Boym also recalls Arendt's phrase 'the banality of evil' and her support of reflective thinking, which if not followed, could contribute to and participate in political evil (ibid.). Following Nabokov, Boym summarises the ethics of reflective nostalgia as follows: 'through shudders and gaps, through labyrinths and gaps, through ironic epiphanies and the bullet holes of memory' (ibid.: 340).

Since the 1990s the theme of the past, memory and how to respond to it have been taken up by many authors reflecting specifically on the South African experience. Andre P. Brink, in one of the first volumes on the theme calls for new aesthetic responses to the changing circumstances (1998a: 29). He notes that apartheid curtailed this theme, or at least resulted in certain themes to be prioritised. For Brink it is impossible to separate the political from the personal and history from story (ibid.: 30). He rightly observes that many themes and experiences were not explored by the Truth and Reconciliation Commission and that there is space for literature and the imagination to 'extend, 'complicate' and 'intensify' (ibid.: 30). Concerning fiction, he remarks that the 'real' is never only represented but that it is also always imagined – this is of course also true for how the past is represented through the archive, and the law (ibid.: 30). Brink aptly refers to the 'editing' and 're-editing' of memory (ibid.: 31). He explains how history often coincides with story, and refers to the work of Charles van Onselen as bringing forth a new view of history in his narration of *The Life of Kas Maine, a South African Sharecropper 1894–1985* (Brink 1998a: 32; Van Onselen 1996). Brink underscores a critical approach to memory and argues for new ways of thinking about the past (Brink 1998a: 33).

Jacob Dlamini, in his work titled *Native Nostalgia*, might be a good example of exactly what Brink is calling for. He summarises his main question as follows: 'What does it mean for a black South African to remember life under apartheid with fondness? What does it mean to say that black life under apartheid was not all doom and gloom and that there was a lot of which black South African could be, and indeed, were, proud?' (Dlamini 2009: 13). Dlamini pre-empts possible critiques by continuing: 'Only lazy thinkers would take these questions to mean support for apartheid. They do not. Apartheid was without virtue' (ibid.). For him it is important to bring to the surface that the freedom of black South Africans did not come about 'courtesy of a liberation movement' (ibid.). With reference to Jonny Steinberg he confirms that apartheid brought forth a 'deformed world', a world in which 'order and depravity became confused with state violence and depravity' (ibid.). However, this doesn't mean that black life under apartheid was caught up in a 'moral void' (Dlamini 2009: 13). Dlamini's view here stands in contrast to how black life under apartheid has often been described, and could be compared for example with Johan van der Walt's equation of black life under apartheid with Giorgio Agamben's description of 'bare life' (Van der Walt 2005). Dlamini, following Lewis

124   Karin van Marle

Nkosi, says that every act of a black person was not done in response to apartheid (2009: 14).

Dlamini notes the criticism against nostalgia, that to be nostalgic is seen to be bad, to be called nostalgic is an 'affectionate insult' (2009: 16). However for him there is no need for it to be like this. Nostalgia is not necessarily a longing for a past to be recovered and a rejection of the present and future. For him, to be nostalgic about apartheid entails remembering 'social-orders and networks of solidarity that made the struggle possible in the first place' (ibid.: 17). Reference can be made here to other writings on social movements in the past, the workings of local groups who later formed the Mass Democratic Movement and their struggle against apartheid in all forms (for example Tshepo Madlingozi, who does not frame his work within the terms of nostalgia but he does write positively about an active politics that existed in the past that cannot so easily be subsumed by the master narrative of the liberation struggle; see e.g., Madlingozi 2009).

Dlamini relies strongly on Boym and her distinction between restorative and reflective nostalgia. It is in the latter version that he finds inspiration for his own work. He sees his book as part of a wider concern about a 'distorting master narrative' about apartheid that dominates all history (Dlamini 2009: 18; Walker 2008). What bothers him most about this master narrative is that it asserts that all black South Africans 'experienced apartheid the same way, suffered the same way and fought the same way against apartheid' (Dlamini 2009: 18). This unified and one-dimensional version of the past denies the richness and complexity of the lives of black South Africans. I read Dlamini's project in the guise of a counter-archive. By questioning the mainstream narrative, the forced consensus, by reflecting nostalgically on the past he is disturbing the ideas that there is only one world view, and bringing another one into the picture. He refers specifically to what he sees as 'the anti-politics machine of the ANC' that created a new order dominated by 'political entrepreneurs' and 'racial nativists' (ibid.: 20). Dlamini recalls a conversation with an official of the Ekurhuleni Metropolitan Council – established in 2000 as part of the African National Congress' (ANC) local government reform that amalgamated formerly black and white municipalities – in which he asked permission to view archival material on the old Germiston and Katlehong townships. The official, after hearing that he is writing a book on Katlehong responded: 'But, bro, Katlehong doesn't exist anymore. Why don't you write a book about Ekurhuleni instead?' (ibid.: 21).

Dlamini explains that the use of the word 'native' in his book has two meanings – on the one hand it follows the literal meaning of indigenous, from a certain place, but on the other hand it also takes up the colonial and segregationist meaning of referring to a person of African descent. He refers to views by Bronisław Malinowski and Karl Polanyi that challenged

Counter-archive as staging dissensus 125

the idea that an African could be urbanised, that one could be African and living in a city at the same time, that Africans can be 'native to a city' (Dlamini 2009: 150–151). He wants readers to understand the book and the title of the book against this view. He describes his work as a meditation on 'a time out of joint', a term used also by Boym (ibid.: 153). He refuses the reduction of black South Africans to 'PDIs' (previously disadvantaged individuals). In the same vein townships have been relegated to 'places in need of service delivery' and 'sites of struggles' renamed as 'sites of development' (ibid.). Eusebius McKaiser, in a review of Dlamini's book, picks up on the latter issue by noting the tendency in the social sciences to make broad statements and generalised conclusions (McKaiser 2010; Truscott 2010). By 'examining sites' rather than 'experiencing places' the complexity of township life is denied (Dlamini 2009: 153). McKaiser highlights Dlamini's emphasis on the 'senses' (seeing, feeling, hearing, smelling, touching) in order to understand the everyday lives and relations in communities (ibid., 2010).

David Medalie, in a piece on how the past is dealt with in post-apartheid literature, observes that a recurring idea in many post-apartheid works is the idea that the past is simultaneously known and unknown, it is familiar and strange (2013). He refers to various views on the question whether literature could and should play the role of a unifying force (ibid.: 5). Guy Butler in the 1950s asked if literature could have 'a substantial effect on society' and whether it could 'help to bring about the cohesion necessary for a common culture (as quoted by Medalie 2013: 5; Butler 1994). Nat Nakasa in 1963 raised a similar question concerning 'shared nationhood' and a 'common experience' (see Nakasa 1975) and Es'kia Mphahlele in 1983 bemoaned the 'absence of a national literature' (see Mphahlele 2002). Lewis Nkosi later hoped for the 'creation of a single national culture … with local variations' (as quoted by Medalie 2013 p. 5; Nkosi 1994). Medalie responds to these views by saying that this will not be achieved, mainly because of the small readership, in other words that the role of literature is so minor that no shared identity can be forged (2013: 5). However, he then turns to the possible effect of the literature on those that do read – what do they say about 'the textures of newness in a reconstituted society, and about the trace of the past as an element in that reconstitution'? (ibid.: 5–6). For my purpose, the question is how these works contribute to the archive, to a possible counter-archive. For Medalie, post-apartheid South Africa in J.M. Coetzee's *Disgrace*[2] is characterised as the site for struggles

---

2   J.M. Coetzee's novel *Disgrace* (1999) tells the story of David Lurie who leaves Cape Town after an illicit affair with a student that ends with him taking early retirement from his university. He visits his daughter, Lucy, who lives on a small holding in the Eastern Cape where they are both attacked, and she raped by youth from the community. The story deals with the complexities of his own personal life intertwined with that of life in South Africa.

about land, ownership and possession, as well as a place where history and stories unfold. Coetzee in this sense is doing what Brink calls for – he complicates, extends and intensifies past, present and future through his work. Coetzee had been doing such work long before apartheid South Africa became 'post-apartheid', and his works can be regarded indeed as an archive/counter-archive of the country's history. Medalie depicts Marlene van Niekerk's *Agaat*[3] as an 'intricate investigation' of the relationship between South Africa's past and present: '[I]n *Agaat* the past is still being discovered, still emergent, still being born, still dying' (Medalie 2013: 10). He refers to the character Jakkie, who in his return to Grootmoedersdrift notes 'an abundance that never suffices' (Van Niekerk 2008: 677) and interprets this reference in light of the novel as 'a desperate attempt to fill the spaces left by loss, displacement and hollowness' (Medalie 2013: 11). Medalie highlights the theme of artifice and of 'making' in the novel, in the many references to stitching, sewing and embroidery (ibid.). Another character in *Agaat*, Milla, declares that 'sewing is an attempt to "reconcile the world with itself"' (as quoted by Medalie 2013: 11; Van Niekerk 2008: 387). Medalie recalls Milla's depiction of *Agaat* as her 'archive', 'parliament' and 'hall of mirrors' (Medalie 2013: 12; Van Niekerk 2008: 554). Even though Milla wishes for another language in which they could converse, one that is not caught up in the fraught relation of power, this will not materialise – 'such a language does not exist' (Medalie 2013: 12).

'That things could be different': The imagination, disappointment and staging dissensus

Mark Antaki considers to what extent the legal imagination could successfully respond to Max Weber's description of disenchantment as the fate of modernity (2012: 1; Weber 1946: 129). For Weber, at the root of this disenchantment is rationalisation, and the idea that 'one can, in principle, master all things by calculation' (1946: 129). As part of our re-configuring the archive and thinking a counter-archive, we should consider to what extent the imagination could respond to this state of disenchantment. However, Antaki warns that most, if not all, imaginary attempts might fail for being too firmly rooted in the rationality and functionalism of modernity, which could also be true if by countering the archive we are limited by the givenness of the official one (2012: 4).

---

3   Marlene van Niekerk's novel *Agaat*, as Coetzee's *Disgrace* takes off but then departs from the tradition of the farm novel. Agaat, according to apartheid racial categories, a brown woman, is adopted by Milla as a young child and initially brought up and loved as her own but is rejected when Milla falls pregnant with her husband, Jak's child. The story traces the relationship between these two women as Agaat ends up as the main carer for Milla at the end of her life.

Antaki considers four types of legal imagination – the theoretical imagination, the progressive imagination, the transformative imagination and the nostalgic imagination. He argues that many aesthetic turns – the turn to the imagination included – are part and parcel of disenchantment. For him the nostalgic imagination comes closest to the possibility of acquiring some distance from the endless rationalisation of modernity, because it is not a project that requires mastery, but rather asks 'us to let go, and to cultivate the capacity to be struck, to be arrested, to be struck in wonder' (Antaki 2012: 15). Antaki turns to the work of Critchley, who identifies 'disappointment – and not wonder – as the primordial human attunement' (Antaki 2012: 16; Critchley 2004). He explains that Critchley, although not letting go of a transformative imagination, accepts it as an imagination that understands its own limits and (im)possibility. He cites Critchley on Wallace Stevens:

> Stevens's undoubted romantic naïveté resides in his offer of a resistance to reality through the violence of the imagination. This offer is minimal. It is not the offer of a new place, new habitat, or Ur-Heimat. Nor is it the promise of a utopia, a new Pantisocracy on the banks of the Susquehanna River, or the promise of a New America. ... It is rather the offer of a new way of inhabiting this place.
>
> (Antaki 2012: 17)

The vision that we find here is not transformative in the sense that it puts forward a blueprint or even framework for a 'new place'. However, as Antaki states, 'reality is still to be resisted, transfigured' (2012: 17). In Critchley's words 'we have to expect less from the imagination and accustom ourselves to more minimal transfigurations of reality' (2004: 17). Critchley's response to nihilism and disenchantment is in the vein of 'delineating' rather than 'overcoming' (ibid.). The reason for this is that the attempt to overcome, to transform, to change, almost inevitably originates from the same place as the disenchantment or nihilism. One could place this need to overcome and to transform in the same vein as restorative nostalgia, the longing for a homecoming. For Critchley, this does not mean that we shouldn't reflect on the possibility that things could be different (ibid.). Reflective nostalgia might open exactly the possibility for such a reflection.

Turning to dissensus, I draw on Rancière's response to Hannah Arendt's distinction between the realm of the public or the political and the realm of private life in her identification of three human conditions as labour, work and action. For Rancière, this very distinction between the public and the private opened the possibility of depoliticisation (2004: 290). With reference to the work of Agamben he contends that 'the radical suspension of politics in the exception of bare life is the ultimate consequence of

Arendt's archipolitical position, of her attempt to preserve the political from the contamination of private, social, apolitical life' (Rancière 2004: 301; Agamben 1998). The desire to keep politics pure, results in its disappearance and creates what Rancière calls an 'ontological trap' (2004: 302). In order to get out of this trap, he argues we should rephrase the question on the rights of man and in particular the question on the subject of politics. Following Arendt, according to Rancière, the rights of man are either the rights of the citizen, meaning the rights of those that have rights, which amounts to a 'tautology' or they are the rights of the stateless, those who have no rights, which amounts to a 'void' (ibid.). Rancière puts forward a third way: 'the Rights of Man are the rights of those who have not the rights that they have and have the rights that they have not' (ibid.).

Rancière unpacks this as follows: we should approach rights in two steps. First, as written rights, as 'inscriptions of the community as free and equal ... as configuration of the given' (2004: 303). Second, they are 'the rights of those who make something of that inscription' (ibid.). This means more than making 'use' of the right, it means to build a case to enact whatever is promised by the inscription of the right. For Rancière, Arendt wrongly limits the sphere of politics and argues that the question of politics is exactly about the decisions of what politics entail: 'The point is, precisely, where do you draw the line separating one life from another? Politics is about that border. It is the activity that brings it back into the question' (ibid.). Rancière invokes the example of Olympia de Gourges, a French woman in the time of the Revolution who stated that 'if women are entitled to go to the scaffold, they are entitled to go to the assembly' (ibid.). Of course, at that time women had no political rights, they were not regarded as equal citizens and they had no access to the public realm, being limited to the private. However, the fact that they could be sentenced to death meant that they were not totally excluded from politics, totally reduced to bare life. 'If, under the guillotine, they were as equal so to speak, "as men", they had the right to the whole of equality, including equal participation to political life' (ibid.: 303–304). Rancière notes that this kind of understanding could not have been 'endorsed' or 'heard' but it could have been 'enacted' by way of voicing a 'dissensus' (ibid.: 304). 'A dissensus is not a conflict of interests, opinions or values; it is a division put in the "common sense": a dispute about what is given, about the frame within which we see something as a given' (ibid.). I am interested in this notion of staging a dissensus by placing a division in the common sense. In thinking about a counter-archive and countering the traditional archive, it is exactly this notion of dissensus, of disputing what is presented as common, that is at stake. Because we are not thinking about replacing one official or master narrative with another, the suggestion of putting two worlds together beckons possibilities.

The case of *Baphiring*

The case of the Baphiring Community tells a story of nostalgia, of a community's longing to return to the land from which they were evicted under apartheid law. The court case tells us that the issue on the table 'concerns a land claim under the Restitution of Land Rights Act 22 of 1994' (*Baphiring Community v Tshwaranani Project* CC 2014 (1) SA 330 (SCA)). In the judgment, we are told that the community lived on land 'colloquially known' as old Mabaalstad that was 'expropriated through racially discriminatory laws' in 1971. The community was forcibly moved or as the court record states 'relocated' to land given to them as 'compensation'. The land given to the community to replace their land was 80 km north of the expropriated land and is now known as 'new Mabaalstad'. The case that is the focus for my purpose is an appeal from the Land Claims Court to the Supreme Court of Appeal. The main issue that the court had to decide on was the issue of 'restoration.' The case was preceded by three previous decisions. In the first, in the Land Claims Court, the court had to consider a number of preliminary issues, such as whether the communal property association in question could bring the claim, what the nature of the 'rights in land' were that were being reclaimed and what the extent was of compensation received at the time of expropriation (*Baphiring Community v Uys* (Unreported) (LCC 64/98) [2002] ZALCC 4 (29 January 2002)). The court found that the community was competent to bring the claim, that the dispossessed right was ownership (including mineral rights) and the compensation received amounted to R181 million in current terms. In the second decision, the court had to rule on the question whether the compensation that had been received at the time was 'just and equitable' (within the meaning of section 2(2) of the Restitution Act) with the effect that it precluded the claim for additional relief (*Baphiring Community v Uys* (Unreported) (LCC 64/98) [2003] ZALCC 27 (5 December 2003)). The court found that the compensation was not just and equitable and that the community was thus not prevented from seeking restitution. In the third decision, that went on appeal to the Supreme Court of Appeal, the Land Claims Court had to rule on the question whether it was 'feasible' (according to section 33 (cA) of the Act) to 'restore' the land to the community (*Baphiring Community v Uys* 2010 (3) SA 130 (LCC)). The court in this case decided that it was not 'feasible' to restore the land and held that the community was entitled to 'equitable redress', being further financial compensation or alternative land, but not restoration. The appeal court thus had to decide on the non-restoration order. The appellants argued that this order was made in the absence of a proper feasibility study, that there was not sufficient material evidence from the state to indicate that restoration was not feasible. The appeal court explicitly stated that a claimant for restitution of dispossessed land is entitled to restoration whenever feasible and unless it is to the detriment of the public interest (*Baphiring Community v Tshwaranani Project* CC 2014 (1) SA 330 (SCA)). Other forms of compensation may be considered, whether alternative land or monetary compensation, only after the issue of feasibility has been considered. The court upheld the appeal in light of the absence of a feasibility study and referred the matter back to the Land Claims Court, for it to decide again whether restoration is feasible, once it had been presented with a proper report from the State on feasibility.

It is important here to start off by examining the issue of land reform within the broader discourse on the shifts and changes required for political, social and legal transformation in South Africa. Central to these shifts and changes is the engagement with the past, with memory. I have referred to the two possible ways of approaching the Constitution as suggested by Du Plessis – monumental or memorial – and how these approaches might connect with Boym's distinction between restorative and reflective nostalgia. Taking this line, monumental constitutionalism, similar to restorative nostalgia, might rely on idealised versions of the past and over-optimistic plans for the present. Memorial constitutionalism, as reflective nostalgia, would be more cautious to claim grand scale success, will act with restraint and might be more attuned to everyday practices. I have raised the question above of whether memorial constitutionalism could be linked in a sense with a politics of refusal. In other words, that an awareness of the constitution (and processes of transformation emanating from the constitution such as land reform) as limited, might open a more reflective and thoughtful way of engagement. Central to slowness and reflection is also an awareness of materiality, it is a more embodied and embedded approach. This for me then raises the question of the possibility of resisting, of refusing a monumental approach to constitutional reform and restorative nostalgia – a politics of refusal. The discourse on land reform has arguably been performed in the guise of the monumental, with a strong reliance on restorative nostalgia. Cheryl Walker has referred to the 'master narrative' on land reform telling a one-dimensional story of black South Africans being dispossessed of their land under apartheid to be restored after a successful liberation struggle by government (Walker 2008; Walker, Bohlin, Hall, and Kepe 2010). She has urged for everyone involved to realise the limits of land reform, to recognise the discontinuities and that the process of land reform is open-ended and inconclusive. The mainstream discourse, master narrative, has chosen to present a 'selective simplified past' to explain history as if it occurs in a direct and linear way, starting from a fixed place (Walker 2008: 229). Walker has commented also on the mismatch between the expectations that were created, in terms of the monumental and restorative, and the potential of land reform (ibid.: 231). By highlighting the limits of the master narrative of rural dispossession and restoration, Walker is not denying the truth of it, but she argues that it is

Counter-archive as staging dissensus   131

insufficient as a basis for understanding the challenges that confront transformation in South Africa at present (ibid.: 233). An interesting point that she raises is the extent to which urban issues have been neglected. Even though far more urban claims were made, scholarly analyses and public political commentary have focused much more on rural claims and rural land issues (Walker *et al.* 2010: 3; Bohlin 2004). The issue of urban land is from the start much more fractured than the rural and more attuned to the everyday, the ordinary, reflective nostalgia and the restrained constitution. We should recall Dlamini's references to the views that regarded it impossible to be urban and African at the same time. Derrick Fay and Deborah James note how restitution can be seen as a combination of 'modernity's romantic aspect, nostalgia for the lost rootedness of landed identity' with more technical and bureaucratic features of the state (2010: 41). The discourse on land reform has significant implications for how the past is remembered, but also for the understanding of rights, citizenship, state formation and nation building in the present and future (Fay and James 2010: 43–44).[4] In describing land reform as not only a spatial process but also a temporal one, Fay and James identify six phases. Concerning the final phase they point to the realisation that 'restitution may never occur' (Fay and James 2010: 48).

Returning to the Baphiring community one could ask after the memory – what kind of nostalgia, what kind of archive is at play here? Let's look at some of the circumstances that surround the specific claim of the Baphiring community. Prior to the community's removal by the apartheid government in 1971, the community was faced with a challenge already in 1906 when the Royal Bafokeng Nation requested the Minister to register all the farms in the area owned by different owners in the Bafokeng tribe in the name of the Royal Bafokeng Nation. A number of people within the Bafokeng tribe opposed this request and argued that the land should be registered in the name of the original buyers. The land was rightfully bought by various communities, amongst others the Baphiring, around 1871. The Bafokeng land buyers recall that it was Chief August Mokgatlhe who during his reign, from 1897–1906 'plotted to register all the farms, bought privately by sections of the "tribe", in his name' (Nape 2009). In this recollection the Bafokeng Land Buyers Association underscores the extent to which chiefs were used by colonial governments, including the apartheid government. The registration of the community's farms in 1906 in trust for August Mokgatlhe was a result of on the one hand the 'co-operation' between the chief (because of his 'obedience' to the government)

---

4   In a chapter for a volume dedicated to the work of South African scholar Lourens du Plessis, I elaborate on these aspects of land reform and connect it to the notions of constituent and constituted politics.

and the government, and on the other the handing over of title deeds to August Mokgatlhe by the wife of a deceased missionary who was faced with huge debts related to the land (Nape 2009). The court decided in 1908 against the request of registering the land in the name of the original owners.

On 8 December 2009, a media statement of the Bafokeng Land Buyers Association stated: 'We hope that since the decision of the Court in 1908 was based on racially discriminatory laws of that time, which made it impossible for our forefathers to have our lands registered in our names, it is possible in our democratic, constitutional state that such transference and registration as we wish take place'. They added: 'We will oppose and contest the Bafokeng application until we have the land of our forefathers, our land, back. We will not be apologetic for that' (Nape 2009). A central part of the narrative as told by the community is how the 'ANC-led government always [prefers] to work with the rich and mighty Bafokeng than with the meek and poor rural community who wants to assert and entrench their constitutional right to land' (Nape 2009). The Bafokeng land buyers also raise the concern that the Royal Bafokeng Nation's administration may not be a 'democratic institution' and that 'it is not representative of all the bona fide members of the "tribe"' (Nape 2009). They note that the people 'representing' the tribe might be 'controlled by certain powerful people or companies who are not members of the "tribe"' (Nape 2009). They make specific reference to mining companies 'who are looting the platinum wealth ... with the support of unscrupulous government officials and politicians' (Nape 2009). The resemblance between the former colonial (and in particular apartheid) government and the present powers is striking. In this vein the Baphiring community's refusal to accept the ruling of the Land Claims Court can be regarded as one of resistance, as a continuance of a politics of refusal that started many years ago and as again asserting a dissensus.

At the same time, the insistence on restoration by the Baphiring community seems to reflect a longing for home, belonging and the rediscovery of identity. As noted above, 'Giving land back to the people' has been central in the post-apartheid discourse on how to respond to the past. I have referred to Dlamini's and Walker's engagement with the way in which the ANC has constructed a unified discourse of the past that underlies the institutional process for land reform and restitution. To invoke the metaphors of monument and memorial, or restorative and reflective nostalgia, one could argue that the Land Restitution process stands in the guise of monument and restoration that not only excludes certain narratives of the past but also negates the experiences and real needs for reform in the present. The emphasis (and perhaps even overemphasis) placed on the rural, singles out those displaced under the 1913 Land Act ('the Act'). The limit of law's time is underscored by the firm line drawn here by including in the

Restitution process only those who fall within the ambit of the 1913 Act. Restitution of one claim that amounts to full restoration could amount to millions spent by the state that might be to the detriment of other urgent socio-economic issues like access to housing in urban areas; education and healthcare. One could ask what is at stake in the Baphiring community's insistence on full restoration. Juanita Pienaar in a reflection on the Land Restitution process pays attention to how in her view the Land Claim's Court in the case of Baphiring fulfilled the requirement of 'good governance' (Pienaar 2011: 41). Pienaar underscores the fact that the land (Old Mabaalstad) was not developed in any commercial sense and that only farming on a small scale and on a subsistence basis took place (ibid.). The land formerly owned by the Baphiring community was subsequently developed by a number of different owners and became highly commercialised. The Baphiring community did not succeed in establishing anything beyond subsistence farming in New Mabaalstad. Pienaar highlights the four criteria that were identified to assist in ascertaining if restoration would be feasible: 1) the costs of the acquisition; 2) the disruption of the lives and economic activities of the present land owners; 3) the ability of the claimant community to use the land and, 4) the public interest including the extent of state resources (ibid.: 42).

The court raised a number of reasons why full restoration was not possible. Amongst other reasons, high costs, disruption of the lives and economic activities of those who live presently on the land, negative impact on food production, and that so far not one resettlement project in the whole North West Province was successful (Pienaar 2011: 43). The court also held that restoration would entail that some of the members of the Baphiring community will 'downgrade their living space and that new houses and infrastructure would have to be provided' (ibid.). The court also argued that not all the members of the Baphiring community were in favour of moving back. Importantly, the court decided that small parts of the land that contain graves could be restored (ibid.). Pienaar finds it unfortunate that the court did not comment on the issue of public interest, but argues that in light of the high restoration costs the court probably found it unnecessary to elaborate on the public interest (ibid.). The options available to the court were: 1) to award specific restoration; 2) to award alternative land; 3) to award compensation or 4) a combination of all four. For Pienaar, the Land Claims Court is central in mapping out a path for restitution and restoration. Throughout her discussion of the Land Claims Court she relies heavily on the metaphor of restitution as a journey and the court as the map or GPS that should show the way. She formulates the following four questions that the Land Claims Court should consider: What would be in the best interest of everyone involved? How can these interests be determined? How is the final analysis made? How to consider on the one hand discourses of redress/redistribution and on the other hand economic development/ sustainability (ibid.). In her concluding paragraph, Pienaar firmly states that the role of the court is to decide on the 'end destination' by not only showing 'the path' but by mapping the 'exact route', by 'setting the beacons clearly in place and fixing time lines as to when and how markers should be reached' (ibid.: 44). The clarity of her analysis and suggestions for the Land Claims Court should be appreciated, and yet the specific story of Baphiring (like most probably the stories of many others) show that the paths, directions, maps and times are more complex, multidimensional and layered.

Boym's understanding of nostalgia as a utopia that works 'sideways' provides us with a more complex response to the issue of land reform, restitution and restoration to the extent that it challenges the attempts to build a linear, one-dimensional and oversimplified version of past and future. As explained above, Boym's understanding of utopia is not directed to the future or to the past, but is rather an attempt to break with the confines of time and space. She supports a nostalgia that longs for a different place and time, a time that is 'other' to modern notions of history and progress. A critical or reflective nostalgia is not a longing for a restoration or a rediscovery of identity or a longing to return to 'the actual home'. How could an approach of 'off-modern', as formulated by Boym, respond to the issue of land reform? Recalling Critchley's support of disappointment, an off-modern approach would know that restoration is an impossible hope and claim, it would temper and restrain the grand narrative of dispossession and reform that is mapped in a linear and chronological path. In the 'off-modern tradition' we find a mix of reflection, longing, estrangement and affect (Boym 2001: xvii). Following Goodrich, the law can only assert its autonomy and the possibility to restore by forgetting its relations to philosophy, to stories, to other laws (1995: 137). As Goodrich argues, by remembering exactly what the law wants to forget, possibility of critique is created (ibid.). In what way could we engage with land restitution in a critical manner? By raising these questions the aim is not to deny the gravity of land deprivation, forced removals and the multiple injustices that resulted because of this. However, to the extent that unified discourses all hold the potential of limiting critical thinking and ultimately absconding responsibility we should be cautious. At the same time we should be true to our support of ambivalence and equivocation.

The Baphiring community could be read as being caught up in restorative nostalgia, buying into the master narrative of rural dispossession and restoration, hoping for a restoration that could ensure a return to home, and finding their lost identity. In this vein they also partake in the master narrative of past land dispossession and present restitution that although not untrue, negates the losses of those who do not fall within the ambit of the restoration framework, but also the continuance of homelessness and evictions in the present. At the same time the Baphiring community might

Counter-archive as staging dissensus   135

be aware of the possibility that restitution might disappoint; aware of what has been described as the 'loss of the loss' (Du Toit 2000: 82).[5] How then could we read the refusal to accept the deal handed to them by an apartheid government, and affirmed by the Land Claims Court to the extent that it did not grant restoration? It might be that their insistence on restoration is not a claim for a nostalgic return but a refusal to consent to the consensus, the common sense of governments old and new enforced on them. As was clear from the statement by the Bafokeng Land Buyers Association, communities have been involved in a struggle with the powers-that-be since 1906. The Baphiring community could be seen as bringing their world to the world of the law, 'putting two worlds together' (Rancière 2004: 306). In this sense their nostalgia might not be restorative, or purely restorative, but also reflective. By remembering a past, they are challenging law's claim to autonomy and judgment seemingly devoid of history and politics. The approach here could be seen as what Boym calls 'off-modern' – as mixing reflection, longing, estrangement and affect. By weaving the similarities between tradition and revolution into heterogenous times and approaches, a certain ethics of and an insistence on responsibility (Levinasian 'anarchic responsibility') come to the fore. The insistence on restoration here might be sensitive rather than sentimental, to mean exactly 'something more beyond restoration', 'a public acknowledgement of wrong' (Fay and James 2010: 53–55).

Before I conclude it is necessary to flag an aspect that is central to any discussion of land restitution and reform, such as that played out by the Baphiring case above, namely spatiality and spatial justice. The main aim of this chapter was to consider how nostalgia could be regarded as a critical approach in contrast to how it is traditionally perceived as conservative. In particular I aimed to think of nostalgia along the lines of a counter-archive and dissensus, with reference to the Baphiring community's insistence to have the ownership of its land restored. However, although an in-depth discussion of the spatial politics is beyond the scope of this chapter, the importance of space as something produced by social relations (Lefebvre 1991; Foucault 1986) should be at the forefront of the consideration of the issue of land reform and restoration. To the extent that nostalgia is about a longing for another place, spatiality is also of relevance for a critical consideration of nostalgia. Henri Lefebvre has exposed space as embedded

---

5   It might be valuable here to note the Baphiring youth's objection against the Traditional Courts Bill, suggested legislation that will have dire consequences to the position of rural women. In joining other organisations in resisting the excesses of the Royal Bafokeng Nation and the power attached to traditional chiefs, the community is showing that they are not engaged in some kind of longing for a past to be restored. Then again their objections to the Bill might be more narrowly aligned with their claim to restore the ownership of the land in their name (Jara 2012: 45–46).

in history, part and parcel of the development of various modes of production and affected by conflicting processes (Lefebvre 1991; Tally 2013: 117). His work presents us with a triad through which to understand and explore space, namely perceived space, conceived space and lived space (Lefebvre 1991: 33–40; Tally 2013: 118). All three of these are involved in discourses of nostalgia, memory and land. David Harvey has exposed the ambiguity, contradiction and struggle that lie behind what is often offered as common-sense and natural ideas about space and time (Harvey 1990: 205; Tally 2013: 112). In thinking about reflective nostalgia as a possible way of staging dissensus or countering the archive, the notion of spatial justice becomes prominent. Andreas Philippopoulus-Mihalopoulos defines spatial justice as 'the conflict between bodies that are moved by a desire to occupy the same space at the same time' (2014: 5). He does not set up spatial justice as 'the answer' to a number of conflicts, it is not a question of 'what can happen', but rather 'what happens' (ibid.: 5). 'Spatial justice emerges from a movement of withdrawal from the atmosphere' (ibid.: 6). He describes atmosphere as 'the perfect enclosure' (ibid.). 'Withdrawing from the atmosphere is a movement that allows a momentary rupture' (ibid.). As already indicated, the specific aim and focus of this chapter do not allow further and deeper investigation here, so I end on a rather unsatisfactory note of including a mere trace of something to be pursued later. However, for now I want to tie, albeit tentatively, nostalgia, dissensus and spatial justice together.

Conclusion

The aim of this chapter was to reflect tentatively on possible connections between nostalgia and a politics of resistance/staging dissensus. Boym and also Dlamini's work on nostalgia, and their support of reflective nostalgia, open the possibility of memory to offer a critique on unified versions of the past. The distinction between restorative and reflective nostalgia, the former concerned with truth and belonging, the latter with ambivalence and belonging, provides a useful framework through which to view various engagements with the past. Critchley's view of a philosophy rooted in disappointment elaborates on and adds to the notion of reflective nostalgia as a nostalgia that understands the impossibility of belonging or home coming. I attempted to read Rancière's understanding of staging dissensus by troubling a forced common sense as a way to challenge also a version of the past or a response to the past that does not allow other versions or responses. Finally, I interpreted a community's longing for restoration of the land from which they were forcibly removed by an authoritarian and racist government in light of the above. The aim was not to reach a final conclusion or clear answer but rather to underscore the complexities and ambiguities at play. I end with the late South African author Andre P. Brink from his novel, *Devil's Valley*: 'We fabricate yesterdays for ourselves which we can live with, which make the future possible, even if it remains infinitely variable and vulnerable, a whole bloody network of flickerings, an intimate lightning to illuminate the darkness inside' (1998b: 287; Burger 2015: 18).

References

Agamben, G. 1998, *Homo Sacer: Sovereign Power and Bare Life*, trans. D. Heller-Roazen, Stanford University Press, Stanford.

Antaki, M. 2012, 'The Turn to Imagination in Legal Theory: The Re-enchantment of the World?', *Law and Critique*, vol. 23, no. 1, pp. 1–20.

Arendt, H. 1963, *Eichmann in Jerusalem. A Report on the Banality of Evil*, Penguin, London.

Bohlin, A. 2004, 'A Price on the Past: Cash as Compensation in South African Land Restitution', *Canadian Journal of African Studies*, vol. 38, no. 3, pp. 672–687.

Boym, S. 2001, *The Future of Nostalgia*, Basic Books, New York.

Brink, A.P. 1998a, 'Stories of History: Re-imagining the Past in Post-apartheid Narrative' in S. Nuttal and C. Coetzee (eds), *The Making of Memory in South Africa*, Oxford University Press, Cape Town.

Brink, A.P. 1998b, *Devils' Valley*, Secker and Warburg, London.

Burger, W. 2015, 'A "Contrary" Man Who Stood by His Principles', *The Sunday Independent*, February 15, p. 18.

Butler, G. 1994, 'South African Literature', in S. Watson (ed.), *S. Guy Butler: Essays and Lectures 1949–1991*, David Philip, Cape Town.

Cavarero, A. 1995, *In Spite of Plato: A Feminist Rewriting of Ancient Philosophy*, Polity Press, Cambridge.

Coetzee, J.M. 1999. *Disgrace*, Secker and Warburg, London.

Critchley, S. 2004, *Very Little … Almost Nothing: Death, Philosophy, Literature*, Routledge, London.

Dlamini, J. 2009, *Native Nostalgia*, Jacana Press, Auckland Park.

Du Plessis, L.M. 2000, 'The South African Constitution as Memory and Promise' *Stellenbosch Law Review*, vol. 11 pp. 385–394.

Du Plessis, L.M. 2008, 'The South African Constitution as Monument and Memorial, and the Commemoration of the Dead' in R. Christensen and P. Bobo (eds), *Rechtstheorie in rechtspraktischer Absicht. Freundesgabe zum 70. Geburtstag von Friedrich Muller*, Berlin, Duncker and Humblot, pp. 189–205.

Du Toit, A. 2000, 'The End of Restitution: Getting Real about Land Claims', in B. Cousins (ed.) *At the Crossroads: Land and Agrarian Reform in South Africa into the 21st Century*, Programme for Land and Agrarian Studies, University of the Western Cape and National Land Committee, Cape Town and Johannesburg.

Fay, D. and James, D. 2010, 'Giving Land Back or Righting Wrongs? Comparative Issues in the Study of Land Restitution' in C. Walker, A. Bohlin, R. Hall and T. Kepe (eds) *Land, Memory, Reconstruction and Justice: Perspectives on Land Claims in South Africa*, University of KwaZulu-Natal Press, Pietermaritzburg, pp. 41–60.

Foucault, M. 1986, 'Of Other Spaces', *Diacritics*, vol. 16, no. 1, pp. 22–27.

Goodrich, P. 1995, *Law in the Courts of Love: Literature and Other Minor Jurisprudences*, Routledge, London.

Harvey, D. 1990, *The Condition of Postmodernity: An Enquiry into the Origins of Cultural Change*, Blackwell, Cambridge.

Jara, M.K. 2012, 'Tribal Courts: Land, Power *and* Custom', *Amandla*, vol. 28, no. 1, pp. 45–46.

Klare, K. 1998, 'Legal Culture and Transformative Constitutionalism', *South African Journal on Human Rights*, vol. 14, pp. 146–188.

Kundera, M. 1996. *Slowness*, Harper Collins, New York.

Lefebvre, H. 1991, *The Production of Space*, Blackwell, Oxford.

Madlingozi, T. 2009, 'Hayi Bo! Refusing the Plan: Acting, Thinking and Revolting by Post-apartheid Social Movements and Community Organisation' in K. Van Marle (ed.), *Refusal, Transition and Post-apartheid Law*, Sun Media, Stellenbosch, pp. 79–100.

Medalie, D. 2013, '"To Retrace your Steps": The Power of the Past in Post-apartheid Literature' *English Studies in Africa*, vol. 55, no. 1, pp. 3–15.

McKaiser, E. 2010, 'Remembering Apartheid with Fondness', viewed 14 October 2014, <www.politicsweb.co.za/politicsweb/view/politicsweb/en/page/page 71619?oid=1527>.

Mphahlele, E. 2002, 'South African Literature Versus Political Morality', *Es'kia*, Stainbank Associates and the Es'kia Institute, Rivonia.

Nakasa, N. 1975, 'Writing in South Africa', in E. Pattel (ed.), *The Works of Nat Nakasa: Selected Writings of the Late Nat Nakasa*, Ravan/Bateleur, Johannesburg.

Nape, G. 2009, Bafokeng Land Buyers Association Press Release, cited in the Appendix to MA thesis by L. September, 2010, *The Social Dimensions of Mining: Expectations and Realities of Mining Induced Relocation*, University of the Witwatersrand.

Ndebele, N. 2003, *The Cry of Winnie Mandela*, David Philip, Cape Town.

Nkosi, L. 1994, 'Constructing the Cross-border "Reader"', in E. Boehmer, L. Chrisman and K. Parker (eds), *Altered State? Writing and South Africa*, Dangaroo Press, Sydney.

Philippopoulus-Mihalopoulos, A. 2014, *Spatial Justice: Body, Lawscape, Atmosphere*, Routledge, London.

Pienaar, J. 2011, 'Restitutionary Road: Reflecting on Good Governance and the role of the Land Claims Court', *Potchefstroom Electronic Law Review*, vol. 13, no. 3, pp. 30–48.

Rancière, J. 2004, 'Who is the Subject of the Rights of Man?' *South Atlantic Quarterly*, vol. 103, no. 2/3, pp. 297–310.

Snyman, J. 1998, Interpretation and the Politics of Memory, *Acta Juridica*, pp. 312–321.

Tally, R.T. 2013, *Spatiality*, Routledge, New York.

Truscott, R. 2010, 'Confronting Found Memories of Apartheid', *Psychology in Society*, viewed 14 October 2014, <www.scielo.org.za/scielo.php?script=sci_arttext& pid=S1015-604620100002000>.

Van der Walt, J.W.G. 2005, *Law and Sacrifice: Towards a Post-apartheid Theory of Law*, Birkbeck Press, London.

Van Marle, K. 2003, 'Law's Time, Particularity and Slowness', *South African Journal on Human Rights*, vol. 19, pp. 239–255.

Van Marle, K. 2008, 'The Spectacle of Post-apartheid Constitutionalism', *Griffith Law Review*, vol. 16, no. 2, pp. 411–429.

Van Marle, K. 2009, *Refusal, Transition and Post-apartheid Law*, Sun Media, Stellenbosch.

Van Niekerk, M. 2008, *Agaat*, trans. M. Heyns, Jonathan Ball, Jeppestown.

Van Onselen, C. 1996, *The Life of Kas Maine, a South African Sharecropper 1894–1985*, Hill and Wang, New York.

Walker, C. 2008, *Landmarked: Land Claims and Land Restitution in South Africa*, Jacana Press, Johannesburg.

Walker, C., Bohlin, A., Hall, R. and Kepe, T. 2010, *Land, Memory, Reconstruction and Justice. Perspectives on Land Claims in South Africa*, University of KwaZulu-Natal Press, Pietermaritzburg.

Weber, M. 1946, 'Science as Vocation', in H.H. Gerth and C.W. Mills (eds), *Max Weber: Essays in Sociology*, Oxford University Press, New York, pp. 129–156.

Case law

Baphiring Community v Uys (Unreported) (LCC 64/98) [2002] ZALCC 4 (29 January 2002)

Baphiring Community v Uys (Unreported) (LCC 64/98) [2003] ZALCC 27 (5 December 2003)

Baphiring Community v Uys 2010 (3) SA 130 (LCC)

Baphiring Community v Tshwaranani Project CC 2014 (1) SA 330 (SCA)

Legislation

Black Land Act 27 of 1913

Constitution of the Republic of South Africa Act 200 of 1993

Constitution of the Republic of South Africa 1996

Restitution of Land Rights Act 22 of 1994

Chapter 7

Constitutions are not enough

Museums as law's counter-archive

Stacy Douglas

Sovereignty, the state, liberalism, democracy – none of these can be without their scriveners...

(Paul Passavant 2012: 57)

No archive without outside.

(Jacques Derrida 1995: 11)

Introduction

Many legal scholars concerned with the production and reconstruction of political community in post-colonial and post-conflict societies turn to the constitution as their central tool. This approach casts its attention on the text of the foundational document of a nation to contemplate how best to negotiate complex questions of history, belonging and citizenship after periods of violent conflict, civil unrest, and institutionalised exclusions. However, what is missed in this privileging of the constitution is the way in which negotiations of political community also occur at other sites. I am interested in the important role that museums play in these negotiations and the need to consider them as central producers of imaginations of political community. Museums, when paired with constitutional reform, can act as law's counter-archive, helping to create imaginations of political community that resist simple narratives of 'community' amidst contested histories. Drawing on research from South Africa, I contend that this approach is critical for legal scholars intent on reconstructing relations in post-colonial societies but who are, as of yet, equipped only with the constitution.

The chapter title presupposes a central dilemma: that museums and the law are two separate things. Such a distinction is overstated at least in as far as law as heralded as an autonomous system with which museums can then 'interact'. This implied separation functions to perpetuate an image of the law as a self-defining structure that is ordered and coherent, an image that is central to law's continued exaltation as the pinnacle tool with which we exact precise measurements of justice. While the aim of this chapter is to show that, importantly, museums do things that constitutions cannot, to overdraw a distinction between the two is counterproductive. As such, I want to capitalise on a distinction between constitutions and museums and, simultaneously, resist the almost irresistible trap of articulating this distinction.

The chapter is divided into three parts. I begin the chapter by giving a truncated argument about the limits – both substantively and functionally – of constitutions. My focus here is the South African context. Museums can operate as a helpful resource in fostering reflexivity about these limitations. In this way, museums may serve as law's counter-archive. However, the dilemma in defining 'law' – a necessity for defining its alternative ('counter-archive') – is one that has been encountered by many juridical thinkers. In the second section of this chapter I explore various attempts made by positivists and their critics to define 'law', as well as the common problem they encounter. This pursuit of law's origins fails to recognise law's inherent contingency and belies a belief in law as an authentic and autonomously functioning system. In the third section of this chapter I turn to Derrida's work on archives to further explicate the chimerical promises of authenticity in the pursuit of defining 'law' or its antithesis. I propose that rather than thinking of law as a system that occasionally interacts with other things (i.e., systems, archives, language), 'law' is better thought of as constituted by those very things. Attempting to disentangle these interactions in the quest for an objective definition of law keeps us tied to a positivist legacy that is both impossible to fulfil, and one that actively contributes to the continued lionisation of the Western juridical order.

The limits of constitutions

This paper starts from the premise that constitutions are often considered to be the primary devices with which to construct new political communities in post-revolutionary, post-colonial and post-conflict societies. New constitutions in South Africa in 1996, in Kenya in 2010, as well as in Tunisia and Egypt in 2014, to name but a few, were all adopted to signal a shift in the political and legal apparatus of their respective nations. Importantly, these shifts are also meant to signal a kind of cultural shift away from legally entrenched inequality, and towards idealised notions of democracy, transparency and the rule of law.

In these scenarios, new constitutions become the vehicles for achieving grand transformation beyond legal change – they are the devices that are deployed to articulate aspirations of renewal. It comes as no surprise then that the Preamble to the 1996 Constitution of the Republic of South Africa claims with unflinching nerve that the constitution aims to 'Heal the divisions of the past ... Lay the foundations for a democratic and open society ... Improve the quality of life of all citizens and free the potential of each person; and Build a united and democratic South Africa'.

However, the centralisation of the constitution and its presumed deliverance of democracy – or what I call constitutional fetishism – conflates the everyday management of populations with the vast horizons of political possibilities. Indeed, the constitution and those theorists who promote it as the key device with which to negotiate political community, monumentalise the production of sovereignty – both of the nation and the atomised subjects within it. The poverty of this conflation is readily apparent in the South African context. There, centring the document as the key tool in the navigation of political community denies the messy realities of subjectivities, and glosses over persistent issues of inequality. Significantly, it is not only new, transitional constitutions that perpetuate this problem, but rather a dilemma inherent to constitutions themselves. Constitutions, whether drafted in post-conflict times or otherwise, cannot help but delimit and legally ground political community. Indeed, this is not to be lamented – to make such a distinction is the constitution's main function. Yet, if the task is to trouble these sovereign imaginations of community and of the individual, the constitution cannot be looked to as the key tool for transformation. Rather than concretise community, we should look to devices that help us un-imagine sovereignty, in order to attend to the plurality of the world. Museums are one such site that can help us interrupt steady and strong conceptions of community that orient the political imaginations and sovereign desires of Western legal regimes.

I take my inspiration here from Jean Luc Nancy who contends that there can be no isolated, autonomous individual or community (1991). Nancy argues that every time we draw a border around an absolute – whether it be an individual or a community – we supply that thing a mythological autonomy (ibid.: 2–3). He stresses that no thing is absolutely alone – it is always in relation to that which is outside of it (ibid.: 6). For example, a human being relies on the intake and excretion of air, water, and food; its relation is an inherently contingent one. Nancy calls this inherent relationality – which is the reality of existence for all things – 'being-in-common' (ibid.: 40). The world is made up of relations of sharing, and this truth destabilises any attempt to postulate secure demarcations between beings – in fact, there are no 'beings', there is only being-in-common (ibid.: 38–39). Projects of representation deny this ontological primacy of the world and, therefore, participate in the production of the mythology of autonomy. The task then is to interrupt these productions of community so as to render legible the infinite sharing of the world.

Nancy's challenge to the thinking of community poses a dilemma for constitutionalism. For how can the constitution, the framework for the articulation of political community *par excellence*, avoid the inevitable delimitation of political community? As I argue above, constitutionalism is imagined to be *the* authorised site from which to draw these lines. While it is certainly true that the constitution is open to amendment and change, its principle function is the delimitation of community – the constitution bounds a body politic. In this contention, I align with Emilios Christodoulidis, who claims that authors' attempts to pair reflexivity with the institutional constrictions of constitutionalism leads to an inevitable 'constitutional irresolution' (2003). Constitutionalism cannot be asked to both found political community and hold it open. Indeed, it cannot be entirely reflexive or else it would forsake its own project, thereby eliminating the very organisation that it is meant to give expression to. The constitution cannot be asked to accommodate radical reflexivity because it is structurally bound to build and bind community.

Therefore, for Christodoulidis the only way to get at, or rather get away from, this institutional dilemma is not from within law, but from politics. He develops a theory of politics that emanates from a constituent power. He turns to the potential of civil society to push the boundaries of the constitutional arrangement (Christodoulidis 2003). For Christodoulidis, it is only this external pressure that can stretch constitutional possibilities. However, this response continues to hinge on a logic of communion; indeed, his theory of resistance is founded on the absolute immanence of a collective subject. Christodoulidis hangs on to the possibility of absolute immanence through his theory of the multitude that he takes from Antonio Negri (1999). This approach merely replaces the stifling proclivities of constituted power with the romanticisation of the potential of constituent power. This move does not undo or interrupt the production of community but rather instantiates it in a new form. In this context, the self-assured political community of the constitution is merely replaced with the self-assured boundaries of the multitude. Consequently, while I follow Christodoulidis in his turn to an alternative site from which to launch imaginations of political community, I do not follow his endorsement of the potential of the multitude, which merely substitutes the monumentalisation of the constitution with monumental politics. In contrast, I contend that the museum and its counter-monumental memorialising practices offer potential for a counter-monumental constitutionalism that de-centres the constitutional arrangement *and* interrupts the communing logic of the multitude.

Museums, like constitutions, are a place for the launching of imaginations of political community. As they share in the project of representation, they are often, like constitutions, invested in producing an idea of a knowable community. Certainly this is a historical claim levelled at museums. For example, Tony Bennett documents the civilising rituals of the museum, demonstrating how its incarnation as a public institution in England in the mid-eighteenth century was used as a training ground for middle class values. In this setting it was imagined that the working class would attend the museum, see their esteemed compatriots acting in good manners and, subsequently, emulate the appropriate behaviour (Bennett 1995: 47). In short, middle class museum visitors were to set an example for the working class populations (ibid.: 100). In addition to this history of mandated pedagogical citizenship, museums, like constitutions, have been criticised for the their imperialist, colonial, and otherwise exclusionary legacies (Edwards *et al.* 2006; Simpson 2001; Sleeper-Smith 2009). These critiques often articulate a feeling that the museum tells a story about a particular community – i.e., the victors' or the settlers' – as if it were the universal story, or (and sometimes 'and') that it is telling a mythological story about the community itself – i.e., how the colonisers are more inherently developed than the colonised. These critics too point to the ways in which such narratives tell a story about political community, about who is entitled to sovereignty, land, recognition and history.

Like constitutions, it may seem hard to imagine how a museum could do otherwise. Is a museum's *raison d'être* not to represent a community, whether based on ethnocentric, nationalist, or anthropocentric premises? While this is often the case, museums do not have to function this way. Significantly, they are not subject to the same structural limitations as the constitution and can proffer reflexivity over the form and substance of the 'community' they represent. They may even be able to represent that the unrepresentable exists (le Roux 2007: 69–70). In other words, memorialising practices can be deployed in both monumental and counter-monumental ways. South African constitutional theorists take up the difference between these practices in the context of the 1996 constitution (de Vos 2001; Du Plessis 2000; le Roux 2007; Snyman 1997; Van Marle 2007a, 2007b, 2007c). Whereas monumental practices perpetuate a persistent theme of community by fostering the logic of communion, counter-monumental practices destabilise smooth and secure conceptions of community.

The District Six Museum offers one such example of counter-monumental memorialising practices. The interactive adult educational programs at this small community-based museum in Cape Town, South Africa, offer examples of memory practices that *interrupt* rather than *produce* a stable conception of community (Douglas 2011). Indeed, they privilege the questioning and conversing over who or what constitutes 'community'. Staff at the District Six Museum see their role not as producers of community but as catalysts in creating a crisis of community (Sanger 2008: 102; Soudien 2008: 24). This task is crucial for them as they attempt to re-imagine South Africa in anti-apartheid and anti-capitalist ways. This project is vital because legacies of colonialism and apartheid have drastically shaped imaginations of political community in South Africa. Staff claim that in order to articulate an alternative politics, they must re-consider the very categories they have been taught to think with. These disruptive re-imaginations are the primary subject of concern at the museum. Elsewhere I have more thoroughly demonstrated how their approach resists the exaltation of liberal equality that erases difference and, instead, promotes contestation and disagreement (Douglas 2011). Here, I explore one example to illustrate.

District Six Museum staff claim that contemporary classifications of race are steeped in the vocabulary of apartheid. Therefore, they are constantly engaged in processes of interrogating its meaning (Staff Interviews 2009). Staff draw on the work of Nazir Carrim in order to try and 'break with the singular racialised identities that have continued to press down on [the youth of South Africa] and define them in narrow ways' (Sanger 2008: 107). According to Carrim:

> one could be a daughter in a family, a pupil in a school, a friend in the neighborhood, a human rights worker in the community and a South African or British for example. It is also important to note that these identities are in the same person all of the time and operate simultaneously. In addition, these identities also change. One could get married and become a wife in the family, one could move to another country, and so on. It is also important to note that these multiple identities are not always in harmony or balanced. They may be in tension with each other and, at moments, may even contradict each another.
> (Carrim 2006: 52)

Staff employ this approach both in their educational programming and in the practices of the museum more widely. For instance, museum staff and members of the community are deeply invested in disrupting the characterisation of District Six as a 'coloured space'. While the city of Cape Town places demands on the museum to present itself as a representative of a 'coloured' community, the museum refuses to adopt what they feel is an overly-simplistic and homogenising characterisation (Soudien 2008. p. 23). Anwah Nagia, the Chairperson of the District Six Beneficiary Trust claims that 'this politics is the very politics which was responsible for the dismemberment of the District Six – a poisoned racialised way of understanding the world. Whites here, Africans there, and "coloureds" over there' (Soudien 2008: 23).

However, this does not mean that the District Six Museum retreats from making critiques of racism and race-privilege. Rather, staff at the museum also focus on the way in which racism continues to animate the South African landscape. According to staff this means that their imaginings of restitution are imagined at a distance from state-based legislation that covers up the persistence of material inequalities. In contrast to the constitution, as well as those representations on offer at other museums, the promise of the future, as well as the potential for the role of law in the struggle for a post-apartheid city, is contested at the District Six Museum. According to staff:

> memory in this reckoning is an engaged space in which agents invoke and perform multiple, ambiguous and contradictory subjectivities shot through with the push and pull of the ambient politics of the past, present and the future. These multiple inflections surrounding memory force it into a crisis at the moment of its enunciation, at the moment when it is having to be pulled together into a statement of what it is.
>
> (Soudien 2008: 24)

According to staff, these practices are necessary to challenge the state descriptors and categories of race that have been inherited by the apartheid regime, and continue to animate the potential of political imaginings. In engaging in these agonistic exercises about memory and belonging, they participate in the necessary writing of the interruption community. Their practices offer insight into the poverty of over-investing in the potentials of representation and constitutionalism.

However, while the District Six Museum may offer a unique and dynamic example of the possibilities of writing the interruption of community, its existence does not erase the persistent demand to speak to the everyday politics of government and constitutional decision-making. I want to underscore that I am not ignoring the continued role of constitutions in the negotiation and navigation of political community. Rather, the problem is its centralisation as the key tool from which to re-imagine how to be together in the world and its presumed ability to be sufficiently reflexive about its exclusions. Although some constitutional scholars attempt to attend to the constitution's limits by drawing attention to its reflexive potential, such reflexivity is impossible. The constitution cannot simultaneously be asked to delimit political community and undo it – an external site is required. However, where Christodoulidis turns to the potential of politics for such reflexivity, his approach continues to hinge on the role of a knowable immanent community (a constituent power) for change. The challenge is to unthink the compulsion to sovereignty – therefore we need to avoid the romanticisation of immanentism. Rather than attempt to make the structure of the constitution turn on itself, or look to another sovereign collective with which to push the parameters of the constitution, the museum can function as an external site from which such reflexivity about the limitations of sovereign political communities and its atomised legal subjects can be fostered. While the constitution continues to operate as a legal device that assists us in the inevitable decision-making that is necessary for any political community, it does not have to be fetishised as the primary tool with which we shape our political horizons. As such, the museum can act as law's counter-archive, telling a story about political community that the constitution is unable to.

Constitutions are not enough 147

However, substantive questions persist. How can the museum and the constitution 'be brought together'? What does such a pairing look like in real life? What kind of a relationship does this argument assume exists between these two institutions? These inquiries conjure a central underlying dilemma of my argument: while I want to note the distinctive operations of constitutions and museums, I also want to be cautious about describing the operations as absolutely distinct. Museums and constitutions share many foundational precepts and operational techniques. For example, both are deeply invested in the project of representation, in telling stories about human communities, about remembering pasts and imagining futures (Douglas 2015). My point is not to argue that constitutions need to formally recognise or be in conversation with museums, but that they always already are. In other words, my argument is not that law *can* or *should* interact with museums in important ways, but that law *always* interacts with museums in important ways because 'law' is not limitable to a human-made set of legal orders. While I have just argued that the museum can function as law's counter-archive, I also want to resist the very paradigm, inherited from a positivist legacy, that establishes 'law' on the one hand and 'the museum' on the other.

The positivist trick

Many legal thinkers have attempted to formulate a concrete definition of law. Formidable engagements, set out by countless scholars, attempt to draw a boundary around what law is. These theorists draw schemas for an understanding of law as either an autonomous system or as a structure that is inherently infused by its social environment. In the former, legal positivists claim that law is definable by identifying its central organising force, such as a basic norm (Kelsen 1967) or a set of primary and secondary rules (Hart 1961). In the latter, socio-legal scholars argue that law is not reducible to such simple definitions and, rather, is constituted by a complex network of social phenomena, but which can still be identified by, for example, a binary code (Luhmann 2004) or documenting how people talk about 'law' (Ewick and Silbey 1998). In both cases, however, law stands as a knowable, meaningful category that 'is'. The presumed independence of law is further illustrated by vaunted academic dualisms such as 'law and society', 'law and economics', and 'law and literature', to name but a few. In these pairings, law is something that is autonomous, its distinct quality is highlighted by the coupling. These binaries tell us that law 'is', and that it is not the other thing; law 'is', yet it is also *not* literature, economics, or society.

In an example seemingly explicating law's heteronomy, legal thinker Carl Schmitt similarly begins with a critique of positivism. His *Political Theology*, originally published in 1922, is a sustained argument against positivist legal scholars like Hans Kelsen. According to Schmitt, liberal constitutionalists think that a positive order of laws is the ultimate tool that humans need to make decisions and manage conflict (Schmitt 1922/2005: 18–19). Schmitt claims that these thinkers misunderstand the reality of human life and the limits of law (ibid.: 15). Schmitt's poignant contribution is that there will always be situations that arise that cannot be accommodated by this positive set of law. Such situations exceed the bounds of constitutions and charters and, therefore, require the human element of judgment and decision. Constitutionalists neglect to see this human element as central to legal dynamics. Where thinkers like Kelsen attempt to stifle this necessary human decision-making power, Schmitt wants to excavate it. This is not to suggest that Schmitt is hostile to having a positive set of laws; he is certainly a constitutionalist. However, he warns against the over-reliance on positive law both because it is unrealistic and because such clouded thinking is a threat to the maintenance of state sovereignty (ibid.: 59).

Schmitt's critique of the positivist impulse does not only concern the role of the decision. His theory is also fundamentally predicated on the primacy of human action, which law is then built upon. In *The Concept of the Political* (1996) he explains that, before the state is even formed, there is a distinction made between individuals concerning who is a 'friend' and who is an 'enemy'. This distinction is the 'concept of the political' and is what orients all future state formations and attendant juridical orders. The norms of any particular legal system are then fundamentally predicated on the primacy of human action and the friend/enemy distinction. In this way Schmitt helps us understand that law does not appear as an absolutely autonomous tool before us. Rather, law is produced by preceding notions of community (Schmitt 1996; Strong 2005: xv).

However, while Schmitt is critical of positivism, he too falls for the positivist trick. While he seeks to illustrate law's contingency on human judgment and decision, it is these additions that give him his working definition of law. Although he warns against pre-emptively defining its exact content, Schmitt too circumscribes 'law' to a place, even if those places are multiple. For both Hart and Schmitt then, law is not only a positive set of dictates – it also relies on the decision of a sovereign or a complex of interconnected rules. However, these elaborations merely expand the definitional border of the concept and persist in their assertion of the possibility to circumscribe 'law'.

Peter Fitzpatrick has long been a critic of this notion of law. He has consistently demonstrated the way in which this story of law's independence hinges on myth. He emphasises that, in modernity, the West's attachment to a juridical structure as an objective, rational legal system is fundamentally predicated on a rejection of an imagined uncivilised savagery that it is *not* (Fitzpatrick 1992). This foundational presumption means that the West is psychically bound to and, therefore, inherently

Constitutions are not enough 149

contingent, on this primordial fear as its self-defining other. However, the lionised view of Western law refutes this relationality, choosing instead to suffocate this reality in the pursuit of an image of law as absolutely autonomous. Even when its societal influences are considered, as in the work of many socio-legal studies scholars, it remains a transcendent tool whose existence as an independent system is rarely questioned:

> Law transcends society yet it is of society. The boundaries of law are inevitably and palpably set in relation to society but even in the face of the overwhelming evidence of law's social limits, popular belief in its transcendent efficacy persists. ... This is not a matter of inconsistency or delusion. It is ... a matter of myth.
>
> (Fitzpatrick 1992: 9)

Hence, for Fitzpatrick, law's autonomy is fictitious. The fictive quality of law allows it to simultaneously purport to be stable and unchanging as it adapts to new situations in order to maintain its relevance and authority: 'law fuses its seeming stability, its determinate "order", with a receptive creativity' (Fitzpatrick 2012: 194). But at its heart, law has no absolutely independent content or origin, despite its mythological claims otherwise. It is always in relation to its 'outside', that which it rejects and purports not to be (ibid.: 204).

The danger in the assertion of law as autonomous (and knowable through an authentic origin story) is that it perpetuates a mythological image of law as ordered and coherent. This image of law is vital to its continued romanticisation as the lauded and objective mediator of all conflict. In its celebration as a precise instrument of justice, law's messy and contingent truth is suppressed. The positivist trick relies on this story; it purports to tell us that law is definable through its autonomy. It is this myth that rests at the foundation of the questions about my project – what is law's relationship to museums? How do they interact? My response is not that law and museums are alike (which improperly suggests that they both operate via their own unique and independent logics) but that the very formulation that sets them apart misunderstands their mutual imbrication. This relationship can be helpfully illustrated through an analysis of the archival logic that animates both their content as well as their imagined institutional boundaries.

The archival promise

Archives return us to the problem of beginnings. According to Derrida, the word invokes two interrelated principles, to commence and to command: 'the principle according to nature or history, there where things *commence* – physical, historical, or ontological principle – but also the principle according to the law, there where men and gods *command, there* where authority, social order are exercised ...' (Derrida 1995: 1, original emphasis). Archives then, as Derrida suggests, are the place where things begin and where authority is articulated, or perhaps more aptly, archives are the site from which political authority is articulated and, hence, where law begins. Moreover, the Greek origins of the word clearly render legible the spatiality of the concept; the *arkheion* is the actual place where *archons* (those who command) reside, where official documents are filed. In other words, the archive is the *house* of the law (Derrida 1995: 2–3). What Derrida suggests here is that the enunciation of law is predicated on the collection of files and that this archive is the site from which authority is exercised. But where is this house? What is the address of this command centre?

Some would suggest that the archival seat of authority is found in a supreme court or perhaps a legislative assembly. Indeed, these are sites where official documents are collected and stored, and where sovereign declarations are presumed made. However, a further reflection on Derrida's invocation surfaces other possibilities. If, as he says, the archive is the place where signs are gathered together with the aim of coordinating a single corpus – what he calls archontic power (Derrida 1995: 3) – then the archive is not only found on parliament hills and in court rooms. Rather, the archive is any place where this project of anamorphosis takes place – it is the museum *and* the courthouse *and* the encyclopaedia, to name but a few. Importantly, he is not insinuating that these articulations of coherence utter a truth about their contents. Derrida's point, one that is at the centre of much of his writing, is exactly to argue that archives offer promises of authentic unity where no such cohesion exists. As such, the archontic power of the archive is everywhere (not only in formal institutions), yet the truth claim at its foundation is nowhere. Lawmakers draw on and perpetuate their archive under the pretence of making precise, rational calculations of justice, forgoing rumination on the necessary exclusions such decisions entail (Van der Walt 2005b). However, this archontic articulation is not exclusive to law. The seductive influence of the illusory archival promise is so prevalent in late modernity that Derrida likens it to an illness that he calls 'archive fever'.

To elaborate, in *Archive Fever* (1995), Derrida illustrates the persistence of origin stories and their chimerical promises of authenticity. In this work, he traces the efforts of Sigmund Freud, and psychoanalysis more broadly, to reveal the layered contingency of representation (i.e., how people's representations of themselves in language and action are dependent on psychic underwritings). Yet this very premise paradoxically rests on an assertion of an authentic layer 'beneath the surface'. Derrida refutes the existence of any such 'original copy' (1995: 3). The persistent search for this unknowable origin, which is also an attempt to assert sovereignty, is what he pathologises as 'archive fever' (Van der Walt 2005a: 290). Aptly put by Brien Brothman, 'neither texts buried in the interior subconscious and retrievable through psychoanalysis nor public documents stored in archives preserve authentic, immutable permanent records, that is, a foundational – provincial – site of inscription' (1997: 191). For Derrida there are no sovereign subjects and no sovereign archives – there are only ever traces and impressions.

In an insightful and exhaustive article, Renisa Mawani also turns to the relationship between law and the archive. She argues that law is the archive, claiming that

> law continually produces, protects, proliferates, and destroys documents and records that ground its authority and that are contained and preserved in state and non-state archives ... law is the archive: generating, compiling, referencing, absorbing, and disregarding statutes, precedent, and other forms of knowledge.
>
> (Mawani 2012: 351)

Here, Mawani emphasises the fact that law's authority, its seat of command, comes from archival inscriptions. These inscriptions are what constitute law and its claims to supremacy:

> the British common law as legal precedent continually and explicitly makes reference to what came before, asserting its sovereignty and maintaining its legitimacy through its own archival production and proliferation. Precedent – as recall, translation, and reinterpretation – is how law continues to maintain the relevance of its own history to the present and future.
>
> (Mawani 2012: 354)

Mawani's argument brilliantly demonstrates the way legal regimes use archives in order to articulate sovereign claims (and maintain colonial legacies). The repetition and repeatability of these archival claims is central to its continued legitimacy. However, law not only draws on archives of official court documents, it also draws on wider discourses such as utterances and inscriptions from the museum for its legitimacy.

As the museum articulates conceptions of community and history, it tells us a story of who is and who is not legitimate to think of as belonging to that community, and what is and what is not legitimate to think of as belonging to that history. For example, Constitution Hill, a museum in central Johannesburg, claims that 'nowhere can the story of South Africa's turbulent past and its extraordinary transition to democracy be told as it is at Constitution Hill' (Constitution Hill 2009). According to the narrative proffered by Constitution Hill, South Africa's 'turbulent' history has been replaced with the advent of a new era of democracy.

Visitor materials, as well as interviews with staff at Constitution Hill, also tell the story about the arrival of democracy in South Africa. This contemporary period is differentiated from a vaguely construed 'past' (i.e., apartheid). Significantly, the arrival of democracy is consistently imagined as inherently linked to the 1996 Constitution. Indeed, senior staff emphatically claim that the museum fosters democracy by educating people about their newly found constitutional rights. They state, for example, that the museum participates in bolstering democracy by providing visitors with the opportunity to learn 'about their constitutional rights, as entrenched in our law books' (Staff Interviews 2009). Through this veneration of the 1996 document and its attendant ushering in of democracy, apartheid is imagined as a distant and bygone phenomenon, eradicated by the arrival of the new constitution.

The sure-footedness of Constitution Hill's conception of democracy – and its intimate relationship with an exaltation of the powers and potentials of the new liberal democratic constitutional order – constructs and maintains what is legitimate to think of as the political in the South African context. It centralises the role of constitutionalism and glosses over contestations about the legacies of apartheid under a narrative that proclaims the arrival of democracy. Further, this notion of democracy is inherently linked to the promises of the Constitutional Court and its attendant 'law books' (Staff Interviews 2009). This narrative asserts that these legal institutions provide a foundational stability for a progressive teleology that will continue to carry South Africans away from their 'dark past' to an increasingly democratic future (Staff Interviews 2009). As such, the given categories of the liberal democratic legal system are infused with grand promises for South African political community. Indeed, these legal precepts are presumed to be adequate tools with which to address the deep legacies of colonialism and apartheid. In short, the political project at Constitution Hill is bounded by a presupposed equation between the promises of the new constitution and democracy.

More than merely stressing that law draws on multiple sets of archives, I suggest that the very distinction between 'law' and 'archive' is overdrawn. In other words, I want to go further than saying that law relies on archives (past, present, and future) for its continued authority. Taking inspiration from the Constitution Hill example above, I ask, where does law end and the archive begin? Where does the constitution end and the museum begin? Both constitutions and museums need to tell a story about a 'we':

> We see how a past and with it an identity impresses itself upon us so that we inherit that impression as it constitutes us as a *we*. We also see that the archive is inherently troubled in that it always involves *us* in interpreting the trait of being, and indeed authorizing it as that which is a mark of an identity. The archive in that sense both encircles and

marks us, and it is through that encirclement that we endlessly find ourselves in a spiral of reinterpretation that opens out into a future as we continuously reaffirm what are and what are not the authoritative traits of an identity.

(Cornell and Van Marle 2011: 347)

The archival promise is central to both the content *and* definitional boundary of law and the museum. As Derrida claims, 'archivization produces as much as it records the event' (Derrida 1995: 17). The archive doesn't just showcase content, the archive *produces* the institution it is associated with. A clear delimitation of what constitutes law's archive maintains an image of law as a distinct and autonomous system and, with it, the mythology of its sovereign authority.

Conclusion

The concept of 'law's counter-archive' requires that we have an exclusive definition of 'law' as well as its 'archive' in order for us to consider its alternative. The danger is that doing so perpetuates an image of law as clearly delimitable. At the same time, however, it is possible to recognise law's functional limitations and to look elsewhere for alternatives. Where the constitution is unable to provide the kind of reflexivity that is imperative (namely, a reflexivity that challenges the very logic of delimitation), museums can. This is because the two institutions have different functions. Whereas the constitution's task is to delimit community, the museum has no such mandate. The museum can pursue such ends but it is not functionally or structurally committed to doing so. It is this functional differentiation that represents the potential for museums to function as law's counter-archive, doing the kind of interruptive work of community that constitutions are unable to.

However, although the museum offers sites of reflexivity to the limited thinking of community found in constitutions, it is important not to over-draw the differences between the two. Indeed, constitutions and museums share a common investment in the archontic principle and, as demonstrated through my example from Constitution Hill, serve to mutually constitute each other. Constitutions and museums also share in their guarantees of order and sovereign authority even as they systematically fail to deliver on these promises. We must resist the seductive allure of the pursuit of origins at the heart of circumscriptions of 'law' and of law's 'archives' as these authentic origins are nowhere to be found.

References

Bennett, T. 1995, *The Birth of the Museum: History, Theory, Politics*, Routledge, London.

Brothman, B. 1997, 'Archive Fever: A Freudian Impression'. *Archivaria*, vol. 43, pp. 189–192.

Carrim, N. 2006, *Exploring Human Rights Education: Framework, Approaches, and Techniques*, British Council of South Africa, Cape Town.

Christodoulidis, E. 2003, 'Constitutional Irresolution: Law and the Framing of Civil Society', *European Law Journal*, vol. 9, no. 4, pp. 401–432.

Constitution Hill 2009, [Visitor Brochure], *Constitution Hill.*

Cornell, D. and Van Marle, K. 2011, 'Exploring *Ubuntu:* Tentative Reflections', in D. Cornell and N. Muvangua (eds), *Ubuntu and the Law: African Ideals and Postapartheid Jurisprudence*, Fordham University Press, New York, pp. 344–366.

de Vos, P. 2001, 'A Bridge Too Far? History As Context in the Interpretation of the South African Constitution', *South African Journal of Human Rights*, vol. 17, no. 1, pp. 1–33.

Derrida, J. 1995, *Archive Fever: A Freudian Impression*, trans. E. Prenowitz, University of Chicago, Chicago.

Douglas, S. 2011, 'Between Constitutional Mo(nu)ments: Memorialising Past, Present, and Future at the District Six Museum and Constitution Hill', *Law and Critique* vol. 22, no. 2, pp. 177–187.

Douglas, S. 2015, 'Museums As Constitutions: A Commentary on Constitutions and Constitution-Making', *Law, Culture, and the Humanities*, vol. 11, no. 3, pp. 349–362.

Du Plessis, L. 2000, 'The South African Constitution as Memory and Promise', *Stellenbosch Law Review*, vol. 11, no. 3, pp. 385–394.

Edwards, E., Gosden, C., and Phillips, R.B. 2006, *Sensible Objects: Colonialism, Museums, and Material Culture*, Berg, New York.

Ewick, P. and Silbey, S. 1998, *The Common Place of Law: Stories from Everyday Life*, University of Chicago Press, Chicago.

Fitzpatrick, P. 1992, *The Mythology of Modern Law*, Routledge, London.

Fitzpatrick, P. 2012, 'Reading Slowly: The Law of Literature and the Literature of Law', in R. Buchanan, S. Motha and S. Pahuja (eds), *Reading Modern Law: Critical Methodologies*, Routledge, London, pp. 193–210.

Hart, H.L.A. 1961, *The Concept of Law*, Oxford University Press, Oxford.

Kelsen, H. 1967, *Pure Theory of Law*, trans. M. Knight, University of California Press, Berkeley.

le Roux, W. 2007, 'War Memorials, the Architecture of the Constitutional Court Building and Counter-monumental Constitutionalism', in W. LeRoux and K. Van Marle (eds), *Law, Memory, and the Legacy of Apartheid: Ten Years After AZAPO v. President of South Africa*, Pretoria University Law Press, Pretoria, pp. 65–92.

Luhmann, N. 2004, *Law as a Social System*, Oxford University Press, Oxford.

Mawani, R. 2012, 'Law's Archive', *Annual Review of Law and Social Science*, vol. 8, pp. 337–365.

Nancy, J-L. 1991, *The Inoperative Community*, trans. S. Sawhney, P. Connor (ed.), University of Minnesota Press, Minneapolis.

Negri, A. 1999, *Insurgencies: Constituent Power and the Modern State*, trans. M. Boscagli, University of Minnesota Press, Minneapolis.

Passavant, P. 2012, 'Democracy's Ruins, Democracy's Archive', in R. Buchanan, S. Motha and S. Pahuja (eds), *Reading Modern Law: Critical Methodologies and Sovereign Formations*, Routledge, London, pp. 49–73.

Sanger, M. 2008, 'Education Work in the District Six Museum: Layering in New Voices and Interpretations' in B. Bennett, J. Chrischené, and C. Soudien (eds), *City-Site-Museum: Reviewing Memory Practices at the District Six Museum*, District Six Museum, Cape Town, pp. 96–109.

Schmitt, C. 1996, *The Concept of the Political*, trans. G. Schwab, University of Chicago Press, Chicago.

Schmitt, C. 2005, *Political Theology: Four Chapters on the Concept of Sovereignty*, trans. G. Schwab, University of Chicago Press, Chicago

Simpson, M. G. 2001, *Making Representations: Museums in the Post-Colonial Era*. Routledge, London.

Sleeper-Smith, S. 2009, *Contesting Knowledge: Museums and Indigenous Perspectives*, University of Nebraska Press, Lincoln.

Snyman, J. 1997, 'Interpretation and the Politics of Memory', *Acta Juridica*, pp. 312–337.

Soudien, C. 2008, 'Memory and Critical Education: Approaches in the District Six Museum', in B. Bennett, J. Chrischené and C. Soudien (eds), *City-Site-Museum: Reviewing Memory Practices at the District Six Museum*, District Six Museum, Cape Town, pp. 110–119.

Staff Interviews 2009, Conducted by S. Douglas at Constitution Hill, Johannesburg and District Six Museum, Cape Town.

Strong, T. 2005, 'Foreword' in *Political Theology: Four Chapters on the Concept of Sovereignty*, trans. G. Schwab, University of Chicago Press, Chicago, pp. vii–xxxv.

Van der Walt, J. 2005a, 'Interrupting The Myth Of The Partage: Reflections On Sovereignty And Sacrifice In The Work Of Nancy, Agamben And Derrida', *Law and Critique*, vol. 16, pp. 277–299.

Van der Walt, J. 2005b, *Law and Sacrifice: Towards a Post-Apartheid Theory of Law*, Birkbeck Law Press, London.

Van Marle, K. 2007a, 'Constitution as Archive' in S. Veitch (ed.), *Law and the Politics of Reconciliation*, Ashgate, Aldershot, pp. 215–228.

Van Marle, K. 2007b, 'Law's Time, Particularity and Slowness', in W. LeRoux and K. Van Marle (eds), *Law, Memory, and the Legacy of Apartheid: Ten Years After AZAPO v. President of South Africa*, Pretoria University Law Press, Pretoria, pp. 11–32.

Van Marle, K. 2007c, 'The Spectacle of Post-Apartheid Constitutionalism', *Griffith Law Review*, vol. 16, no. 2, pp. 411–429.

Chapter 8

Archiving victimhood
Practices of inscription in international criminal law

Sara Kendall

> For the written to be the written, it must continue to 'act' and to be legible even if what is called the author of the writing no longer answers for what he has written.
>
> (Jacques Derrida 1982: 316)

> It is a big problem that people think they are in by virtue of filling in a paper.
>
> (Common Legal Representative for Victims in *Prosecutor v. Ruto and Sang*, ICC, Nairobi, 4 July 2013)

The term "archive" suggests many referents at once. It refers to a set of practices, or what some anthropologists have described as the "living archive" of social relations and forms of governance. Laura Bear describes India's Eastern Railway Headquarters as the 'medium through which social relationships were contested and formed' in the postcolonial state (2007: 15); meanwhile, Ann Stoler regards Dutch colonial archives as 'an arsenal of sorts that were reactivated to suit new governing strategies' (2009: 3). In this sense archival practices mediate relationships as well as produce forms of governance. Yet as Achille Mbembe (2002) and Jacques Derrida (2002) have observed, the term also connotes a place: a space of memorialisation or containment (or both), where material is deposited and perhaps later abandoned. This chapter considers efforts within the field of international criminal law to inscribe and transform the experience of suffering into legally recognisable categories. Here the victimary archive also works as both practice and place: the archival work of international criminal law seeks to contain a material history of atrocity within law while presenting the place of justice and redress in particular institutional locations, suggesting that people are 'in', for instance, 'by virtue of filling in a paper'.

The above statement from a victim's legal representative at the International Criminal Court (ICC), formally mandated to represent conflict-affected individuals who qualify as victim participants, reveals a tension in the field of international criminal law's victimary archive. In order to appear within the frame of positive law, victimhood must be inscribed to be rendered legible for recognition. At the same time, the lived experience of suffering and grievance is depersonalised and reified, enclosed within the terms of a legal field that will transform it into something else: as data to be contained and managed in relation to juridical time. Such inscriptions take place through the artefact of the application form, which travels through a filtering process of filing, adjudication, and bestowal (or denial) of victim status as a legal category.

'Filling in a paper' brings practice and place together, where the inscription of suffering happens at an institutional site that offers itself as a form of redress for victims of grave crimes. Court officials have maintained that victims are the ICC's '*raison d'être*' (Arbia 2012); meanwhile, proponents of international criminal law assert that 'the voice of victims may be heard' through trial proceedings (Orie 2002: 1478). Yet the individuals who fill in papers, provide proof of their identities, and make claims about loss and harm are less significant in their concrete particularity for the project of international criminal law. They are displaced by the figure of the abstract victim, as suggested through common tropes that collapse a plurality of voices and interests into a singular 'voice of victims'. International criminal law attempts to legitimate itself through referencing an abstract victimhood that is said to be ventriloquised or 'heard' through this legal field.[1] The victim thus appears within this scene as a double body – first, as a corporeal body seeking redress through law, and second, as part of the abstract body of generalised victimhood; as Pierre Bourdieu describes it, as 'a mystical body incarnated in a social body, which itself transcends the biological bodies which compose it' (1991: 208).

This chapter traces the production of the victim before the ICC through its institutional practices and technologies of inscription.[2] It takes up a series of sites and artefacts that reveal the limits of international criminal law's restorative turn, which introduces the figure of the victim within a fundamentally punitive field. It considers the role of the forms and practices that interpellate individuals as victims of mass atrocity crimes. If the victim's abstract body is produced through the claims of court proponents, its corporeal body is brought into the frame of the court through printed forms and spreadsheet 'registers' that distil jurisdictionally relevant details for legal processes. Building upon Jacques Derrida's claims about the nomological power of the archive, a power that makes law as well as produces respect for law (1995: 7), this chapter illustrates how the abstract

---

1   I take up this argument in greater detail in Kendall and Nouwen (2014). See also Fletcher (2015).

2   The content of this chapter is based upon an empirical project tracking the ICC's work in Kenya and Uganda, which involved interviews and participant observation over a three-year period.

victim is invoked to shore up the authority of international criminal law, while the corporeal body is subjected to a calculus that will include or exclude based upon categories that appear arbitrary from outside the legal frame. The 'emblematic wound', an outgrowth of juridical logics, begins to unsettle this archive through revealing its biopolitical implications. Finally, a letter of withdrawal from a large group of court-recognised victims contests the form of justice carried out in their name. If the victimary archive is produced through inscribing and compiling characteristics of those who have suffered, its nomological power is unsettled by subjects who speak back, countering the court's authority and, in turn, revealing the tenuous authority of international criminal law as a space of redress.

Inscribing victimhood

International criminal law now forms part of the global humanitarian continuum, with its attendant political dream of saving lives and alleviating suffering. From its origins in a traditionally punitive form of justice, the field has undergone a restorative turn marked most clearly by the inclusion of victims' rights at the ICC, the sole permanent institution where international crimes are adjudicated. Early proponents viewed the ICC's development of a 'victim mandate' as a 'great advance in international criminal procedure' (Cassese 1999: 167–168) and 'a new step forward' (Jorda and de Hemptinne 2002: 1387). The statute agreed in Rome in 1998 included victim participation provisions and the right to legal representation, protection, and reparations. In language that draws upon familiar tropes from the field of transitional justice, commentary on these provisions contends that 'international justice must provide redress for these victims in the name of securing peace, drawing a line between the present and the past and facilitating the healing and forward movement of society' (Donat-Cattin 2008: 1279). A historically punitive field is thus recast in relation to the aims of healing, restoration and transition.

More than forms of transitional justice such as truth commissions, however, international criminal law is subject to juridical and jurisdictional constraints. This is most evident with the field's relationship to individuals and communities who have suffered from mass crimes as they are interpellated as subjects of international criminal law. As a juridical process, the practice of bestowing victim recognition is unable to recognise the intricacies of suffering and grievance outside of positive law's limited terms. Instead the practices of victim recognition produce and consolidate a victimary archive that is used toward the ends of international criminal law, or toward fostering the field as an end in itself. This archive serves a particular narrative of a conflict told through the court's jurisdiction: the archive contains only those whose suffering falls within the temporal and subject matter jurisdiction of the ICC, producing remainders in the form of liminal individuals and remnants of conflict-affected populations who do not qualify within juridical logics.

To appear within the frame of the ICC, conflict-affected individuals must apply to be recognised as a victim within the meaning of the court's statute. The production of the victimary archive emerges through the court's requirement, stated in its rules of procedure, that individuals must apply in order to participate in proceedings. This act of applying is usually carried out through the material site of the application form. The form is submitted to the relevant chamber, which may reject it if the chamber determines the applicant is 'not a victim or that the criteria set out in Art 68(3) are not otherwise fulfilled' (ICC RPE 89(2)). The relevant statutory provision offers little detail, stating that:

> where the personal interest of the victims are affected, the Court shall permit their views and concerns to be presented and considered at stages of the proceedings determined to be appropriate by the Court and in a manner which is not prejudicial to or inconsistent with the rights of the accused and a fair and impartial trial.
>
> (ICC RS 68(3))

This framing in the court's constitutive documents left interpretive discretion to the judges about who could participate, at what stages of the proceedings, and in what ways, unbound by precedent from other chambers. As a consequence, early jurisprudence on victim participation varied widely. This has led to different approaches in different 'situations', the court's term used to describe sets of events with shared territorial and temporal dimensions (such as the Situation in Darfur, Sudan and its related cases). Although most chambers have employed the practice of collecting application forms for potential victim participants, a different approach was developed for the Kenyan situation, where an overburdened judiciary experimented with new practices of victim participation, developing a process of what it termed 'registering' victims. Both the collected forms considered here and the Kenyan 'register' considered below produce juridical archives of a conflict, determining who appears within the frame of the situation or case and who falls outside. Though the victimary archive of international criminal law may appear contingent and arbitrary from the standpoint of conflict-affected communities, it sits easily within juridical logics that seek to evaluate, divide, distil causality, and rule in favour or against the ascription of legal identities.

The application form is central to the bestowal of participatory rights for most situations before the ICC. Completing it entails a series of prior acts: individuals have to already know or be informed that the court exists and that its mandate enables them to possibly 'be heard' there; they then need to access resources, such as court personnel, possible interpreters, and the relevant documents; finally, they must be able to demonstrate their identity through acceptable documentary evidence.[3] Knowledge about the court is disseminated through outreach practices that cultivate the impression that the ICC is the appropriate forum for hearing conflict-related grievances. In response to increased awareness of the ICC's restorative mandate, staff members employ a counter-discourse of 'managing expectations', caught in a tension between promoting the court and articulating its limits.[4]

The ICC's victim participation form inscribes individual experience into categories that can be more readily translated into juridical terms. Details of suffering are not only recorded, but also brought into an epistemic frame that is oriented toward criminal accountability. These inscriptions are not neutral acts of documentation, but instead serve as classifying techniques that translate trauma and loss into terms that can be viewed in relation to perpetrated harms. In their work on governmental practices, Peter Miller and Nikolas Rose draw upon Bruno Latour's notion of 'inscription devices' to illustrate the role of record-keeping in the operation of power:

> Information in this sense is not the outcome of a neutral recording function. It is itself a way of acting upon the real, a way of devising techniques for inscribing it in such a way as to make the domain in question susceptible to evaluation, calculation and intervention.
>
> (Miller and Rose 2008: 66)

The very process of recording information entails acting upon it, rendering it available and opening it to future use in ways that build upon the intervention of the inscription. Inscription is an act of interpretive framing and selection, enabling relationships to be established between different elements and across space, containing and consolidating as well as opening the inscribed to new possibilities. In her account of colonial governance read through the site of Dutch archives, Ann Stoler claims that archival documents are 'active, generative substances with histories, as documents with itineraries of their own' (2009: 1). Such acts of inscription are productive, furthering the operation of colonial power. Stoler tracks

---

3   The application form states: 'It is a requirement that the victim provide proof of identity. This can include, for example, national identity card, birth certificate, voting card, passport, driver's license, student or employee card, letter from a local authority, camp registration card, card from a humanitarian agency, tax document or other document identifying the victim'.

4   For example, a policy document on external relations includes among its goals 'managing expectations, engaging in dialogue and obtaining feedback'. See International Criminal Court, *Integrated Strategy for External Relations, Public Information and Outreach*, viewed 27 July 2015, <www.icc-cpi.int/NR/rdonlyres/425E80BA-1EBC-4423-85C6-D4F2B93C7506/185049/ICCPIDSWBOR0307070402_IS_En.pdf>.

'archiving-as-process rather than archives-as-things'; in this sense, colonial archives 'were both transparencies on which power relations were inscribed and intricate technologies of rule in themselves' (ibid.: 20).

International criminal law's restorative turn also operates as a form of governance, and its practices produce effects that are in tension with its restorative premises. The ICC's 'inscription devices' are directed at conflict-affected populations. Both the means through which archived material is contained, such as forms and certificates, as well as the substance of what is inscribed and contained work as actants, producing identities as well as shoring up the power of individuals and institutions who bestow or withhold recognition. The court seeks to include and contain those who have suffered from mass crimes within a juridical field that claims it 'gives voice' to their suffering. For example, an official court guidebook asserts that

> in order to ensure that the voices of victims are heard and their inter-ests are taken into account during proceedings, victims at the ICC enjoy rights that have never before been incorporated in the mandate of an international criminal court.
>
> (ICC: 12)

Some proponents press even farther, claiming that participation in the project of international criminal justice is 'the first step toward giving victims back the dignity they had lost through these crimes' (Victims Rights Working Group 2012). Institutional recognition of victimhood is credited with producing a space for articulating loss and a platform for rights asser-tions, and restoring fundamental aspects of the humanist frame – a secular conception of dignity – on which the field depends. In this way it operates as a form of what anthropologist Didier Fassin (2012) terms 'humanitarian governance', the introduction of moral sentiments into political projects.

As Michel Foucault (2002) has observed, the archive operates as a system of statements, as rules of practice that shape what can and cannot be said. As an 'inscription device' that archives suffering, the victim partic-ipation form is a critical actant in producing who constitutes a victim before the ICC. This happens through modes of address, choices of terms, the kinds of information requested and the amount of space allocated for responses. The standard form used in most situations is addressed in the third person: 'Has the victim already submitted an application for partici-pation or for reparations to the ICC?'[5] Although the court permits other

---

5   All subsequent references to the form refer to the International Criminal Court, *Request for Participation in Proceedings and Reparations at the ICC for Individual Victims*, viewed 29 April 2015, <www.icc-cpi.int/NR/rdonlyres/48A75CF0-E38E-48A7-A9E0-026ADD32553D/0/SAFIndividualEng.pdf>.

individuals to write on behalf of aspiring victim participants, those directly affected may also fill in forms. The individual seeking formal recognition who personally fills in the form must step outside herself, recognising herself as 'the victim' and presenting herself as the object of an address made in the third person. Not 'you' or even 'the individual', she is already hailed as 'the victim', an identity that appears to belong to the individual applicant, but is in fact bestowed by the court through these official documents and may be withdrawn at a later point. By filling in the form, conflict-affected individuals are brought into a state of waiting for institutional recognition of an identity that they already seem to inhabit by virtue of being hailed as 'the victim'. As the form travels through the juridical process, the court regulates the distinction between the victim who has suffered in a context where the court is active and the victim as a form of institutional recognition. Two different conceptions of victimhood thus share the same referent as 'victim': the unqualified victim, addressed in the third person through the form itself, and the qualified victim, officially confirmed by an ICC chamber as one who has met the membership criteria within a specific case. This polysemy produces confusion when the unqualified victim, the form's addressee, is later informed that she is not a victim according to the juridical logic of the court.

In addition to regulating identity at the individual level, the form and its uptake produce and reproduce biopolitical categories at the level of the population. The form has an optional 'tribe/ethnic group' category, revealing an assumption that the ICC works and will continue to work where these categories carry social and political weight. The question is also directed at establishing elements of crimes where targeting a particular group is legally relevant, as with the presumed ethnic distinctions between the Hema and Lendu people in the eastern Democratic Republic of the Congo or between Kikuyus and Luos in Kenya. Yet this desire to document tribe or ethnicity – to include it within the archive of victimhood – also re-inscribes existing conceptions of identity that may have contributed to conflict-related grievances. In this sense, court forms act into the situation by furthering identity categories based on taken-for-granted (and frequently colonial) signifiers. Capturing such 'data' through the form may serve statistical purposes for the court, helping it to chart the demography of conflict-affected populations. Yet this iteration of identity may further cement identity-based grievances, reminding the self-identified Lendu individual that it was the Hemas who attacked her community. When her application to participate is not granted due to issues of time and place, the promise of institutional redress recedes, but her grievance remains.

The form's main purpose – of linking those who have suffered to charged crimes – is revealed through the substance of the address to 'the victim'. It devotes half a page to 'what happened', inviting individuals to attach additional paper if this space is not enough. This contrasts starkly with the jurisdictional questions that follow: when, where, and by whom. 'Who does the victim believe is responsible for the event(s)? If possible, explain why the victim believes this'. Two blank lines are available for answering this critical question that seeks to establish a nexus to the charged crimes. Has the form-filling subject been informed of the weight of this inscription – that it might make the crucial difference between being a 'case victim' with participatory rights or a victim of the broader 'situation'? The form's very architecture, its allocation of space in relation to questions, belies the relative gravity accorded to different responses from a juridical perspective.

Finally, the form's architecture produces expectations for what the court is capable of providing as specific types of redress. After asking whether 'the victim' would like to apply for reparations, it prompts 'what would the victim want?' A marginal note elaborates: 'What is the victim expecting if the accused person is found guilty? Reparations can be anything which can help the victim to repair the harm suffered.'

As ICC staff members working for the court's Victim Participation and Reparations Section have noted, individual responses can be quite specific, such as requesting compensation for lost livestock. As part of their effort to 'manage expectations', staff members must explain that specific losses are unlikely to be compensated by the court despite the form's suggestions to the contrary.

As inscription technologies, then, victim application forms simultaneously produce or re-inscribe identities and desires as they gather material for the ICC's victimary archive. The individuals filling them out – 'unqualified' victims – are hailed as participants in the process of determining the court's reparative policy ('what would the victim want?') even as the data gathered through the forms themselves are scrutinised, disarticulated, used for the court's own demographic purposes, and subjected to juridical time. Distinct from the temporality of lived experience, juridical time operates according to its own internal logics – court calendars, judicial recesses, and the contestations of different parties. As a consequence, in some situations, the court applicants have waited years before hearing anything about their status.[6] Furthermore, since the field emphasises locating an individual doer behind a deed, hinging redress to international criminal law produces new vulnerabilities among those who have suffered, creating

---

6   A 2012 ASP resolution noted '*with continued concern* reports from the Court on the persistent backlogs the Court has had in processing applications from victims seeking to participate in proceedings' (emphasis added): see Resolution ICC-ASP/11/Res.7, 'Victims and Reparations', 21 November 2012. Meanwhile, the inability to process and adjudicate forms before significant events on the judicial calendar has resulted in hundreds of individuals not receiving a determination from the Court before the confirmation of charges hearing in the *Mbarushimana* case in 2011.

164   Sara Kendall

a taxonomy of victims and re-inscribing identities among divided populations. If charges are dropped in a particular case, there are implications for court-recognised victims whose recognition is tied to those charges, with consequences for exercising substantive rights and the prospect of material assistance.

The register as archive

A related archival function is served through the practice of 'registering' victims in the Kenyan situation before the court. Yet this shift to different procedures – ostensibly in the interests of improving efficiency – shores up the power of the victims' legal representative to speak the 'voice of the victim' while simultaneously reducing the number of participant applications to be judicially vetted. The relevant decision states that:

> The purpose of this registration is threefold: first to provide victims with a channel through which they can formalise their claim of victimhood; second, to establish a personal connection between the victim and the Common Legal Representative ... third, to assist the Court in communicating with the victims and in preparing the periodic reports referred to in paragraph 54 below.
> (*Prosecutor v. Ruto and Sang* (Decision on Victims' Representation and Participation) ICC-01/09-01/11 (3 October 2012))

In its recursive structure, the paragraph claims that the court's Registry will maintain a 'registration database' that will be used by the court's victim participation section to 'provide detailed statistics about the victims' population' to the Chamber, that will be supplied through a 'comprehensive report on the general situation of the victims as a whole, including registered and non-registered victims' (Decision on Victims' Representation and Participation 2012, para. 54). In this sense the practices associated with registering victims – producing a database and generating reports to the chambers – both individuates and massifies, collating data on individuals while simultaneously collapsing the distinction between 'registered and non-registered victims'.

As an archival technology, the practice of 'registering' victims serves more of an overtly demographic, biopolitical purpose than the victim participation form. An ICC staff member explained that the purpose of registration was 'to keep the details of the victims', adding, 'they need to have the information stored somewhere' (Interview with member of Victim Participation and Reparations Section, Nairobi, 2 July 2013). The relevant decision elaborates that this database will contain 'names, contact details as well as information as to the harm suffered', to be administered by the Registry and made available to the Common Legal Representative

(Decision on Victims' Representation and Participation 2012, para. 48). One legal representative for the Kenyan situation described this archive as 'useless' – 'probably some Excel file somewhere in the Registry' whose purpose was still not evident over a year and a half after the decision had been issued (Interview with Common Legal Representative, Nairobi, 29 January 2014). Yet if, as Annelise Riles contends, 'documents are paradigmatic artifacts of modern knowledge practices' (2006: 2) then the register as a phenomenon reveals what the court considers significant.

The victim registry operates archivally both as a practice and as a place – a practice of distilling identifying details and demographically significant facts and containing them in an electronic database, a closed archive accessible only to the court itself. The database would not be made available to humanitarian organisations, for example, and it was not clear whether it could be accessed by the court's affiliated Trust Fund for Victims, which carries out an assistance mandate empowered to provide medical care. It is a space outside judicial scrutiny where victim representatives 'validate' the authenticity of the archived details and determine which individuals might meet the legal criteria as victim participants.[7] Ultimately it is the space where individuated details are collapsed into a mass of largely inaccessible data. While granting that in some instances victims will be unable to register, perhaps because they 'may be subject to social pressure not to report the crimes they claim to have suffered or be afraid of intimidation or ostracism in the event that their registration becomes known in their community' (Decision on Victims' Representation and Participation 2012, para. 50), their views 'shall nevertheless be voiced, in a general way, through common legal representation' (Decision on Victims' Representation and Participation 2012, para. 51). Thus while the case is at trial, 'all victims, regardless of whether they have registered or not, will be represented through common legal representation' (Decision on Victims' Representation and Participation 2012, para. 52). All are contained within the victimary archive, irrespective of their particular desires.

The register thus harbours its own archival logic, entombing suffering through a set of disarticulated details that are then massified – 'a multiple body, a body with so many heads that, while they might not be infinite in number, cannot necessarily be counted' (Foucault 2003: 245). As a conduit of power, the register is directed at the level of conflict-affected populations, aggregating individual details into a body of information that can then be 'represented' and spoken for within a juridical frame. Following Derrida, it can be read as both a place from which order is given and a place where the memory of mass violence is contained. The claim to represent 'all victims'

---

7   The decision notes that 'registration does not imply any judicial determination of the status of the individual victims' (Decision on Victims' Representation and Participation 2012, para. 37).

is invoked to shore up the humanitarian aspirations of the court; in a nomological sense, as what institutes and conserves respect for law. Yet this power is not merely a sovereign power of deduction and seizure, of bestowing and withholding recognition, but also a biopolitical power that would foster life while simultaneously subjecting it to forms of regulation and control. This is perhaps most evident in the work of the ICC's affiliated Trust Fund for Victims, which is empowered to provide medical and livelihood support to populations falling within the court's temporal jurisdiction.

The emblematic wound

The Trust Fund for Victims was established through the court's founding statute as a complementary institution that would support programs to address harms arising from crimes under its jurisdiction. The Fund's two mandates include implementing reparations orders following convictions as well as providing 'victims and their families in situations under Court jurisdiction with physical rehabilitation, psychological rehabilitation, and/or material support' (Trust Fund 2004: 4). As one of its representatives recounted, 'we are like a donor' (Interview with Trust Fund for Victims representative for Uganda, Kampala, 25 October 2011): grants are given to 'partners' who agree to provide assistance within the court's jurisdictional parameters. In this sense the Trust Fund's work acts broadly, as with the register, restricted only by the situation rather than tied to specific cases and charges. Yet even here the court's in-country work classifies and divides populations. In Uganda, for example, where the conflict transpired over the course of two decades, only individuals who suffered harm since the ICC came into effect in 2002 can receive assistance.

In providing assistance to conflict-affected communities, the Trust Fund employs the discourse of 'targeting' to explain its logics of classification and categorisation. Its public reports explain that 'in some cases, assistance was targeted to specific categories of victims, such as victims of sexual violence or children and youth associated with armed forces. Elsewhere, assistance targets affected communities, such as villages victimised by pillage, massacre, and/or displacement' (Trust Fund 2014: 6). Despite the claim that its work is untethered from specific cases and charges, the Fund's practices of targeting appear to track the logics of international criminal law, with categories derived from recognisable crimes (the use of child soldiers, sexual violence, pillage, and displacement).

As ethnographic accounts of care provision have shown (Ticktin 2011; Fassin 2012), providing assistance is imbricated with forms of governance. ICC assistance operates according to biopolitical logics aimed at individual bodies as well as at the broader population (Foucault 1980: 139). For example, the Fund explains that the purpose of physical rehabilitation is 'to address the care and rehabilitation of those victims who have suffered physical injury, in order to recover and resume their roles as productive and contributing members of their societies' (Trust Fund 2014: 5). Individual narratives of Trust Fund beneficiaries emphasise their economic productivity and reintegration into their respective communities.[8] At the broader level of the population, the Fund supports 'savings and lending groups' to foster economic security and promote entrepreneurialism as well as 'community therapy sessions' to encourage community reconciliation. Care provision operates as a means of managing life, rendering populations more physically secure and economically productive.

The provision of medical assistance is the most overt instance of the court's biopolitical power to '"make" live and "let" die' (Foucault 2003: 241). As with other forms of assistance, medical assistance through Trust Fund support is channelled through targeting practices: victims of sexual violence are referred for surgical procedures, and amputees are provided with prosthetic limbs. A Trust Fund representative explained that the Fund tries to address people who have medical injuries that are 'emblematic of the conflict', such as burn victims and amputees (Interview with Trust Fund for Victims representative for Uganda, Kampala, 9 December 2011).

This choice of terms is revealing: conflict-related suffering in its plurality of forms is narrowed to the emblematic wound, the violence inscribed on the body that archives a conflict's history as it intersects with juridical logics. If the victimary archive divides, classifies, individuates and massifies, recognises and refuses recognition, treats and denies treatment, then its efforts to provide an authoritative account of suffering are unsettled through confrontations with individuals whose suffering falls outside its categories or those who refuse its form of redress.

Such unsettling does not necessarily happen through the terms of the victimary archive, with its attendant truth-claims and desire for jurisdictional precision. For example, a narrative of the Trust Fund's biopolitics, told by one of its implementing partners, already reveals the tenuous nature of the ICC's claims to redress. Whether it can be verified or not – thus apocryphal, neither demonstrably true nor false – it shows how the promise of international criminal law's restorative turn may be untenable. The story was told by a young Ugandan activist from the north of the country, who had grown up in an internally displaced persons camp. His organisation's task was to 'mobilise' individuals needing care; assisting with identifying them and helping to transport them to medical facilities. This man described a patient mobilisation that took place in 2009 in Pader, northern Uganda, paraphrased here from fieldnote inscriptions:

---

8   For example, the Fund's annual report recounts the case of 'Mary' from northern Uganda, who 'became actively involved in economically-productive activities' following Trust Fund-supported counselling (Trust Fund 2014: 32).

They had mobilised people to screen for possible care. There was a man who could not stand. He had been caught by Lord's Resistance Army rebels and was abducted. At the time he had been wearing gumboots and did not realise that they were army gumboots. The rebels accused him of being a soldier, tied him up, and filled his boots with hot charcoal. His feet and legs were badly burned, with wounds to the bone that were still open. The team of surgeons there for the screening said they were only treating plastic surgery cases such as burns, and not orthopedic cases as this injury would require.

(Interview with staff member of non-governmental organisation, Kampala, 1 November 2011).

The Trust Fund partner claimed that he had explained the situation to the Trust Fund representative, who said it was not a plastic surgery case and therefore did not fall within the terms of this particular treatment. When the partner returned three weeks later, he discovered that the man was dead.

The desire to document injustice within the terms of law bears its own limitations. What the Trust Fund partner had claimed could not be verified – in a later interview the country representative would not address specific cases, but spoke instead of injuries that are 'emblematic of the conflict' and invoked institutional categories. The terms of the two narratives appeared incommensurable – one impassioned and specific, the other cautious and general. The unsettled nature of the former contrasts with the desire for certainty of the latter: the former account was given over two years after the relevant events to an outside party with limited ability to verify its truthfulness, countering the epistemological claims to archived 'facts' that would document the conflict in an authoritative way. In this sense, efforts to contest the court's archive of suffering and to reveal its remainders may not be recognisable within the terms of the authoritative framework that the court relies upon.

Archival contestations

Contesting the authority of the court's victimary archive also challenges the juridical hold on memory and redress, and with it, the terms of response to mass violence. As the domain of law expands, with an attendant 'tribunalization of violence' (Clarke 2009: 45), the turn to legal institutions as spaces of redress becomes increasingly naturalised. The violence of conflict is framed as a violation of rights, and legal discourse proliferates in the locations where the court intervenes. In the eastern Democratic Republic of Congo, for example, a Trust Fund implementing partner taught community members about 'different texts protecting the rights of women (Rome Statute, Protocol on the Statute of the African Court of Justice and Human Rights, etc.) and how to identify violations of those rights' (Trust

Fund 2014: 24). Although knowledge of rights alone does not carry talismanic value, the proliferation of rights and accountability discourse in post-conflict settings is regarded as a form of assistance, which also extends the reach of legal institutions as spaces of redress.

The court's archival practices direct the terms and techniques through which institutional recognition can be sought, and, once engaged, they bring their own temporalities to bear that are bound up with juridical time. The time in which law carries out its work remains indifferent to embodied experiences of suffering and loss. For this reason the Trust Fund claims that its support 'is not linked to a conviction, but key to helping repair the harm that victims have suffered, by providing assistance to victims in a timelier manner than may be allowed by the judicial process' (Trust Fund 2014: 4). Yet even this attempt to break from the slow time of law, with its dialectical patterns of filings and responses, is constrained by the terms of the institution to which the Fund is tied. Assistance projects require judicial approval to ensure that they do not 'predetermine any legal issue before the Court or hinder the rights of the accused' (ibid.: 35); this also entails responses from the parties before a 'portfolio' of assistance is approved.[9] The Kenyan situation has been the site of ongoing deferral: despite claims that representatives would carry out an assessment in 2012 (Interview with Trust Fund for Victims representative for Uganda, Kampala, 25 October 2011, Kampala) it has been delayed by three years and will then require vetting and judicial approval. The Fund's 'timelier manner' of providing assistance can thus remain perpetually over the horizon.

The deferrals and remainders produced through the restorative turn in international criminal law is partly a product of the recursive logic of institutionalisation. Ethnographic accounts of institutional knowledge-production and practices have noted how technologies of representation are developed internally that then shape and colonise how we come to perceive appropriate responses, re-inscribing the authority of the institution: 'Institutions systematically direct individual memory and channel our perceptions into forms compatible with the relations they authorize' (Douglas 1986: 92). Observing a development aid project, Richard Rottenburg contends that the organisational structures through which it is carried out are detached from social and political contexts, 'an issue of representing reality through technologies of inscription and organizational procedures that have been detached from other subsystems of society in such a way that they cannot be

---

9   Trust Fund activities for the Democratic Republic of Congo do not have a physical rehabilitation mandate because it was not originally requested from the chamber. To alter this would require approaching the chamber, which would then have 45 days to decide on the proposal, and observations would need to be made by all parties (Interview with Trust Fund for Victims representative for the Democratic Republic of Congo, Kampala, 12 July 2012).

subjected, for instance, to social, political, or economic criteria' (Rottenburg 2009: xxiii). The autopoietic tendency of law and its attendant institutions pose similar problems. The system takes on a life of its own, decontextualised and self-sustaining, and the interests of those most affected by its work – including potential court-recognised victims – are overshadowed by institutional and discursive self-perpetuation.

Law's desire for certainty and enclosure is unsettled by political and contingent acts of countering the ICC's victimary archive. Resisting efforts to emplace (victims) in an archive, such practices are reactions to the impulse to contain and to create an authoritative institutional narrative. Countering the archive is not only reactionary: it also contests the massified production of the abstract victim by a return to the concrete particularity of individuals. In June of 2013, ninety-three individuals connected to the Kenyan situation submitted a letter to the court requesting that their names be 'removed from the list of victims'.[10] Contending that 'we are no longer confident that the process which is going on at the court is beneficial to our interests', the letter provides an account of unchosen legal representation, impersonal treatment from the court, the use of victims as conduits for prosecutorial case-building, and the court's failure to guarantee individual compensation. The letter claims that its signatories had indicated the name of the lawyer that they wanted to represent them in their application forms, as the forms provide a space for listing a lawyer and contact details. In spite of this, and despite writing directly to the court, the ICC had appointed other lawyers to act on their behalf.

As an artefact, the letter provides a contrasting narrative to the ICC's authoritative claims about victim representation. Most strikingly, it bears the names, identification numbers, and signatures of all of the individuals. Unlike their anonymity within the victimary archive, they individuate themselves and declare their identities to the public, with the signatures on the letter acting as counter-inscriptions to their signatures on the victim participation forms. As with the story of the Trust Fund told above, the validity of the claims cannot be clearly established. The legal representative had to work through the list of signatures to determine whether they were court-recognised victims of the case (with participatory rights) or of the situation (and therefore only 'registered'). He also was required to consult with each individual to ensure that they had consented to withdraw; there was some suspicion that the mass withdrawal may have been

---

10 Letter to the Victims and Witness Office from the Chairman, Amani Peace Building and Welfare Organisation, 5 June 2013, on file with author. For an official account of the letter, see *Prosecutor v. Ruto and Sang* (Common Legal Representatives for Victims Comprehensive Report on the Withdrawal of Victims from the Turbo Area by Letter dated 5 June 2013) ICC-01/09-01/11 (5 September 2013).

driven by Kenyan political actors as an effort to weaken the court.[11]

Although the motivations behind this act of contestation and refusal can be read in multiple ways, including as a product of regional politics in the wake of the 2013 election that brought individuals accused before the ICC to power, the letter's signatories disrupt the court's authoritative claims to represent their interests. The letter offers a counter-narrative of misrecognition and neglect, and articulates a different conception of redress from that on offer at the ICC. The letter states that its signatories 'went to the high court in Nairobi and petitioned the Kenyan government for compensation. We hold the Kenyan government responsible and not individuals. … Our peaceful co-existence as communities is of much more importance than the prosecution of people we did not even complain against'. Contending that responsibility for having failed to protect the Kenyan population from violence following the disputed 2007 election lies with the Kenyan state, the letter questions the authority of the ICC, as a transnational actor, in carrying out individual prosecutions against select individuals on behalf of the Kenyan people. It prioritises reconciliation over accountability, contesting a fundamental premise of the court's work and the broader *raison d'être* of the field of international criminal law.

Archival remains

The sites and artifacts considered here – the form, the register, the emblematic wound, the apocryphal narrative, the letter of withdrawal – offer openings for critical reflection on the claims of international criminal law as a space for redressing suffering. As the material sites through which international criminal law's archive of victimhood is produced and contained, the form and the register can be read as inscription technologies through which victimary identity is bestowed and withheld. Forming part of a broader process of categorisation and evaluation that travels through juridical channels, participation forms and registers first individualise before massifying (Foucault 2003), producing an abstract victimhood to be represented and, by extension, to legitimate the institution as a site of redress. The concept of the emblematic wound serves a similar role of classification, arranging suffering on a spectrum of proximity to what is considered most 'emblematic of the conflict', where

---

11 One of the ICC indictees was William Ruto, a popular politician from the North Rift, where the individuals were based. He had become Deputy President of Kenya following the March 2013 elections. An Eldoret-based 'intermediary' claimed that a government agent was attempting to persuade victims to withdraw from the ICC process. 'Civil Society Consultative Meeting', Nairobi, 28 June 2013, author's notes. For an account of the relationship between the ICC intervention in Kenya and the domestic political context, see Kendall (2014).

individual bodies are assessed based upon which kinds of wounds are considered treatment priorities.

As objects of critique, the form and the register reveal the precarity of juridified victimhood. Through addressing the individual applicant as 'the victim' and asking about losses and desired forms of redress, the form suggests a responsiveness to its addressee that is constrained in practice by its subjection to juridical time and court decisions. When charges are dropped against an accused person or indictments are altered, this carries implications for court-recognised victims. A case victim with participatory rights may be re-categorised as a victim of the broader situation when her nexus to a charged crime is lost, leaving her in a similar position as individuals whose data are 'registered' in line with the Kenyan decision. For its part, the register appears to serve more demographic purposes, enabling the court to chart a conflict as it was inscribed across the body of a population. The stories of conflict-affected individuals are disarticulated into pieces of data to be filed and perhaps forgotten, particularly in the archive produced through the Kenyan register.

Countering the victimary archive unsettles the binarism on which it depends: between qualified and unqualified victims, case and situation victims, and, less rigidly, wounds that are considered to be 'emblematic' and those that are not. Such distinctions are of great significance for the work of law, in the sense that law is that which 'cuts' into justice, rendering it calculable and determinate (Derrida 1990; Fitzpatrick 2001). Yet from outside the legal frame, from the standpoint of conflict-affected communities, these determinations fail to adequately grasp the contours of embodied suffering and to recognise individuals in their concrete singularity. In this way the apocryphal story of 'letting die' reintroduces the individual person, irreducible to the wound as a site of screening and treatment. It illustrates the perils of engaging institutions constrained by juridical categories in the practice of providing medical assistance.

Such narratives remind us that wounds are not reducible to representational emblems standing for something else – the iconic atrocities of a particular conflict – but rather embodied and material threats to lives requiring care. The limitations posed by screening and determining treatment priorities are not unique to the ICC's Trust Fund; as Alex de Waal observes, humanitarian care provision in general entails forms of cruelty when workers are placed in the inescapable position of needing to turn people away (de Waal 2010). Yet linking humanitarian care to juridical categories produces more severe and intractable limitations than other institutions providing medical assistance would face. As a Trust Fund representative observed, 'we are not a humanitarian body': beneficiaries receive assistance as a product of a harm suffered, not as a response to a need (Interview with Trust Fund for Victims representative for the Democratic Republic of Congo, Kampala, 12 July 2012).

The figure of the emblematic wound appears as the counterpart to the spectacular crime upon which the field of international criminal law depends. Both circulate in the court's symbolic economy (Clarke 2011), but with one always subordinated to the other: the wound is subordinated to the crime, and the victim to the criminal in a field originating from punitive desire. The account of the untreated individual offers a contrasting narrative to what is often told by court proponents: that victims turn to the ICC as a way of restoring dignity and alleviating suffering. This story unsettles the victimary archive by revealing its limits, which are especially pronounced when it comes to stretching a field oriented around judgment and punishment, centred on the crime and the criminal, toward restorative ends, where the figure of the victim enters the frame.

Similarly, the letter offers a counterpoint to what court proponents would claim. As a counter-archival inscription, it contests the court's claim as the proper site of redress, arguing instead that the state should provide them with compensation. Withdrawing in protest, the letter's signatories refuse the terms of victimhood in which they had been cast, where they were unable to choose who would represent their interests and where they disagreed with the course the prosecution had taken. Through the performative inscription of a signature, these individuals emerge from out of the anonymity of the victimary archive to assert themselves as political actors, refusing the form of justice carried out in their name. They also sever their ties to particular individuals charged with crimes, which was a condition of possibility of their recognition as case victims, maintaining instead that the Kenyan government should be considered responsible for their suffering. Claiming that 'Kenyans had reconciled', the signatories designate themselves as members of communities seeking 'peaceful co-existence' rather than prosecutions.

The emplaced materiality of the archive, with its inscription practices – the form and the register – and its restricted account of suffering marked by the emblematic crime, narrow the field of what international criminal law can recognise in the aftermath of mass violence. Loosening its hold requires a broader critique, calling into question how victimhood itself is conceived at this site and through its terms. A critique along these lines might draw upon François Laruelle's observation that victimhood may be regarded as a condition of generic being, common to humanity, as a means of refusing classification schemes and the hierarchies they produce, as well as countering the appropriation of the figure of the victim by others to serve their own purposes (Laruelle 2012).[12] Here victimhood has meaning

---

12 Laruelle is particularly concerned about claims to represent the victim by *engagé* intellectuals: 'The engaged intellectual. ... must restore harmony to the two poles which occupy him, power and the victim, by subjecting the whole thing to a Principle of Intellectual Reason, an Idea or Ideal to which he aspires and which guides or legitimates

because it is grounded in an individual's concrete particularity and experience, and not as a transcendent concept to be deployed toward other ends, such as the 'bad conscience' of those who speak on their behalf (Laruelle 2015). This point of departure also works to contest the figure of the abstract victim imagined as the beneficiary and *raison d'être* of the International Criminal Court. It may be that victimhood as a legal category must be rethought more fundamentally, as the logics of categorising beings derived from a juridical frame produce as many remainders as they provide redress.

References

Arbia, S. 2012, Registrar to the 11th session of the Assembly of States Parties, The Hague, 14 November.

Bear, L. 2007, *Lines of the Nation: Indian Railway Workers, Bureaucracy, and the Intimate Historical Self*, Columbia University Press, New York.

Bourdieu, P. 1991, *Language and Symbolic Power*, Harvard University Press, Cambridge.

Cassese, A. 1999, 'The Statute of the International Criminal Court: Some Preliminary Reflections', *European Journal of International Law*, vol. 10, pp. 144–171.

Clarke, K. 2009, *Fictions of Justice: the International Criminal Court and the Challenge of Legal Pluralism in Sub-Saharan Africa*, Cambridge University Press, Cambridge.

Clarke, K. 2011, 'The Rule of Law through its Economies of Appearances: the Making of the African Warlord', *Indiana Journal of Global Legal Studies*, vol. 18, no. 1, pp. 7–40.

Derrida, J. 1982, *Margins of Philosophy*, University of Chicago Press, Chicago.

Derrida, J. 1990, 'Force of Law: the "Mystical Foundation of Authority"', *Cardozo Law Review*, vol. 11, pp. 919–1046.

Derrida, J. 1995, *Archive Fever: A Freudian Impression*, University of Chicago Press, Chicago.

Derrida, J. 2002, 'Archive Fever in South Africa', in C. Hamilton, V. Harris and G. Reid (eds), *Refiguring the Archive*, Kluwer, Dordrecht.

De Waal, A. 2010, 'The Humanitarians' Tragedy: Escapable and Inescapable Cruelties', *Disasters*, vol. 34, pp. 130–137.

Donat-Cattin, D. 2008, 'Article 68: Protection of Victims and Witnesses and Their Participation in the Proceedings', in O. Triffterer (ed.), *Commentary on the Rome Statute of the International Criminal Court: Observers' Notes, Article by Article*, 2nd edn, Hart Publishing, Oxford.

his action.' (2015: 52). The same might be said of court proponents, who invoke victims not as ends in themselves but as means toward their own objectives. Here the proper orientation is one of compassion, of shared suffering, rather than of pity: 'As much as pity is a theologically dominated sentiment derived from piety and its interiority, which is linked to an exteriority, so compassion appeals to lived passivity, being felt, with a minimum of representation, from one individual to the next.' (ibid.: 46).

Douglas, M. 1986, *How Institutions Think*, University Press Syracuse, Syracuse.

Fassin, D. 2012, *Humanitarian Reason: A Moral History of the Present*, University of California Press, Berkeley.

Fitzpatrick, P. 2001, *Modernism and the Grounds of Law*, Cambridge University Press, Cambridge.

Fletcher, L. 2015, 'Refracted Justice: The Imagined Victim and the International Criminal Court,' in C. De Vos, S. Kendall and C. Stahn (eds), *Contested Justice: The Politics and Practice of International Criminal Court Interventions*, Cambridge University Press, Cambridge.

Foucault, M. 1980, *The History of Sexuality, Vol. 1: An Introduction*, Vintage Books, New York.

Foucault, M. 2002, *The Archaeology of Knowledge*, Routledge, London.

Foucault, M. 2003, *Society Must be Defended: Lectures at the Collège de France, 1975–76*, Picador, New York.

International Criminal Court, *Rules of Procedure and Evidence*, Adopted by the Assembly of States Parties, First Session, New York, 3–10 September 2002, ICC-ASP/1/3.

International Criminal Court, Rome Statute of the International Criminal Court, entry into force 1 July 2002.

International Criminal Court, *Victims Before the International Criminal Court: A Guide for the Participation of Victims in the Proceedings of the Court*, viewed 15 September 2014, <www.icc-cpi.int/en_menus/icc/structure%20of%20the%20court/victims/participation/Pages/booklet.aspx>.

Jorda, C. and de Hemptinne, J. 2002, 'The Status and Role of the Victim', in A. Cassese, P. Gaeta and J. Jones (eds), *The Rome Statute of the ICC: A Commentary*, Oxford University Press, Oxford.

Kendall, S. 2014, '"Uhuruto" and Other Leviathans: the International Criminal Court and the Kenyan Political Order', *African Journal of Legal Studies*, vol. 7, no. 3, pp. 399–427.

Kendall, S. and Nouwen, S. 2014, 'Representational Practices at the International Criminal Court: The Gap between Juridified and Abstract Victimhood', *Law and Contemporary Problems*, vol. 76, no. 3–4, pp. 235–262.

Laruelle, F. 2012, *Théorie générale des victimes*, Mille et une Nuits, Paris.

Laruelle, F. 2015, *General Theory of Victims*, Polity Press, Cambridge.

Miller, P. and Rose, N. 2008, *Governing the Present: Administering Economic, Social and Personal Life*, Polity Press, Cambridge.

Mbembe, A. 2002, 'The Power of the Archive and its Limits', in C. Hamilton, V. Harris and G. Reid (eds), *Refiguring the Archive*, Kluwer, Dordrecht.

Orie, A. 2002, 'Accusatorial vs. Inquisitorial Approach in International Criminal Proceedings Prior to the Establishment of the ICC and in the Proceedings Before the ICC', in A. Cassese, P. Gaeta and J. Jones (eds), *The Rome Statute of the ICC: A Commentary*, Oxford University Press, Oxford.

Riles, A. 2006, 'Introduction: In Response', in A. Riles (ed.), *Artifacts of Modern Knowledge*, University of Michigan Press, Ann Arbor.

Rottenburg, R. 2009, *Far Fetched Facts: A Parable of Development Aid*, The MIT Press, Cambridge.

Stoler, A. 2009, *Along the Archival Grain: Epistemic Anxieties and Colonial Common Sense*, Princeton University Press, Princeton.

Ticktin, M. 2011, *Casualties of Care: Immigration and the Politics of Humanitarianism in France*, University of California Press, Berkeley.

The Trust Fund for Victims/Fonds au Profit des Victimes 2004, *Programme Progress Report*, Summer 2014.

Victims Rights Working Group, 2012, *Statement presented at the 11th Assembly of States Parties*, 15 November, The Hague, <www.icc-cpi.int/iccdocs/asp_docs/ASP11/GenDeba/ICC-ASP11-GenDeba-VRWG-ENG.pdf>.

Chapter 9

The conspiracy archive
Turkey's 'deep state' on trial

Başak Ertür

The phrase 'deep state' in Turkish popular parlance refers to powers operating with impunity through and beyond the official state structure.[1] It is considered to be a state within the state, a network of illegitimate alliances crisscrossing the military, the police force, the bureaucracy, the political establishment, the intelligence agency, mafia organisations and beyond; lurking menacingly behind the innumerable assassinations, disappearances, provocations, death threats, disinformation campaigns, psychological operations, and dirty deals of the past several decades. The currency of such a phrase points to a public consensus around the existence of non-democratic leadership, state-sponsored extralegal activities, state protection and perpetuation of particular forms of political violence, and more generally corruption within state institutions. Recently, a number of criminal trials brought the deep state into Turkey's courtrooms. My focus in this chapter is on the most famous of these, the so-called Ergenekon trial. I offer a reading of the Ergenekon case file as comprising an archive of the Turkish deep state, not because it successfully captures its history and facticity, but rather because it allows insight into the rationalities and passionate investments that culminate in the reification of the deep state. Two concerns guide my inquiry here: the problem of producing knowledge about the deep state, and the performative production of the state in trials involving state crimes. These two issues are inevitably related, since ways of knowing the political are intimately tied to ways of reifying it (Abrams 1988). In Pierre Bourdieu's words, the state 'thinks itself through those who attempt to think it' (1994: 1). The case file in the Ergenekon trial has its own way of conjuring the state, in a bizarre amalgam of fact, fiction, fantasy, desire and disavowal – an amalgam best understood,

---

1   Similar terms are in use elsewhere. I understand that 'para-state' signifies comparable structures of non-transparency in Greece. Since Hosni Mubarak's fall in February 2011, and more frequently since the military coup of July 2013, English language reports have been referring to Egypt's 'deep state'. Occasional references to Russia's 'deep state' are also found in political analyses and commentaries.

I argue, in terms of the conspiratorial imagination. I conclude the chapter with a consideration of a way of knowing the deep state beyond the limits of legal and conspiratorial imagination, an articulation that mobilises the legal archive for a counter-conspiracy against the conspiring case files.

Ergenekon is a sprawling criminal process that began in June 2007 with the police discovery of a cache of hand-grenades in a residential building in Istanbul. The investigation expanded in numerous directions to include coup plots, bomb attacks, assassination plans, further secret arms caches and the like. The first hearing of the first Ergenekon trial began in October 2008 with 86 defendants. By the time the verdict was passed in August 2013, twenty-three other indictments had been integrated into this trial, raising the total number of defendants to 275.[2] The defendants included retired and active senior and junior military officials, police chiefs, civil leaders, ultranationalist militants, politicians, bureaucrats, journalists, writers, academics, lawyers, businessmen, mafia bosses and small-time gangsters. Only twenty-one defendants were acquitted in the August 2013 verdict, and most of the others were convicted on charges relating to leadership of, membership in, or aiding an armed terrorist organisation, referred to in the main indictment as the 'Ergenekon Terrorist Organisation' (ETO). Ostensibly, this is Turkey's deep state trial, purporting to purge patterns of corruption and illegality within the state. The prosecutors in the indictments, as well as the judges in the verdict, claim that the ETO is synonymous with what has come to be known as the deep state.

An occasion for countless conspiracy theories in its obscurity, the notion of the deep state and the kind of activities and alliances that it refers to have to be understood against the background of Turkey's extended history of military tutelage (Söyler 2013), its military coup tradition (Ünver 2009) and the special privileges of unaccountability and impunity that the army has enjoyed throughout the republic's history, up until very recently.[3] Against this background of military tutelage, historians, investigative journalists and commentators attempting to get a more credible hold on this nebulous concept tend to focus on state institutions that are considered to

---

2   At the time of writing, the trial is still at the appeals stage and there will likely be a retrial.
3   Arguably, the second term of the current Justice and Development Party (AKP) government have witnessed the consolidation of an appearance of representative democracy, owing to a series of 'purges' (including the Ergenekon trial itself) aimed at tackling military tutelage, which in turn is often understood to be the sole source of the wide range of phenomena evoked with the phrase 'deep state'. And yet, as I propose in this chapter, the deep state should be understood not as a field of measurable deviance, the gradual elimination of which will lead to democratisation (as argued, for example, by Söyler 2013), but rather as a particular amalgam of governmental rationality and fantasy that perpetuates a state tradition. Unlike various analyses that focus on the military as the one and only source of the problem of the deep state, this approach is able to address the recent episodes in Turkish politics whereby the phantom of 'the state within the state' continues to hover in new guises.

be conducive, due to their structural non-transparency, to the continuation and prospering of such activities and alliances. Focusing on institutions rendered unaccountable by design yields a relatively long history of the Turkish deep state, stretching beyond the republican era to the Ottoman Teşkilat-ı Mahsusa ('Special Organisation'), an early type of unconventional warfare organisation considered by historians as the key operational structure behind the 1915 Armenian Genocide. Later, an important locus of deep state activity from the early 1950s onwards is identified as the NATO-related Özel Harp Dairesi (ÖHD; 'Special Warfare Department'). Designed to build an infrastructure of civilian-military mobilisation against a possible Soviet occupation like other NATO stay-behind units in Europe, ÖHD was later revealed to have been behind the 1955 Istanbul pogrom primarily directed at the city's Greek minority. In the 1970s ÖHD was implicated in assassinations of communist intellectuals and young activists on the left, among other deeds. In the early 1990s, as the war against the insurgent Partiya Karkerên Kurdistan (PKK; 'Kurdistan Workers' Party') was intensified, ÖHD was restructured into Özel Kuvvetler Komutanlığı ('Special Forces Command'). Another key unit that emerged at this time, and was virtually synonymous with the deep state for a while, is known as JITEM, an acronym for 'Gendarmerie Intelligence and Counterterrorism Group Command' in Turkish. Although it was officially disavowed for many years, and said to have never existed, testimonies implicate JITEM in the majority of the thousands of disappearances and extrajudicial executions that peaked during the 1990s, primarily targeting Kurds, as well as in illegal arms trading and drug trafficking in the Kurdish regions.

While the style and structure of deep state plots render them easily recognisable to a public that has become all too familiar with them, such familiarity does not alleviate the epistemological problem concerning the deep state. Official secrets, denials, cover-ups, suppression or outright elimination of witnesses or researchers, psych-ops, and barrages of misinformation all weave a web of opacity, casting the deep state as a wilderness of mirrors, and endless fodder for conspiracy theories. After all, conspiracy theories may be seen as so many attempts 'to give form to, and thus exercise a certain amount of control over, a fearful, ghostly reality of violence' (Aretxaga 2005: 197). There was, however, a key moment in the mid-1990s, at the height of the war against the PKK, when a justification offered itself up for a wide array of suspicions, briefly illuminating the murky depths of the Turkish state in a flash of lightning. It took the form of a car accident. On 4 November 1996, a speeding Mercedes crashed into a lorry in the town of Susurluk. The passengers in the car included Sedat Bucak, parliamentarian and the leader of a Kurdish clan in close cooperation with the Turkish authorities in the war against the PKK, providing about 2,000 of the notorious paramilitary 'village guards'. Then there was Hüseyin Kocadağ, the director of the Istanbul Police Academy and former

180 Başak Ertür

Deputy Police Chief of Istanbul. A third passenger was Abdullah Çatlı, who was wanted by not only the Turkish police for alleged participation in the massacre of seven members of the Turkish Labour Party in 1978,[4] but also by Interpol for his 1982 escape from a Swiss prison where he had been held on drug smuggling charges. Of this unholy trinity of warlord parliamentarian, police chief and nationalist mafia boss, only the first survived, and he claimed a complete loss of memory. At the time of the accident, the mafia boss Çatlı was found to be carrying diplomatic passports and a licence to carry weapons, the latter bearing the original authorisation signature of Mehmet Ağar, the then Minister of Interior. This alone crystallised something of the essence of what the phrase 'deep state' tries to communicate: the documents had been forged, but the signatures were authentic. Fourteen individuals linked to the so-called 'Susurluk gang' were tried on charges of organised crime, though efforts to bring to light the entire set of connections and culpabilities failed spectacularly. The trial came to a conclusion in 2001, neither addressing the full range of implications, nor satisfactorily ensuring prosecution.

According to its prosecutors and judges, the Ergenekon trial picks up where the Susurluk process left off. The claim is seemingly corroborated by the incorporation of some key figures from the Susurluk process into the Ergenekon trial as defendants. The first indictment in the Ergenekon trial provides its own definition and history of the Turkish deep state. It claims that the deep state is 'a key obstacle to Turkey securing the Rule of Law', having been 'active for many years in the country' as 'the dark force behind countless actions', involved in mafia and acts of terror, such as 'unknown assailant killings of intellectuals' (*Ergenekon Case*, First Indictment 2008: 46–47). It further suggests that the Susurluk investigation shed some light on the ETO, but could not be deepened sufficiently due to the organisation's influence and power at the time (ibid.). Both the indictment and the judgment provide partial and extremely vague histories of the deep state with references to ÖHD. They refer to the purge of NATO-related paramilitary organisations in the early 1990s in other European countries, especially highlighting Italy's *Mani plute* operation. The prosecutors and the judges thus present the Ergenekon trial as the belated Turkish counterpart to these Europe-wide clean-up operations.

While the Ergenekon case file merely gestures towards it, the global historical context is indeed quite key in understanding the covert and extralegal functions of the Turkish state over the past several decades. On the one hand, the period we can identify as the ÖHD/NATO stretch (1953–1991) cannot be divorced from the general context of the Cold War

---

4   At the time of the massacre, Abdullah Çatlı was a member of Grey Wolves, the ultranationalist youth organisation that was allegedly recruited by the ÖHD as its 'civilian elements' in acts of political violence targeting communists.

and similar extralegal formations in other European countries (Ganser 2005). Turkey's 1980 coup d'état finds its precursors in the Southern Cone coups of the mid-1970s (Klein 2007) in terms of its economic and political rationales and objectives (Ahmad 1981). Likewise, the extralegal methods utilised by the Turkish state during the so-called 'low-intensity warfare' against the Kurdish insurgency are comparable to state-sponsored terror that goes under the guise of anti-terror measures across the world: Britain's deployment of the Military Reaction Force against the IRA in the early 1970s (*Britain's Secret Terror Force* 2013); Spain's grotesque tactics in the Basque conflict (Aretxaga 2000); Argentina's 'dirty war' (Suárez-Orozco 1992); state-sponsored terror in Guatemala (Afflitto 2000) and so on.

Although institutional histories of the deep state are important in revealing what kind of bureaucratic structures allow the monopoly of violence to be distributed beyond the bureaucracy, they also risk a misconception of the deep state as solely a unit within the state, a hub of extralegality within a larger context of constitutional operation, a rotten spot that can be carved out and discarded, isolated and thus easily purged. Indeed, in the aftermath of the Susurluk accident, one of the points that the more theoretical approaches insisted on was precisely that the deep state *is* the state. The editorial preface for the critical journal *Birikim*'s 1997 special issue on 'the state in Turkey [Türkiye'de Devlet]' suggested that the *état de droit* and the deep state are like the solid and liquid forms of the same matter' (Anon 1997: 16). In the same issue, Ömer Laçiner described the deep state as not so much a special unit within the state system, which carries out and commissions criminal activities and conducts secret operations, but rather institutions and establishments that operate on the basis of the understanding that the state will inevitably engage in such activities (1997: 18). Tanıl Bora advocated for a technical rather than moralising terminology to refer to the kind of operations exposed in the Susurluk accident, because

> although such activities are indeed 'dark', 'dirty' and 'horrific', they are activities that are part of the nature of the modern state apparatus – therefore they are normal. In the case of our particular nation-state these natural organs are especially well developed.
>
> (Bora 1997: 53)

The governmental rationality operative in these types of activities can be identified very generally in terms of *raison d'état*, whereby the legitimacy of a state's activities is solely grounded in the preservation and perpetuation of the state itself. The self-referential legitimation means that according to this rationality a state's activities should not be subject to any external law – positive, natural, moral, nor divine (Foucault 2007). In Michel Foucault's account, the relationship between *raison d'état* and the sphere of legality is one that is determined according to the convenience of the former. The field of legality is never a proper external limitation to *raison d'état*, but rather always already accessorial – overridden and suspended if need be.[5] Admittedly, in doctrine, the two concepts of *raison d'état* and the rule of law seem to be diametrically opposed as bases of governmental legitimacy. This opposition is particularly pronounced in the genealogies of the two concepts.[6] In its inception, the idea of the rule of law is understood as an attempt to impose external limitations on *raison d'état* by recourse to law, namely 'juridical reflection, legal rules, and legal authority' (Foucault 2008: 9). However, the history of the relationship between *raison d'état* and the rule of law may be more complicated than the doctrinal origins suggest.[7] Reflecting on the co-existence of and the tension between *raison d'état* and the rule of law, Turkish legal scholar Mithat Sancar suggests that the two doctrines are not as incommensurable as they may seem (1997, 2000). Sancar identifies the different ways in which a combination of the two can be brought about: in a normativist interpretation of the rule of law, *raison d'état* can be incorporated into legal norms (1997: 84). In an approach that may be referred to as the '*raison de l'état de droit*', *raison d'état* can be rendered the organising principle of the constitution (Sancar 1997: 84). Sancar further proposes that the entire history of the bourgeois constitutional state can be read as the history of its marriage to the doctrine of *raison d'état* (1997: 85). While opposition is weak and the system has confidence in itself, the rule of law can be foregrounded. But in times of crisis

---

5   Notably, Foucault identifies the *coup d'état* as the epitome of the absolute priority of *raison d'état* vis-à-vis the field of legality. In the *coup d'état*, *raison d'état* asserts itself unequivocally. The *coup d'état* is 'the self-manifestation of the state' (2007: 262). It is interesting to consider in this light of the analysis one often finds in Turkish political literature to the effect that the country's relatively frequent *coups* are precisely moments when the deep state and the state become one.

6   Foucault notes that the idea of *Rechtsstaat* (the rule of law) was developed in the eighteenth century in Germany very much in opposition to *Polizeistaat* (the police state), which in turn was 'the form taken by a governmental technology dominated by the principle of *raison d'état*' (2007: 318). Danilo Zolo's broader perspective arrives at a similar conclusion, comparing the different historical experiences that led to the formulation of the analogous concepts of the Rule of Law in Great Britain and North America, *Rechtsstaat* in Germany, and *état de droit* in France (Zolo 2007).

7   This complication can also be traced, albeit somewhat circuitously, in Foucault's genealogy of governmental rationalities (2007). While the emergence of the rule of law doctrine is intimately bound with the attempt to propose an external limitation on *raison d'état*, its proper appropriation within a governmental rationality occurs with liberalism, and only as a principle of internal limitation, that is, solely to do with formal interventions in the economic order. In other words, in liberalism, the rule of law is not an end in itself, but a principle defining the scope of legal interventions by the state in the economy. This shift from external limitation to internal rule regulation can be understood to take the rule of law out of an axis of opposition to *raison d'état*.

or a substantial opposition, a variety of methods can be employed to render *raison d'état* operative (Sancar 1997: 85).[8]

The ultimate instability of the opposition between *raison d'état* and the rule of law creates complications for legal processes like the Ergenekon trial. The rule of law is idealised in liberal democracies as the sole basis and legitimacy of political decisions, whereas the extralegal activities of a state stem from certain political decisions that operate beyond the sphere of legality and override the rule of law. The criminal prosecution of such activities is usually meant to subject the entire affair to the rule of law. In transitional justice settings or in trials that involve a jurisdictional remove, this dynamic can be stage-managed to maximal effect as a grand 'return' to the rule of law. Both scenarios allow at least the appearance of a conflict between the prosecuting authorities and the defence concerning what a state's relation to legality ought to be. Thus in a felicitous prosecution in either type of scenario, the trial may serve to performatively enact the very rule of law to which it purports to submit. However, in the absence of either a transitional framework or jurisdictional remove that allows for a high enough definition of the line that separates the prosecutors and the prosecuted, we have a particularly complex political trial scenario. When state crimes come before the law of the very state suspected of criminal activity, the state becomes both the law and its transgression (Aretxaga 2000: 60). In trials involving the public prosecution of a state's own crimes, this blurring of the prosecution, the defence, and the court as arbitrator produces a surplus of meaning that cannot be easily managed.

In the Ergenekon trial, this surplus is evident already in the criminal legal framing of the matter: the object of prosecution, the deep state, translates into criminal legal perception as a 'terrorist/criminal organisation'. In turn, the alleged crimes of the deep state translate into 'crimes against the state'. The former designation recasts the ghostly agency of the deep state in terms of a wilful aggregation and cooperation of individuals, who can be held liable collectively and separately. The latter designation does two things at once: it indemnifies the state as perpetrator, and relegates it to the status of injured party. Beyond the structural failures of the criminal legal imagination (Sabuktay 2010), a more significant way in which the unmanageable surplus emerges in the Ergenekon trial is as a deep ambivalence on the part of the prosecutors concerning how much state there actually is in the 'deep state'. The first indictment purports that 'it is obvious that the Ergenekon terrorist organisation has crucial contacts within

---

8   Sancar summarises such methods under three general headings: those that stay within the purview of legality (i.e. partial suspension or relativisation of human rights); those that blur the limits of legality (i.e. state of emergency); and those that dispense with legality altogether (i.e. counterinsurgency tactics such as extrajudicial executions) (1997: 85–86).

state institutions' (*Ergenekon Case*, First Indictment 2008: 47). But then it disavows this claim at every opportunity. In a section entitled 'Could there be such a structure as Ergenekon within the State?', the prosecutors serenely explain that they have officially written to the offices of the Chief of General Staff, the secret service and the police, to ask 'whether there is such a formation within their organisation' (ibid.: 48–50). Having received negative answers from all these official bodies, the prosecutors conclude that:

> The Ergenekon organisation which describes itself as the 'deep state' has no connection or relation to any official institution of the state ... [it is thus understood that] the Ergenekon organisation masquerades as the deep state ... but unlike the definition of the deep state which involves the benefit and vested interests of the state, it attempts to govern the state in accordance with its own ideological views.
>
> (*Ergenekon Case*, First Indictment 2008: 54–55)

Amidst a plethora of inconsistencies that make up the first Ergenekon indictment, perhaps this is the most significant one: the defendants are at once identified as 'the deep state' and as people who 'masquerade as the deep state'; while the deep state is at once described as the dark force behind countless bloody actions and as the body that protects the interests of the state. Here, *raison d'état* rears its head to reveal a prosecutorial rationality that is deeply ambivalent about the rule of law, to which the Ergenekon trial is supposed to represent a return. The trial is supposed to purge the deep state, but the only way the prosecutors can bring themselves to do so is by denying that the prosecution has anything to do with the state. It is as if the purge of extralegality from within the state is magically enacted by a prosecutorial disavowal: 'Now you see it, now you don't! It never was there anyway, but we will get rid of it!'

If the consideration of institutional histories, global politico-economic context and governmental rationalities are indispensable to a knowledge of the deep state, the Ergenekon case file betrays that affective investments into a notion of the state are also quite crucial. In other words, the unmanageable surplus is not only a surplus of meaning but also one of affect. In the Ergenekon trial the blurring of the differences between the prosecution and the defence becomes most pronounced around these passionate investments. They can be traced in the disavowals of the prosecution and the judges in the indictments and the first verdict, as well as in the correspondences and wire-tapped phone conversations of the defendants – the latter making up a significant part of the indictments themselves. While it is impossible to attempt to address the various configurations of fantasy and desire in the Ergenekon case file in detail here, I will highlight one general configuration that marks the case as a whole, and is perhaps best described

The conspiracy archive 185

in terms of what we may call 'the conspiratorial imagination'. This is, first of all, evident in the legal idiom of the trial, as the crux of the prosecution is an allegation of conspiracy among the defendants.[9] Second, it is discernible in the public life of the trial, since trial is widely perceived as a government conspiracy against the old guard: those suspicious of the governing party AKP's commitment to secularism have been concerned that Ergenekon is a witch-hunt carried out by the pro-Islam government against the deep-seated secularist establishment whose ranks include the Turkish army. But there is a third and more significant way in which the conspiratorial imagination is operative: the case file as a whole comprises an enormous conspiracy archive.

There are specific reasons for this. One is that some of the better-known Ergenekon defendants happen to be prominent conspiracy theorists. For example, defendant Erol Mütercimler is a writer, researcher and public figure, famous for hosting TV shows with names like 'Conspiracy Theory' and 'Behind the Mirror'. The Ergenekon judges identify him as 'an expert on conspiracy theories and strategy' and quote a high-profile journalist's description of him as 'one of the most important conspiracy doctors in Turkey' (*Ergenekon Case*, Detailed Judgment 2014, IIA: 116–167). Similarly, defendant Yalçın Küçük, once a widely respected socialist intellectual, now almost exclusively trades in conspiracy theorising, with a particular obsession about the 'Sabbatian Jewish' plot. Defendant Doğu Perinçek, the leader of the Maoist-turned-ultranationalist Workers' Party (now renamed the 'Patriotic Party'), has been publicly conspiracy theorising for decades with remarkable consistency in style, though the contents or 'plots' of his theories have changed considerably. The public utterances and writings of these figures are incorporated into the case file as evidence and drawn upon in the indictment. But the conspiratorial archive is not solely down to these figures. Other materials integrated into the case file as evidence include the personal documents and notes of almost all of the defendants, third-party testimonies, as well as the archives of Perinçek's party, mainly consisting of documents and information leaked from official bodies, as well as faked official leaks. Ploughing through this material, which adds up to tens of thousands of pages, it is staggering to notice the currency of the conspiratorial imagination in how the defendants and other trial participants conceive of the world and the political.

The conspiratorial imagination contaminates the entire case file, particularly through the pivotal role accorded to a collection of documents obtained by the police from Ergenekon defendants. According to both the prosecutors and the judges, these documents comprise the main body of

---

9　Although there is no conspiracy doctrine as such in Turkish criminal law, the specific offences that the defendants are charged with would best correspond to the common law conspiracy offence.

evidence concerning the very existence of a terrorist organisation called Ergenekon, as well as certain defendants' affiliation with it. The indictment refers to this collection as 'organisational documents'. They consist of structural guidelines, action plans and reports on contemporary events produced by and for a secret organisation that refers to itself alternately as 'the deep state' or 'Ergenekon'. In addition to serving as a trail in the police operations, these documents assist the prosecutors in making their case: the indictment directly quotes them in describing the overall structure, different units, as well as the functions and aims of Ergenekon. There are approximately 20 of these documents, adding up to 700–800 pages in total. The avowed centrality of these documents to the case file is somewhat astonishing as they read like a mishmash of internal bureaucracy and wild conspiratorial fantasy. One entitled 'Ergenekon Analysis Restructuring Management and Development Project' is considered by the prosecution to be Ergenekon's 'constitution' and a cursory summary of the document will perhaps explain what I mean by mishmash. The document begins by stating that 'it aims to contribute to the reorganisation of Ergenekon which operates from within the Turkish Armed Forces' (*Ergenekon Case*, First Indictment 2008, Appendices vol. 236: 85). The proposed restructuring is for Ergenekon to organise and incorporate influential members of the civilian public. It is indicated that Ergenekon's 'own successful JITEM experience' must be seen as a precursor to this restructuring (ibid., Appendices vol. 236: 96). Then the following suggestions are made: Ergenekon needs to establish its own non-governmental organisations and gain control over foreign-funded NGOs that are currently active in Turkey; it must secure control over the media and establish its own media outlets; it must attain ideologically desired politico-economic conditions by becoming a key player in international trade and banking; it must gain control over drugs trafficking; it should consider undertaking chemical weapons production so as to exercise control over terrorist organisations worldwide, and so on. Whether fabricated or genuine (i.e. whether produced by the police force tasked to investigate the case or by deep state actors) the very existence of these documents and their incorporation into the case file as the crux of the evidence against the defendants convey something of the fantasies of the deep state that are operative in the trial.

Further, the prosecutors pile together potential though unverified fragments of information pertaining to past deep state activities, gleaned from secret witnesses, tapped phone conversations and the vast cache of confiscated documents. This compilation amounts to a bewildering amalgam of fact and fantasy whereby the two cannot be told apart. Thus the case file operates as a chaotic archive of conspiracy in which the conspiracy theories cannot be distinguished from actual conspiracies pertaining to the past. In this sense the case file itself can be said to conspire to obfuscate the truth of past atrocities. The judgment makes strategic use of this mess to simultaneously include *and* exclude the past deeds of the deep state. It evokes them constantly to capitalise on their rhetorical uses and cites them explicitly to demonstrate the self-evident existence of the deep state. Past atrocities are also brought in as instruments of self-justification, meant to verify not only the necessity but also the soundness of the judgment itself. However, all the cited deep state activities are then fully excluded as actual objects of judgment. Instead, the only non-inchoate or complete criminal acts that the defendants are convicted of pertain to a number of violent attacks from 2006. The rest of the offences that the defendants are convicted of are either possession crimes or inchoate offences, including incitement and the Turkish anti-terror version of the crime of conspiracy.

As evinced by their oddly defensive preamble to the judgment, the judges are fully aware of the glaring absence of any proper inquisitorial process concerning the past deeds of the deep state in the trial. Responding to challenges that the court should expand the purview of the trial to adjudicate the state-sponsored activities of the late twentieth century, the judges suggest that such a proposal:

> has no standing in practice. First and foremost, a court judges the acts involved in the case before it. Further, it is also evident that it is very difficult to take into consideration events that have taken place in the distant past. Additionally, there is neither a legal nor a conscientious basis for an approach that says 'How can you judge the present if you are not judging the past'.
>
> (*Ergenekon Case*, Detailed Judgment 2014: 1)

The judgment's inclusion/exclusion of the past activities of the deep state bolsters the zone of unaccountability that these deeds have traditionally occupied by reframing it within an insufficient legal account of the past. In other words, the judgment empowers the ghostly hold of past atrocities on the present by letting them remain apparent but not established, rousing them but not laying them to rest, conjuring them but not demystifying them.

The relation between actually existing conspiracies and conspiracy theories requires careful thought. Often conspiracy theories are dismissed as pathological at the expense of the possibility of producing knowledge about actual conspiracies. Carlo Ginzburg touches on this matter in *The Judge and the Historian* (1999), his book about the miscarriages of justice in the 1988–91 trial of Adriano Sofri, a leftist leader accused and eventually convicted of ordering the murder of a policeman in the early 1970s in Italy. The murder was an integral part of a series of acts of political violence that are understood to have launched the Italian 'Years of Lead' (*anni di piombo*), a period that could be attributed to the Italian 'deep state', if that

188 Başak Ertür

usage were in place.[10] Convinced of his friend Sofri's innocence, Ginzburg has to work with this labyrinthine backdrop of the trial. His account is legibly haunted, if not driven, by a sense that the entire judicial process may be a conspiracy. In trying to make sense of the machinations involved, Ginzburg has to negotiate a potential accusation of engaging in *dietrologia*, a pejorative term coined in Italy to refer to conspiracy theorising.[11] While acknowledging that narratives concerning conspiracies amount to 'a vast library of foolishness, often with ruinous consequences', Ginzburg notes that conspiracies do exist in the world, as evidenced by the period in question (1999: 64). So how to make sense of conspiracies without lapsing into conspiracy theorising?

Ginzburg does not rule out the latter as a form of methodology, especially in trying to decipher affairs as murky as the one under consideration. On the contrary, he suggests that an outright dismissal of '*dietrologico* attitudes' would be detrimental to the effort 'if by *dietrologia* we mean a clear-eyed interpretative scepticism, unwilling to settle for the surface explanations of events or texts' (Ginzburg 1999: 65). However, while Ginzburg's preferred methodology may share a spirit of inquiry with conspiracy theorising, he suggests that the problem with conspiracy theories is their inability to take into account the rule of heterogeneity that presides over how wills are executed, intentions are materialised, and actions are enacted:

> every action directed towards an objective – and therefore, *a fortiori*, every conspiracy, which is an action directed towards particularly chancy objectives – enters into a system of unpredictable and heterogeneous forces. On the interior of this complex network of actions and reactions, which involve social processes that cannot easily be

---

10 Following the bomb planted in the Agricultural Bank in Milan in 1969, 'the first major event that revealed the conspiratorial character of Italian politics' (Aureli 1999) widely known as the Piazza Fontana bombing, two anarchists were arrested as suspects. One fell off the window of a police station and died, an incident which inspired Dario Fo's famous play *The Accidental Death of an Anarchist* (1970). The window from which he fell was that of the office of the policeman whose eventual murder Sofri was accused of. The period launched by the Piazza Fontana bombing is attributed to the 'Strategy of Tension', which refers to the engineering of political instability in order to prepare the grounds for an authoritarian takeover. A series of terrorist attacks, later found to be carried out by neofascist groups (Bull 2012) linked to the Italian NATO stay-behind unit Gladio, were used both to create an eminently governable atmosphere of terror and to target those on the left by attributing them the responsibility for these incidents.

11 *Dietrologia* literally translates as 'behindology', i.e. the science of uncovering "what lies behind". Ginzburg offers a number of definitions of the term in a footnote (1999: 126n45).

manipulated, the heterogeneity of objectives with respect to the initial intentions is the rule.

(Ginzburg 1999: 65)

Thus conspiracy theories err because they do not take account of the necessary and myriad infelicities that can interfere between the will and its execution, the intention and the action, the action and the objective it is meant to achieve. The equation of individual intentions with objectives reduces the causes behind events to individual wills. Notably, Ginzburg identifies this kind of equation posited by conspiracy theories as an 'extreme form of judicial historiography', which reduces the task of understanding an event to the attribution of liability to individuals (1999: 65).

In a short essay on this problem of knowing that conspiracies pose, and the need to address actually existing conspiracies without falling into the traps and limitations of conspiracy theorising, Ferhat Taylan turns to another text by Ginzburg, his famous essay 'Clues: The Roots of an Evidentiary Paradigm' (hereinafter, 'Clues'), to formulate the problem with what he refers to as 'the conspiratorial perception' in a slightly different register:

> Conspiratorial perception does not interpret traces, it contents itself with presenting them as the evidence for an unarticulated 'theory'. In this sense, it is like a child who points at the traces and shouts 'there!': traces alone enable the emergence and the verification of the so-called 'theory'. The trace, deemed to be the evidence, turns into the sole constituent of the hypothesis that is expected, in and of itself, to yield an explanation.
>
> (Taylan 2011: 17)

What is at work in conspiracy theorising is a metaphysics of presence whereby signs and traces are perceived to unambiguously stand for, and therefore reveal, the content they are assumed to originate from. Against this, Taylan proposes something like a conspirology based on what Ginzburg delineates as the conjectural paradigm (2011: 16).

Ginzburg's formulation of the conjectural paradigm in 'Clues' departs from a consideration of the similarity of methods in the works of the art connoisseur Giovanni Morelli, Sigmund Freud's psychoanalysis and the detective-work of Sherlock Holmes in Arthur Conan Doyle's novels. Ginzburg suggests that it is the key significance of minor details in their methodology that bring these figures together: 'In each case, infinitesimal traces permit the comprehension of a deeper, otherwise unattainable reality' (1990: 101). Noting that Morelli, Freud and Doyle were all physicians, Ginzburg connects the conjectural paradigm to traditional medical semiotics whereby the analysis, classification and interpretation of directly observed symptoms lead to hypotheses about underlying causes. Though he understands this form of knowledge to have emerged in the humanities sometime around the late nineteenth and early twentieth century, he suggests that its roots may be traced back to the kind of knowledge practiced by the hunter, who had to be attuned to traces, smells, and minute signs, such as clusters of hair, excrement and broken branches in the chase of the prey (ibid.: 102). Pitting the conjectural paradigm against a natural scientific paradigm of knowledge that is anti-anthropocentric, anti-anthropomorphic and quantitative, Ginzburg describes it as a form of sentient knowing that draws on our animalistic properties of senses, instincts, insights and intuitions. These 'imponderable elements' provide passage from directly observed and/or experienced data to knowledge concerning what is, strictly speaking, unknowable.

Notably, Ginzburg's main examples for the conjectural paradigm pertain to resistant objects of knowledge. Morelli's was a technique developed to distinguish original artworks from their copies, which strove to pass for the original. Sherlock Holmes attunes himself to details that are imperceptible to most in seeking authors of crimes, who were clearly invested in covering over their tracks. Freud attempted to formulate a methodology for 'divin[ing] secret and concealed things from unconsidered or unnoticed details, from the rubbish heap, as it were, of our observations' (cited in Ginzburg 1990: 99), despite and against what he identified as a complex psychic apparatus of repression. They are similar in this sense to the deep state, which is by definition secretive and non-transparent – it jealously guards evidence of itself, and presumably mobilises the entire state apparatus to do so. In all of Ginzburg's scenarios the clues are revealed when the sovereign agency of the 'authors' falter: the art historian looks for the unimportant details that the copyist paints inattentively, Holmes and Freud seek clues in details that escape intentional control. Thus the conjectural paradigm presumes what the conspiratorial imagination denies: the field of unpredictability and heterogeneity that every action and intention is subject to.

The conspiratorial imagination that pervades the Ergenekon case file can be identified as one that sustains a fantasy of absolute sovereignty on the part of the deep state and its agents, whose wills are understood as fully self-present and their acts as absolutely felicitous. Although the trial has so far played out as a classic political trial with the usual clamour of a seemingly radical, incommensurable difference between the defendants on the one hand and the prosecutors and the judges on the other, the shared conspiratorial imagination reveals a deep consensus among the warring parties. Beyond all the noise and commotion, the accusations and counter-accusations of conspiracy, this consensus produces the 'deep' state as something of a fetish in the scene of the trial. The state is co-produced and reproduced through the case file that functions as a conspiracy archive.

The trial becomes the scene for the performative enactment of the public thing called the state, which comes into being as a collective misrepresentation (Abrams 1988).

But there may be other ways of knowing the deep state without investing it with the power of a fetish, and Taylan may be correct about the potentials of conjectural knowledge here. One such vein of inquiry is undertaken by lawyer Fethiye Çetin, who has been involved in another deep state trial, albeit one that is not officially identified as such. The trial concerns the assassination of the Armenian-Turkish journalist Hrant Dink in Istanbul in 2007. Although the deep state is inscribed all over the case file (including the chain of events that led to Dink's assassination, the assassination itself, as well as the ensuing criminal process), the entire investigation and trial has been marked by its disavowal. Thus the criminal justice process operates as an extension of the crime itself. As the Dink murder trial has been mostly concurrent with the Ergenekon process,[12] its spectacular, though convenient failures, can be interpreted as revealing the disingenuity of the claim that the Ergenekon trial is a wholesale purge of extralegal operativity within the state. The Dink murder trial operates on a logic of discontinuity, disconnection, dissociation and fragmentation all meant to cover up state involvement in the assassination. Çetin represented Dink in the trials that plagued him in the lead-up to his assassination. After the assassination, Çetin acted as the representative for the Dink family in the murder trial, through a provision in Turkish criminal procedure that allows the victim (or in case of homicide, their relations) rights of representation in the trial.

Çetin eventually wrote a book about the assassination and its aftermath, to make public her knowledge of the case, her findings as well as intuitions. She points at certain figures who may be key to the assassination but have never been investigated, and tries to make sense of a wide range of connections, events and dynamics in seeking the truth of the assassination. Her methodology is, indeed, conjectural. She writes of frequently encountering 'traces and signs' of cover-ups in the case files: 'I had intuitions but was not able to demonstrate anything concretely' (Çetin 2013: 24). She also writes of a solution based on experiential knowledge:

> What I knew of, lived through, saw in the case files and read in the press made me realise that the truth must be sought not in what is shown and visible in the case files but rather in what is not shown, what is hidden.
>
> (Çetin 2013: 227)

---

12 Underway since 2007, the Dink murder case is currently being retried after the verdict of the first trial was appealed.

Çetin proposes the study of the negative spaces of the case files, of the traces and signs of that which has been deleted or not presented. Notably, she reads not only the Dink murder case file, but also the Ergenekon case file closely for signs of Dink's assassination. She scans what has been left out and trains her gaze to focus on the gaps and absences. On a number of occasions, she specifically focuses on the ellipses, literally, in the Ergenekon case file. Honing in on what has been left out by the Ergenekon prosecutors in their quotations of the Ergenekon defendants' online chat records and wiretap transcripts, she conjectures on the basis of that which has been rendered invisible behind three dots.

The conspiracy archives of the Ergenekon trial hide, rather than reveal, the truth unless one devises ways and means of deciphering them. A reading practice like Çetin's mobilises the traces of that which has been left out, censored and repressed, against the conspiring case files. This is something of a counter-conspiracy, a kind of knowing that at the same time divests the fetish of the 'deep' state of its powers. It requires attunement to the mishaps and vagaries of intentionality, the inadvertent omissions in the tightly-woven plot, and the heterogeneity of forces that all actions and intentions are subject to. The counter-conspiracy works with and against law: rather than staking claims on the legal spectacle and therefore allowing it to fulfil or frustrate (and thus orchestrate and co-opt) the desire for truth and justice, it mobilises law's archive against itself. The aim is not only to seek the truth of past violence but also to discern the traces of the forces, patterns, imaginaries and affective investments that facilitate the perpetuation of particular forms of violence. The line between conjectural knowledge and conspiratorial imagination is perhaps fine and shifting, but treading it with care may be the only way to strike a judicious balance between working with and against law in addressing the petrifying memory and ghostly reality of state violence.

References

Abrams, P. 1988, 'Notes on the Difficulty of Studying the State', *Journal of Historical Sociology*, vol. 1, no. 1, pp. 58–89.

Afflitto, F.M. 2000, 'The Homogenizing Effects of State-Sponsored Terrorism: The Case of Guatemala', in J.A. Sluka (ed.), *Death Squad: The Anthropology of State Terror*, University of Pennsylvania Press, Philadelphia, pp. 114–126.

Ahmad, F. 1981, 'Military Intervention and the Crisis in Turkey', *Merip Reports*, January, pp. 5–32.

Anon. 1997, Türkiye'de Devlet, *Birikim*, no. 93/94, pp. 16–17.

Aretxaga, B. 2000, 'A Fictional Reality: Paramilitary Death Squads and the Construction of State Terror in Spain', in J.A. Sluka (ed.), *Death Squad: The Anthropology of State Terror*, University of Pennsylvania Press, Philadelphia, pp. 46–69.

Aretxaga, B. 2005, *States of Terror: Begoña Aretxaga's Essays*, Centre for Basque Studies, University of Nevada.

The conspiracy archive 193

Aureli, A. 1999, 'The Usual Suspects', in G.E. Marcus (ed.), *Paranoia within Reason: A Casebook on Conspiracy as Explanation*, University of Chicago Press, Chicago, pp. 197–224.

Bora, T. 1997, 'Devlet ve Ülkücüler: Karşılıklı Bir Aşk', *Birikim*, no. 93/94, pp. 53–62.

Bourdieu, P. 1994, 'Rethinking the State: Genesis and Structure of the Bureaucratic Field', trans. Loic J. D. Wacquant and S. Farage, *Sociological Theory*, vol. 12, no. 1, pp. 1–18.

Britain's Secret Terror Force 2013, television program, BBC Panorama, BBC One, 21 November.

Bull, A.C. 2012, *Italian Neofascism: The Strategy of Tension and the Politics of Nonreconciliation*, Berghahn, New York.

Çetin, F. 2013, *Utanç Duyuyorum! Hrant Dink Cinayetinin Yargısı*, Metis, Istanbul.

Ergenekon Case (First Indictment) 2008, Republic of Turkey, Istanbul Office of the Chief Public Prosecutor, Investigation no: 2007/1536, Case no: 2008/968, Indictment no: 2008/623.

Ergenekon Case (Detailed Judgment) 2014, Republic of Turkey, Istanbul 13th High Criminal Court, Case no: 2009/191, Judgment no: 2013/95.

Foucault, M. 2007, *Security, Territory, Population: Lectures at the Collège de France 1977–1978*, trans. G. Burchell, Palgrave Macmillan, New York.

Foucault, M. 2008, *The Birth of Biopolitics: Lectures at the Collège de France, 1978–79*, trans. G. Burchell, Palgrave Macmillan, New York.

Ganser, D. 2005, *NATO's Secret Armies: Operation Gladio and Terrorism in Western Europe*, Frank Cass, London.

Ginzburg, C. 1990, 'Clues: Roots of an Evidential Paradigm', in C. Ginzburg, *Myths, Emblems, Clues*, trans. J. Tedeschi and A.C. Tedeschi, Hutchinson Radius, London, pp. 96–125.

Ginzburg, C. 1999, *The Judge and the Historian: Marginal Notes on a Late-Twentieth-Century Miscarriage of Justice*, trans. A. Shugaar, Verso, London.

Klein, N. 2007, *The Shock Doctrine: The Rise of Disaster Capitalism*, Penguin, London.

Laçiner, Ö. 1997, Türk Toplumunun Devleti. *Birikim*, no. 93/94, pp. 18–25.

Sabuktay, A. 2010, *Devletin Yasal Olmayan Faaliyetleri: Susurluk Olayı'na Hukuk-Siyaset Kuramından Bakış*, Metis, Istanbul.

Sancar, M. 1997, 'Devlet Aklı', Hukuk Devleti ve 'Devlet Çetesi', *Birikim*, no. 93/94, pp. 80–90.

Sancar, M. 2000, 'Devlet Aklı', *Kıskacında Hukuk Devleti*, İetişim, Istanbul.

Söyler, M. 2013, 'Informal Institutions, Forms of State and Democracy: the Turkish Deep State', *Democratization*, vol. 20, no. 2, pp. 310–334.

Suárez-Orozco, M. 1992, 'A Grammar of Terror: Psychocultural Responses to State Terrorism in Dirty war and Post-Dirty War Argentina', in C. Nordstrom and J. Martin (eds), *The Paths to Domination, Resistance, and Terror*, University of California Press, Berkeley, pp. 219–259.

Taylan, F. 2011, 'Many Signs Have Come to Pass: The Concept of Conspiracy and Conspiratorial Perception', in B. Ertür (ed.), *Manual for Conspiracy*, Sharjah Art Foundation, Sharjah, pp. 7–18.

Ünver, H.A. 2009, 'Turkey's 'Deep-State' and the Ergenekon Conundrum', *The Middle East Institute Policy Brief*, 23 April, viewed 17 November 2014, <www.mei.edu/content/turkeys-deep-state-and-ergenekon-conundrum>.

Zolo, D. 2007, 'The Rule of Law: A Critical Reappraisal' in P. Costa and D. Zolo (eds), *The Rule of Law: History Theory and Criticism*, Springer Publishing Company, Dordrecht, pp. 3–72.

Chapter 10

Making a treaty archive
Indigenous rights on the Canadian development frontier

Miranda Johnson

> The archive takes place at the place of originary and structural break-down of ... memory.
>
> (Jacques Derrida 1995: 11)

> There is no doubt in my mind that their testimony was the truth and represented their best memory of what to them at the time must have been an important event. It is fortunate indeed that their stories are now preserved.
>
> Justice William Morrow (*Re Paulette and Registrar of Land Titles*, 1973: 313)

In this chapter I tell a story of an archive-in-the-making. Like all archives, the one I write about was constructed in a very particular social, political, and economic context and for reasons emerging from, though not reducible to, a historical moment (Duff and Harris 2002). In the early 1970s, Dene leaders in the Northwest Territories (NWT) of Canada began to document their own communities' understandings of treaties made with them earlier in the century in order to assert continuing land rights in the Mackenzie Valley. This was a time of rapid economic change in the region as the Canadian government sought to open up the north of the country to large new mining and development projects, in this particular instance the building of massive oil and gas pipeline. It was also period of national political ferment as disputes deepened across Canada and internationally concerning the rights of indigenous peoples to the maintenance of their lands and collective identities. In these tumultuous circumstances, Dene leaders sought recognition of their land rights. They also wanted to more firmly establish their distinct standing in the nation-state as first peoples and solidify their own peoples' historical identity. They did so by creating what I call a treaty archive. The treaty archive – which I regard in this chapter as an historical artefact itself, as well as a repository from which new historical narratives could be made – was created with particular political purposes in mind. The archive transformed 'law's archive' by countering the official story of treaty-

196 Miranda Johnson

making told by the Canadian state about treaties with indigenous peoples as expedient instruments of empire (Mawani 2012). The treaty archive also helped to frame a new Dene political consciousness.

Central to this archive was the testimony of Dene elders who were present at treaty signings and were asked to remember the promises made to their communities during those events. The testimonies were key evidence in a legal case that Dene leaders brought in 1973, as a consequence of specific events I narrate below. Guided by lawyers and the judge in the case, Dene people were asked to turn their stories of treaty-making into legal tales. Their testimonies were to demonstrate how they had maintained unextinguished customary land rights according to a particular legal doctrine known as 'aboriginal title'. The process of archiving that was already underway in Dene communities was of particular use in the case as those involved in research and in giving oral history interviews could be called on again to provide testimony to the court. Furthermore, the records that were produced in the case – notably, court transcripts of those testimonies – enlarged the treaty archive.

The legal transcript that I discuss in this chapter documented something else, and did so perhaps more clearly and certainly more poignantly than either the judge or others involved in archiving would readily admit. The transcript records the difficulties that Dene elders experienced in presenting accurate memories that they thought the court wanted to hear. Indeed, the reader frequently comes across the failure of such efforts at translation. Readers of the transcript might become alert to when the pressure of expectation became too much for 'witnesses', being asked to recall events of 50 years earlier – events that may not have even been of much significance to them at the time, yet were achieving a new significance in the politics of the present.

In drawing attention to the failures of memory recorded in the transcripts, I bring into relief the contradictions of the archiving impulse itself. On the one hand, the archivist hopes that the documents collected will preserve the past for those in the present and thus the archive will protect a record that others may make use of in the future. On the other hand, that very aspiration is formed in the face of loss, at the place of the 'originary and structural breakdown of memory', for instance, when the subject, asked to remember something for the court, struggles to put what they embody into words (Derrida 1995: 11). The archive is thus a repository of memory as it has been translated, transcribed, and replaced – as it no longer is.

This essay begins where I began my research (discussed in greater detail elsewhere):[1] with the 1973 legal case. I then turn to the making of the

---

1   In my forthcoming book, *The Land Is Our History: Indigenous Claims and the Transformation of the Settler State.*

archive that the legal case drew on and helped to augment, focusing on the historical work of one 'archivist' in particular: a long-time resident of the north and Oblate priest, René Fumoleau. He was principally concerned with two treaties, made in 1899 and 1921 respectively. I will examine the treaty of 1921 as "event" and as "memory" in his work, and in the proceedings of the 1973 legal case where the treaties' meanings were also at issue. I return to the site of law as a particularly interesting and important site of archive-making and even nation-building.

The legal case

On 3 April 1973, a young Dene chief, François Paulette, along with 15 others, applied to lodge a caveat under the Land Titles Act 1970 in order to protect their communities' interests to 400,000 square miles of land that a proposed oil and gas pipeline would cross. The caveat that they sought from the Northwest Territories Supreme Court would not recognise Dene peoples' land rights in the first instance, but it would serve to demonstrate their interest in the land prior to an investigation of their title to it. Because of the unusual nature of the caveat – that it was based in a claim to aboriginal title and treaty rights – the Registrar of Titles forwarded it to the Northwest Territories Supreme Court. The Court had been in operation for less than 20 years (it was created in 1955) and it was mostly concerned with criminal cases in Indian settlements (Eber 1997; Morrow and Morrow 1995). This was the first time that this court had been asked to broach the question of aboriginal title and the land rights of northern people.

The legal case, *Re Paulette and Registrar of Land Titles* (No. 2) (1973) 42 DLR (3d) 8, commonly referred to as 'the Caveat case', must be contextualised in the larger economic, political, and legal scene in Canada at the time. Here I focus on three issues. First, the opening up of the north to new mining and development. Second, the political activism of Indians across Canada, and their assertions of distinct rights as self-determining indigenous peoples. Third, the precedent for examining distinct land rights established in the recent case heard by the Supreme Court of Canada, *Calder et. al. v Attorney-General of British Columbia* (1973) SCR 313.

In 1970, the Canadian Liberal government tabled guidelines for the construction and operation of a northern oil and gas pipeline in the Northwest Territories. An engineering feat, the Mackenzie Valley pipeline was only now possible because of new technology and considerable capital available for such projects. It would be the largest of its kind, transporting oil and gas from Arctic reserves and connect up with existing pipelines in the south. The construction of the pipeline would realise Canada's 'northern vision' as Prime Minister Diefenbaker had imagined it in 1958. This vision would, he claimed, 'create a new sense of national purpose and national destiny' (Diefenbaker 1958). Notably, in the imagination of

Diefenbaker and that of subsequent politicians, the majority population that inhabited the Arctic and Canada's far northern regions – indigenous peoples – was not to play a part in this national story.

The publication of the guidelines caused consternation among northerners wary of how their communities and livelihoods would be affected by such a pipeline (Berger 1977; The Dene Nation 1984). In particular, no mention was made of the recognition of the land rights of Dene, Métis and Inuit peoples whose lands the pipelines would cross.[2] Moreover, the government had not consulted about the proposals directly with individual chiefs nor with their representative organisation, the Indian Brotherhood of the Northwest Territories.

This lack of consultation was particularly galling to Indian leaders who had recently been pressing for their rights as 'citizens plus'. This term referred to the idea that Indians in Canada were entitled to additional rights, over and above their equal civil rights to other Canadian citizens. These rights derived from treaties made with the Canadian government in the past which recognised their distinct ways of life on the land (Hawthorn 1966: 13; Cairns 2000). Indian peoples' demands for the recognition of their distinct rights came to a head in Canada in 1969, following government proposals to do away with special 'treaty status'. This status was awarded to members of some communities by virtue of their inclusion in treaties made in the nineteenth and early twentieth centuries. So, those who signed on to treaties in the Northwest Territories became 'status' or 'treaty' Indians. They were distinguished administratively from Indians without treaties, or those who had accepted land 'scrip' or freehold title to small plots of land, according to the Indian Act, first passed in 1876 and successively amended (Miller 2009). The Act placed status Indians under the administration of the Department of Indian Affairs and established rules about how treaty payments and other moneys promised in treaty agreements would be paid. It laid out how reserve lands and the bands that lived on them would be managed. Significantly, it set out how status itself could be maintained or lost (Jamieson 1978).[3]

In 1969, the recently-elected Liberal government issued a White Paper proposed doing away with this status. The White Paper also proposed that

2   The term 'Indian tribes' or 'bands' was in contemporary usage in the early 1970s and I use them here to mark the fact that this was a historical period distinct from our present. Today in official and scholarly prose as well as in public, the terms 'First Nations' and 'Aboriginal people' are preferred, though some indigenous peoples in Canada continue to refer to themselves as 'Indians'. I also use other local terms of self-designation, notably 'Dene', which literally means 'the people'.

3   Until changes in 1985, for instance, status Indian women who married non-status (Indian or non-Indian) men lost their status and became Canadian citizens, whereas white women who married status Indian men gained Indian status without losing Canadian citizenship. The selective gender bias of the legislation tended to diminish the numbers of those who claimed status, since more status Indian women married non-status men.

dissolving the Department of Indian Affairs, which administered treaty Indians, in the interest of establishing greater equality between Indian and non-Indian citizens in Canada (Weaver 1981). According to Prime Minister Pierre Trudeau, treaty status made Indians wards of the state. What was needed, in the age of the 'Just Society', he argued, was for 'our Indian and Inuit population ... to assume the full rights of citizenship through policies which will give them both greater responsibility for their own future and more meaningful equality of opportunity' (Trudeau 1998: 19).

Indian activists and leaders vigorously opposed the idea of a Just Society if that meant that their distinctive rights would be abolished, rights founded in long-standing treaty promises. They argued that the government's universalist position denied the political significance of treaties as establishing 'peace and friendship' between the Canadian government and their own nations (Miller 2009). As prominent Cree activist Harold Cardinal put it, treaties were 'honourable dealings in good faith' that obliged ongoing discussion and consultation between the Canadian government and Indian communities (Cardinal 1969: 30).

In a global context in which the idea of self-determination had become the clarion call of colonised peoples, indigenous peoples in Canada sought to re-establish themselves on their own lands and in accordance with their own histories. Although indigenous minorities in settler states did not press for full independence, in Canada they did argue for recognition as 'citizens plus'. The importance of this political claim cannot be underestimated. It marked a radical departure from the demands of many Indian leaders earlier in the century who had mainly mobilised for equal, civil rights. In a polemic titled *Citizens Plus*, published to counter the government's proposals, the Indian Association of Alberta – one of the oldest provincial indigenous organisations in the west – closely bound together the preservation of cultural practices and individual memories with the recognition of rights and status and the protection of a distinctive identity. 'The only way to maintain our culture is for us to remain as Indians. To preserve our culture it is necessary to preserve our status, rights, lands and traditions. Our treaties are the basis of our rights' (Indian Chiefs of Alberta 1970: 5; Drees 2002: 169).

By going to the law, Dene leaders drew on this recent assertion of Indians as 'citizens plus'. They hoped that by winning legal recognition of what they believed was theirs, the government would be forced to consult with them about matters of deep concern to their communities. Indeed, the Indian Brotherhood strongly criticised the 'sham game of consultation' that the government had thus far engaged in regarding the building of the oil and gas pipeline ('Indian Brotherhood explains freeze' 1973) 'When the government decides that they will develop a dialogue and deal with us on just terms then we can move out of the courts and to the more civilized bargaining table,' the Brotherhood explained in its recently established newspaper on the eve of the caveat hearings (ibid.).

Asserting their claim over the unpatented Crown land, the applicants made two arguments, represented by the Indian Brotherhood's lawyer, Gerry Sutton. First, they argued that the treaties their leaders had signed with Canadian authorities in the past were promises of 'peace and friendship' rather than land cession deeds. Second, they argued that they had used and occupied the area since time immemorial and therefore maintained customary aboriginal title over the entire area. This interpretation of those treaties – as establishing peace and friendship rather than land cession – which would be substantiated by Indian elders' own memories and stories about what had been understood and promised in them, was crucial evidence in establishing the unextinguished aboriginal title of northern indigenous peoples.

The argument for indigenous land title was radical. It countered assumptions by the Canadian government that such rights had been extinguished explicitly through treaties or implicitly through settlement. However, by 1973, aboriginal title claims were on the verge of becoming justiciable. In the 1960s, Nisga'a leaders in British Columbia reignited their long-standing demand for recognition of their land rights and hired lawyers to prosecute their claim in court. After two rulings against the plaintiffs in the lower courts, on 31 January 1973 the Supreme Court of Canada found in *Calder v Attorney-General of British Columbia* (the 'Calder case') for the first time in Canadian legal history that aboriginal title did exist according to the British Proclamation of 1763. That proclamation had limited legal settlement in the thirteen colonies east of the Appalachian mountains and recognised 'Indian territory' west of the proclamation line. However, the justices split (3–3) evenly on the issue of whether or not such title had been extinguished and the seventh judge found against the Nisga'a claimants on a matter of jurisdiction rather than fact (Foster, Raven and Webber 2007). The Nisga'a claimants failed on a technicality, but the case marked a turning point in legal opinions about the possibility of recognising Indians' land rights. The Calder case had a significant political effect: Prime Minister Trudeau reversed his opinion that aboriginal title rights could not be recognized in Canada ('Indians have more land rights than he [Trudeau] thought' 1973). Moreover, it encouraged other Indian communities including the Dene to push forward their own claims to aboriginal title. In the case of the Dene, they also pushed for recognition of their understanding of treaty agreements.

The Caveat case that the Dene leaders pursued in 1973 was therefore not a singular event. It arose in a wider context of indigenous political and legal activism. Nonetheless, the case was a significant, if under-analysed one, mainly because of the evidentiary process that the Chief Justice of the Supreme Court of the Northwest Territories, William Morrow, deployed in hearing individual Dene witnesses' testimony. Indeed, Justice Morrow prided himself on the court's evidentiary flexibility in admitting the testimonies of Indian elders, even where they might otherwise fall foul of hearsay rules, and on his special understanding and appreciation of Dene people. In order to hear such testimony, Justice Morrow made a number of adjustments to the court's evidentiary process. He took the court party out to the local settlements to hear witnesses' testimonies in their own venues and even homes rather than requiring them to come to a central location such as Yellowknife. During court hearings, Morrow allowed lawyers to lead some evidence and he permitted witnesses to digress to some extent. Furthermore, he acknowledged his own role as one resembling that of inquisitor actively seeking facts as much as an objective and distant adjudicator. He appointed a lawyer as *amicus curiae* (friend of the court) who would cross-examine witnesses and provide counter-argument (*Re Paulette and Registrar of Land Titles*, Morrow and Morrow 1995).

In the Caveat case, the memories, traditions and stories of local Dene people *themselves* would become critical evidence to understanding communities' occupation and use of the land as well as their political understandings of what they had been promised in the past. The evidence offered by priest-cum-historian René Fumoleau, and anthropologists who worked with Dene communities, was also important, though perhaps not as persuasive to Morrow. Nonetheless, a further condition of possibility for the legal case was the archive of treaty-making and Dene history more generally that was already under construction in the north and elsewhere.

The politics of the treaty archive

In the late 1960s and 1970s, as politics in the north heated up, a number of individuals and organisations began to carry out research into Dene history particularly about land rights and treaties. One of those was Fumoleau, a French priest of the Oblates of Mary Immaculate who had lived in the NWT since 1953. In 1975, he published the first history of Treaties 8 and 11 as they affected people in the NWT. *As Long As This Land Shall Last* is still regarded as the seminal account of the two treaties. In the preface, he explained his intentions for collecting the documents presented in the book, which he found scattered all across Canada, and which were used in the Caveat case and by the Indian Brotherhood for other purposes (Fumoleau 2004: xx). Fumoleau wanted to make these documents available for 'Indian and non-Indian Canadians' and he disavowed any moral or political objectives in his research (ibid.). 'The documents are presented here neither to justify nor condemn, to moralize nor to philosophize, to apologize nor to plea … [they] must speak for themselves to show exactly what was known, thought, said, or done at a given period in the past' (ibid.: 14).

By disavowing such a purpose, Fumoleau underplayed his own role in selecting from the documents (from which he quoted extensively) and ordering them into a coherent and elegantly narrated history. Those for whom the history had the most immediate relevance were not so coy. The then president of the Indian Brotherhood of the Northwest Territories, James Wah-Shee, was much more direct in his foreword to the book. 'It is to be hoped,' wrote Wah-Shee:

> that this book will help to clear away much of the ignorance that has blinded those charged with responsibilities toward the Indian people. If the book achieves the readership it deserves, it will engender a new respect for the Indian position and considerable sympathy for the recent historical experience of the Indians of the Territories.
>
> (Fumoleau 2004: xvii)

Fumoleau was not alone in seeking to recover the history of treaties in Canada. In the early 1970s, Indian organisations and a recently created Indian Claims Commission, which was examining how treaty breaches might be investigated, began to undertake wide-ranging research into the treaties made with Indian communities across the country. This renewed interest in the wider history of the treaties – and their historical and contemporary meaning to Indian people themselves – was a consequence of, and helped to further enhance, the new wave of rights activism mentioned above.

However, as Fumoleau observed in carrying out his own research, there was little in the extant historical record about what Indian signatories and their wider communities thought they were agreeing to in signing treaties. Had Indians actually understood that they were ceding all their land rights? Did traditional communities even have a concept of land possession and alienation inherent to common law notions of property rights? If the treaties were understood by the signatories as promising other kinds of relationships – those of 'peace and friendship' as many activists now claimed – did they actually have the kind of validity that the Crown assumed they did? And how could such be ascertained if evidence of the signatories' understanding was not available in the written record?

Research into treaty-making prompted a new historical approach, as well as the drawing together of 'scattered' documents. In order to find out what Indian communities themselves understood and remembered about treaties, Indian organisations, other state-sponsored groups, anthropologists and historians, initiated oral history projects with elderly community members. In the Northwest Territories, oral history projects were undertaken in 1966 by the Company of Young Canadians (a federally sponsored youth organisation modelled on the American peace corps), the Indian Brotherhood of the Northwest Territories (founded in 1969), and students and anthropologists from the University of Iowa, some of whom had long worked with Dene people. As well as citing documents produced by state officials, Department of Indian Affairs employees, and the accounts of missionaries involved in treaty-making, Fumoleau drew extensively on the transcripts of these interviews in filling out the Indian side of the story.

However, the transcripts of the interviews reveal much more complexity and uncertainty in elderly peoples' memories than either Fumoleau or other political leaders generally admitted. For instance, in an interview conducted in January 1973 with Ted Trindel, a Métis man who was 20 years old when the treaty was signed at Fort Simpson in 1921, he recalled how the Treaty commissioners wanted a man known as Old Norwegian to be chief, 'but he said no because he didn't understand what it was all about' (Fumoleau 2004: 225). Trindel continued,

> The Indians didn't know what treaty was. In fact, I swear they didn't know what it was all about … [I]n the Treaty book it says that you'll be subject to the Law, and it says that after the Treaty you had to abide by whatever rules come along, but at Treaty time the Treaty party didn't tell them that. It was still your country. The Treaty was more or less to keep peace in the family.
>
> (Fumoleau 2004: 225)

Understanding the meaning of treaties from an Indian perspective thus incited the construction of an even broader archive. This was one that was supplemented and considerably expanded by the oral histories undertaken with elderly people in the local communities. According to Fumoleau such an archive was necessary to provide a history of treaty-making, in which the facts 'must speak for themselves' and educate the wider Canadian public (ibid.: xx). The treaty archive was constructed in the context of considerable political change in Canada: that is, of the forceful assertion of *distinct* rights by Indian activists. Several of those activists had been educated at universities in the major cities and had participated in the new democratic organisations, such as the Company of Young Canadians. Yet they did not want to be assimilated into the mainstream of Canadian life. Moreover, the treaty archive was needed for restoring Indian traditions and reconnecting young Indian people with their culture. These goals underpinned a larger political project of asserting peoplehood.

Dene leaders clearly and consciously asserted the political goals of achieving a recognisably distinct peoplehood. As the Indian Brotherhood of the Northwest Territories declared in its 1970 constitution, the organisation's mandate was to 'give voice to the opinions of the Peoples of the NWT' (The Dene Nation 1984: 25). In doing so, the Indian Brotherhood began to undertake a variety of economic, political, and cultural projects. These included the establishment of food cooperatives, leadership courses, and language learning. As the authors of a book celebrating 'Denedeh' or Dene country wrote in 1984, 'the Dene revival took many forms' (ibid.: 20).

The organisation also embarked on preservation projects, collecting the histories of their elders who might not survive the next decade, and making those histories available as a resource especially for younger Dene people who may not have been as familiar with their communities' traditions on the land. In the early 1970s most Dene people lived in permanent settlements, attended government-run schools, and consumed popular culture on TV and through other media. In a funding request to the national Indian Claims Commission that the Indian Brotherhood made in August 1973, it argued that carrying out field research in local settlements would be a 'very valuable self-study and learning process for our people [...] The eventual settlement agreed upon by us with the Minister will provide nothing less than the resource base for our future as independent Canadians' (Indian Brotherhood of the N.W.T. 1973). The argument countered the obvious fact that the broader history of the treaties had previously been of little interest to the Department of Indian Affairs, once the treaties had been signed and the title to lands that Indians may have had rights to was extinguished.

The treaty-as-event

So what was the treaty and what did it enforce or promise? Here, I will give an account of Treaty 11, signed during the summer of 1921. Several witnesses in the later Caveat case of 1973 had attended these signings as young men and women and were asked to recall their memories of them during the later court hearings. In one sense, the treaty signings began in a journey: the party that was convened in the summer of 1921 to secure the signatures of Indian chiefs to Treaty 11 travelled down the Mackenzie River on a barge in order to access the remote settlements of the region. Known as 'Dehcho' (which means 'Big River' in Slavey, one of the dialects of the region), it is the largest river system in Canada, rising out of the Great Slave Lake and emptying in the Beaufort Sea. The boreal forests that carpet the valley are home to Athabaskan linguistic groups including Chipewyan, Beaver, Slave, and Kaska nations, who have occupied the area according to seasonal food availability for as long as 10,000 years. From the eighteenth century, many of these peoples had become involved in the fur trade. The river system acquired its European name from Alexander Mackenzie, the first European to travel the river, on bark canoe, in 1789. He hoped to find a water passage to the Pacific on behalf of the North West Company that was seeking to extend its fur trading enterprise and discover a faster route to markets in Europe. The Company established a fur trading enterprise there based around the Fort of Good Hope, working 'largely within Dene law and jurisdictions' (Promislow 2012: 35).

The treaty of 1921 – the last of the numbered treaties that the Canadian government made with Indian groups – was also the most recent instantiation of an established political tradition in Canada. However, the Canadian government entered into treaty-making in the northern Mackenzie district reluctantly (Miller 2009). Despite requests for a treaty that some Indian leaders made to the government earlier in the century, and the regular concerns expressed about the state of Indian people in the region by the Treaty 8 Inspector, H. A. Conroy, the department refused to make a treaty north of the 60th parallel. In a letter to the Department of Indian Affairs in Ottawa, Conroy claimed that there was a 'universal' desire on the part of Indian people to be included in a treaty. He thought that Treaty 8, made in 1899 with communities in the Lesser Slave Lake area and northern Alberta, could be extended to Indians further north (Fumoleau 2004: 159). The Department officials, however, argued that people in the north were best left to their own devices. Without a treaty, they could continue their subsistence hunting and trapping livelihood rather than becoming subject to treaties. In the official mind, treaties were instruments of assimilation, deployed to encourage Indians to take up a sedentary agricultural life on the reserve lands that the so-called numbered treaties established on the plains to the south. The Department also claimed that some provision was already made for the destitute in the north by issuing supplies through the Hudson's Bay Company (Coates and Morrison 1986).

The Department's attitude changed around 1920, after oil drilling commenced at Fort Norman, auguring rapid changes in the north. At that moment, the need to ensure that Indians' land rights in the area were clearly extinguished became more urgent as the government sought to assert its sovereignty over the area. The humanitarian objective of offering some protection to northern Indians in the form of reserves and annuities offered to the tribes also seemed more pressing. Conroy was appointed to be the treaty negotiator, assisted by the Oblate Bishop Gabriel Breynat who had been appointed to the Mackenzie region in 1901. Breynat viewed the invitation to be a part of the treaty party as an 'uncommon sign of esteem and a public recognition of the influence the Catholic Missionaries have on those people whose friendship the Government desires to win' (Fumoleau 2004: 208). He continued, 'my signature will be seen forever, together with those of our great chiefs . . . to bear witness, for future generations, to the good faith of the contracting parties' (ibid.).

However, both Breynat and Conroy were sorely disappointed with the terms of the treaty they were obliged to take to the Indians. Treaty 11 required the cession of 'all [the signatories'] rights, titles, and privileges whatsoever' to approximately 372,000 square miles of land; it assured the Indians that they could continue hunting and trapping activities, subject to regulation and public works projects, though it did not stipulate fishing rights; it promised the establishment of reserves; offered annuity payments, treaty medals and flags to the chiefs, and a variety of implements including axes, saws, augers, and hunting tools and supplies (Aboriginal Affairs and

206 Miranda Johnson

Northern Development. n.d.). Breynat later expressed his frustration with this non-negotiable document: the treaty terms 'were prepared in advance to be imposed upon them rather than freely discussed in a spirit of reconciliation and mutual concessions' (ibid.: 163).

Conroy and Breynat, with other members of the treaty party including Indian interpreters, nonetheless carried out the wishes of the Department. Notice was given in the Mackenzie district that the treaty would be taken first to Fort Providence on July 5, 1921, then Fort Simpson and so on, ending at Fort Rae on August 23, 1921. As Fumoleau discovered in compiling his documentary history of the treaty-making process, little in fact was written about discussions of the treaty on the ground in each settlement either in official documents or in press reports.

It was clear, for instance, that when the party arrived at Fort Simpson, the second stop on the river journey, there was little enthusiasm for a treaty. This was despite Conroy's earlier and repeated insistence to the Department that there was a universal desire on the part of the Indians throughout the Mackenzie for such an agreement. Yet all Conroy noted in his minutes to the Department was that, 'At first the Indians at this point were nearly unanimous in their decision to let "well enough" alone and to remain in the condition in which they had been heretofore, but after several talks and explanations, they all entered into Treaty, and elected their chief and headmen entirely to the satisfaction of myself' (Fumoleau 2004: 173). What the 'talks and explanations' consisted of, and how exactly the chief who signed on behalf of Fort Simpson residents was chosen, Conroy did not elucidate. There was little media reportage of the treaty signings. The Hudson's Bay Company's recently established historical magazine, *The Beaver,* observed that 'there is nothing spectacular about the payment of the treaty [11] ... and long-winded speeches by the Indians, tom-tom concerts and tea-dances are strictly taboo. Nothing but straight business goes' (ibid.).

The changes that the Department of Indian Affairs officials feared were about to come to the Northwest Territories did not eventuate in the interwar period. It was too difficult and costly to transport the oil from the far north to the south and the mining projects lagged. However, the Indian population of the NWT continued to grow and was also becoming increasingly impoverished, particularly once the bottom fell out of the fur trade market in the post-World War II era (Ray 1990). In the 1950s, Canadian governments once again began to look north. Governments expanded infrastructure including extensions to the highway from Edmonton that reached Yellowknife, the largest town in the NWT, in 1961, and by 1971 was heading towards Fort Simpson in the west. In the same period, the population across the NWT grew exponentially. In 1941, the total population of the NWT was 12,028; by 1971 it was 34,805; and in 1976 it had reached 42,610 (Helm 2001: 133). In 1971, the 'treaty Indian' population was 7,108, an absolute increase of over 60 percent from 30 years earlier – the majority of whom were young, under 25 years old (ibid.). The non-Indian population in the NWT increased over 600 percent, from 2,290 in 1941 to 16,225 in 1971 (ibid.).

Although Treaty 11 promised reserve lands for those who signed, those were never established. In 1959, a commission of inquiry was charged with recommending remedies for the unfulfilled treaty provisions of Treaties 8 and 11, in particular, the failure of the government to set aside reserves. Lamenting that reserves had not been established in the past, the commissioners nonetheless recommended *against* establishing reserves for contemporary Indians who were in a 'transitional stage' (Nelson *et al.* 1959). They pointed out that the idea of reserves smacked of paternalism. The government's job was now, the Commission opined, to encourage Indians to enter into the mainstream economy so that they would 'eventually become integrated into the Canadian way of life' (ibid.). Therefore, the commissioners recommended individual Indians should be provided individual or fee simple title to the plots of land they resided on and that bands should be given cash settlements for the lands they had ceded and annuity payments from mineral gas and oil resources. Payments to bands should be held in trust by the government (ibid.). None of the commission of inquiry's recommendations were put into effect.

The treaty-as-memory

As I explained earlier, when the Dene leaders brought their application for a land caveat to the NWT Supreme Court, they argued that the treaties their leaders had signed were agreements of 'peace and friendship' rather than agreements to land cession. They claimed ongoing aboriginal title rights. In order to prove such title, lawyers called on elderly witnesses who could remember the treaty signings, attest to what had or had not been promised, and also talk about Dene peoples' life on the land.

Michael Landry, an 87-year-old of Fort Providence who had attended a signing of Treaty 11 in 1921, was a key witness. Landry told the court he remembered that local people were given nets, shells, and flour when the treaty 'money' was first paid, and that there was a policeman who gave out the goods. The judge (referred to in the transcript as 'The court') sought more information, through the sworn interpreter, about Landry's personal circumstances and his way of life (Transcript, *Re Paulette and Registrar of Land Titles*, 17 July 1973: 347–348).

The court:	Is he not married?
The Interpreter:	He is married and still lives like the old days. He is nomadic. He goes to his old trapping grounds and now gets a pension.

The lawyer acting as *amicus curiae*, Dietrich Brand, then continued the examination, referring more particularly to what Landry remembered about the treaty signing:

Q:	Before the Treaty was signed, did you consider your-self to be a Canadian?
A:	Yes, he said before the white men came, he figured it was his own land.
The court:	When they made their 'X''s, can he remember if each man made his 'X' like that, or did somebody else take the pen and push their hand?
The Interpreter:	Yes, he says it is pretty hard for him to tell. Nobody knew how to write in those days.

Many Dene witnesses struggled to remember what had happened at treaty signings earlier in the century. Few witnesses gave clear or particularly detailed descriptions of treaty signings over 50 years earlier when most of those who had been present at or in the vicinity of the signings were in their teens and early twenties. The comments of several of those who appeared before the court suggested that the treaty signings had been insignificant to them.

According to June Helm, an anthropologist from the University of Iowa who had written her dissertation on Dene people, and who appeared as an expert witness in the Caveat case, land rights were not discussed locally prior to 1967. Before that, most complaints she heard were about hunting and trapping rights. In that year, she said that some of her Dogrib friends began expressing concerns – provoked by the visit of a Department of Indian Affairs official – that they were to be 'put on a reserve', an idea they found very distressing. She emphasised that no one thought the treaties were about land: 'It was not understood before,' she explained to the judge, 'and I understood in previous years [that the treaties were land cession deeds] although I did not bring this up with them and I wish I had brought it up before now feeling a sense of responsibility' (Transcript, *Re Paulette and Registrar of Land Titles*, 20 August 1973: 569–571; Asch 2002: 31–32).

During cross-examination, a number of witnesses' accounts became more confused, an experience that seemed to provoke anxiety for them as they worried, for instance, that the lawyers asking the questions thought they were lying even though they had sworn oaths. Elise Murphy, a 64-year old resident of Fort Rae and one of the few Dene women to give evidence in the caveat hearings, recalled how her father was reluctantly made chief during the treaty discussions in 1921. Her father accepted the treaty payments, she said, because an agreement was reached that as 'long as the sun is rising in the east and setting in the west and the river flows and as long as they never changed, there won't be any laws about the game, and also he mentioned about the map, how big the land he is going to use for his people. This is how the Treaty was paid' (Transcript, *Re Paulette and Registrar of Land Titles*, July 30 1973: 493). Gerry Sutton, the lawyer for the Indian Brotherhood, pressed her on this point, asking whether a particular piece of land was mentioned in the treaty. Murphy changed the story: no land was mentioned at the treaty signing. 'They hadn't mentioned anything about land, they didn't say they were getting money for the land' (ibid., July 30 1973: 495–496). Murphy admitted that she could not 'see' a map nor could she read or write. 'I don't know how to write,' she stated, 'I can't tell you a lie, I must tell you the truth. Do you feel I am not telling you the truth because you keep asking me these questions?' (ibid., July 30 1973: 497–498).

Perhaps most poignant was the testimony given by Jimmy Sibbeston. The court party (including the judge, two lawyers, and a court reporter) went to visit Sibbeston at his home in Hay River towards the end of the hearings on 23 August 1973. Justice Morrow explained to Sibbeston through his daughter that the court was there, 'to protect aboriginal rights and we are here to get his story' (Transcript, *Re Paulette and Registrar of Land Titles*, 23 August 1973: 879). But Sibbeston, who had worked as an interpreter for the treaty party in 1921 and had travelled down the river with them, could not remember what had been said exactly at the treaty signing back in 1921. 'He said he sits with the group and he interprets but he just forgets and he is just repeating his words. He says he sits with the group and he just forgets,' explained Sibbeston's daughter, Sarah, to the court party. It was too bad, she commented, that they weren't there a few years back, before he had suffered a stroke, when his memory was still good (ibid., 23 August 1973: 881–882).

Mr Sibbeston (or Sibbiston as his name appears in the Hudson's Bay Company records) died on 10 February 1974 when he was 100 years old (Hudson's Bay Company Archives). The transcript that I refer to in this chapter, and that I located in the special collections at the University of Calgary, must have been produced after this date, for he is named in it as the 'late Jimmy Sibbeston' (Transcript, *Re Paulette and Registrar of Land Titles*, 23 August 1973: 878).[4] Sibbeston did remember some of what happened at Fort Simpson where local people were reluctant to sign the treaty. 'For three days Norwegian [a leader in the settlement] showed no

---

4   In a letter to the Honourable Justice T. R. Berger the following year, in 1974, Morrow noted that Berger's staff had picked up copies of the transcripts and he enclosed accounts for the two court reporters who had produced them (Morrow 1974). Berger had recently been appointed to preside over the Mackenzie Valley Pipeline Inquiry that followed after the Caveat case that I discuss in this chapter. It is not clear why Morrow was expecting Berger's commission to pay the court reporters.

interest in Treaty,' Sibbeston told Morrow's court, recalling that he asked Norwegian why he wouldn't be a 'chief' for his people (ibid., 23 August 1973: 880). 'He said there were three Chiefs who wanted to go at it and he said he didn't want to see his land go. Therefore he did not want to take Treaty ... another guy they called Mustard became the chief' (ibid., 23 August 1973: 881). But when one of the lawyers pressed him for more details of the discussion at other treaty signings, Sibbeston demurred. He just couldn't remember more of what went on. The judge sympathetically intervened: 'I gather he can see the picture in his mind as he goes down the river,' said Morrow, 'but he can't tell us about it. I can see that.' 'It is true,' responded his daughter. 'That is what he means' (ibid., 23 August 1973: 882).

A journalist, Steve Hume, who was reporting on the case for the *Edmonton Journal* also referred to this testimonial moment. Observing the irony that Sibbeston's daughter 'was interpreting for a man who, himself, interpreted for the government in that summer when the northern Indians took treaty,' Hume referred to Sibbeston's struggle to remember (1973a). It is unclear whether Hume was in Sibbeston's house as well, or whether he wrote his account based on what others told him and the court reporter's notes.

Despite the struggle to remember, which a number of the elderly witnesses in this case experienced, Hume characterised the examination of Sibbeston and others as a kind of re-enactment. 'Again and again the judge had explained the purpose of the hearing as he flew from settlement to settlement hearing the testimony of the Mackenzie Valley's old people,' Hume emphasised, 'the ones who had seen another man come to give them Treaty 51 summers earlier' (1973a). With even more flourish, Hume had written in *Oilweek* the month before the examination of Sibbeston:

> The history in this case deals with human beings, not the interpretations of scholars writing after the fact. These old men, whom the court is seeking out in the settlements down the 1,200 mile length of the Mackenzie, are the very stuff of Canadian history. In them lies the origin of what the North is today and what it will be tomorrow, and in their memories rests first-hand knowledge of the wilderness Canada was and will never be again.
>
> (Hume 1973b)

Justice Morrow echoed this romantic vision in his decision on the case. 'I think almost every member of the Court party felt that for a short moment the pages of history were being turned back and we were privileged to relive the treaty-negotiating days in the actual setting,' he wrote, nonetheless qualifying his observation with the comment that such 'may not be pertinent to this Judgment' (*Re Paulette and Registrar of Land Titles 1973*: 313).

Despite the problems attending to many of these testimonies, Justice Morrow was convinced that Indians in the north maintained aboriginal title rights. According to him, this was a matter of fact, derived from the testimonies of Indian elders. They had convinced him that they were descendants of those who lived in 'organized societies and us[ed] the land as their forefathers had done for centuries'. The Canadian government therefore had a constitutional obligation, Morrow averred, to protect the rights of the claimants (*Re Paulette and Registrar of Land Titles 1973*: 339–340).

Conclusion: Archives and the site of law

The story of the treaty archive that I have described here was constructed in a context of significant and pressing political and economic change. As I have argued, the archive that was co-created by people such as René Fumoleau and June Helm, as well as organisations including the Indian Brotherhood for the Northwest Territories, was produced in the first instance in the service of new assertions of rights – in a broad sense to demonstrate how Indians were 'citizens plus'. The fact that the treaty archive was produced in this context, and for particular ends, does not make it less authentic or more opportunistic than any other archival project. However, I have suggested that the use and expansion of this archive in the site of law as Dene leaders sought recognition of their *legal* rights was particularly important.

In the court, two important things happened to the 'treaty archive'. First, the components of the archive that I have identified in this essay were given *legitimacy*. The set of official documents referring to treaties or other promises made to indigenous peoples in the past, which researchers had collected, were examined by the judge and lawyers and could be challenged or supported by other expert evidence. Even more significantly, the Indian elders who provided oral testimonies under oath were examined and cross-examined, and any potential inconsistencies laid bare – as was the case for Elise Murphy. Thus, both kinds of record, official documentation and historical memory, were juridically authorised. The archive that Fumoleau and the Brotherhood created outside of the law did not have the same kind of authority since it was not subjected to legal evidentiary process. This mattered in terms of how the state would recognise the claims of indigenous peoples and even how those claims could achieve recognition by settler publics too.

The examination and elaboration of the treaty archive in the site of law was particularly important for a second reason. The histories provided were given added authority as stories of *peoplehood*. This happened in two, somewhat divergent ways. The first was the legitimation of a growing sense of collective Dene peoplehood. In the face-to-face setting of the court, Dene

212 Miranda Johnson

people asserted who they were and who they were not. Most hearings were attended by other members of the settlements as well as Dene people from across the region. They listened to and supported or challenged each others' tales. The articulation of their present-day struggles, as well as their claims to ancient pasts, and even their struggles to remember accurately what had happened, offered the possibility of establishing a diverse but also coherent 'Dene-ness', as recorded in the legal testimonies and the treaty archive more broadly. Morrow recognised Dene peoplehood in his decision, when he referred to the claimants as descendants of the original inhabitants of the area.

The second way that archives in the site of law operated to establish, or newly ground, a sense of peoplehood was by incorporating Dene people into a story about *Canadian* nationhood. Again, the face-to-face interactions in the court encouraged Indian and non-Indian people to think about what they had in common and how they were different. For Justice Morrow, and reporters like Steve Hume, the common themes in the case strongly evoked a sense of frontier nostalgia. These 're-enactments' of history, as Hume put it, added to the case something of *national* value, that is, of value to the Canadian nation. Stories of frontier hardship and struggle might also be told from the archive constructed by Fumoleau and the Indian Brotherhood. However, that archive would not have come to have the wider public significance that it did, had the legal case not drawn attention to the demands of Indian activists. The process of constructing a *legal* archive through the hearing Indian elders' testimonies, had an added effect: publicising the stories of these northerners to a national audience and incorporating their memories of a (vanishing) history into national tropes of the frontier. Constructed in the face of loss, the 'treaty archive' that Dene leaders and others developed in the course of a legal claim offered new, diverse, even unexpected possibilities of imagination for Dene people themselves and for those who encountered them, and it may well have laid the ground for new disputes.

References

Aboriginal Affairs and Northern Development Canada. n.d., 'Treaty texts — Treaty 11', viewed 1 January 2015 <www.aadnc-aandc.gc.ca/>.

Asch, M. 2002, 'From *Terra Nullius* to Affirmation: Reconciling Aboriginal Rights with the Canadian Constitution', *Canadian Journal of Law and Society*, vol. 17, pp. 23–40.

Berger, T. 1977, *Northern Frontier, Northern Homeland: the report of the Mackenzie Valley Pipeline Inquiry*, Minister of Supply and Services Canada, Ottawa.

Cairns, A. 2000, *Citizens Plus: Aboriginal Peoples and the Canadian State*, UBC Press, Vancouver.

Cardinal, H. 1969, *The Unjust Society: The tragedy of Canada's Indians*, M.G. Hurtig, Edmonton.

Coates, K.S. and Morrison, W.R. 1986, *Treaty Research Report No. 11 (1921)*, Treaties and Historical Research Centre, Indian and Northern Affairs Canada, Ottawa.

Derrida, J. 1995, *Archive Fever: A Freudian Impression*, trans. E. Prenowitz, University of Chicago Press, Chicago and London.

Diefenbaker, J. 1958, 'A New Vision', opening campaign speech, 12 February, Winnipeg, <www.usask.ca/diefenbaker>.

Drees, L.M. 2002, *The Indian Association of Alberta: A History of Political Action*, University of British Columbia Press, Vancouver.

Duff, W.M. and Harris, V. 2002, 'Stories and Names: Archival Description as Narrating Records and Constructing Meanings,' *Archival Science*, vol. 2, pp. 263–285.

Eber, D.H. 1997, *Images of Justice: A Legal History of the Northwest Territories as Traced Through the Yellowknife Courthouse Collection of Inuit Sculpture*, McGill-Queen's University Press, Montreal.

Foster, H., Raven, H., and Webber, J. 2007, *Let Right Be Done: Aboriginal title, the Calder case, and the future of Indigenous rights*, UBC Press, Vancouver.

Fumoleau, R, 2004, *As Long as This Land Shall Last: A History of Treaty 8 and Treaty 11, 1870–1939*, University of Calgary Press, Calgary.

Hawthorn, H.B. 1966, *A Survey of the Contemporary Indians of Canada: A Report on Economic, Political and Educational Needs and Policies in Two Volumes*, vol. 1, Indian Affairs Branch, Ottawa.

Helm, J. 2001, *The People of Denedeh: Ethnohistory of the Indians of Canada's Northwest Territories*, McGill-Queen's University Press, Montreal and Kingston.

Hudson's Bay Company Archives. n.d., 'Biographical Sheets', viewed 1 January 2015 <www.gov.mb.ca/chc/archives/hbca/biographical/s/sibbiston_james-jimmy1902-1927.pdf>.

Hume, S. 1973a, *Edmonton Journal*, 24 August.

Hume, S. 1973b, *Oilweek*, 30 July.

'Indian Brotherhood explains freeze' 1973, *Tapwe*, 11 April.

Indian Brotherhood of the N.W.T. 1973. 'Budget Submission Regarding Research Leading to a Settlement of Indian Land Claims in the N.W.T. August 1, 1973,' *Indian Claims Commission Files 1970–1976*, RG 33-115, 9-2-5, Libraries and Archives Canada, Ottawa.

Indian Chiefs of Alberta 1970, *Citizens Plus*, A Presentation by the Indian Chiefs of Alberta to the Right Honourable P.E. Trudeau, Prime Minister and the Government of Canada, June, Edmonton.

'Indians have more land rights than he [Trudeau] thought' 1973, *Globe and Mail*, 8 February, p. 8.

Jamieson, K. 1978, *Indian Women and the Law in Canada: Citizens Minus*, Advisory Council on the Status of Women, Ottawa.

Mawani, R. 2012, 'Law's Archive', *Annual Review of Law and Social Science*, vol. 8 pp. 337–365.

Miller, J.R. 2009, *Compact, Contract, Covenant: Aboriginal Treaty-Making in Canada*, University of Toronto Press, Toronto.

Morrow, W.G. 1974, 'Morrow to Berger', 28 August 1974, Morrow Fonds, MS 261, Box 18/166, Special Collections, University of Calgary.

Morrow, W.G. and Morrow, W.H. 1995, *Northern Justice: the memoirs of Mr. Justice William G. Morrow*, University of Toronto Press, Toronto.

Nelson, W.H. *et al.* 1959, *Report of the Commission Appointed to Investigate the Unfulfilled Provisions of Treaties 8 and 11 as They Apply to the Indians of the Mackenzie District*, The Commission, Prince Albert, Saskatchewan.

Promislow, J. 2012, '"It Would Only Be Just": A Study of Territoriality and Trading Posts along the Mackenzie River, 1800–27', in L. Ford and T. Rowse (eds), *Between Indigenous and Settler Governance*, Routledge, New York, pp. 35–47.

Ray, A.J. 1990, *The Canadian Fur Trade in the Industrial Age*, University of Toronto Press, Toronto.

Re Paulette and Registrar of Land Titles (No. 2), 42 D.L.R. (3d) 8 (1973).

The Dene Nation 1984, *Denedeh: A Dene Celebration*, The Dene Nation, Yellowknife.

Transcript of *Re Paulette*, July-August 1973, Morrow fonds, MS 261, Box 50/166, Special Collections, University of Calgary.

Trudeau, P. 1998, 'Official Statement by the Prime Minister: The Just Society [1968]', in R. Graham (ed.), *The Essential Trudeau*, McClelland & Stewart, Inc., Toronto.

Weaver, S.M. 1981, *Making Canadian Indian Policy: The Hidden Agenda, 1968–70*, University of Toronto Press, Toronto.

Chapter 11

Schmitt's *Weisheit der Zelle*

Rethinking the concept of the political

Jacques de Ville

Introduction

In *Constitutional Theory* (1928), Carl Schmitt contends that liberal constitutionalism represses the political component of the modern constitution,
especially the question of sovereignty (Schmitt 2008: 93, 187). According to
Schmitt, the political component should in fact guide the understanding of
the constitution, rather than the rule of law component, with, at its foundation, first the idea of freedom existing prior to and superior to the state,
and second the limitation of state powers through the principle of separation of powers. Schmitt reflected on the concept of the political itself in the
1927 text *The Concept of the Political* (Schmitt 2007a; hereinafter, *The
Concept*). In the latter text, Schmitt shows the centrality of human nature to
the concept of the political, with the latter to be understood as the drawing
of a distinction between friend and enemy, with war as its most extreme
possibility. Schmitt finds support for his definition of the concept of the
political specifically in the reflections of political thinkers who acknowledge man as a 'dangerous and dynamic' being (2007a: 61). Schmitt is
consequently of the view that attempts to repress or deny the political
cannot succeed, being inescapable due to human nature.

In the 1947 essay 'Wisdom of the Prison Cell' (*Wisdom*) in *Ex Captivitate
Salus* Schmitt relies on his own precarious situation to further reflect on the
issue of human nature (Schmitt 2010: 79–91). He analyses the so-called
'new man' of technology and a number of texts, specifically Max Stirner's
The Ego and Its Own (1910/2006), to reflect on this issue, as well as on a
certain 'abyss', which appears to be at stake here (Schmitt 2010: 81).
Schmitt also returns to his reflections on the enemy in *The Concept* (2010:
88–90). In so doing, he moves beyond simple opposition, for example that
between good and evil, to arrive at the 'structure', or what Jacques Derrida
would call the 'differantial stricture' of the human being (1987: 351). The
aim of this chapter is to establish the implications of Schmitt's *Wisdom* for
the concept of the political, which could, in the sense in which Schmitt
views it in *Constitutional Theory*, and in view of the theme of the present

collection of chapters, be referred to as law's 'counter-archive'. This enquiry will take place primarily through an analysis of *Wisdom*, and of Derrida's *Politics of Friendship*, where he discusses Schmitt's *Wisdom* (Derrida 1997: 159–167). Before we start with the analysis of *Wisdom*, let us first look briefly at the context within which it was written.

After the Second World War, Schmitt was interned briefly by the Russians in April 1945 and thereafter again on two occasions by the Americans, from September 1945 to October 1946 and from March 1947 to May 1947. During his second detention he was interrogated by Robert Kempner at Nuremberg to determine whether he should be charged with participating, directly or indirectly, in the planning of wars of aggression, war crimes and crimes against humanity (Bendersky 1987, 2007; Schmitt 1987, 2007b). During his time in Nuremberg, Schmitt wrote a number of smaller texts, including *Wisdom*, which was published in 1950 under the title *Ex Captivitate Salus* (Schmitt 2010). In *Wisdom*, Schmitt again takes up the issue of the enemy, which played a central role in his reflections in *The Concept*, and which would again come to the fore in *The Theory of the Partisan* (1963) (*The Theory*). In *Wisdom* the enemy is not, however, or at least not in the first place, the enemy confronted in external or civil war, as in *The Concept*, or the partisan, as in *The Theory*, but the self, or the brother. Schmitt suggests that the self, and by implication, the concept of the political, is haunted by a force of self-destruction. If the concept of the political is indeed law's counter-archive, this force of self-destruction calls for a certain 'radicalisation' of the notion of the counter-archive. The concept of the political, with reference to which law is ultimately to be understood, in *Wisdom* implodes on itself. At stake in the counter-archive would then not be something against, counter to, or opposed to the archive, which perhaps still remains too complicit in archive production,[1] but perhaps rather some 'thing' archive destroying.

Defining man: Nakedness

Schmitt starts his reflections in *Wisdom* by asking himself which of the definitions of man in circulation appears self-evident. For him, this is the fact that the human being (*der Mensch*) is naked. The most naked is the human being who, without clothes, appears before another who is clothed; someone who has been disarmed, appearing before someone who is armed; someone who is powerless, appearing before someone powerful. Schmitt notes that this is an experience that Adam and Eve already had when they were driven from paradise (2010: 79). This raises the further question whether the definition of the human being is to be attached to the first or

---

1 The example here would be constituent power, which can abolish a constitution and set a new, perhaps more inclusive one in its place.

Schmitt's *Weisheit der Zelle*   217

the second category of person in every instance, and in addition, which of these is closer to paradise. Schmitt leaves open the question, posed in such stark oppositional terms. In the versions of paradise promoted in the present age, Schmitt comments, human beings go around clothed (ibid.). In contrast, Schmitt sees himself as clearly naked and proceeds to quote Theodor Daübler's *Perseus*: 'Now you stand naked, naked as at birth [*geburthaft nackt*], in desert expanses [*in wüsten Weiten*] (cited in Schmitt 2010: 79). The pieces of clothing that were left for him, he says, only confirm his nakedness in an objective sense. Even more so, the clothing underlines his nakedness in a highly ironic, as well as unpleasantly accentuated manner. One experiences oneself being thrown back onto one's last reserves, Schmitt notes (2010: 80). Further emphasising his own vulnerability, he notes that his remaining physical powers can very easily be extinguished (ibid.). Then, continuing his reflections on the definition of man, Schmitt recalls the sentence in Richard Wagner's *Twilight of the Gods* (*Götterdämmerung*) (1876): *Einzig erbt ich den eigenen Leib, lebend zehr ich ihn auf* ('Singularly do I inherit my own body, living, I feed on it') (cited in Schmitt 2010: 80). This passage is sung by Siegfried in what Schmitt refers to as 'a wonderful collapsing and crashing interval' (ibid.). It captures in unparalleled fashion an exuberant physical feeling of happiness, Schmitt says, which still rides upon the waves which led to the 1848 revolution in Germany (ibid.). Schmitt however notes that the passage is originally found in Max Stirner,[2] and that with Stirner we approach the idea of paradisiacal nakedness (in contrast to modern versions of paradise where, as we saw, man is clothed) (ibid.). At stake here appears to be Stirner's insistence on the self's identity with itself, which Schmitt clearly finds problematic:

> Thus at any rate: glorious solidarity: We could call to millions in the choir 'nothing is beyond me, and I am I'. You can perhaps say that of yourself as well as the millions in your choir who shout with you. I can unfortunately only say of myself that I don't know whether I am I/ego [*ob ich Ich bin*] and whether nothing is beyond me. I do not know how things stand with this I/ego/self of mine [*wie es sich mit diesem meinem Ich verhält*], whether it is a fixed star or a marsh light, or both. Are you singular [*ein Einziger*] or are you a thousand and countless selves in your I/ego/self [*bist Du tausend und zahllose Ich in Deinem Ich*]. All of this I do not know. I do not know who I am. If you know who you are, all the better. Let your knowledge serve you.
>
> (Schmitt 1991: 48)

2   The reference here is most likely to Stirner where he says: 'this, that I consume myself, means only that I am [*dass Ich Mich verzehre, heisst nur, dass Ich bin*]' (2006: 135) and where Stirner refers to the mortal creator of the self 'who consumes himself [*der sich selbst verzehrt*]' (2006: 324). Schmitt elsewhere refers to these passages, which he appears to approve of, though somewhat mockingly (1991: 48).

Stirner, his ego and modern technology

Schmitt notes that he read Stirner in High School (*Unterprima*) and that this prepared him for many recent events, which would otherwise have surprised him (2010: 80–81). Stirner's *The Ego and Its Own* was published in 1844 and Schmitt notes that the European thought process from 1830–1848 prepares one also for present world events (2010: 81). What Schmitt refers to as the debris field (*das Trümmerfeld*) of the self-decomposition (*der Selbstzersetzung*) of German theology and idealist philosophy, had since 1848 developed itself into a force field of theogonic and cosmogonic approaches (ibid.). What is exploding in the present, Schmitt notes, was already prepared before 1848 (ibid.). The fire that is burning in the present was built then. There are, he continues, with clear reference to the at-the-time recently developed atom bomb, some uranium mines of intellectual history (*Uran-Bergwerke der Geistesgeschichte*), which include the pre-Socratics, some church fathers and also certain writings of the time before 1848 (ibid.).[3] The poor Max (Stirner), Schmitt notes, also falls perfectly within this category (i.e. of atomic thinkers) (ibid.). This categorisation of Stirner should, as also appears from the use of the adjective 'poor' (*arme*) not be read as unqualified praise. 'On the whole', Schmitt says, Stirner is hideous, boorish, pretentious, boastful, a tormentor (*ein Pennalist*), a depraved student (*ein verkommener Studiker*), oafish (*ein Knote*), an egomaniac (*ein Ich-Verrückter*), obviously a serious psychopath (*ein schwerer Psychopath*) (ibid.). Stirner, Schmitt continues with his mocking, crows with a loud, unpleasant voice: 'I am I. I feel no authority over me', and his word-sophisms are unbearable (ibid.). This vehement denunciation of Stirner can, as we saw above, partly be ascribed to Stirner's view in relation to self-identity, which is for Schmitt the issue at stake here. As noted above, in *The Concept*, Schmitt ascribes to inter alia Thomas Hobbes's view on the nature of man and declares that 'all genuine political theories presuppose man to be evil, i.e. by no means an unproblematic but a dangerous and dynamic being' (Schmitt 2007a: 61).[4] In *The Nomos of the Earth*, in a discussion of Hobbes's *homo homine lupus*, Schmitt mentions Stirner as one of those who had (erroneously) denied the truth of this maxim (Schmitt 2006: 96). Yet perhaps he did not deny it completely, as we will see shortly.

---

3   Schmitt strikingly refers to the revolutionary events around 1848, which appeared under the slogans of socialism, communism, anarchism, atheism and nihilism (2002: 100–101), with which Schmitt associates Stirner (Schmitt 1991: 21) as an abyss (*Abgrund*) opening up.

4   Tying in closely with the analysis that will be undertaken here of *Wisdom*, Emily Zakin points out that Schmitt in *The Concept* problematises 'the liberal assumption that human nature is "good and educable" and that a suitable regime can thus remake this nature in a feat of human engineering' (Zakin 2011: 98).

Apart from the backhanded compliment that Stirner counts among the atomic thinkers of the nineteenth century, Schmitt also gives Stirner credit for realising that the 'I' (*das Ich*) is not an object of thought (*Denkobjekt*).'[5] This is likely to be at least partially a reference to Stirner's earlier statement that the 'I' has to be found 'behind thoughts' (ideas, conceptions, faith, the truth), that is, as their creator and owner (Schmitt 1995: 17). How is this ambivalence towards Stirner to be understood? If we take account of the fact that the same Stirner, also in the reading of Schmitt,[6] did battle with ghosts, which he showed to continuously haunt the 'I', we can make sense of Schmitt's ambivalence (1991: 48). Schmitt appears to adopt a reading here of Stirner similar to that of Derrida in *Specters of Marx* in terms of which Ego equals ghost. Derrida puts this as follows:

> Stirner has often been read, in fact, as a Fichtean thinker. But this Ego, this *living individual* would itself be inhabited and invaded by its *own specter*. It would be constituted by specters of which it becomes the host and which it assembles in the haunted community of a single body. Ego=ghost [*Moi=fantôme*]. Therefore 'I am' would mean 'I am haunted'. ... Wherever there is Ego, *es spukt*, 'it spooks'.
>
> (Derrida 2006: 166)

In further support of this reading, we see that Schmitt, after expressing his admiration for the title of Stirner's *Der Einzige und sein Eigentum* – declaring it to be the most beautiful, or in any event, the most German (*deutschesten*) book title in the whole of German literature – notes that in this moment Max is the only one/the Ego [*der Einzige*] who visits him in his prison cell (2010: 81–82).[7] This visit, Schmitt says, with perhaps a tint of irony, touches him deeply in view of Stirner's rabid egoism (ibid.: 82). The Ego/ghost haunting Schmitt in his prison cell, as we will see further below, can be said to stand at the 'origin' of thought, which perhaps explains why Schmitt confirms that it cannot be the object of the latter (ibid.: 81). The ghost thus appears to tell Schmitt something about the definition of the human that he is searching for.

The ultimate drive (*letzten Antrieb*) or true longing (*wahre Sensucht*) of the 'I'-lunatic (*Ich-Verrückten*) Stirner is, according to Schmitt, to be found expressed in a letter written by Stirner (Schmitt 2010: 82). With this we

---

5   Schmitt likewise comments as follows after having quoted a passage from Stirner's *The Ego and Its Own*: 'I am I; I am no object of thinking, but I; no idea and no concept' [*Ich bin Ich; Ich bin kein Denkobjekt, sondern Ich; keine Idee und kein Begriff*]' (1991: 100).

6   'The remarkable thing about Max Stirner is ... the desperation of his struggle with the fraud [*Schwindel*] and ghosts [*Gespestern*] of his time' (Schmitt 1991: 48).

7   Schmitt reports that he was given a copy of Stirner's *Der Einzige und sein Eigentum* by Peter Heinrich Kirchoff at 0600 on 17 February 1948 (1991: 100).

220 Jacques de Ville

return to the Stirnerian paradise mentioned above. In this letter, Stirner declares that the new paradise will consist of an overcoming of self-estrangement and self-alienation in a perfect bodily presence (ibid.). Man would then again become like the animals of the forest and the flowers in the fields. Schmitt compares Stirner's paradise to Hieronymus Bosch's *The Garden of Earthly Delights* (1500). In this paradise there will be a pure identity of man with himself. Over the next few pages, which for the purpose of this chapter cannot be explored in great detail, Schmitt points by contrast to the monopolisation of the 'I' by the artificial paradise of modern technology (2010: 83–86). The latter however only benefits the new elite, i.e. the gods of the new paradise.[8] Returning to the opening question of the definition of the human and his being clothed or naked, Schmitt speculates about the abilities of modern technology to make clothing obsolete, at least for the new elite. He describes the new human, to be produced by modern technology, as the totally other (*das ganz Andere*), as incalculable (*unberechenbar*), and as neither naked nor clothed, but transformed into radiation (*Strahlung*) (ibid.: 86).

Being placed in question

We pick up Schmitt's analysis again in more detail when he raises the question of whether he has been placed on earth to ensure through his labour that technology can transform us into radiation (Schmitt 2010: 86). If this is indeed the case, he asks, whose command must I subject myself to, in order to undertake my labour? He raises this question, he notes, because he has for a long time not been alone or lonely, but organisationally monopolised (*organisatorisch vereinnahmt*) (ibid.).[9] Schmitt however cuts himself short. The above questions may actually no longer be asked in the new world. In fact, questions may no longer be asked at all. One must instead answer the questions posed to oneself. Questionnaires are now prepared by others, which place one in question together with one's questions (*die dich mitsamt deinen Fragen in Frage stellen*).[10] Schmitt makes a call to

8 Schmitt's analysis here corresponds with Schmitt (2002: 114) about Donoso Cortés' recognition of man's tendency to terrorise and destroy all others who do not submit to him, as well as the rise of the superhuman, with his murderous counter-concept, the subhuman, which opens the terrible abyss of enmity. The subhuman 'deserves' only extermination and destruction in the eyes of the superhuman (see also Schmitt 2007a: 54).

9 As we will see below, Schmitt appears to suggest with this that one is always already confronted by the evil genius of Descartes, represented here by modern technology.

10 See in this respect the opening pages of *Ex Captivitate Salus* where Schmitt reports that he was asked towards the end of 1945 by Eduard Spränger to fill in a questionnaire (in 14 points about his Nazi sympathies and anti-Semitism) (2010: 9–10). Spränger, at the time Rector of the Friedrich Wilhelms University and member of an executive committee tied to the Berlin local authority with the function of investigating political affiliations to National Socialism, told Schmitt that what he had thought and said may be interesting

Schmitt's *Weisheit der Zelle* 221

the reader (and to himself perhaps) to finally grasp what this means (ibid.: 87). In the opening essay of *Ex Captivitate Salus* ('Conversation with Eduard Spränger') we see something similar when Schmitt notes that he finds the prosecutorial function, to which he is being subjected, even more uncanny (*unheimlicher*) than the inquisitorial (ibid.: 11).[11] He ascribes this to his own theological roots, because, as he points out, *Diabolos* means prosecutor (*Ankläger*) (ibid.). His experience of his own prosecution, Schmitt suggests, places him in a similar position as Descartes who was confronted by the *spiritus malignus* (ibid.: 87).[12]

Following Derrida, we can say, also with reference to what happens later in *Wisdom*, that the posing of the questions 'Who is then my enemy? Who can I then ultimately recognise as my enemy?' and the answer to the questions, 'Obviously only he who can place me in question. Insofar as I recognise him as enemy, I recognise that he can place me in question. And who can really place me in question? Only I myself. Or my brother' (Schmitt 2010: 89) is inscribed into a self-questioning, that is, a being-placed-in-question (Derrida 1997: 162–163). This self-questioning, as Derrida points out, is no longer a theoretical question, a question of knowledge or recognition (ibid.).[13] The question is posed by someone, who first of all puts the question to himself, as an attack, a wound, a complaint, the calling into question of the one who questions. The enemy and the question are therefore inseparable, as also expressed in Däubler's *Hymne an Italien*: 'The enemy is our own question as figure', which Schmitt quotes on the second-last page of *Wisdom* (Schmitt 2010: 90).[14] Yet one poses the question of the enemy, as Schmitt does, only because one is first of all being placed in question by it (Derrida 1997: 150).[15]

The 'question' which is at stake here is clearly not simply any question, but the philosophical question itself, which as Martin Heidegger has

and clear but that it was never clear who he was as a person. Schmitt refused to complete the questionnaire. He however referred to himself on this occasion as a Christian Epimetheus, which Meier makes much of in his analysis of Schmitt as a political theologian (Meier 1998). We will explore the implications of Schmitt's statement further below with reference to what it tells us about the (philosophical) question.

11 Schmitt appears to also be alluding to the criminalisation of the enemy in general, whereby the very humanity of a section of mankind is denied, that is, placed in question (see Schmitt 2007a: 54–55).

12 See par 'Descartes and the self as enemy' below.

13 See similarly the section above entitled 'Defining man: Nakedness' on Schmitt's analysis of Stirner.

14 Däubler (1919: 65): 'Der Feind ist unsre eigne Frage als Gestalt. Und er wird uns, wir ihn zum selben Ende hetzen [And he will hound us, and we him, to the same end/for the same purpose]'. References to this passage in Däubler can also be found in Schmitt (1991: 213; 2004: 61).

15 See similarly Derrida and Dufourmantelle (2000: 3–5) on the question of the foreigner, who places me in question.

222 Jacques de Ville

shown, is closely connected to the nature of man (2005: 32).[16] Derrida is indeed alluding here to Heidegger, and one could explore the issue at stake also through a reflection on the essence of language, as Derrida does in more detail elsewhere (1997: 150).[17] In *Politics of Friendship*, Derrida notes that the whole history of the (philosophical) question, starting with the question of Being, as well as the whole of history which has been governed by the latter question (i.e. philosophy, epistemology, history, research, investigation, inquisition, etc.), has been accompanied by polemical violence, strategy and arms techniques (ibid.).[18] Without suggesting that the question itself should be renounced, Derrida notes that what is at stake in *Wisdom* can be said to be a movement beyond and before the question, before and beyond all war, which enables the deployment of the question; in other words, a movement towards 'the perhaps', towards that 'space' and 'time' that 'precedes' the friend and enemy passing into each other in the form of the brother (1997: 150).[19] One would, Derrida suggests, have to hear an exclamation mark before the question mark (ibid.). The Aristotelian 'O my friends, there is no friend!' and the Nietzschean reversal, 'O enemies, there is no enemy!', point for Derrida towards this movement (ibid.). This double outcry would be addressed both to the friend and to the enemy who is no longer or not yet (ibid.). What is at stake is, in other words, a friendship – exceeding all measurement, moderation, and calculation, and involving no concern for the self, thereby characterising the perfect gift – before the friend/enemy distinction of the political as well as the Schmittian/Däublerian notion of the enemy as our question as figure, in this way leading to a repositioning of the political (ibid.: 244, 249).[20] Schmitt appears to also allude to this when, after having quoted Däubler to the effect that the enemy is our own question as figure, he (implicitly) refers to the sayings of Aristotle and Nietzsche, whilst insisting (as in *The Concept*) on the necessity of making this distinction:

16 'This understanding of being [*Seinsverständnis*], which comes to expression in philosophy [i.e. of the being of beings], cannot be invented or thought up by philosophy itself. Rather, since *philosophising is awakened as a primal activity of man* [das *Philosophieren als Urhandlung des Menschen in diesem selbst erwacht*], arising thus from man's nature prior to any explicit philosophical thinking, and since an understanding of being is already implicit in the pre-philosophical existence of man (for otherwise he could not relate to beings at all) philosophy's understanding of being expresses what man is in his pre-philosophical existence. This awakening of the understanding of being, this self-discovery of the understanding of being, is the birth of philosophy from the Dasein in man.' (Heidegger 2005: 32)
17 See also Derrida (1991: 129–136).
18 See also Derrida's engagement with Heidegger's Rectorate address (1993a: 201–202).
19 'The question is already strict-uring, is already girded being [*La question est déjà stricturante, l'être ceint*]' (Derrida 1990: 191a).
20 See also Derrida on the friend as the figureless (*le sans-figure*) (1991: 175).

Woe to him who has no *friend*, as his enemy will judge him.
Woe to him who has no *enemy*, as *I* will become his enemy on the day of judgment.

(Schmitt 2010: 90)

Self-deception

Again underlining his own/man's vulnerability in the new world, Schmitt, having invoked the issue of being placed in question by questionnaires, notes that it would show a lack of taste to delude oneself (like Stirner, perhaps) due to the luxury of one's solitary confinement into thinking that one is simply forlorn (*vereinsamt*) in the cell and not already for a long time monopolised (*vereinnahmt*) (2010: 87). Schmitt concludes the section by asking himself/the reader whether he wants to succumb anew to deception (ibid.). This can of course be read as an admission of having been misled by National Socialism, but read in the context of Schmitt's reflections on his own/man's non-autonomy, being placed in question and being prosecuted, at stake here (in addition) seems to be the question of the structure of the human, particularly the relation to self-deception.

Self-deception, Schmitt notes, belongs to isolation (2010: 87).[21] Someone who is isolated thinks by himself and speaks to himself, and in soliloquy we of course speak to a dangerous sycophant (*einem gefährlichen Schmeichler*).[22] The moralists, Schmitt says, are correct in regarding an autobiography as a sign of vanity (ibid.).[23] Yet vanity would be the most harmless and amiable of the motives that come into play here (that is, in Schmitt's quasi-autobiography), he comments (ibid.).[24] The holy, he notes further, in

---

21 Above we saw that Schmitt also links 'isolation' with monopolisation (by technology). Self-deception and monopolisation both appear to announce a break with self-identity.

22 In *The Theory*, Schmitt alludes to this division within the self with reference to General Salan who fought both against the French and the Algerian front: 'Is it not a sign of inner division to have more than one single real enemy? The enemy is our own question as *Gestalt*. If we have determined our own *Gestalt* unambiguously, where does this double enemy come from?' (2004: 60–61).

23 Gopal Balakrishnan contends, with reference to the opening sentence of *Ex Captivitate Salus* (Who are you?/*Wer bist du?*) that Schmitt in this text answers the question 'who was Carl Schmitt?', which would make *Wisdom* a kind of autobiography (Balakrishnan 2000: 256).

24 In seeking to understand what Schmitt may be alluding to here, we can refer to Derrida (2011: 86–87) who, in an analysis of Defoe's *Robinson Crusoe* points out that 'every autobiography ... presents itself through this linguistic and prosthetic apparatus – a book – or a piece of writing or a trace in general ... which speaks of him without him, according to a trick that constructs and leaves in the world an artefact that speaks all alone [*tout seul*] and all alone calls the author by his name, renames him in his renown [*le renomme en sa renommée*] without the author himself needing to do anything else, not even be alive. The fantasy (of being buried alive), which provokes such writing as well as technology (see also Derrida 2011: 130), we will come across again below.

224 Jacques de Ville

a quasi-confession of guilt, do not write autobiographies (ibid.). In the deepest core of the prison cell, he says, lies soliloquy and self-deception (ibid.). Schmitt compares this to the excruciating dread of Descartes who philosophises in his solitary room by the fireplace, and who thinks only of escaping the evil, deceptive spirit, that is, the *spiritus malignus* from whose treachery we are never safe, the least when we think ourselves secure (ibid.). In the fear of deception, Descartes becomes a masked man, *l'homme au masque* (2010: 87–88). Similar to the new man, whom Schmitt spoke of earlier, the masked man is no longer naked and also no longer clothed. '*Larvatus prodeo* [I proceed wearing a mask]', he says (about himself), quoting Descartes (Schmitt 2010: 88). The dread, Schmitt says, is so much more excruciating, as one comes closer to the source (*zur Quelle*), where there are ever more deceptions (ibid.: 87). Someone who thinks only of evading deception walks straight into it (ibid.: 88). The deceptions at stake here, Schmitt comments, casting the net as wide as possible, are those of feeling and of mind, of flesh and spirit, of vice and virtue, of man and of woman (ibid.). Schmitt notes, again in a quasi-confession, that he always again succumbs to deception (ibid.). Yet, he says, he has always again evaded it, presumably, in view of what Schmitt just said, after having at first faced up to its inescapability.[25] Also with the final jump, Schmitt says, he will succeed in doing so. He ends the paragraph with a call: 'Come, dear death [*Komm, geliebter Tod*]' (ibid.).

After having made this call to death, perhaps expressing thereby his deepest desire,[26] Schmitt nonetheless acknowledges that death too can deceive us. He mentions two problematic understandings of death here: as a jump into the sphere of freedom,[27] and as the sweet heathen/heaths dying (2010: 88).[28] Schmitt's mention of death in the same breath as deception, suggests that he sees death as the ultimate deceiver.[29] All deception, Schmitt notes in support of this reading, is and remains self-deception (ibid.). The self-shielding (*Selbstverpanzerung*) of Stirner, Schmitt notes, is self-deception of the highest order (2010: 88). Stirner's combination of harmlessness and cunning, honest provocation and deceitful swindle,

---

25 See also Derrida (1997: 160).

26 See par 'Echo' below.

27 An allusion to Engels (1894: 318): 'It is only from this point that men, with full consciousness, will fashion their own history; it is only from this point that the social causes set in movement by men will have, predominantly and in constantly increasing measure, the effects willed by men. It is humanity's leap from the realm of necessity into the realm of freedom (*Es ist der Sprung der Menschheit aus dem Reiche der Notwendigkeit in das Reich der Freiheit*).'

28 An allusion to Däubler's (1916) 'Grünes Elysium' in *Das Sternenkind*: 'Die Pflanzen lehren uns der Heiden sanftes Sterben' [plants teach us the sweet heathen/heaths dying].

29 See also on the relation to death, Derrida (1993b: 67, 76–77; 1987: 363). Derrida likewise refers to the evil genius of Descartes as 'the deceitful one par excellence' (1997: 160).

Schmitt's *Weisheit der Zelle* 225

Schmitt describes as 'hideous' (*häßlich*) (ibid.). Like every person obsessed with the 'I' (*jeder Ich-Verrückte*), he sees in the non-I the enemy.[30] In this way, the whole world becomes his enemy and he imagines that they must believe it when he, non-committally (*freibleibend*), offers them a brotherly kiss (ibid.).[31] He hides himself before the dialectical splitting force of the 'I' and seeks to escape the enemy by deceiving him. However, the enemy is an objective power. He (i.e. Stirner, and perhaps also humanity in general) will not escape from him and the real enemy (*echte Feind*) does not allow himself to be deceived.[32]

Descartes and the self as enemy

In the last two pages of *Wisdom*, Schmitt reflects further on the enemy, asking, as we saw above, who one can ultimately recognise as one's enemy, and concludes that this can only be someone who can put me in question (2010: 89).[33] When I recognise someone as enemy, he continues, 'I accept that he can place me in question. And who can really place me in question?' (ibid.). He then asks, and answers: 'Only I myself. Or my brother [*Nur ich mich selbst. Oder mein Bruder*] (ibid.)'[34] In his analysis of this passage, Derrida notes that the '*oder*/or' in this sentence fulfils the function of both an alternative and of equivalence, that is, 'myself as my brother: myself or, if it is not me, my brother' (1997: 163).[35] With the notion of being one's own enemy, Derrida further comments, Schmitt both confirms and contradicts everything he had said about the enemy up to this point (1997: 163). We find in *Wisdom* the same insistence on correctly identifying the enemy, as in *The Concept* and *The Theory*. Yet whereas Schmitt's concern in these two texts is to guard the borders of the self, that is, of the proper, here the enemy is said to be lodged within the proper, the familial, the own home, at the heart of resemblance and affinity, within the *oikeiotes*, where actually, in terms of the logic of *The Concept* and *The Theory*, only the friend should

---

30 Schmitt elsewhere charges Germans with at first seeing in every non-I the enemy, and then, in coming to their senses, treating the whole world as friend (1991: 220).

31 This appears to be an allusion to, on the one hand, all the 'enemies' to ownness that Stirner detects in the family, community, society, the state, the nation, mankind, religion, fixed ideas, etc., and, on the other, to Stirner's epoch of egoism where there will be a union [*Verein*] of egoists, but where one will nonetheless continue to live egoistically (2006).

32 The name 'Stirner' here appears to serve as metonym for the German nation.

33 These two pages could also be explored with reference to their Hegelian heritage, but space does not allow for this here.

34 See likewise Schmitt (1991: 217).

35 In *Politics of Friendship* Derrida refers to what is regarded as the crime of crimes, and which Schmitt was accused of participating in: the crime against humanity; Derrida contends that this crime should be understood in terms of fratricide as 'the general form of temptation, the possibility of radical evil, the evil of evil (1997: 273).

226 Jacques de Ville

have been lodged (Derrida 1997: 163, 172). The enemy as the most improper, as Derrida points out, is here identified with the proper, with the self (ibid.: 163). The most proper is in other words the most foreign, the most *unheimlich*. The enemy did not appear only after the friend, to oppose or negate him, but was always already there (ibid.: 172).

Schmitt arrives at this point, as we saw, by seeking a definition of man with reference to his own situation as well as of humanity in general in the new era. Descartes' evil genius, through which he places in question the metaphysical foundations of knowledge, as we saw above, plays an important role here as well. Descartes asks in this respect what the position would be if the God he believes in, and has always trusted in, were an evil genius who is deceiving him so that all his certainties are actually deceptions (Descartes 1968: 100). To understand what is at stake here, it will be useful to briefly look at Derrida's 'Cogito and the History of Madness' (Derrida 1978: 31–63).[36] The evil genius invoked by Descartes can, Derrida contends, be likened to a 'total madness' which exceeds metaphysics, that is, 'a total derangement over which I could have no control because it is inflicted upon me – hypothetically – leaving me no responsibility for it' (1978: 52–53). After this invocation, Descartes quickly seeks to reassure himself that he is not mad (ibid.: 54). He does so by way of language, which is, as Derrida points out, necessarily tied to reason, and therefore in itself entails a break with madness (ibid.: 54–55). Madness in this sense continues to haunt philosophy, as we can also see from the reflections of Stirner and Schmitt on the Ego/ghost. The typical reaction of philosophy, when daring to go to the limit, is to immediately seek reassurance, as Descartes for example does by relying on God and reason to support the cogito. Philosophy, Derrida contends, can in fact only exist insofar as it imprisons madness, that is, the mad man within us (ibid.: 61). Schmitt, as we saw above, realises that one cannot simply escape the deception of the evil genius – one walks straight into it. Derrida, in his analysis of *Wisdom*, points out that Schmitt's invocation of Descartes in this context, necessarily has important implications for the enemy, which as we saw is central to Schmitt's concept of the political, and therefore at the same time for his definition of man:

> Without an enemy, I go mad, I can no longer think, I become powerless to think myself, to pronounce '*cogito, ergo sum*'. For that I must have an evil genius, a *spiritus malignus*, a deceitful spirit. Did not Schmitt allude to this in his cell? Without this absolute hostility, the 'I' loses reason, and the possibility of being posed, of posing or of opposing the object in front of it; 'I' loses objectivity, reference, the ultimate stability of that which resists; it loses existence and presence, being, *logos*, order,

---

36 For a more detailed analysis, see de Ville (2011: 95–112).

Schmitt's *Weisheit der Zelle* 227

necessity, and law. 'I' loses the thing itself. For in mourning the enemy,[37] I have not deprived myself of this or that, this adversary or that rival, this determined force of opposition constitutive of myself: I lose nothing more, nothing less, than the world.

(Derrida 1997: 175–176)

Echo

Schmitt ends his reflections in *Wisdom* by invoking wordplay. His own imprisonment is again the focal point: 'This is the wisdom of the prison cell. I lose my time and gain my space (*Raum*) (2010: 90).[38] Suddenly I am overcome by the quiet/silence/peace/rest (*Ruhe*)[39] which shelters the meaning of words' (ibid.). Schmitt then points to the association between *Raum* (space) and *Rom* (Rome), declaring them to be the same word (ibid.).[40] Schmitt proceeds by pointing to the wonders of the German language, specifically its spatial and germinal powers (*die Raumkraft und die Keimkraft*) (ibid.). The German language, he notes, made possible the rhyming of 'word' (*Wort*) and 'place' (*Ort*) (ibid.: 90–91). Even the word 'rhyme' (*Reim*) has retained/conserved (*bewahrt*) its spatial sense and allows poets to utilise the dark play (*das dunkle Spiel*) of 'rhyme' (*Reim*) and 'home/country' (*Heimat*) (ibid.: 91).

In rhyme, Schmitt contends, a word searches for the sibling sonority of its meaning (*den geschwisterlichen Klang seines Sinnes*) (2010: 91). German rhyming is not the kind of bonfire (*Leuchtfeuer*) rhyme of Victor Hugo (ibid.). German rhyme is in the nature of Echo, clothing and decoration/finery (*Echo, Kleid und Schmuck*) and at the same time a divining rod (*Wünschelrute*) to localise meaning (ibid.). The words of the prophetic poets Theodor Daübler and Konrad Weiß, Schmitt comments, now take hold of him (*ergreift mich*) (ibid.). The dark play of their rhyme, he notes, becomes meaning and entreaty (*wird Sinn und Bitte*) (Schmitt 2010: 91). 'I listen to their word', Schmitt says, 'I hear and suffer and acknowledge, that I am not naked, but clothed and on my way to a house/home' (*zu einem Haus*) (ibid.). Schmitt concludes *Wisdom* by first paraphrasing Weiß's poem '1933' ('I see the defenceless rich fruit of the years [*die wehrlos reiche Frucht der Jahre*], the defenceless rich fruit, upon which the law of meaning [*dem Recht der Sinn*] grows') and then quoting from it (cited in Schmitt 2010: 91):

---

37   That is, if one loses the enemy, as Schmitt complains in *The Concept*, is happening in the twentieth century.
38   See likewise Schmitt (1991: 60).
39   *Ruhe* also has the meaning of 'resting place' or 'death': *die ewige Ruhe/die letzte Ruhe finden*.
40   See likewise Schmitt's essay 'Raum und Rom – Zur Phonetik des Wortes Raum' (Schmitt 1995: 491–495).

Echo wächst vor jedem Worte,	Echo grows before every word
wie ein Sturm vom offnen Orte	like a storm from open places
hämmert es durch unsre Pforte	it pounds through our gates

Echo stands here for rhyme, which Schmitt suggests is there from the first word, and which has a certain containing power (Connors 2011: 148). With this emphasis on meaning, home and place, we appear to have moved far away from Descartes' *spiritus malignus*, Stirner's ghostly Ego and being placed in question, that is, from delocalisation, meaninglessness, madness, *Unheimlichkeit*.[41] If we further follow Derrida, then Schmitt's invocation of meaning, home and place at this point, amounts to a response to the deterritorialising effect of modern technology, that is, the expression of a drive for rootedness, for presence, in view of that which technology announces: our own death (Derrida and Stiegler 2005: 38–39). Technology, as Derrida shows in a reading of Defoe's *Robinson Crusoe*, is in the first place a response to our foundational phantasm (fear and desire) of being dead while alive, more specifically the image of being buried or swallowed alive (2011: 77, 82, 117). Technology mimics the functioning of this phantasm or self-destructive power, which itself functions in a mechanical fashion thereby disobeying the interest of reason and the law (ibid.: 84–85).[42] Ovid's *Metamorphoses* can be read as testifying to the same phantasm. Echo does not simply repeat the words of Narcissus, which she hears, as Schmitt seems to suggest (2010: 91). In repeating his (narcissistic) words ('Is anyone here?', 'Come!', 'Why do you run from me?', and 'Here let us meet') she gives them a new meaning which speaks of her overflowing love for him (Derrida 2005a: xii). When speaking in this inaugural fashion, she still keeps literally to, yet at the same time disobeys the law, that is, the prohibition/limitation placed upon her by the goddess Hera (Derrida 1997: 24, 160, 165–167; 2005a: xi–xii). When she tries to embrace Narcissus upon his invitation to the voice he hears, he flees from her when he sees her, with the words 'Hands off! Embrace me not! May I die before I give you power o'er me!', she repeats 'I give you power o'er me!' (Ovid 1951, Book III). Here we again touch on delocalisation, meaninglessness, madness and *Unheimlichkeit*.[43] The Echo which storms through the portals invoked by Weiß and Schmitt, now in fact appears to be a threatening and self-destructive force, which disrupts meaning and home.

41 See also Connors (2011: 146–147).
42 This interlinkage between life and death again returns us to the question of spectrality (Derrida 2011: 117).
43 See likewise Derrida on Paul Celan's poetry, more specifically the impossibility of appropriating language as well as its spectrality (2005b: 97–107).

The haunting of the political

We saw in the above analysis that in *Wisdom*, Schmitt does not reject his earlier view of human nature or of the political, yet a certain development does take place. He refers to his own vulnerability, his nakedness, his being placed in question, his persecution, his being haunted by a ghost, his wearing of a mask, and his subjection to deception by Descartes' evil genius. The new man, to be transformed by modern technology, is in turn portrayed as the totally other, as the incalculable, and as radiating. Schmitt invokes Stirner's 'atomic' thinking and his idea of the self consuming itself. He mocks Stirner's belief in self-identity, and speaks of the enemy as ultimately the self, or the brother. All of the above, as we saw in our analysis of Schmitt by way of Derrida's texts, speak of a division in the self, that is, of a self being haunted by a force of self-destruction; or rather, of the 'self' becoming a self only through a binding of this force of self-destruction (Derrida 1987: 402). Schmitt no doubt stands sceptical towards the modern era and the 'overcoming' of man that is taking place, yet it appears from his analysis that this overcoming is a 'symptom' and that its appearance today is only possible because it is 'written' in man from the beginning. Schmitt's analysis of what can be termed the 'differantial stricture' of the human being has important implications for the concept of the political with its friend/enemy distinction (ibid.: 351). Schmitt's text shows the latter concept to be haunted, similar to every (human) being, by a force of self-destruction. Freud identified this force in 'Beyond the Pleasure Principle' as the death drive (2001: 7–64). In *Archive Fever*, Derrida calls this force *anarchivic, archiviolithic*, or archive destroying (1995: 10–11). It incites the annihilation of memory, a forgetfulness thus, beyond repression, and also commands the radical effacement of the documentary archive (ibid.: 11, 19). At stake in this 'force' would be a kind of friendship, that is, an act of loving, which Derrida refers to as 'lovence' (*aimance*), which is disproportionate, without calculation, with no concern for the self, with no expectation of any return (1997: 7–8). Constitutional theory, through its inevitable engagement with law and with the political, has no option but to navigate between the force fields of the preservation and the destruction of the archive.

Acknowledgements

Funding from the South African National Research Foundation is gratefully acknowledged.

References

Balakrishnan, G. 2000, *The Enemy: An Intellectual Portrait of Carl Schmitt*, Verso, London.

Bendersky, J.W. 1987, 'Carl Schmitt at Nuremberg', *Telos*, no. 72, pp. 91–96.

Bendersky, J.W. 2007, 'Carl Schmitt's path to Nuremberg: A sixty-year reassessment', *Telos*, no. 139, pp. 6–34.

Connors, C. 2011, 'Derrida and the Friendship of Rhyme', *The Oxford Literary Review*, vol. 33, no. 2, pp. 139–149.

Däubler, T. 1916, 'Das Sternenkind', in *Die Deutsche Gedichtebibliothek*, accessed 16 July 2014, <http://gedichte.xbib.de/gedichtband_Das+Sternenkind_D%E4ubler,32,0.htm>.

Däubler, T. 1919, *Hymne an Italien*, Insel-Verlag, Leipzig.

de Ville, J. 2011, *Jacques Derrida: Law as Absolute Hospitality*, Routledge, Oxford.

Derrida, J. 1978, *Writing and Difference*, University of Chicago Press, Chicago.

Derrida, J. 1987, *The Post Card: From Socrates to Freud and Beyond*, trans. A. Bass, University of Chicago Press, Chicago.

Derrida, J. 1990, *Glas*, trans. J.P. Leavey, Jr. and R. Rand, University of Nebraska Press, Lincoln.

Derrida, J. 1991, *Of Spirit: Heidegger and the Question*, trans. G. Bennington and R. Bowlby, The University of Chicago Press, Chicago and London.

Derrida, J. 1993a, 'Heidegger's Ear: Philopolemology (*Geschlecht* IV)', in J. Sallis (ed.), *Reading Heidegger: Commemorations*, Indiana University Press, Bloomington, pp. 163–218.

Derrida, J. 1993b, *Aporias*, Stanford University Press, Stanford.

Derrida, J. 1995, *Archive Fever: A Freudian Impression*, trans. E. Prenowitz, University of Chicago Press, Chicago.

Derrida, J. 1997, *Politics of Friendship*, trans. G. Collins, Verso, London/New York.

Derrida, J. 2005a, *Rogues: Two Essays on Reason*, trans. P.A. Brault and M. Naas, Stanford University Press, Stanford.

Derrida, J. 2005b, *Sovereignties in Question: The Poetics of Paul Celan*, T. Dutoit and O. Pasanen (eds), Fordham University Press, New York.

Derrida, J. 2006, *Specters of Marx: The State of Debt, the Work of Mourning, and the New International*, trans. P. Kamuf, Routledge, New York and London.

Derrida, J. 2011, *The Beast and the Sovereign II*, The University of Chicago Press, Chicago.

Derrida, J. and Dufourmantelle, A. 2000, *Of Hospitality*, trans. R. Bowlby, Stanford University Press, Stanford.

Derrida, J. and Stiegler, B. 1995, *Echographies of Television: Filmed Interviews*, trans. J. Bajorek, Polity Press, Cambridge.

Descartes, R. 1968, *Discourse on Method and The Meditations*, Penguin, London.

Engels, F. 1894, *Herr Eugen Dühring's Revolution in Science (Anti-Dühring)*, New York International Publishers, New York.

Freud, S. 2001, *The Standard Edition of the Complete Psychological Works of Sigmund Freud*, vol. XVIII, J. Strachey (ed.), Vintage, London.

Heidegger, M. 2005, *The Essence of Human Freedom*, Continuum, London.

Meier, H. 1998, *The Lesson of Carl Schmitt: Four Chapters on the Distinction between Political Theology and Political Philosophy*, trans. M. Brainard, The University of Chicago Press, Chicago and London.

Ovid, 1951. *Metamorphoses*, trans. F.J. Miller, Harvard University Press, Cambridge.

Schmitt, C. 1987, 'Interrogation of Carl Schmitt by Robert Kempner (I–III)', *Telos*, no. 72, pp. 97–129.

Schmitt, C. 1991, *Glossarium: Aufzeichnungen der Jahre 1947–1951*, Duncker and Humblot, Berlin.

Schmitt, C. 1995, *Staat, Großraum, Nomos: Arbeiten aus den Jahren 1916–1969*, Duncker and Humblot, Berlin.

Schmitt, C. 2002, 'A Pan-European Interpretation of Donoso Cortés', *Telos*, no. 125, pp. 100–115.

Schmitt, C. 2004, 'The Theory of the Partisan: A Commentary/remark on the Concept of the Political', trans. A.C. Goodson, *The New Centennial Review*, vol. 4, no. 3, pp. 1–78.

Schmitt, C. 2006, *The Nomos of the Earth in the International Law of the Jus Publicum Europaeum*, trans. G.L. Ulmen, Telos Press, New York.

Schmitt, C. 2007a, *The Concept of the Political: Expanded Edition*, trans. G. Schwab, University of Chicago Press, Chicago.

Schmitt, C. 2007b, 'The "Fourth" (Second) Interrogation of Carl Schmitt at Nuremberg', *Telos*, no. 139, pp. 35–43.

Schmitt, C. 2008, *Constitutional Theory*, Duke University Press, Durham.

Schmitt, C. 2010, *Ex Captivitate Salus*, 3rd edn, Duncker & Humblot, Berlin.

Stirner, M. 1910/2006, *The Ego and Its Own*, Cambridge University Press, Cambridge.

Zakin, E. 2011, 'The Image of the People: Freud and Schmitt's Political Anti-Progressivism', *Telos*, no. 157, pp. 84–107.

Index

Aboriginal Protection and Restriction of the Sale of Opium Act of 1897 72
Aboriginals Ordinance 1918 (NT) 80, 81
aboriginal title, doctrine of 196, 200, 207
Aborigines 72–3; aboriginal title 196, 200, 207; assimilation 80, 83; blood-based racial categorisation 73; definition of 84; derogatory language in archives 73; government control over 92; *see also Cubillo v Commonwealth* case (2000); Gunner, Peter
Abrams, P. 177
absolute immanence 143, 146
Accidental Death of an Anarchist, The (Fo) 188n10
Adam and Eve 216
Adorno, Theodor 27
affect markers 45
Agaat (van Niekerk) 126
Agamben, Giorgio 123
A ar, Mehmet 180
Agricultural Bank (Milan) 188n10
Albert, Stephen 114
Allen, Danielle 22
American Revolution 21
ANC (African National Congress) 124, 132
Ancient Rome 27
Andrew, Brook 71n2
Antaki, Mark 126–7; legal imagination 127
apartheid 44–5, 123; dealing with the past 125; dispossession of land 130; lives of black people under 123, 124; nostalgia about 124; PDIs (previously disadvantaged individuals) 125; urban land 131

apology, in musical improvisation 62–3
aporia 5
Applications for Remand 106
Archaeology of Knowledge, The (Foucault) 24
archive fever 5, 19, 56
Archive Fever: A Freudian Impression (Derrida) 5, 7, 56, 150–1, 229
archives: authentic unity 150; beginnings 149–50; colonial 75; listening to 34–48; oral 77
archive, the: archival contestations 168–71; archival remains 171–4; archontic power 150; creative practices 91–2; epistemological struggle 76; form of 2–5; forms as evidence 79–90; house of the law 150; and law 151; materiality 77; ontological character of sources 71; principle of provenance 85; purpose of 25; reciting 23–6; redefinition of 24; unremembering 55–7; *see also* counter-archive
archons 1, 4, 23
Arendt, Hannah 8; act of beginning 26–7; appreciation of reflections 29–31; banality of evil 123; counter-archival sensibility 17; dark times 27; facts 18; making sense of phenomena 19–20; personal experience 27; political and social spheres of government 20; power of citation 18–23; tradition 27; *see also* 'Reflections on Little Rock' (Arendt)
Argentina: dirty war 181
arkheion 1, 23
Armenian Genocide (1915) 179
Arrest Memo 106

Index   233

artefacts 70–94; administration 76; archival forms as evidence 79–90; archives on the Aborigines 73; buildings to house records 76; centrality to the law 78–9; creative anachronism 91–2; documents as 70; evidentiary sources 72; files 78–9; forms 79; history of the emergence of 78; material conditions of creation 70; material qualities of 71; objects and texts 72; recovering archives 72–8
assimilation policy 80, 83; census 83
assistance projects 169
Auschwitz 35
Australia: *Aboriginals Ordinance 1918* (NT) 80, 81; archival documents 71; archival records as evidence 77n7; claims by Indigenous people 71; files 86; Peter Gunner case 80–5, 87, 88–9; *Welfare Ordinance 1953* (NT) 80, 83, 84; *see also* Aborigines; *Cubillo v Commonwealth* case (2000); Gunner, Peter
autonomy 142

Bachelard, Gaston 24
Baehr, Peter 27
Bafokeng Land Buyers Association 131, 132, 135
Baldwin, James 38
Ballantyne, Tony 76
Baphiring Community 129–36; Bafokeng Land Buyers Association 131, 132, 135; compensation 129, 130; court hearing 133; expropriation of land 129; feasibility 129–30; Land Act (1913) 132–3; Land Claims Court 129, 132, 133; Land Restitution process 132–3; Mabaalstad 129, 133; nostalgia 129; politics of refusal 132; reflective nostalgia 135; restitution 134–5; restoration 129, 129–30, 132, 133, 134, 135; Royal Bafokeng Nation 131, 132
Baphiring Community v Tshwaranani Projects case (2014) 11, 117, 129, 130
Baphiring Community v Uys case 129
Barker, Joanne 22n5
Bar-On, Dan 38
Barthes, Roland 19

Basque conflict 181
Bear, Laura 156
Beaver nation 204
Beaver, The 206
beginning: act of 27
beginnings 149–50
being-in-common 142
Bell, Richard 71n2
benevolent world 38, 39
Benhabib, Seyla 16n2
Benjamin, Walter 8, 22, 23
Bennett, Gordon 71n2
Bennett, Jane 75
Bennett, Tony 143
Bernasconi, Robert 21
Birikim's 181
Birth of the Clinic, The (Foucault) 8
Birulés, Fina 27
Blommaert, Jan *et al.* 45
Blommaert, Jan 44
Bock, Mary 44
Bora, Taml 181
Borges, Jorge Luis 103–4; *The Garden of Forking Paths* 114
Borgo, David 50, 52, 53; improvisation 58–9
Bosch, Hieronymus 219
Bourdieu, Pierre 157, 177
Boym, Svetlana 10, 116; distinction between nostalgia and melancholia 119; habits 122; mapping 120; nostalgia 118–19, 121; off-modern tradition 119, 134, 135; reflective nostalgia 119, 120, 121, 122, 123; restorative nostalgia 119, 121, 122; utopia 134
Brand, Dietrich 208
Breynat, Oblate Bishop Gabriel 205, 206
Brink, Andre P. 122, 123, 136–7
Brison, Susan 39, 48
Brothman, Brien 151
Brown v. Board of Education of Topeka case 8, 17, 20, 21
Bucak, Sedat 179
Burton, Ann 25, 76
Butler, Guy 125

Cage, John 50, 65
Calder v Attorney-General of British Columbia case 200
Canada: aboriginal title 196, 200, 207; Canadian nationhood 212; citizen

234 Index

plus rights 198, 199; economic change 195; fur trade 204, 206; indigenous peoples of the northern regions 197–8; Just Society policy 199; land rights 13, 195; land rights of Nisga's 200; Northwest Territories Supreme Court 197; oil and gas pipeline 197; oil drilling 205, 206; Registrar of Titles 197; Treaty 8 205; Treaty 11 204, 205–6, 207; treaty status 198–9; White Paper 198; *see also* Caveat case (1973); Dene leaders; Indian peoples (Canada)
Cardinal, Harold 199
Carrim, Nazir 145
Çatlh, Abdullah 180
Cavarero, Adriana 120
Caveat case (1973): aboriginal title 196, 200, 207; adjustments to evidentiary process of court 200–1; Canadian nationhood 212; citizen plus rights of Indian peoples 198, 199; Dehcho 204; Indigenous peoples of the northern regions 197–8; lack of consultation 198; land rights of Indigenous peoples ignored 198; *As Long As This Land Shall Last* 201–2; Northwest Territories Supreme Court 197; oil drilling 205, 206; peace and friendship 200, 207; peoplehood 211–12; politics of the treaty archive 201–4; Registrar of Titles 197; research into Dene history 201; reserve lands 207; transcripts of interviews 203; Treaty 8 205; Treaty 11 204, 205–6, 207; treaty archive 211–12; treaty-as-event 204–7; treaty-as-memory 207–11; witnesses 207–10; *see also* Indian peoples (Canada)
Central Forensic Science Laboratory 107
Çetin, Fethiye 191–2
Chand, Constable Suraj 105
Chesterman, John 83
Chipewyan nation 204
Christodoulidis, Emilios 143, 146
circulating reference 100, 110
citation, power of 18–23
citizen plus rights 198
civil rights movement 19, 22
Clanchy, Michael 78
Clues: The Roots of an Evidentiary

Paradigm (Ginzburg) 189
Code of Criminal Procedure (India) (1973) 104
code switch 62
Coetzee, J.M. 125–6
Cogito and the History of Madness (Derrida) 226
Cold War 180–1
Coleman, Ornette 56, 57
colonial archives 3, 71; hierarchical categories of evidence 77
colonialism: archives 71; historians of 71; written documents 75
colonial state: nature, extent and accuracy of archives 77
Coltrane, John 52
commissions, truth 37
common law: archives 78; legal precedent 60
Common Legal Representative 164
Company of Young Canadians 202, 203
Compte, August 23
Concept of the Political, The (Schmitt) 148, 215, 222–3; centrality of human nature 215
conjectural knowledge 191
conjectural paradigm 189–90
Conroy, H.A. 205, 206
consent, form of 80–5
consignation 6
conspiracy theories 185–6, 186–7, 188, 189
conspiratorial perception 189
constitution 11
constitutionalism 143, 152
Constitutional Theory (Schmitt) 13–14, 215
Constitution Hill 151–2
constitutions 140–53; constitutional fetishism 142; limits of 141–7; political communities 141, 142–3; Preamble to the 1996 Constitution of the Republic of South Africa 141–2; *see also* museums
contextualisation: justice 3–4
Cook, Terry 24, 25, 26
Corbett, J. 51
Cornell, D. and Van Marle, K. 152–3
counter-archive 5–8; improvisation 51–2; power of citation 18–23; reciting the archive 23–6; sense 8–14; sensibility 16–31; stimulating further reflection 17

Index   235

counter-monumental memorialising practices 144
Counterpath (Derrida) 57
court cases, India: Applications for Remand 106; Arrest Memo 106; case diaries 106; Central Forensic Science Laboratory 107; chargesheets 107–8; Code of Criminal Procedure (1973) 104; Daily Diaries 104, 105; defence strategy 111–12; Delhi High Court Rules (1967) 104; Explosive Substances Act (1908) 105; file mapping 104; First Information Reports (FIRs) 104, 105, 106; Indian Evidence Act (1872) 104; Indian Penal Code (1860) 105; Indian Police Act (1861) 104; legal paperwork 104; *malkhanas* 107, 110; Mohammed Hanif trial 104–5; police accountability 104; presentation of the evidence 109–10; presentation of the facts 109; *pulandas* 107; Punjab Police Rules 104; Rukka 105; Seizure Memos 106–7; trial before Sessions Court 108; Unlawful Activities Prevention Act (1967) 105–6
courtrooms 97
creative practices 91–2
Critchley, Simon 116, 127, 136
critical improvisation 55
critical reflection: tradition of 119
Critical Studies in Improvisation (CSI) 63
Cry of Winnie Mandela, The (Ndebele) 120
Csikszentmihalyi, Mihaly 59
Cubillo, Lorna 79–80, 81
Cubillo v Commonwealth case (2000) 10, 70, 79–80, 81, 86
Culbert, Jennifer 8
Culture Warriors 72n4
customs 122

Daly, Mabel 92
Daübler, Theodor 217, 221, 222, 227
Davis, Miles 56n8
death 224
death drive 5
deception 223–5
deep listening 62
deep state, the 12; amalgam of governmental rationality and fantasy

178n3; conspiracy theories 179; Ergenekon Terrorist Organisation (ETO) 178; history of 179; integral part of the state 181; low-intensity warfare against Kurds 181; meaning of 177; Özel Harp Dairesi (ÖHD) 179; style and structure of plots 179; Susurluk gang 180; *see also* Ergenekon trial
de Gourges, Olympia 128
Dehcho 204
Dehlin, Erlend 58, 59, 61
Delhi High Court Rules (1967) 104
democracy: in South Africa 152
Democratic Republic of Congo (DRC) 168; Trust Fund for Victims 169n9
Dene leaders 13; difficulties presenting accurate memories 196; doctrine of aboriginal title 196, 200, 207; documenting treaties 195; land rights ignored 198; legal case *see* Caveat case (1973); recognisably distinct peoplehood 203; recognition of land rights 195, 196; testimony of elders 196; treaty archive 195–6, 211–12
Dene people: lifestyle 204; peoplehood 211–12
Department of Indian Affairs (Canada) 198
depoliticisation 127–8
Der Einzige und sein Eigentum (Stirner) 219
DERRIDA (film) 57
Derrida, Jacques 140; analysis of Wisdom 226–7; *Archive Fever: A Freudian Impression* 5, 7, 56, 150–1; archives 150, 153, 195; archons 1, 4; archontic power 150; beginnings 149–50; creation and protection of the archive 4; differential stricture 215; improvised text 57; lovence 229; metaphor of exterior and interior 6; participation at jazz festival 56–7; relationship between preparation and improvisation 57; technology 228
Descartes, René 221, 224; the self as enemy 225–7
de Souza, Colin 44–5
determined improvisation 59
de Tocqueville, Alexis 27
de Ville, Jacques 13

236 Index

Devil's Valley (Brink) 137
de Waal, Alex 172
Dialogic Evidence: Documentation of
  Ephemeral Events project 55
Diefenbaker, John, Prime Minister
  197–8
dietrologia 188
Dink, Hrant 12, 191–2
discontinuity 7
disenchantment 126, 127
Disgrace (Coetzee) 125–6
dissensus 116–36; definition 128
District Six Museum 11, 144–6
Dlamini, Jacob 123, 123–4, 131
documents *see* artefacts
Dolezal, Rachel 22n5
Douglas, Heather 83
Douglas, Stacy 11, 169
du Plessis, Lourens 117, 118, 120
Dworkin, Ronald 30

Eastern Railway Headquarters 156
Edmonds, Penelope 71–2
Edmonton Journal 210
Ego and Its Own, The (Stirner) 215, 218
Egypt 141
Eichmann, Adolf 20, 21, 29, 30
Ekurhuleni Metropolitan Council 124
Ellis, Simon 55
emblematic wound 166–8, 172, 173
empire building 76
entrepreneurialism 167
Ergenekon Terrorist Organisation
  (ETO) 178
Ergenekon trial 12, 180–92;
  conspiratorial imagination 185–6,
  186–7, 190, 192; definition and
  history of the deep state 180;
  Ergenekon Analysis Restructuring
  Management and Development
  Project 186; fantasy and desire
  184–5; First Indictment 183–4;
  global historical context 180–1; past
  activities of the deep state 187;
  purging of the deep state 184;
  restructuring 186; scale of 178; *see
  also* deep state, the
Ertür, Başak 12–13
ethics 122
ethnographic images 91
evidence: Australian archives 77n7;
  Dialogic Evidence: Documentation
  of Ephemeral Events project 55;

Exhibit R93 88–9; files 79; forms
  79–90; hierarchical categories of 77;
  see also form of consent
Ex Captivitate Salus (Schmitt) *see
  Wisdom* (Schmitt)
Exhibit A21 87–8
Exhibit R93 88–9
Explosive Substances Act (1908) 105

Fabri, Mary 36
facts 18
Fassin, Didier 161
Fay, Derrick 131
Featherstone, M. 25
Feiler, H. 36
fever: archive 5–6, 19, 56
files 97–114; colonial administration in
  Australia 86; contesting itself
  110–12; emblems of state power 101;
  as evidence 79; foundation of legal
  activity 78–9; fragility of state
  documents 101–2; hypertextual
  113–14; Indian colonial state 101;
  making of 104–10; media
  technology of 78; Mohammed Hanif
  trial 97–100; performative and fact
  producing 79; power of 102–4;
  reality contained in 110–11;
  relationship to the world 101–2;
  usage in law 78; world-consuming
  110–11; *see also* paper
Fire Next Time, The (Baldwin) 38
First Encyclopaedia of Tlön Vol. XI 103–4
First Information Reports (FIRs) 104,
  105, 106
Fischlin, D. and A. Heble 51
Fischlin, D. *et al.* 53, 54, 55
Fish, Stanley 117
Fitzpatrick, Peter 66, 148–9
Fo, Dario 188n10
Foley, Fiona 71n2
form of consent: *Cubillo v
  Commonwealth* case (2000) 86;
  Exhibit A21 80–5, 87–8; Exhibit R93
  88–9
Form of Information of Birth 89–90
forms 79; as evidence 79–90;
  standardisation of 85–6
Fort Norman 205
Fort Simpson 206
Fortunoff Video Archive for Holocaust
  Testimonies 35
Foucault, Michel 7–8; archival

Index

approach 76; the archive 161; *raison d'état* of the state 181–3; redefinition of the archive 24, 24–5
found improvisation 60
fragility 39–40
free improvisation 59
French Conseil D'État 86
French Revolution 23, 128
Freshwater, H. 25
Freud, Sigmund 150, 189, 190, 229
Frisk, H. 56
Fumoleau, René 197, 201; *As Long As This Land Shall Last* 201–2; transcripts of interviews 203
fur trade 204, 206
Future of Nostalgia, The (Boym) 116

Gabbard, K. 59
Garden of Earthly Delights, The (Bosch) 219
Garden of Forking Paths, The (Borges) 114
genuineness of creativity 58
German language 227
Giese, Harry 87–8, 89
Gines, Kathryn 19, 22
Ginzburg, Carlo 187, 188, 188–90
Gobodo-Madikizela, Commissioner 43
Goodrich, Peter 117, 134
grants 166
Grassian, Stuart 46
Grunenberg, Antonia 27
Guatemala 181
Guenther, Lisa 46
Gunner, Peter 79–80, 80–1, 87, 88–9; form of consent 80–5

habit 56, 122
Hacking, Ian 3
Hanif, Mohammed 10, 97–100; Identification Memo 98, 99, 100; Pointing Out Memo 97–8, 100
Hannah Arendt and the Negro Question (Gines) 22
Harper, Richard 89
Harris, Verne 3–4
Hart, H.L.A. 148
Harvey, David 136
Hayner, Priscilla 37, 42
Heidegger, Martin 221–2
Helm, June 208
Herman, Judith 38, 39
heterotopic space 104

Historical Ontologies (Hacking) 3
historical selfconsciousness 118
historiography: genealogical approaches to 76
History 6–7; archives as historical agents 75; description of 24; development of 23; oral 77; postcolonial scholarship 76–7
Hobbes, Thomas 218
Hobsbawm, Eric 28
Holmes, Sherlock 189, 190
Holocaust 8, 38
Horkheimer, Max 27
Hudson's Bay Company 205, 206
Hull, Matthew 103
human nature 215
human rights: abuses 47; of women 168–9
Human Rights Violations 43
Hume, Steve 210, 212
hypertextual files 113–14

Identification Memo 98, 99
images 91
imagination, legal 127
implicated subjects 5
improvisation: apology 62–3; certainty 53; code switch 62; counter-archival in nature 51–2; critical 55; deep listening 62; determined 59; failure 55; found 60; free 59; genuineness of creativity 58; improbable inevitability 53; and jazz 59; and the law 60–1; mistakes 65; musical *see* musical improvisation; organisational 58; predetermined 59; predictability 53; and preparation 57; process of evolving 61; recognising failure 50; rememberings into the present 58–62; as social practice 51; spontaneity 58, 60; and time 62
India: court cases *see* court cases, India; Eastern Railway Headquarters 156; government by paper 101; Identification Memo 98, 99, 100; Mohammed Hanif trial 97–100; paper files in courtrooms 97; Pointing Out Memo 97–8, 100; Special Cell anti-terror police 97
Indian Act 198
Indian Association of Alberta 199
Indian Brotherhood of the Northwest

238 Index

Territories 198, 199, 202; economic, political and cultural projects 203; preservation projects 204
Indian Claims Commission (Canada) 202, 204
Indian Evidence Act (1872) 104
Indian Penal Code (1860) 105
Indian peoples (Canada): citizen's rights 198; comprehension of treaties 203; government removal of special treaty status 198, 198–9; Indian Act 198; Indian Claims Commission 202, 204; Just Society policy 199; lack of consultation 198; recognition as citizens plus 199; self-determination of 199
Indian Police Act (1861) 104
Indigenous art 91
Indigenous peoples: elders 77–8; hyper-surveillance of 77; self-determination of 199; *see also* Indian peoples (Canada)
inscription: act of 160; filling in paper 157; victimhood 157, 158–64
institutionalised nostalgia 121
International Criminal Court (ICC) 156; delays for court applicants 163; inscription devices 161; registration 164–5; victim mandate 158; victim participation form 159–60, 161–3; victims 157
international criminal law: global humanitarian continuum 158; juridical/jurisdictional constraints 158–9; legitimation 157; restorative turn 161; tension 156–7
interviewers 35–6
Isaacson, Grace 73, 92
isolation 46–7
Italy: deep state 187–8; *dietrologia* 188; *Mani plute* operation 180; Years of Lead 187

James, Deborah 131
Janoff-Bulman, Ronnie 38, 39
jazz: and racism 59
Jazz a la Villette festival 56
JITEM (Gendarmerie Intelligence and Counterterrorism Group Command) 179
Johnson, Miranda 13, 77–8
Judge and the Historian, The (Ginsburg) 187

judgements, legal 60–1
judges 7
justice 3–4; contextualisation 3–4; to the past 4
Justice and Development Party (AKP) 178n3
Justice as Improvisation: The Law of the Extempore (Ramshaw) 66

Kafka, Ben 102–3
kagazi case 102
Kammen, Michael 118
Kaska nation 204
Kelsen, Hans 147, 148
Kempner, Robert 216
Kendall, Sara 11–12, 66
Kenya 141, 169; registers 172; registration of victims 159, 164–5; victims' request to be removed from list 170–1, 173
Khutwane, Yvonne 42–4
Kitching, Harry 84n12, 86–7
Klare, Karl 118
Kline, Dana 40
Kluger, Ruth 39
Kocadag, Hüseyin 179–80
Krog, Antjie 37
Küçük, Yalçın 185
Kühn, Joachim 56
Kundera, Milan 120
Kundrilba, Topsy 81, 81–3, 84, 85, 87, 89
Kurdistan Workers' Party (PKK) 179
Kurds 179; low-intensity warfare against 181

Laçiner, Ömer 181
Land Act (1913) 132–3
Land Claims Court 132, 133
Landgraf, E. 51
land reform: rural land 131; in South Africa 130; urban land 131
land rights: in Canada 13, 195, 196; Indigenous peoples 198; Nisga's 200
Landry, Michael 207–8
Land Titles Act (1970) (Canada) 197
Langer, Lawrence 36, 40, 41
Laruelle, François 173–4
latent power 75
Latour, Bruno 86, 88, 100, 103, 110; inscription devices 160
Laub, Dori 37–8
law: archival inscriptions 151; and the

Index 239

archive 151; beginning in archives 150; common 60; definition 147, 148; documentary practices 78–9; fictive quality of 149; files 78–9; forms 79; improvisation 51, 60–1; independence of 147, 148–9; interacting with museums 147; linearity 61; materiality and movement of documents 86; media technology of files 78; and melody 61; melos 61; nomos (reasons) 61; origins of 78; produced by preceding notions of community 148; rule of 182, 183; singularity 6; thesmos (commands) 61; and time 119–20; truth, state and subject 78; unpredictability of legal judgement 60–1
Lefebvre, Henri 135–6
legal imagination 127
legal judgements 60–1
Lesser Slave Lake area 205
Levinas, Emmanuel 122
Lewis, G. 51
linearity, in law 61
listening 9; deep 62; failing to hear 37–9; fragility 39–40; Hanna F. interviews 35–7, 40–1; narratives of suffering 44–5; responsiveness 47
Locke, Jill 20
As Long As This Land Shall Last 201–2
Luker, Trish 9–10

Mabaalstad 129
MacKenzie, Alexander 204
MacKenzie River 204
Mackenzie Valley 195, 197
Madlingozi, Tshepo 124
Madness and Civilization (Foucault) 8
Mahinder, Sub Inspector 105, 106
mal 5, 6
Malinowski, Bronislaw 124
malkhanas 107, 110
Mandela, Winnie 120
mapping 120
Mass Democratic Movement 124
Mawani, Renisa 81, 151
Mbembe, Achille 75, 156
McCormick, Kay 44
McCoy, Mr 89
McGrath, Professor Ann 88
McKaiser, Eusebius 125
McNamee, E. 52

Medalie, David 125, 126
medical assistance 167
melancholia 119
'Meletti and Law's Mindfulness of Time' (Postema) 61
melody 61
melos (melody) 61
Members of the Yorta Yorta Community v State of Victoria and Ors case (1998) 71n3, 77n7
memorial constitutionalism 117, 118, 120, 130
memory 11; trauma of 55–7
Men in Dark Times (Arendt) 27
Metamorphoses (Ovid) 228
Michelet, Jules 6–7
Military Reaction Force 181
Miller, Danie 71n2
Miller, Peter and Rose, Nikolas 160
Mingus, Charles 51
Minow, Martha 42
mistakes 52–5; archiving 50, 50–1; improvisation 65; in law 50
modernity 16
Mokgatlhe, Chief August 131–2
Montfort, Nick 114
monumental constitutionalism 117, 118, 120, 130; monumental practices 144
Morelli, Giovanni 189, 190
Morrow, Justice William 195, 200–1, 209–10, 211, 212
Morrow, Ruth 58n12
Mphahlele, Es'kia 125
Mukharji, Projit 26
Murphy, Elise 208–9, 211
Murphy, Timothy 56–7
museums 11, 140; civilising rituals in England 143–4; conceptions of community in history 151; Constitution Hill 151–2; democracy 152; District Six Museum 11, 144–6; imaginations of political community 143; interacting with the law 147; raison d'être 144; separation from law 140–1
musical improvisation 9, 50, 51; apology 62–3; audience participation 54; contingency 52; exploration of uncertainty 52; failure 53–4; musicking 54; practice and dedication 52; and time 62, 63
musicking 54

240 Index

Musicking (Small) 54
Mütercimler, Erol 185

Nabokov, Vladimir 122
Nagia, Anwah 145
Nakasa, Nat 125
nakedness, of man 216–17
Nancy, Jean-Luc 142
natality 8
National Archives of Australia 85
National Association for the
   Advancement of Colored People
   (NAACP) 22
National Indigenous Art Triennial
   2007 72n4
native, meaning of 124–5
nature, human 215, 218
Ndebele, Njabulo 120
Negri, Antonio 143
New York Times 22
Nisga leaders 200
Nkosi, Lewis 125
nomos (reasons) 61
North West Company 204
Northwest Territories Supreme Court
   197
nostalgia 11, 116; Baphiring
   Community *see* Baphiring
   Community; critical approach 135;
   criticism of 124; of disappointment
   117–26; distinct from melancholia
   119; homecoming 119;
   institutionalisation 121;
   interdisciplinarity of 119; reflective
   116, 120, 121, 122, 123, 127, 136;
   restorative 121, 122, 136; restorative
   and reflective 119; utopian 118–19;
   working sideways 121

objects: as texts 72
off-modern tradition 119, 134, 135
Oilweek 210
Oliveros, Pauline 62
Olney, Judge 77n7
O'Loughlin, Justice 80, 80–1, 84–5, 88
ontology 3
oral archive 77
oral history 77
Order of Things, The (Foucault) 8
organisational improvisation 58
Organization Science 58n11
Origins of Totalitarianism, The (Arendt)
   27

Orr, Wendy 42
Özel Harp Dairesi (ÖHD) 179, 180
Özel Kuvvetler Komutanlı ı (Special
   Forces Command) 179

paper 76; courtrooms 97; government
   by 101; gravitational pull of 97–101;
   Hanif, Mohammed trial 97–100;
   paper case 102; paper truths 102;
   psychic life 102
paradise 216–17
paranoid reading 34, 38
Passavant, Paul 140
Between Past and Future (Arendt) 27
Patriotic Party 185
patterns 25
Paulette, François 197
PDIs (previously disadvantaged
   individuals) 125
Penelope (Cavarero) 120
Perinçek, Do u 185
Perry, Adele 77
Peter Froggatt Centre 64
Peters, Gary 52, 53
Philippopoulus-Mihalopoulos, Andreas
   136
Piazza Fontana bombing 188n10
Pienaar, Juanita 133–4
Plato 27
plausibility 26
Pledger, Mavis 92
Plessy v. Ferguson case (1896) 20–1
Pointing Out Memo 97–8, 100
Polanyi, Karl 124
political community: and constitutions
   141, 142–3; and museums 143
Political Theology (Schmitt) 147
politics: concept of the political 148;
   point of 128
Politics of Friendship (Derrida) 216, 222
politics of refusal 120, 130, 132
politics of resistance 116
Polizeistaat (the police state) 182n6
positivism 147–9
Postema, Gerald 61
predetermined improvisation 59
principle of provenance 85
Prosecutor v. Ruto and Sang case 156,
   164
provenance, principle of 85
psychoanalysis 150
public schools 20
pulandas 107

Punjab Police Rules 104

Queensland Aboriginals Protection and Restriction of the Sale of Opium Act 1897 (Qld) 92
Queensland Centenary of Women's Suffrage and Forty Years of Aboriginal Suffrage 73
Queensland State Archives 73, 75

racial legislation 20
Ramshaw, Sara 9, 51, 59n15, 65, 66–7
Rancière, Jacques 117, 127–8, 136; ontological trap 128; politics 128; rights of man 128
rape 43
rationalisation 126, 127
recognition 1
'Reflections on Little Rock' (Arendt): access to what really happened 19; appreciation of 29–31; context of photograph 18; definitive answers to questions 19; girl's father 22; inspiration of photograph 17, 18; traditional archival work 18–19; white friend 22
reflective nostalgia 11, 116, 119, 120, 121, 122, 123, 127, 136; Baphiring Community 135
registers 164–6, 171, 172
Registrar of Titles 197
Registration of Births, Deaths and Marriages Ordinance 1941 (NT) 89
rehabilitation 166–7
remembering: memorial 117, 118, 120; monumental 117, 118, 120
reparations 1, 166
reparative reading 34–5
Re Paulette and Registrar of Land Titles (No. 2) (1973) *see* Caveat case (1973)
representation 150
resilience 47–8
responsibility 1
restorative justice movement 39
restorative nostalgia 119, 121, 122, 136
On Revolution (Hobsbawm) 28
Ridener, John 85, 86
rights of man 128
Riles, Annalise 83–4, 164
Robert, Hannah 87
Robinson Crusoe (Defoe) 228
Roman court proceedings 110

Rome: ancient 27
Ross, Fiona 42, 43, 45
Rothberg, Michael 5
Rottenburg, Richard 169–70
Royal Bafokeng Nation 131, 132
Rukka 105
rule of law 182, 182n7, 183
Ruto, William 171n11

Saint Mary's Church Of England Hostel 83
Sancar, Mithat 182, 183n8
Schmitt, Carl 13–14, 147–8; Echo 227–8; the enemy 221, 225–6; German language 227; haunting of the political 229; human nature 215; interned 216; liberal constitutionalism 215; and Max Stirner 215, 217, 218–20; placement on earth 220–2; and René Descartes 225–7; self-deception 223–5; wordplay 227; *see also Wisdom* (Schmitt)
Scholem, Gersholm 29, 30
Schroeder, Franziska 59, 59–60
Schwartz, Joan 24
Sedgwick, Eve 34
Seizure Memos 106–7
self-deception 223–5
sensibility: counter-archival 16–31
sensitivity 122
Shanks, Michael 28
Sibbeston, Jimmy 209–10
Singh, Sub Inspector Rakesh Kumar 106, 108–9, 113
Slave nation 204
slavery 20
slowness 120
Slowness (Kundera) 120
Small, Christopher 54
Smith, Andrea 22n5
Snyman, Johan 117
sociolinguistic discourse analysis 44
Sofri, Adriano 187, 188
solitary confinement 46
Sonic Arts Research Centre 64
Soudien, C. 146
South Africa: *Agaat* 126; democracy 152; land reform 130; urban land 131; *see also* apartheid; constitutions
South African Constitution 117, 117–18; democracy 152; memorial 118, 120; monumental 118, 120

242 Index

Southern Cone coups 181
sovereignty: personal 41–2
Spain 181
spatiality 135
spatial justice 136
Special Cell anti-terror police 97, 98
Specters of Marx (Derrida) 218
Speers, Michael 59n15
spontaneity 58, 60
Sputnik 19
Stapleton, Paul 9, 55n6, 59n15, 64–6
state law 5; exclusivity 5
State Library of Queensland 73
state, the: deep *see* deep state, the;
    fragility of documents 101–2;
    importance of the archive 23, 76;
    legitimacy of 181–2; not subject to
    external laws 181–2; *raison d'état*
    181–3; rule of law 182
state violence 11
Stauffer, Jill 8–9, 66
Steedman, Carolyn 6–7; place of the
    archive 24
Steinberg, Jonny 123
Stevens, John 54n5
Stevens, Wallace 127
Stirner, Max 215, 217, 218–20, 229;
    self-deception 224–5
Stolen Generations 10, 70, 80
Stoler, Ann Laura 2–3, 76, 156; archival
    documents 160–1
storytelling 18; power of 16n2
Suresh, Mayur 10
Susurluk gang 180
Sutton, Gerry 200, 209

Talking to Strangers (Allen) 22
Tarlo, Emma 102, 112
Taylan, Ferhat 189, 191
tear gas 44–5
Territory Health Services 88–9
texts: as objects 72
Thakur, Inspector Akash 106
Theory of the Partisan, The (Schmitt) 216
thesmos (commands) 61
time 119–20; slowness 119–20
Tlön, Uqbar, Orbis Tertius (Borges)
    103–4
torture 37, 44
totalitarian regimes 27
tradition 27; break from 16n1; critical
    reflection 119; off-modern 119, 134,
    135

transitional justice 1; and the law 2;
    mistakes in law 50
trauma 39
Trindel, Ted 203
Trudeau, Pierre 199, 200
Trundle, C. and Kaplonski, C. 76
Trust Fund for Victims 165, 166–8;
    assistance projects 169; Democratic
    Republic of Congo (DRC) 169n9;
    entrepreneurialism 167; grants 166;
    medical assistance 167; reparations
    166; victim support 169
Truth and Reconciliation Commission
    (TRC) 8, 37; Commissioners'
    patience 42, 43
truth claims 79
Ts'ui Pen 114
Tunisia 141
Turkey: deep state *see* deep state, the;
    influence of the military 178; Justice
    and Development Party (AKP)
    178n3; low-intensity warfare 181;
    Southern Cone coups 181
Turkish Labour Party 180
Twilight of the Gods (Wagner) 217

Uganda 166
'under the act' (Watson) 72
United States of America (USA):
    Constitution 20; Fourteenth
    Amendment 20–1; public schools
    20; racial legislation 20; racial
    prejudice 38
United States Supreme Court 20
Unlawful Activities Prevention Act
    (1967) 105–6
Unspeakable Truths (Hayner) 42
urban land 131
utopia 118–19, 134

van der Walt, Johan 123
van Marle, Karin 10, 11
van Niekerk, Marlene 126
van Onselen, Charles 123
Between Vengeance and Forgiveness
    (Minow) 42
victimhood 12; documenting
    tribe/ethnicity 162; inscription 157,
    158–64; international recognition
    161; mandate 158; participation
    form 159–60, 161–3; qualified victim
    162; registering 164–6; unqualified
    victim 162, 163

Index   243

violence: narratives of 8; state 11
Vismann, Cornelia 9, 78–9, 110, 111
von Ranke, Leopold 23
von Zinnenburg Carroll, Khadija 91

Waddell, Timothy 58n12
Wagner, Richard 217
Wah-Shee, James 202
Walker, Cheryl 130–1
Waterman, Elle 62
Watson, Judy 9, 71n2, 91, 92; archival
   sources 72–3; commissioned by the
   State Library of Queensland 73;
   exhibited works 73–4; latent power
   75; 'under the act' 72

Weber, Max 126
Weiß, Konrad 227
Welfare Ordinance 1953 (NT) 80, 83, 84
Winnicott, D.W. 24
'Wisdom of the Prison Cell' (Schmitt)
   see Wisdom (Schmitt)
Wisdom (Schmitt) 222; the enemy 216;
   nakedness of man 216–17;
   prosecutorial function 221
women: political rights 128

Zehr, Howard 39